Bliss Bibliographic Classification

Bliss Bibliographic Classification

Second Edition

J. Mills and Vanda Broughton

with the assistance of Colin Neilson

School of Information and Communication Studies
The University of North London

Class S
Law

BOWKER
SAUR

LONDON • MELBOURNE • MUNICH • NEW PROVIDENCE, NJ

First edition by Henry Evelyn Bliss
Volumes 1 – 4. (1940 – 1953)

Second edition 1996

British Library Cataloguing in Publication Data
A catalogue record for this book is available from the British Library

Library of Congress Cataloging in Publication Data
A catalog record for this book is available from the Library of Congress

Published by Bowker-Saur, a division of Reed Elsevier (UK) Ltd
Maypole House, Maypole Road, East Grinstead, West Sussex RH19 1HU, UK
Tel: +44 (0) 1342 330100 Fax: +44 (0) 1342 330191
E-mail: lis@bowker-saur.co.uk
Internet Website: http://www.bowker-saur.co.uk/service/

Bowker-Saur is part of REED REFERENCE PUBLISHING

ISBN 1-85739-067-9

Printed on acid-free paper
Printed and bound in Great Britain by Antony Rowe Ltd, Chippenham, Wiltshire

Contents

Outline of the complete BC2 classification

2	Physical forms and forms of arrangement of documents
3	Phenomena: objects of knowledge
	Prolegomena
5	Knowledge, information
	Disciplines: forms of knowledge
A	Philosophy
AM	Mathematics
AY	Science
B	Physical sciences
E	Biological sciences
H	Human sciences and human studies
	Physical anthropology, health and medicine, psychology
J/T	Social sciences and humanities
U/V	Technology and useful arts
W/Y	The arts (including music and philology)

Second outline

2 Generalia: physical forms & forms of arrangement of documents
3 Phenomena: objects of knowledge
* For completely multidisciplinary documents, unclassifiable under any one discipline.
Attributes, activities & processes, entities
Prolegomena
6 Universe of knowledge
Methods of enquiry... Disciplines (general)
7 Information science & technology
Information processing... computers
8 Information work... retrieval
Information systems & services
Primarily reference retrieval... computerised services
9 Primarily document retrieval... libraries
Disciplines: forms of knowledge
A Philosophy & logic
AM Mathematics, statistics & probability
AY Sciences, natural sciences
B Physics
Physics-based technologies
* Alternative only.
C Chemistry
Chemistry-based technologies
* Alternative only.
D Astronomy & space sciences
DH Earth sciences
Geophysics, geology, hydrology, meteorology...
Geography: regional... systematic...
E Biological sciences
EK Microorganisms
F Botany
G Zoology
GR Applied biology
Agriculture & animal exploitation
GY General & human ecology
H Human sciences & human studies
HA Human biology... physical anthropology
HH Health & medicine
I Psychology
J Education
K Society
K9Q Perspectives: sociology, social anthropology...
KAH Social ecology & environment... demography...
KC Social processes: change... social behaviour...
KK Social structure
KLK Collectivities: groups... classes... family...
KRS Inclusive societies... non-literate... literate...
KW Customs, folklore & mythology
LA Area studies
LB Geography
* Alternative only.
LC Travel & description, topography
LD History
LE Study of history... auxiliary sciences: archaeology
LF Prehistory
LG *By social activity*
Social history... political history...
* Alternative only.
[History LD]
By ethnic group
By broad period
LI Ancient history
Modern history
M Favoured country
* For example, UK in British libraries.
N Other countries
As Schedule 2.
O Local history... biography...
* Alternative only for local history.
P Religion... occult... morals & ethics
Q Social welfare & criminology
R Politics... public administration
S Law
T Economics... management of enterprises
U/V Technology & useful arts
Equipment, plant, instrumentation
Systems engineering... control... computers...
Technical testing, maintenance, design... production technology...
Materials handling... packaging... storing...
Energy technologies (general)
Physics–based technologies (nuclear, electrical, thermal, mechanical technologies)
Construction technology... architecture... physical planning...
Environmental technology... safety technology...
Transport technology
Military science & technology
* Alternative only.
Minerals extraction technology... oil & gas well technology...
Process industrial technology... chemical technology.
Manufacture & technology of special products
* Not classed elsewhere.
Agriculture & animal exploitation
* Alternative only.
Useful arts, personal services & technologies
Household management... catering... hotels...
Recreative arts, leisure arts
W Arts, fine arts
W8 Styles, schools, subjects & genres
WC Architecture as an art
WE Plastic arts: sculpture, glyptics, ceramics...
WJ Graphic arts: painting... reprographic arts...
WP Decorative arts
WV Music
WY Performing arts
X Philology: language & literature
XA Linguistics
XL Literature (general & comparative)
Individual languages & their literature
* As Schedule 3 (with modifications), e.g. YV French.
Y Favoured language
* For example, English in British libraries.
Z Religion... occult... morals & ethics
* Alternative is at P.

Volumes in the series

The second edition of the classification will be complete in twenty-two volumes. Twelve have been published so far and are identified by their dates of publication.

Introduction and Auxiliary schedules. 1977.

Class 2/9: Generalia, Phenomena, Knowledge, Information science and technology.

Class A/AL: Philosophy and Logic. 1991.

Class AM/AX: Mathematics, Statistics and Probability. 1993.

Class AY/B: General science and Physics.

Class C: Chemistry.

Class D: Astronomy and Earth sciences.

Class E/GQ: Biological sciences.

Class GR/GZ: Agriculture and Ecology.

Class H: Anthropology, Human biology, Health sciences. 1980. Includes medicine.

Class I: Psychology and Psychiatry. 1978.

Class J: Education. 1990.

Class K: Society. 1984. Includes social science, sociology, social anthropology, customs, folklore and mythology.

Class L/O: History. Includes area studies, travel and topography, and biography.

Class P: Religion, the Occult, Morals and ethics. 1977.

Class Q: Social welfare. 1994. Includes criminology.

Class R: Politics and Public administration. 1996.

Class S: Law. 1996.

Class T: Economics, Management of economic enterprises. 1987.

Class U/V: Technology. Includes household management and services.

Class W: Recreation and Arts. Includes music.

Class X/Y: Language and Literature.

The Bliss Classification Association

Registered charity no. 270580

The Bliss Classification Association is an association of users and supporters of the Bibliographic Classification. It promotes the development and use of the classification, publishes official amendments, enables users to keep in touch and exchange experience, and gives them a say in the future of the scheme. It is a nonprofit organisation, founded in 1967, with members all over the world.

An Annual General Meeting is held each November in London. The Association holds occasional other meetings, organises training in the use of the classification, raises funds, and publishes the Bliss Classification Bulletin each winter.

The Bulletin carries amendments to BC2, news about the Association and the development of the scheme, articles on classification, and reviews. It is available only to members. Membership is open to all organisations and individuals interested in BC2.

The Association's address is:

Bliss Classification Association
The Library
Fitzwilliam College
Huntingdon Road
Cambridge
CB3 0DG
United Kingdom

Please address enquiries about membership or subscriptions to the Hon Treasurer, and other enquiries to the Hon Secretary. The Association is pleased to hear from users and supporters of the classification and to answer questions about it.

Officers of the Association and members of the Committee

During the preparation of the present volume the following members served on the Committee elected at each Annual General Meeting to carry out the work of the Association.

Chair and Hon Editor		
Jack Mills		The Polytechnic of North London
Hon Secretary		
Christina Panagiotidou	1993–1995	University of London Library
Hon Treasurer		
Marion MacLeod	1986–1993	Fitzwilliam College, Cambridge
Angela Haselton	1994–	Tavistock Joint Library, Tavistock Centre
Publicity Officer		
Ed Dua	1993–1994	Department of Health and Social Security
Hon Editor, Bulletin		
Anthony Curwen	1980–	College of Librarianship, Wales
Committee members		
Ken Bell		University of North London
Roger Hughes		Personal member
Marion MacLeod		Fitzwilliam College, Cambridge
Colin Neilson		National Art Library
Chris Preddle		NCH Action For Children

Bliss Classification Association

(Registered charity no. 270580)

Subscription Form for New Members[1]

Subscription rates:	Organisations	£15.00
	Schools and individuals	£10.00

The annual subscription includes the Bliss Classification Bulletin.

Name / Job title ....

Organisation ....

Address ....

....

....

Make cheques, postal orders or international money orders payable to Bliss Classification Association. Overseas subscribers, please send international money orders in pounds sterling.

Signature .... Date ....

Return this form with your subscription to:

Bliss Classification Association
The Library
Fitzwilliam College
Huntingdon Road
Cambridge
CB3 0DG
United Kingdom

[1] Please photocopy this form to prevent damage to the volume

Introduction to Class S
Law

1 This schedule is the result of a rigorous and detailed analysis of the the vocabulary of law, using the techniques of facet analysis. As such, it represents a radical revision and expansion of Class S in the first edition of the Bibliographic Classification (BC1)[1]. The general reasons for making the revision so radical a one are given in the Introduction and Auxiliary schedules[2]. The particular changes in this class are considered in Section 15 below.

2 The Outline on page 1 (after the preliminary pages) is designed to give a clear view of the basic structure. If it is remembered that the schedule is an inverted one (see Section 8) the outline will be seen to show not only the general sequence of facets (categories) and their classes but also the basic operational rule in applying the classification. This is the rule that compound classes (those reflecting the intersection of two or more simpler classes) are located under the class appearing later (lower down) in the schedule. For example, Contract law is SBE; English law is SN; so the compound class English law of contract goes under English law (at SNE) and not under Contract. Similarly, Evidence is S8T; Criminal law is SBW; so the compound class Evidence in criminal law goes under Criminal law (at SBW 8T) and not under Evidence.

3 Scope of Class S and its place in BC2

3.1 The law considered in Class S may be defined briefly as the enforceable body of rules that governs any society. This excludes such constructs as the "laws of nature" and purely moral rules of conduct such as "love thy neighbour". However, moral rules are relevant. Jurisprudence, the theoretical study of the law, examines inter alia exactly what ends the law seeks to achieve, in the sense of what kinds of behaviour should be

[1]Bliss, Henry Evelyn. A Bibliographic classification. New York, The H.W.Wilson Company, 1940/1953.

[2]Bliss bibliographic classification. 2nd ed. by J.Mills and Vanda Broughton. London, Butterworths, 1977- in progress.

deemed legally unacceptable in the society concerned. This also raises the question of what forms of behaviour it is practically feasible to enforce. Another definition (that of Kantorowicz) emphasizes this: a body of social rules prescribing external conduct and considered justiciable.

3.2 The term society in the first definition nearly always means the nation state, or the analogous political aggregates implied by supranational and international law. An enforceable law implies some sort of authoritative source and in the case of the nation state this is the State itself and the political institutions which sustain it. The laws themselves are usually initiated and passed by an executive and legislature and then interpreted and implemented by a judiciary, consisting of judges and other lawyers and the courts within which they operate.

3.3 The location of law in BC2, immediately following politics, reflects the close relationship of the two classes and the fact that most law is ultimately the product of the political process.

3.4 The other main type of society producing a large body of rules prescribing behaviour is that formed by the members of a religion. Insofar as religious law is internal, relating only to its own members, it belongs properly to Class P Religion. But there is often a close connection between the law of a particular religion and that of a country in which that religion is dominant. In the case of established religions, some of the ecclesiastical law is actually part of the national law. Provision is made in Class S for religious jurisdictions.

4 Structure of Class S in BC2

4.1 All classes in BC2 are designed consistently according to a basic pattern which reflects the six fundamental features of a modern documentary classification. In the design operation, these six features are taken in an invariant order, in which each step depends on the preceding ones having first been decided. The steps are, in order: (i) organizing the terms into broad facets; (ii) organizing the terms in each facet into specific arrays; (iii) deciding citation order (between facets and between arrays); (iv) deciding filing order (of facets, of arrays); (v) adding notation; (vi) adding an alphabetical index.

4.2 The theory underlying these features is explained in detail in the Introduction to BC2 (chapters 5 and 6). The application of the features, as they apply to the classification of law, is now considered in some detail in Sections 5/11.

5 Facet structure of law

5.1 The main feature of the schedule is a strict adherence to the principles of facet analysis. A facet consists of all the classes produced when the vocabulary of a subject is divided by one broad principle of division. So the terms making up the vocabulary of law are initially organized into ('divided into') broad facets. Terms representing concepts which stand in the same broad relationship to the containing class are placed in the same facet; e.g. all the terms representing the notion of a jurisdiction (e.g. France, USA, European Union, Islam) are brought together to form a Jurisdictions facet; all the terms representing a particular subject in substantive law (e.g. Persons, Contract, Torts) are brought together to form a Subjects of law facet — and so on.

5.2 Facets in Class S Law

The facets identified by this analysis are summarized below; their scope and relations are considered in more detail under citation order, in Section 7.2.

[1] Jurisdictions — with terms like English law, French law, European Union law, International law, Islamic law...

[2] Substantive law, subjects of law — with terms like marriage law, contract law, property law, criminal law, constitutional law...

[3] Practice and procedure — with terms like courts, hearings, defence, prosecution, evidence, judgement, remedies...

[4] Attributes and principles of law, jurisprudence — with terms like sources of law, philosophical jurisprudence, justice...

[5] Common subdivisions — with terms like persons and organizations in the law, bibliographic form, primary materials...

6 Arrays within facets

6.1 Most facets contain terms which reflect more than one specific principle of division. For example, within the Jurisdictions facet, division may be by political authority (giving English law, European Union law, etc.) or by religious authority (giving Hindu law, Christian law, Islamic law, etc.). Or, within the Substantive law facet, division may be by the type of person affected, the contractual basis of relationships, the nature of the legal interest involved, the particular social activity within which a problem arises (e.g. financial, transport, public administration, etc.). This process may be continued at every level of the classification. For example, within the law of persons, division may be based on age, sex, religion, marital status, ethnicity, etc.

6.2 The terms resulting from division by one specific principle form an array ('subfacet').

6.3 Terms in an array are mutually exclusive; so there is no problem of compounding between them — there can be no class of Christian Islamic law, for example. So the crucial problem of citation order (see Section 7) no longer arises within arrays — only between them.

7 Citation order (combination order)

7.1 This refers to the order in which the elements of a compound class (one consisting of more than one element, whether derived from different facets or from different arrays) are combined ('cited') in a heading. Note that the string of terms making up a heading is called a chain — an important concept in faceted classification. Each term in a chain represents a narrowing of the class defined by the preceding term or terms.

7.11 For example, the subject of a document on women and equal rights in English law could be represented by the chain

English law — Equal rights — Women

However, it could be represented equally meaningfully by five other chains — the total number of combinations of three elements being $3 \times 2 \times 1$; e.g. other chains would be

English law — Women — Equal rights
Equal rights — Women — English law

Citation order decides which of the various possibilities will be followed in the classification.

7.12 Combination order reflects the order of application of the principles of division and determines which concepts are subordinated to others. For example, in the first two headings above, substantive law is subordinated to the jurisdiction and to that extent the literature on any given subject of law would be scattered. But the third heading implies that the literature on a given jurisdiction would be scattered by its subordination to different subjects in substantive law.

7.13 The result of applying a consistent citation order is that the scattering of some subjects because of their subordination to others (a major and inevitable feature of bibliographic classification) is strictly controlled and the location of quite complex classes (reflecting several facets or arrays at the same time) is always predictable. Citation order is the most important feature of a classification system. But clear and consistent rules for it can only be expressed in terms of the facets and arrays involved — hence the prior need to organize terms into facets and arrays.

7.14 Even if the order of the file itself were relatively random as to the subjects of documents, as in an accession-order computer file, say, or in an alphabetically arranged file (where the vagaries of the natural language and the unpredictability of the syntactic forms taken by the different words of a subject description make it a relatively random order) a system of connective references is needed for adequate retrieval. A comprehensive picture of the relations to be accounted for can only be established by a faceted organization of the vocabulary and the application of a controlled citation order.

7.2 Citation order between facets

7.21 In all its classes BC2 seeks to observe as far as possible the 'standard' citation order. For each subject, it seeks to determine the primary (the first-cited) facet by looking for the overall systems in the subject, which systems embody the parts, processes, attributes, etc. peculiar to the subject, on the principle that the whole integrates its parts and gives them meaningful relations. Such systems represent the ultimate object of enquiry in the subject and in many subjects are said to represent the end-product in that subject.

7.22 With the primary facet established, the rest of the standard citation order usually falls into place fairly readily. Each class in the primary facet is divided successively into its types, parts or subsystems, processes, operations (actions on it), agents (of processes or operations). Properties of anything are subordinated to it, whatever category it reflects (type, part, process, etc.). Common facets (history, persons and organizations in the subject, bibliographical forms, etc.) are cited last.

7.23 Citation order of facets in law

7.231 The Jurisdictions facet is cited first. This decision follows directly from the definitions of law given in Section 3 and from a consideration of the legal system as the ultimate object of enquiry in law — i.e. what is the legal position (a propos anything) in a particular jurisdiction?

7.232 The Substantive law facet is cited second. A subject of law in this facet represents that area of activity and behaviour in a society regarding which rules have been established. Such subjects reflect the relationship of subsystem or part of the whole legal system; they are often referred to as branches of the law.

7.233 The Practice and procedures facet is cited third. Procedural law (the term favoured in America) clearly reflects the processes whereby the substantive law is interpreted and judgements made. An important part of the vocabulary of this facet reflects the relationship of agent in these processes, in the form of courts, judges, etc. They are not distinguished as a separate facet since they constitute a 'dependent' facet in relation to the processes.

7.234 The Jurisprudence facet is cited fourth. All the classes of the preceding facets may be examined analytically and theoretically as to their fundamental nature, purpose, origins, etc. The resulting classes combine intellectual operations with consideration of the various attributes of the law. The operations may develop into more concrete ones, as in the case of unification of laws. The term Jurisprudence provides a reasonably accurate and inclusive label for these combined operations and attributes.

7.235 The Common subdivisions of Auxiliary Schedule 1 are cited last (as is usual). The common facets of Time and Place play an important role in defining jurisdictions and in that role are cited first rather than last. However, Time and Place are still needed as common facets (e.g. in specifying local courts). The bibliographical form facet is important; not only does the massive production of official documents call for a special facet to be developed, but it has traditionally been helpful to make a distinction between primary materials (works of law, such as statutes) and secondary materials (works about the law).

7.3 Citation order between arrays

7.31 There are no general principles as yet available for deciding this which are comparable with the standard citation order for citation between facets. Decisions are largely empirical, based on consideration of where a given compound would most helpfully go. For example, in the arrays characterizing types of offences in SBW EQ/SBW WY, the array defined by procedural factors (SBW EQ/EX) reflects a less stable characteristic of division than the others and is therefore cited after them.

7.32 The principles operating in the standard citation order are still applicable to a limited extent; e.g. within Environmental law SBS the array characterizing pollution by location (SBS T/V) is cited before the array by source (SBS RR/ST) since location itself reflects a type of environment whereas the source reflects an agent.

7.33 The number of different arrays is so large that it is out of the question to list them in citation order as is done for facets in Section 7.2. However, the order in which they should be cited is shown clearly by the inverted filing order (see Section 8): an array filing later (further down) in the schedule should be cited before one filing earlier. An example of this is shown in Section 10.51 below for Accessory void contracts (SBE XWC).

8 Filing order

8.1 This is the order in which the individual classes, simple or compound, file one after the other, whether in the schedule, on the shelves or in a catalogue or bibliography. It has two quite separate components — facet filing order and order in array.

8.2 Facet filing order

8.21 This is the order in which the individual facets (each one containing a block of different classes) file one after the other.

8.22 The schedule is an inverted one — i.e. the facets file in an order which is the reverse of the order in which they are cited when compounding terms to form compound classes. So the primary facet (Jurisdictions) files last, the second-cited facet (Substantive law) files next to last, and so on.

8.23 The reason for this (explained more fully in the Introduction to BC2, Section 5.742) is solely to preserve a consistent general-before-special sequence of classes. For example:

S6	Practice & procedure
S9V B	Substantive law
SBW	Criminal law
SBW 6	Practice & procedure

The first class in the above sequence represents Practice & procedure in general. The last class represents Practice & procedure in criminal law; it is a compound class, formed by the intersection of the two 'elementary' classes Practice & procedure and Criminal law; it is a subclass of both these, but is subordinated to Criminal law rather than to Practice & procedure because the citation order rules that the former is cited before the latter. But in filing order, the subclass files after both its 'parents' — the general class in both cases files before the special (the subclass). This is because the filing order of facets is the reverse of their citation order; if it were not so, the following filing order would result:

Substantive law
  Criminal law
    Practice & procedure
Practice & procedure (general)

and general-before-special would not be maintained.

8.24 Similarly, within each facet the arrays are inverted — the first-cited array files last, the second-cited array files next to last, and so on. The two arrays in Environmental law referred to in Section 7.32 above demonstrate this.

8.3 Order in array

8.31 The classes in an array are mutually exclusive and cannot normally be compounded; so their filing order is in no way determined by citation order. Where there is an obviously helpful principle to observe, this is used; e.g. a chronological order is used in S5A 6A (Historical jurisprudence) and SJ/SK (Ancient, medieval and modern law) and (more approximately) in S8L/S9F (Trial proceedings).

9 Alternative treatments and arrangements

9.1 Alternative locations and/or treatments are provided for in a number of cases; i.e. the notation has been designed specifically to allow alterations to be made to the preferred arrangement. In all cases, the preferred arrangement is stated clearly. The general pros and cons of alternatives are explained in the Introduction to BC2 (Sections 5.744, 6.22 and 6.344).

9.2 Alternatives often reflect an underlying theoretical dispute as to where a class is

best collocated (e.g. whether constitutional law should be collocated with constitution making in Class R Politics or with public law in Class S). A number of such problematical cases are considered in Section 12.

9.3 **The main alternatives in Class S are as follows:**

SA/SC Substantive law: two major problems are provided for:

(1) A distinction can be made between traditional branches of law, such as Persons, Contract, Torts, etc. and the law of other special subjects covering most of the general classification, from scientific research to technology and the arts. The preferred arrangement is to locate all substantive law in class S in a general library; but in a library concerned primarily with a particular subject (e.g. social welfare) its law would be subordinated to that subject.

(2) A major cluster of alternatives arises when the citation order between different classes in substantive law is considered (e.g. Contract law — Marriage, or Marriage — Contract law). This question is discussed in Section 12.

SA Conflict of laws (international private law); an alternative (not recommended) is provided under International law, at SDA.

SBS Environmental law; an alternative (not recommended) is provided at SBJ X, where it would be collocated with Planning & development law.

SC Constitutional law; an alternative (not recommended) is provided in Politics, at RF.

SI/SV National jurisdictions; two alternatives (neither recommended) are provided:

(1) Cite the jurisdiction last, not first. The notation of the whole class would then be that of Auxiliary Schedule S1, but each class in S5/SY would be qualified by jurisdiction, using the place facet at S4 (which would take the general works on jurisdictions). For examples, see SHY.

(2) Treat all works other than those explicity dealing with another jurisdiction as though they related solely or mainly to the law of the jurisdiction in which the library finds itself (the 'home country'). So no distinction is drawn between a truly general work on a subject and one on that subject in the jurisdiction of the home country; e.g. in an English library, SE would be used both for general works on contract and works on the English law of contract (further examples are given at SHY. All the law relating specifically to foreign countries would go with those countries.

SL Common law systems (general); an alternative (not recommended) is provided whereby the common law is treated as a single jurisdiction, in which the national juridictions (UK, USA, Australia, etc.) are treated as subclasses and cited after the substantive law within the common law system.

SWF/SYB Law of particular religious systems; this is an alternative (not recommended) to locating in Class P Religion.

10 Notation

10.1 This consists of a base of thirty-five characters — numbers 1/9 followed by letters A/Z. In practice, number one is never used and letter Z only very rarely. Every class represented by one of these characters can be 'divided' by repeating this base indefinitely; e.g. S6 can be divided into S62/S69, S6A/S6Z; then S6N (say) can be divided into S6N 2/S6NZ — and so on.

10.2 The notation is purely 'ordinal' — i.e. it makes no attempt to express hierarchical relations by adding another letter or number to symbolize each step of division. Such an attempt must always fail sooner or later. So BC2 notation concentrates on the primary function of notation, which is simply to maintain the order of classes already determined completely by the theoretical rules governing order (citation order and filing order). By doing this, it secures classmarks which are as brief and as simple as possible. For example:

S6	Practice & procedure
S6E	Courts & court procedure
S8	Actions, lawsuits
S8S	Court actions narrowly, trials, hearings
S8S T	Trial procedure
S9D	Judicial decisions
S9G	Remedies
S9G V	Administrative remedies
S9H	Appeal, Appellate proceedings

Only four of the classmarks in the above chain of nine classes are 'hierarchical' in that they add characters to the classmark of the preceding containing class — S6E, S8S, S8ST, S9GV. On the other hand, the classmarks are shorter than they would have been otherwise; e.g. the last class would need a classmark ten characters long if the notation were hierarchical.

10.3 The notation is fully faceted and synthetic. Compound classes are given classmarks which are built ('synthesized') from their simpler constituent classes according to strict rules. These are explained fully in the Introduction to BC2 (Section 7.4) but the essential ones are repeated here, with examples from law, for convenience.

10.4 The chief method of synthesis is by direct retroactive notation. 'Retroactive' refers to the fact that compounds are formed by 'adding' classes which file earlier — we go 'back' to get them. As a general rule, for any given class in the schedule, all those preceding classes belonging to different facets or arrays (and which are therefore potentially combinable with the class) are available to qualify it by adding the earlier classmark minus its initial letter (in this class, S) directly to the classmark concerned. For example:

S5C	Sources of law
S6	Practice & procedure
S9F	Judgements, awards
SA	Conflict of laws
	(Special concepts in conflict of laws)
SAB	Jurisdiction
	* First enumerated subclass under conflict of laws.

The fact that the first division special to SA (called its First enumerated subclass, or FES) is given the classmark SAB (and not, say, SA2) means that all the classes preceding SA can be added directly (minus the initial S) without clashing with the enumerated classes:

SA	Conflict of laws
SA5C	Sources
SA6	Practice & procedure
SA9F	Judgements, awards
SAB	Jurisdiction

Another example:

SBD	Obligation
SBG	Torts
SBG6	Practice & procedure
SBG8Q	Defence
SBGD	Obligation
SBGG	Liability
SBGH	Public liability
	Kinds of torts
SBGK	Negligence
SBGKL	Voluntary assumption of risk
	* First enumerated subclass of SBGK.

The fact that SBG KL is the first enumerated subclass under SBG K Negligence means that all earlier classes can be added directly to SBG K; e.g. SBG K8Q Defence in negligence; SBG KGH Public liability in negligence. In the last case, the initial SB is dropped before adding, not just the initial S. This is explained in 10.61 below.

10.5 Clearly, direct retroactive synthesis requires that all the letters introducing facets and arrays earlier than the class being qualified must be 'reserved' under the latter; so the first subclass special to it (its first enumerated subclass) must be given a number or letter later in filing order than all those preceding the class. As classes begin with later and later letters of the alphabet, so the number of earlier letters to be reserved increases and the letters available for enumerating the subclasses special to them decreases.

10.51 This presents no problem to a purely ordinal notation, because the next notational array is drawn into service to accommodate these further special subclasses; e.g.

SBE	Contract law
	Types of contracts
SBEWC	Accessory contracts
SBEX	Void contracts
SBEXWC	Accessory void contracts
	* Example of compounding between arrays; see Section 10.6.
SBEYB	Contracts against public policy

Under SBE X, only X/Y are available for enumerated subclasses, since retroactive synthesis uses the letters up to W (as in the example). To gain more notational space for enumerated subclasses, SBE YB, SBE YC, etc. are drawn into use, although hierarchically they do not 'look' like divisions of SBE X.

10.6 Adding classmarks from preceding arrays

10.61 In some cases, two classmarks being linked share the same two initial letters. As a rule, both these letters may be dropped when adding earlier classes; e.g. 'SB' is dropped under SBP Transport law:

SBE	Contract law
SBG	Tort
SBGG	Liability
SBP	Transport law
SBPE	Contract law
SBPGG	Tort liability

This is very common in Class SB which consists entirely of substantive law, making the SB common to all its subclasses.

10.62 Not infrequently it is quite feasible to drop the initial three letters when adding arrays:

SBW	Criminal law
SBWC	Crimes
	Elements in crimes
SBWCE	Commission or omission of offence
SBWCG	Criminal responsibility
SBWD	Criminals, offenders
SBWDM	Mentally ill offenders
	Forms of offence
SBWFP	Petty offences
SBWFPDM	*By mentally ill offenders*

Here, three letters are dropped when qualifying any particular crime by classes SBW A/E. From SBW F onwards, the likelihood of compounding is very much less (by legal definition, most of the types of offences are mutually exclusive). So an intercalator 'F' (see 10.8) is used to introduce all the remaining offences should they be needed as qualifiers or specifiers. For example, Offences against public order (SBW R) can be qualified by Rural crime (SBW GA) to give SBW RFG A. A useful result of this is that the first enumerated subclass under every specific form of offence can begin as early as G, which makes for shorter classmarks. See 10.8 for an explanation of intercalators.

10.7 Forward synthesis

In a very limited number of cases, nearly all within SB Substantive law, it may be necessary to build classmarks forwards rather than retroactively. Such an eventuality is always noted in the schedule and a special Add instruction provided; for an example, see Section 12.46 below.

10.8 Intercalators (facet indicators)

10.81 Another method of synthesis used extensively in Class S is to use a particular letter (or, sometimes, a number) to 'introduce' or indicate a set of classes taken from elsewhere in the classification; these classes are inserted at a required point in the schedule. The selected letter(s) or number(s) at that point are called intercalators. The chief situations where this occurs are:

10.82 Amplification of a class by an auxiliary schedule.

10.821 The most prominent example of this is Auxiliary Schedule S1. This auxiliary reflects a feature of the legal literature which is important in assigning notation. Most of this literature relates to particular jurisdictions and by far the greater part of it will fall within the last (Jurisdictions) facet. Relatively little will be found on the general subjects of (say) torts, or high courts. So optimum brevity of notation has been served by enumerating the detailed vocabulary of practice and procedure and of substantive law in S6/9, SA/SC. All this detail is then available for the qualifying of any jurisdiction, large or small; but instead of squeezing it all into divisions 6/9, A/C of the jurisdiction, the notation has been spread out over the whole base in Auxiliary Schedule S1. The order of classes is quite unaffected.

10.83 Amplification by another class in S outside normal synthesis.

10.831 One example of this is SBW HK Criminal torts, which is divided like SBG K/V Types of torts. It occurs also when normal synthesis is interrupted in order to secure briefer notation when a particular class is expanded in a special context. For example, SBJ is qualified retroactively by SBI. At SBJ IS (from SBI S) normal synthesis is interrupted (to allow a large expansion of rights and interests in property) and is resumed at SBJ O. So 'O' now acts as an intercalator, introducing the remaining classes of SBI — e.g. SBJ OT (from SBI T).

10.84 Amplification by a class taken from outside Class S.

10.841 A major example of this is SBN Economic and commercial law, the entire contents of which are taken from Class T Economics and Management. Compounding of economic and management concepts follows the rules for retroactive synthesis found in Class T. This would clash with the rules for retroactive synthesis within Class S, were the latter applied without adjustment; e.g. International trade is SBN OI (from TOI); Trade agreements is SBN OI AHW (from TOI AHW, taken in turn from TAH W); but this classmark SBN OI AHW would, by the rules for Class S, be something from Conflict of laws in international trade (SAH is a subclass of Choice of laws). So an intercalator (9X) is used throughout SBN to introduce letters taken from Class S.

10.842 Other prominent examples of amplification by outside classes are found in International law (SD), where extensive use is made of classes from Class R Politics, and in SAP/SBC Law of persons, where extensive use is made of classes from Class K Society.

10.85 Enumeration of compounds in schedues

10.851 In principle, a faceted classification consists simply of facets and arrays of relatively elementary terms; all compounds are formed by the classifier assigning classmarks to them by means of synthesis, observing strict rules of citation order. Consequently, the exact location of all potential compounds is fully predictable and compound classes are not usually to be found enumerated in the schedules.

10.852 This principle is modified in BC2 in a number of cases. The most obviously necessary one is where a general concept, on being used to qualify a particular context (in Class S this is usually a particular jurisdiction) generates a special term, peculiar to that context. For example:

SYB	Islamic law
SYB 5C	Sources
	Jurists as sources
SYB 5TF	Shurut

Other obvious examples are the enumeration under English law (SN) of Parliamentary debates in order to accommodate the well-used term 'Hansard' and of High courts to accommodate special terms, like Chancery Division, peculiar to that context.

10.853 Another reason for enumeration of some classes is to assist the indexer to follow the structure of the class. The concepts given under the various facets represent fundamental notions in law; this is demonstrated by the fact that they have been used successfully over and over again to represent those concepts in quite different types of jurisdictions. Nevertheless, each jurisdiction may generate local variations at some points which demand recognition. A prominent example of this is seen under Islamic law (SYB) where the enumerated classes display not only special terminology but in some cases reflect some adjustment to the definition or scope of the general classes used to arrive at them.

In such cases (of a few enumerated compound classes appearing in the schedules) it should not be thought that the detail in that part is limited to the subclasses thus enumerated. When assessing the specificity of the vocabulary in a given class it should always be remembered that the class may be qualified by all earlier facets and arrays, whether this is hinted at by a limited enumeration or not.

The different ways of building classmarks described above may give an impression of daunting complexity at first reading. But so would the simplest action if described in terms of its basic operational steps. The detailed sequence of instructions we need to give a computer for it to process the simplest operation demonstrates this Applying notation is a practical operation. The steps involved are basically simple and quickly become familiar after a little practice. Detailed explanations and examples are given in the Introduction to BC2 (Section 7.4) and a simple flowchart covering all possibilities appeared in the Bliss Classification Bulletin, January 1978.

11 Alphabetical subject index

11.1 The function of the alphabetical index in a classified indexing system is considered in the Introduction to BC2; Section 6.5 gives general principles and Section 7.5 gives practical guidance to a library making its own alphabetical index to its own stock.

11.2 The main points to be remembered for efficient use of the printed index to the schedules of this class will be found on the page preceding the alphabetical index.

11.3 The basic rules are those of chain indexing. If an entry is qualified at all, it is by a superordinate class (a containing class helping to define it). An entry term is never qualified (followed by) a term representing one of its own subclasses in the schedule; e.g.

Contract law SBE
but not
Contracts, Joint SBF CJ

The latter class will have its own entry under Joint contracts; but in the form given above it would simply duplicate the work done in the classified schedule — i.e. displaying the subclasses of contract law.

11.4 The alphabetical index to Class S has been produced largely by automatic selection of terms from the schedules, using a computer program written to this end. The program includes, for example, rules for deleting anti-chain entries such as Contracts, Joint. Entry words are qualified only when the same entry word leads to more more than one classmark and it is necessary to distinguish the different contexts involved.

12 Special problems in Class S

12.1 So far as is feasible, problems of definition and analysis and the practical decisions taken to meet them are noted in the schedules at the point of application. Others are implicit to some extent in the provision of alternatives. But a number of theoretical problems seem to call for more extended consideration and these are given below.

12.2 International law as a jurisdiction

12.21 Although the international community does not have as yet machinery for implementing international law comparable with that wielded by nation states in municipal law or by religious jurisdictions in canonical law, the relationship is essentially the same. It constitutes a body of rules purporting to regulate the behaviour of a community of persons — in this case, of corporate persons in the form of nation states.

12.3 Supranational jurisdictions

12.31 The scale on which the European Union has developed in the past few decades demonstrates the need to recognize this array in the jursdictions facet. The jurisdictional status of many other supranational organizations is less clear. But it seems helpful to locate them all in the same array

12.32 The constitutional structure of the EU is sufficiently different to warrant a special modification of the provisions made for national jurisdictions. It is hoped that this will proved an adequate model for the classification of other supranational jurisdictions.

12.4 Substantive law

12.41 This was decidedly the most difficult facet to schedule. It is divided traditionally into two large classes, private law and public law. Within private law, a fair amount of compounding is possible, which means that several different arrays are present. But it has proved remarkably difficult to name them.

12.42 Bliss named the contents of substantive law the "special subjects" of law. But some would appear to be more special than others. At least, it appears that a number of them, representing mostly well-established branches of law, reflect common and ubiquitous legal relationships; these may be defined by the type of persons involved (e.g. minors), the type of formally legal relationship established (e.g. agreements and contracts), other relationships which the law perforce regulates (e.g. torts) and so on. They are often referred to as the branches of law.

12.43 If the above branches demonstrate common special subjects, others may be thought of as special special subjects. These embrace all kinds of activities — in fact, all human activities susceptible to legal regulation other than those represented by the common special subjects. They range from specialized economic and business activities such as investment, marketing and accounting to social welfare measures, questions of the environment and pollution and cultural matters such as scientific research or archeological enquiry.

12.44 The rough distinction made above (between common and special "special subjects of law") clearly suggests a broad citation order — i.e. special special subjects should be cited before the common (traditional) special subjects. But this still leaves the problem of fairly frequent compounding within the group of traditional subjects of law without, any clear rules for citation order. For example, a prominent class of property relations consists of those established by marriage; in classificatory terms, the product is a type of property and this suggests a citation order: Property — Marriage. The general class Marriage is located under Family — the most fundamental of the groups making up the class Persons. A subclass of Marriage is the process of termination or divorce, and another compound is formed by the question of division of property on divorce. Most of the catalogues and bibliographies consulted in the course of designing class S tended to locate this last subject under divorce law. But this would be inconsistent with the citation order suggested earlier.

12.45 The solution (if it can be called this) to the problem of citation order between the subjects of substantive law was the following filing order under Private law (to be interpreted in the usual BC2 way as the reverse of citation order):

12.451 Persons (as being the enduring common factor in all the relationships regulated).

12.452 Four traditional special subjects, reflecting recurrent legal relationships: Obligation, Contract, Tort, Property.

12.453 A greatly expanded class, covering economic and business relations, to give a systematic context to some further traditional branches such as mercantile law, sale of goods, maritime law, etc.

12.454 All other special subjects, in an order approximating the whole classification.

12.46 But the vagaries of relationships in law have meant that the citation order rules are not quite as strict as is normally the case in BC2. To provide for the extra flexibility implied, all classes in substantive law can be divided by the rest of the class if the relationship demands it. So a few classmarks may be built forwards rather than backwards (retroactively). This will often be the result of the 'pull' of a sub-disciplinary specialization; e.g. SBN H Insurance — Marine (rather than the retroactive Maritime law — Insurance in SBQ A)

12.47 The general rule remains: always cite retroactively unless there is a very strong reason for not doing so.

12.5 Law as a disciplinary class

12.51 The discussion above (Section 12.4) has assumed a substantive law facet which includes all special subjects of law. But the general rule in BC2 is to subordinate social aspects (law, economics, etc.) of a subject with that subject. This rule reflects a dilution of the principle of the 'disciplinary' general classification. In such a classification, the literature on each given form of knowledge (philosophy, history, social science, etc.) is kept together, regardless of its 'subject' or 'phenomenon'.

12.52 BC2 has followed Bliss in rejecting this extreme interpretation of the principle and is more accurately described as a basically discipline oriented scheme (see Introduction to BC2, Section 5.5).

12.53 The problem is posed quite sharply in law. The subordination of law, or any other social science, to a subject reflects the basic indexing relationship of Patient — Action — Agent; e.g. a public library provides a service to the community and the social conditions attaching to that service closely affect that service; these conditions include the law regulating the service. However, that law, although it may sound special to and dependent on the concept of public library, is in many ways even more dependent on the general body of law containing it. For example, most of the relations between the library and its users and staff will be governed by the general law relating to contract, tort, property, etc.; its provision of copying facilities, say, involve copyright law; any levying of charges, say, will involve local government law. Moreover, the primary materials relevant to the subject (statutes, law reports, etc.) will most likely be found in the law class itself.

12.54 The factors just indicated constitute a strong argument for keeping all the law literature together (e.g. locating public library law in S rather than with librarianship). Hence the decision, noted in Section 9.2, to provide for alternative treatments of substantive law (which is the facet largely concerned).

12.6 A particular example of the above problem is constitutional law. In BC1, Bliss argued strongly that it should be subordinated to politics and the penultimate draft of class S in BC2 agreed. However, to the lawyer, constitutional law is the major part of public law (ill-defined as this is in common law systems). It is typically specialized in its legal terminology and inextricably bound up with other branches of law and with the whole apparatus of primary materials in law. Some of its classes (e.g. taxation law in public administration) would seem quite out of place in politics. For these reasons, it was decided to enumerate the class in S rather than in R, although an alternative is provided in R, of course. But the making of constitutions is so crucial a part of the political process that it is still preferred in class R.

12.7 Practice and procedure

12.71 The broad order in this facet is chronological, from the initiation of legal proceedings to the judgements which end them.

12.72 Strict application of facet analysis and indexing rules resolved a number of theoretical problems. Two prominent examples are the recognition of courts as being agents of the legal process rather than systems within which the process wholly goes on, and of forensic science and technology as being an agent of the specific process of establishing the status of evidence.

12.73 The problem of a universally valid vocabulary is particularly acute in this facet. Many terms have a decidedly English flavour, although they include plenty of examples of dog Latin, which tends to the universal. But it is worth emphasising that the schedules are not based on terminology but on conceptual analysis. It is assumed that the minutiae of procedures, from cautioning to questioning to arresting to charging etc. (in the case of criminal procedure, for example) are fundamental to all jurisdictions, whatever the special terminology by which they are locally known.

12.8 Primary materials in law

12.81 This proved a depressingly time-consuming facet to produce. The analytical power of facet analysis which is so effective in organizing special subjects of all kinds (and which is the major factor making possible the production of BC2 with such restricted resources) was only of limited assistance. This is because it is an area in which literary warrant is a powerful determinant in organizing the vocabulary. Bliss's own words prefacing the section of his introduction relating to law (Ref.1) proved very apposite:

> [Law]... does not seem one of the most difficult of the many problems of classification. A system proposed, however, for a general bibliographic classification may not be altogether satisfactory to the legal profession, which needs not only a rational scheme for the literature... [but also] an adequate organization of the resources of the profession in 'practice'...

> the traditional 'sources', and the bodies of codified and statutory law, and the Reports of cases and of decisions in the Courts... The records are innumerable, complicated, elaborate, and widely distributed, and the literature is immense... The problem for bibliographic classification is how to systemize this vast maze of resources.

12.82 Nevertheless, examination of this facet in schedules for numerous jurisdictions (for most of which we have the Library of Congress to thank) revealed a substantial core of common forms of materials. From this core two auxiliary schedules (S2 and S3) were developed — one for national jurisdictions and one for supranational jurisdictions. The latter reflected some of the particular characteristics of international law primary materials (which have been given their own enumerated schedule). Religious jurisdictions have also been given a special schedule for this facet.

13 Practical classification in Class S

13.1 The general rules for classifying by BC2 are considered in the Introduction to BC2 (Section 7) and only a summary of the main points as they apply to Class S appears here.

13.11 Decide first which alternatives are to be used (if any) and delete clearly from the schedules those which are rejected. Once this is done it is done for good and henceforth the alternatives are irrelevant to the library concerned. It also results in a significant simplification of the schedule.

13.111 If several alternatives are adopted, try to be consistent in the decisions taken. If many modifications are made to the standard citation order, the overall predictability in the location of classes is eroded and it becomes less easy to explain the system to library users. The regularity of pattern resulting from the consistent application of a few, simply explained rules makes BC2 much easier to explain than the inconsistent arrangements usually found in older systems (and some newer ones).

13.2 For each document, three distinct operations are necessary:

13.21 Concept analysis

13.211 This means examining the document to decide which concepts are required for a statement of the document's subject. Such a statement should describe what the document is about, using the classifier's own words or words taken from the document. It need not be restricted to the vocabulary of the indexing language. The statement should aim to summarize the overall subject of the document (as distinct from any subsidiary subjects referred to in the document).

13.212 In formulating the concept analysis statement, it is helpful to ask certain questions to ensure that all essential concepts are incorporated. These questions are best posed in the order of the facet structure of the class. The facets themselves are a guide to the kinds of questions to ask. For example, is the document restricted to a particular jurisdiction? To a particular subject in substantive law? To a particular process, etc. in practice and procedure? To a particular concept in jurisprudence? To a particular form of presentation?

13.213 The answers to these questions are then best set out (using the terms of the title, subtitle, etc. so far as appropriate) in a line; e.g. a title "Appealing against the liquor laws [in Maryland]" would be set out as Maryland (USA) — Liquor laws — Appeals. This would imply the following sequence of questions and answers: Any particular jurisdiction? Yes: Maryland, USA. Any particular subject of law? Yes: Liquor (regulation of sale, etc.). Any particular process? Yes: Appeal... In the examples following 13.32 below this sequence for each title is given in abreviated form, so that the title above would appear as:

> [Jurisdiction?] Maryland (USA) / [Substantive law?] Liquor laws / [Practice & procedure?] Appeal...

This approach to concept analysis helps ensure that no significant concept is missed. It also goes a long way to completing the second step — deciding the citation order.

13.22 Deciding citation order

13.221 The second operation is to decide the detailed citation order according to the rules given in Section 7. The string of terms produced in 13.213 is amended, if necessary, to produce a chain — a string of terms in which each term represents a class subordinate to the term preceding it. In the examples below, we give after each term in the citation chain the classmark for that term as it first appears in the schedule — i.e., representing the concept in general, on its own, uncompounded. Normally, these classmarks will be seen to reflect the inverted filing order — i.e., concepts appearing earlier in the chain will have classmarks filing later in the schedule. Apparent exceptions to this are explained in the comments on Title 1 in 13.3.

13.23 Translating the chain into notation

13.231 The third operation is to translate the chain above into a classmark, observing the rules summarized in Section 10.

13.3 Examples of practical classification

13.31 The following examples are chosen primarily to demonstrate problems of relations between constituent concepts in compound classes and the accompanying problems of synthesis. Most of them reflect relatively specific subjects and as the number of constituent elements gets larger, the classmarks get longer, naturally. It should be remembered that a great deal of the literature, particularly at the book level, does not call for such extensive compounding. For all literature, BC2 notation, because of its purely ordinal nature and because of its large base of thirty-five characters, is generally shorter than equivalent classmarks in other general systems.

13.32 Two presentations of the classmark are given as the last step under each example. The first version breaks it into its constituent elements in order to show clearly how the bits are added together. The second version, breaks it into regular blocs of three characters; this is easier to follow when scanning books on a shelf or entries in a classified catalogue and is the recommended form for stating BC2 classmarks on documents, on entries in catalogues or bibliographies, and so on.

[1] **Title:** *Patent infringment litigation costs*

Concept analysis: [Jurisdiction?] nil / [Substantive law?] Patents / Infringement / [Practice & procedure?] / Litigation / Award of costs / [Jurisprudence?] Nil / [Common subdivision?] Nil

Chain: Patent law (SBM) — Torts (SBG) — Special to a context — Infringement (special to intellectual & industrial property) (SBGV) — Practice & procedure (S6) — Actions (S8) — Award of costs (S9FR)

Classmark: SBM GV 9FR (SBM GV9 FR)

Comments:

1. A note in Section 13.221 states that the 'general' classmarks given in the chain will reflect inverted filing order — i.e. those appearing earlier in the chain usually file (in the schedule) after those appearing later. This rule appears to be broken in this example; but it is not. Torts special to a context (SBGV) is dependant on SBG Torts, its general containing class and will always follow it. There is no question of SBGV being 'qualified' by SBG because the latter files before it. SBG is implicit in SBGV.

2. Similarly, Award of costs (S9FR) is a subclass of Actions (S8) which in turn is a subclass of Practice & procedure (S6). Both S6 and S8 are implicit in S9FR and are therefore omitted from the final classmark.

[2] **Title:** *Agency agreements in the export trade*

Concept analysis: [Jurisdiction?] Nil / [Substantive law?] / Agency / Agreements / Export / Trade / [Practice & procedure?] Nil / [Jurisprudence?] Nil / [Common subdivision?] Nil

Chain: Commercial law (SBN) — Overseas economic relations (SBNO) — International trade (SBN OI) — Exports (SBN OO) — Agency (SBFW) — Agreements (SBDJ)

Classmark: SBN OO 9X FW DJ (SBN OO9 XFW DJ)

Comments:

1. Although this work has English law primarily in mind, exports inevitably involve the law of other jurisdictions, so the general class has been preferred.
2. Class SBN is taken entirely from Class T Economics and Management and retroactive synthesis within it follows the rules of Class T, not Class S. So a special intercalator (facet indicator) is needed to distinguish qualification of an economic concept by another economic concept from qualification by a Class S concept. The symbol 9X serves this need and maintains the desired filing order (whereby the special economic subclasses file after the legal ones, since they are cited before them).
3. At SBN 9X an instruction appears to add letters A/Y in Auxiliary Schedule S1 — i.e. synthesis now follows Class S. Letters B/W in Auxiliary Schedule S1 are taken from SBB/SBW; so the initial SB in the classmarks for Agency and Agreements is dropped and FW and DJ are added directly (and retroactively) in the normal way.

[3] **Title:** *Arbitration in international investment agreements*

Concept analysis: [Jurisdiction?] International law / [Sustantive law?] Investment / Agreements / [Practiced & procedure?] Arbitration / [Jurisprudence?] Nil [Common subdivision?] Nil

Chain: International law (SD) — International economic relations (SBNO) — Investment (SBN GL) — Agreement (SBDJ) — Arbitration S9R

Classmark: SD BNO GL 9X DJ 9R (SDB NOG L9X DJ9 R)

Comments:

1. Unlike national jurisdictions, substantive law in international law occupies 9VB/B (from S9VB/SB) rather than 9VB/W. This is in order to provide for a large vocabulary of special subjects in international law (taken largely from Class R Politics). So only the initial S is dropped from SBNO when adding it to SD.
2. Retroactive synthesis within SBN follows the rules in Class T. In Class T, the initial T is dropped; here, the equivalent SBN is dropped — so GL is added directly to SDB NO.

[4] **Title:** *Space law in the United Nations*

Concept analysis: [Jurisdiction?] International law / [Substantive law?] Space / [Practice & procedure?] Nil / [Jurisprudence?] Nil / [Common subdivision?] International organizations / UN

Chain: International law (SD) — Space law (SBQG) — International organizations (SD5LS) — United Nations (SD5N)

Classmark: SD BQG 5N (SDB QG5 N)

Comments:

1. See comment 1 under title 3 above.
2. SD5 LS is implicit in its subclass SD5N and so is not added.
3. Both 5LS and 5N are taken from SD, not from S5 as would normally be the case. This is because the classes at S5 are significantly modified in SD in order to accommodate a number of concepts special to international law.

[5] **Title:** *International law and aboriginal rights*

Concept analysis: [Jurisdiction?] International law / [Substantive law?] Aboriginals / Human rights / [Practice & procedure?] Nil / [Jurisprudsence?] Nil [Common subdivision?] Nil

Chain: International law (SD) — Nationality (SDI) — Indigenous peoples (SCD OO) — Human rights (SDCW)

Classmark: SDI O CW (SDI OCW)

Comments:

1. The class States as international persons (SDEM/SDKU) is an enumerated special subject in international law. But at SDI Nationality it draws on Constitutional law (SC) for its detailed vocabulary; the classes N/P following SCDO (Nationality in constitutional law) are now added to SDI by special instruction, to give SDI O.
2. SDCW Human rights is also an enumerated special subject in international law (although one drawn from Class R Politics). It is therefore added directly to SDI O, dropping the initial SD which is common to both.

[6] **Title:** *The waters around the British Isles*

Concept analysis: [Jurisdiction?] International law / [Substantive law?] Coastal waters / British Isles / [Practice & procedure?] Nil / [Jurisprudence?] Nil / [Common subdivision?] Nil

Chain: International law (SD) — National territory (SDK) — Coastal waters (SDK OL) — British Isles (S4E)

Classmark: SDKOL 4 E (SDK OL4 E)

Comments:

1. SDK is implicit in SDK OL and is omitted in synthesis.
2. The common subdivision for place consists of 4 followed by letters from Auxiliary Schedule 2 (Place). It is not often used in Class S (where place normally defines a jurisdiction) — but this is one such occasion.

[7] **Title:** *Nuclear weapons, the peace movement and the law*

Concept analysis: [Jurisdiction?] International law / [Substantive law?] Nuclear weapons / Peace Movement / [Practice & procedure?] Nil / [Jurisprudence?] Nil / [Common subdivision?] Nil

Chain: International law (SD) — National security (SDOA) — Weapons systems (SDOQ) — Nuclear weapons (SDO R) — Peace movement (SDNQ)

Classmark: SDOR NQ (SDO RNQ)

Comments:

1. SDOA and SDOQ are implicit in SDOR and are omitted from synthesis.
2. SDNQ is added directly to SDOR, dropping the initial SD which is common to both,

[8] **Title:** *Law for accountancy students*

Concept analysis: [Jurisdiction?] English law / [Substantive law?] Nil / [Practice & procedure?] Nil / [Jurisprudence?] Nil / [Common subdivision?] / For particular kind of reader / Accountants

Chain: English law (SN) — In special form of presentation S33 — For a particular kind of reader (S33C) — By subject interest — Accountancy (TO)

Classmark: SN 3 3C TO (SN3 3CT O)

Comments:

1. Special note at S3 instructs addition of 2/3 to get classes 2/3 from Auxiliary Schedule 1 (Common form subdivisions). So 3C is added to S3 to get law books for special readers. The resulting S33C is then added directly to SN, but dropping the initial S (now redundant).

2. In Auxiliary Schedule 1, a special note at 3C instructs addition of numbers and letters from the whole classification to indicate special subject interest. So TO (from the Management class TQ/TY) is added to show Accountants.

[9] **Title:** *Glamorgan Court of Quarter Sessions*

Concept analysis: [Jurisdiction?] English law / [Substantive law?] Nil / [Practice & procedure?] Court of Quarter Sessions / [Jurisprudence?] Nil / [Common subdivision?] Place / Glamorgan

Chain: English law (SN) — Courts (S7) — Higher courts (S7R) — Special to English law — Quarter Sessions (S7RV) — (By place) (S4) — England & Wales — Glamorgan (ERN)

Classmark: SN 7RV 4 RN (SN7 RV4 RN)

Comments:

1. Quarter Sessions is not enumerated at S7RV, but at SN7 RV, since it is special to English law.

2. The common subdivision for Place is used here to indicate local division. Since the concept of the containing country (England & Wales) is already implicit in SN, the initial E of ERN (in Auxiliary Schedule 2 for Place) is dropped.

[10] **Title:** *Damages for personal injury*

Concept analysis: [Jurisdiction?] English law / [Substantive law?] Tort / Personal injuries / [Practice & procedure?] Actions / Damages / [Jurisprudence?] Nil / [Common subdision?] Nil

Chain: English law (SN) — Tort (SBG) — Trespass to person (SBGQ) — Real injuries (SBG QR) — Actions (S8) — Damages (S9M)

Classmark: SN GQR 9M (SNG QR9 M)

Comments:

1. Example of simple retroactive synthesis, following Auxiliary Schedule S1.
2. SBG is implicit in SBG Q and SBG Q is implicit in SBG QR. Similarly, S8 is implicit in S9M. Implicit containing classes are always omitted from the classmark.

[11] **Title:** *Court of Protection and property interests*

Concept analysis: [Jurisdiction?] English law / [Substantive law?] Insane persons / Property interests / [Practice & procedure?] Court of Protection / [Jurisprudence?] Nil / [Common subdivision?] Nil

Chain: English law (SN) — Property (SBH) — Persons (SAP) — Insane (SAYE) — Special courts (S7UF) — Court of protection (special to insane sersons) (S7UG)

Classmark: SN H AYE 7UG (SNH AYE 7UG)

Comments:

1. Simple retroactive synthesis, following Auxiliary Schedule S1.
2. SAP is implicit in SAYE and is omitted in synthesis.

[12] **Title:** *Liability of banks under letters of credit*

Concept analysis: [Jurisdiction?] English law / [Substantive law?] Liability / Banks / Letters of credit / [Practice & procedure?] Nil / [Jurisprudence?] Nil / [Common subdivision?] Nil

Chain: English law (SN) — Economic & commercial law (SBN) — Letters of credit (SBN GJV H) — Banks (SBN FG) — Liability (SBDG)

Classmark: SN NGJVH FG 9X DG (SNN GJV HFG 9XD G)

Comments:

1. See note under Example 2 re use of 9X.
2. This example demonstrates nicely an old indexing criterion for a good chain: can it be read back in the natural language? For example, Liability [of] Banks [for] Letters of credit [in] Commercial law [in] English law.

[13] **Title:** *Women and harrassment at work*

Concept analysis: [Jurisdiction?] English law / [Substantive law?] Women / Harrassment / Work / [Practice & procedure?] Nil / [Jurisprudence?] Nil / [Common subdivision?] nil

Chain: English law (SN) / Employment, work (SBNL) / Employees (SBN LVE) / Women employees (SBN LWM] / Torts against persons (SBGN) / Harrassment (SBG NS)

Classmark: SN NLWM 9X GNS (SNN LWM 9XG NS)

Comments:

1. See note under Example 2 re use of 9X.
2. The classmark for Women employees is enumerated in SBN L (taken from TL), so the general classmark for Women in the law of persons (SAX W) is not used. A general rule in BC2 is that enumerated classes are always preferred to synthetic ones if both provisions occur.

[14] **Title:** *Tanker voyage charter parties*

Concept analysis: [Jurisdiction?] English law / [Substantive law?] Maritime law / Oil tankers / Charter parties / [Practice & procedure?] Nil / [Jurisprudence?] Nil / [Common subdivision?] Nil

Chain: English law (SN) — Maritime law (SBQA) — Carriage of goods (SBPU) — Oil (SBPUYOI) — Special vehicles (SBPSN) — Contract law (SBE) — Special to a context (SBFE/K) — Charter parties (special to maritime law) (SBFJ)

Classmark: SN QA UY OI SN FJ (SNQ AUY OIS NFJ)

Comments:

1. Each form of transport, including sea transport, is divided like SBP Tranport law in general. Simple retroactice synthesis operates throughout SBP, so letters following SBP (UYOI and SN above) are added directly to SBQA.

[15] **Title:** *Crown court practice: sentencing*

Concept analysis: [Jurisdiction?] English law / [Substantive law?] Criminal law / [Practice & procedure?] Crown courts / Sentencing / [Jurisprudence?] Nil / [Common subdivision?] Nil

Chain: English law (SN) — Criminal law (SBW) — Sentencing (S9PL) — High courts (S7R) — Special to a context (e.g. Crown courts in English law) (S7RT)

Classmark: SN W 9PL 7RT (SNW 9PL 7RT)

Comments:

1. The title belongs to a series on crown court practice. The relation between the different aspects of crown court practice would be brought out by a series entry and/or chain index entries (see Section 11) in a catalogue or bibliography.

2. The citation order which cites sentencing before the court reflects a basic indexing principle in BC2; the court is regarded as an agent in effecting the act of sentencing (after trial) of convicted persons.

[16] **Title:** *Impact of Community law on VAT in the United Kingdom*

Concept analysis: [Jurisdiction?] English law / [Substantive law?] Taxation / VAT / [Practice & procedure?] Nil / [Jurisprudence?] Sources / European Union (Community) law / [Common subdivision?] Nil

Chain: English law (SN) — Public administration law (SCL) — Taxation (SCL MPH) — Sources (S5C) — Supranational jurisdictions (European Union) (S5S)

Classmark: SN X LMPH 5S (SNX LMP H5S)

Comments:

1. Citation order observes the basic indexing rule of citing the thing influenced before the influencing factor. But the specific nature of the influence — that of a source of law — is preferred to the vaguer general influence intercalator at S58.
2. Applying Auxiliary Schedule S1, X is used to introduce the divisions of SC.

[17] **Title:** *Mareva injunction*

Concept analysis: [Jurisdiction?] Australian law / [Substantive law?] Nil / [Practice & procedure?] Actions / Mareva injunction / [Jurisprudence?] Nil / [Common subdivision?] Nil

Chain: Australian law (SOS) — Actions (S8) — Remedies (S9G) Injunctions (S9N) — Mareva (S9NV)

Classmark: SOS 9NV (SOS 9NV)

Comments:

1. Simple retroactive synthesis.
2. S8, S9G and S9N are all implicit in S9NV, and are therefore omitted.

[18] **Title:** *Aboriginal land rights in Australia*

Concept analysis: [Jurisdiction?] Australian law / [Substantive law?] Aboriginals / Land tenure / [Practice & procedure?] Nil / [Jurisprudence?] / [Common subdivision?] Nil

Chain: Australian law (SOS) — Real property (SBJ) — Property ownership & possession (SBHJ) — Persons (SAP) — Aboriginals (SBBO)

Classmark: SOS J HJ BO (SOS JHJ BO)

Comments:

1. Note at SBH Property law explicitly instructs the addition of A/IS in Auxiliary Schedule S1 directly to the whole class — which means all its subclasses as well as the general class.
2. The general facet for persons is used to represent aboriginals; were the latter to be given a degree of autonomy akin to that of individual states, a place would have to be found for them under the constitutional law of Australia (SOS X) — at SOS XTV, say. In this case Aboriginals would be cited before property or any other branch of substantive law.

[19] **Title:** *Islamic law in Sudan*

Concept analysis: [Juridiction?] Sudan / [Substantive law?] / Nil / [Practice & procedure?] Nil / [Jurisprudence?] Sources / Islamic law / [Common subdivision?] Nil

Chain: Sudanese law (SVV AS) — Sources (S5C) — Religious law (S5F) — Islamic (SYB)

Classmark: SVVAS 5F YB (SVV AS5 FYB)

Comments:

1. Although religious jurisdictions file after political ones, they are cited after the latter when compounds arise. This minor theoretical inconsistency in Class S is due to historical reasons.
2. An alternative allows all Islamic law to be kept together, with division by country at SYE.
3. A note at S5F instructs the addition of specific religions from SW/SY.

[20] **Title:** *Casebook on Kenyan customary law*

Concept analysis: [Jurisdiction?] Kenyan law / [Substantive law?] Nil / [Practice & procedure?] Nil / [Jurisprudence?] Sources / Customary law / [Common subdivision?] Casestudies

Chain: Kenyan law (SVVUK) — Sources (S5C) — Customary law (S5D) — Casestudies (S33U)

Classmark: SVVUK 5D 33U (SVV UK5 D33 U)

Comments:

1. Simple retroactive synthesis.
2. The common form division Casebook is distinguished here from the special form of cases (law reports).

[21] **Title:** *Succession in the Muslim family*

Concept analysis: [Jurisdiction?] Islamic law / [Substantive law?] Succession / Family / [Practice & procedure?] Nil

Chain: Islamic law (SYB) — Succession (property law) (SBI) — Family (SBCF)

Classmark: SYB BI CF (SYB BIC F)

Comments:

1. Unlike national jurisdictions, religious jurisdictions need the intercalators B/C to introduce general subjects (e.g. succession) from substantive law. This is necessary in order to make room for the large number of special subjects regulated by religious law.
2. An instruction at SBH Property law instructs explicitly the direct addition of classes A/I in Auxiliary Schedule S1 (taken from SA/SC). So CF (from SBCF) is added directly to SYB BI.

14 Multiple entry in the classified catalogue or bibliography

14.1 This means providing as many entries in the classified file as there are different facets and/or arrays in the summarization. In a single-entry system, only the first-cited element has all its literature (represented by entries) collected together. Those elements which are cited second, third, etc. have their literature scattered to an increasing degree. In a multiple entry system each element is systematically brought to the front of a separate entry, thereby collecting together the literature on that particular element.

14.2 The procedure is described fully in the Introduction to BC2 (Section 7.62). Only the bare essentials of notational practice are given here.

14.3 The simplest procedure is to construct a basic classmark consisting of the classmarks of the elementary concepts in the summarization linked together by hyphens. That is, the retroactive synthesis achieved by the dropping of various initial characters is not used. The order of these elementary concepts is then varied by 'rotating' (as though the separate elements were on a wheel) to bring each element to the front in turn.

14.31 Taking Title 10 in Section 13 above, this would be given the following classmarks:

SN — SBGQR — S9M (English law — Personal injuries — Damages)
SBGQR — S9M — SN (Personal injuries — Damages — English law)
S9M — SN — SBGQR (Damages — English law — Personal injuries)

14.32 A practice favoured by some libraries is to use the normal classmark, reflecting the economies of retroactive notation, for the document physically (i.e. putting the relatively brief classmark, broken into groups of three characters, on the back of the book, etc.) and to use the longer, articulated forms to secure multiple entry in the catalogue. The classmark used to locate the document on the shelf must be clearly marked on each catalogue entry.

15 Class S in BC2 compared with BC1

15.1 The reasons for the radical nature of the revision are considered in detail in the Introduction to BC2. Four main features of Class S are compared here: the scope of the class, the order of classes, the notation, and the size of the vocabulary.

15.2 Scope of Class S Jurisprudence and law in BC1 This is very similar to BC2; there are three main points of difference:

15.21 There is no provision for a general class Religious law as a special form of jurisdiction in BC1; the only provision for religious jurisdictions is for Jewish, Islamic law and Hindu law, all subordinated to S3 History of law.

15.22 The alternatives provided for International law, Constitutional law, Public administration law and Military law are preferred in Class R Politics, whereas BC2 prefers them in S. Also, BC1 prefers Medical jurisprudence in Class H Medicine, whereas BC2 does not even refer to an alternative in H (although any special subject may be qualified by its law, using the common subdivisions).

15.23 There is minimal provision in BC1 for the special subjects of substantive law other than the traditional ones like contract, tort, property, etc. In BC2, Substantive law is a major facet.

15.24 A fourth point of difference results from the re-notating of the class (see Section 15.4 below). In BC1, the enumeration of the detailed facets for Substantive law and for Practice and procedure under English and American law (SE), and the assigning to these of a large share of the notation (SE/SQ) gives the appearance of a law class geared primarily to English and American law. In BC2, Auxiliary Schedule S1 provides for the qualification of all jurisdictions equally, including English and American. As a result, BC2 can fairly claim to be an international system in its law class as it is in its other classes.

15.3 Order of classes in BC1

15.31 The overall structure of BC1 is most clearly shown by an outline hierarchy:

S1/9	Common subdivisions
S3	History of law & jurisprudence
S3A	Ancient
	* A mixture of national and religious systems — e.g. Jewish, Roman, Islamic, Chinese, Hindu.
S3B	Medieval...
SA	Jurisprudence
SB/SD	International, Constitutional, Administrative law
	* Alternatives (not recommended) to Class R.
SE	English & American law
SF	USA law (as distinct from English law)
SH	Common law of England & America
SI	Equity, English & American remedial justice
SJ	Civil law, English & American
SJH	Contract... Carriers... Torts... Procedure...
SK	Municipal law
	* Interpreted narrowly as law of towns.
SL	Commercial law, Business law
SM	Property... Persons... Criminal law...
SP	Practice & procedure... Judiciary, Courts
SR/SS	Military law... Medical jurisprudence...
	* Alternatives (not recommended) to Classes R and H.
ST/SY	Law of other countries

15.32 Facets and arrays in BC1

15.321 As is usual in classifications designed before Ranganathan's revolution, characteristics of division are not applied consistently or rigorously. There is no recognition, for example, of the fact that classes in S3A and SB above are the product of division by jurisdiction.

15.322 Again, Bliss recognized the separate class constituted by practice and procedure, and the fact that it was best subordinated to the jurisdiction or special subject of law. But he failed to apply this characteristic to the general class Law. Consequently, BC1 does not possess a general class for this facet; presumably, general works would simply be treated as though they referred only to English and American practice and procedure.

15.323 The same thing occurs in the case of special subjects of law (as Bliss referred to substantive law, a term he did not use). Consequently, there is no general class for substantive law and general works on particular subjects like trusts, contract, property, etc. have to go under English and American law, in SI/SQ.

15.324 BC1 treats as quasi-facets a number of historical concepts whose definitions are now ambiguous and whose application is variable — e.g. common law and equity, civil law, public and private law. In BC2 all these are accommodated as general concepts but without any attempt to subordinate to them their now doubtful progeny. In BC1, an attempt is made to group under them a number of classes historically associated with them; but this is at the expense often of separating them unhelpfully from their own subclasses; e.g. torts in general are located under Jurisprudence (at SAT), under Common law (at SHT) and special types of torts under Civil law (at SJT) and so on.

15.33 Citation order in BC1

15.331 Bliss frequently acknowledged the problem of citation order in his numerous references to 'cross-classification' in the Intoduction (Vol. III, p.49/52). But there is no clear statement of a general rule for it in Class S. However, the major decision (what is the primary facet) is made clearly and sensibly; this is shown in the subordination of both substantive law and practice and procedure to the jurisdiction in SE/SQ. It is seen also in the Systematic Schedule 19, providing for specification under national and other systems of law of the jurisprudence, substantive law and practice and procedure of that system.

15.332 BC1 also acknowledges, in numerous enumerated examples, the citation order Subjects of law — Practice & procedure. But it is nowhere stated as an explicit principle.

15.34 Filing order in BC1

15.341 Without an explicit, overall citation order, and with no awareness of the principle of inversion, BC1 inevitably fails to maintain a fully consistent general-before-special order. As we have seen, it does not even keep together all the arrays and classes belonging to each facet. Its failure to invert consistently is seen, e.g. in the filing of practice and procedure (SP/SQ) after the subjects which it might qualify (SH/SO).

15.342 Nevertheless, the broad filing sequence does reflect inversion, in that the primary facet occupies the whole latter part of the schedule, from SE to SY. Each national jurisdiction is then qualified by its jurisprudence, its subjects of law and its practice and procedure — by enumeration in the case of English and American law SE/SQ and by applying Auxiliary Schedule 19 in the case of the others.

15.35 Alternative arrangements in BC1

15.351 BC1 provides for most of the major alternatives found in BC2, although these do not always agree on the recommended location. But BC2 provides a number of alternatives not found in BC1. For example, Bliss's linking of English and American (USA) law at SE and then enumerating classes SG/SQ as subclasses of the joint class is, in fact, treating Common law systems as one jurisdiction. However, there is no mention of other nations which would form part of such a system (e.g. Canada, Australia). In BC2, the alternative is fully and explicitly worked out.

15.4 Notation

15.41 BC1 provides for only limited synthesis; Systematic Schedule 19 allows qualification of a jurisdiction by some 24 classes; some 10 of these have the same initial letter as the equivalent class in English and American law (e.g. N Persons, where SN is Persons in English law) and in such cases all the detail in the enumerated class (here, SN) may be added if desired. In BC2 any jurisdiction may be qualified by the complete vocabulary of Class S if necessary.

15.42 Replacement of the partial synthesis provided in BC1 by the comprehensive synthesis in BC2 would have by itself resulted in substantial changes in notation. But in addition to this, the changes in order resulting from the imposition of comprehensive rules for citation order and their reinforcement by the inverted filing order have meant a large scale reorganization of Class S. This is despite the fact that the basic groundplan (jurisdictions divided by special subjects divided by practice and procedure divided by jurisprudence) has not been changed.

15.43 This reorganization has been accompanied by a very large expansion of vocabulary and these combined factors together have resulted inevitably in an almost complete re-notating of the class.

15.44 One particular feature of the re-notating has been the decision to treat English and American law on the same footing as that of other national jurisdictions. All jurisdictions may now be qualified by the full vocabulary of the other facets.

15.5 Vocabulary size

15.51 It is very difficult, if not impossible, to give a definite figure for the number of different classes provided by a fully synthetic classification. The number of compound classes which can be synthesized and added to the number of basic classes represented by the 'elementary' terms in their facets is enormous.

15.52 If we consider only those terms enumerated in the schedule, with a specific classmark, BC1 had some 300 elementary terms. To this should be added the full vocabulary of nations and states (provinces) in Auxiliary Schedule 2 which is used to form the national jurisdictions facet at ST/SY — say 500. Another 170 terms could be added for the five main alternatives already noted. A certain number of common form classes could also legitimately be added — e.g. those for the legal profession.

15.53 BC2, on the other hand, enumerates some six thousand terms, excluding many hundreds of enumerated compound classes inserted to help make clear the structure of the schedule at various points (e.g. SBQ AUE Maritime law — Carriage of goods by sea — Contracts). Some of of these terms represent only a selection from much larger vocabularies, all the terms of which can be drawn into Class S if needed. Major examples are at SBN Economic and commercial law (drawing on Class T), SAV/SBC Law of persons (drawing on Class K), SC Constitutional law and SD International law (drawing on Class R). To these must be added all those countries in Auxiliary Schedule 2 not enumerated at SN/SV to give several hundred national jurisdictions. Each jurisdiction may be qualified by all other facets (i.e. the total vocabulary less the jurisdictions). These other facets include the Auxiliary Schedules S2 and S3 for primary materials, each with roughly 100 terms apiece. The full potential vocabulary thus amounts to many hundreds of thousands of named classes.

16 Acknowledgements

We are indebted to a number of colleagues for their help in producing Class S: to Elizabeth Moys, for her comments on the production of the earlier Penultimate draft and for the schedule of primary materials in her Classification scheme for law books (1968), which was used with only slight modifications in that draft; to Dr Steiner, of the Institute of Criminology, Cambridge, for his valuable comments on the Penultimate draft; to Ian Sainsbury, Social Sciences Librarian in the University of Reading and Chair of the Standing Committee on Classification and Cataloguing, British and Irish Association of Law Librarians, for his extremely helpful and thorough comments on a large variety of questions put to him; to my colleagues in the Classification Research Group for their stimulating and helpful discussion of problems presented to the Group. We are pleased also to acknowledge the help received in the matter of vocabulary from some of the Library of Congress Classification Class K schedules relating to primary materials and the judiciary of particular jurisdictions (for the nomenclature of German courts, for example). Also, for some helpful suggestions on the specialized vocabulary of copyright, etc. from Frances Thimann of the Common Law Institute of Intellectual Property. Finally, to those colleagues on the Bliss Classification Association Committee who have given their time unstintingly to the meticulous proofreading of the final schedule.

Summary Outline

This is an inverted schedule: each class may be qualified by all preceding classes so far as they apply — e.g. English conflict of laws SNA.

S **Law**
S2 *Primary materials*
  * Applies only to particular jurisdictions SD/SYB.
S5A Jurisprudence
S6 Practice & procedure, procedural law, Courts & procedure
S6E Courts & procedure
S7 *Types of courts*
S8 Actions, proceedings
S8S Trial proceedings, Hearings
S8T Evidence
S8U Forensic science & technology
S9D Judicial decision... Judgement...
  Other results of litigation
S9Q Compromise... Arbitration...
S9VB Substantive law, Subjects of law
S9W Private law (general)
S9X Civil law (general)
SA Conflict of laws, International private law
SAP Persons
SBD Obligations... Contract... Tort...
SBH Property
SBK Real property... Planning & development law
SBL Personal property... Intellectual property...
SBN Economic & commercial law
SBNQ Business law... Sale of goods... Company law...
SBOY Transport law...
SBTA Social law... Health & safety... Cultural law...
SBW Criminal law
SBY Public law
SC Constitutional law... Administrative law...

SCY Jurisdictions, Legal systems
  * Each jurisdiction may be divided by all preceding classes. See Auxiliary Schedule S1.
  By political authority
SD International law
SE Supranational law, Communities law
SG European Union law...
SHY National law, Municipal law
SI Ethnolaw, Ethnological law
  By broad period & place
SJA Ancient law... Medieval law... Modern law...
SL Common law systems (general)
SN English law... American law...
SR Civil law systems (general)
SVB French law... German law...
  By religious authority
SWE Ecclesiastical law
  Extant religious systems
SWI Hindu law... Christian law... Islamic law...

Outline of Law

Outline of Class S Law

* This is an inverted schedule: the filing order of terms is the reverse of their citation order. So compound classes are formed by citing first the term appearing latest in the schedule; e.g. International law - Criminal - Practice & procedure is SDB W6; Real property - Transfer is SBJ HP.

S Law

S2 . *Primary materials*
. . * Works of law, as distinct from works about the law. This class applies only to individual jurisdictions (SD/SYB). See Auxiliary Schedules S2 and S3.

S3 . *Common subdivisions*
S34 . . Legal profession, persons & organizations
S34 G . . . Study of law, education in law
J . . . Lawyers, attorneys
S37 D . . . . Government law officers... Minister of Justice...
S38 . . . Organizations & agencies, law societies
S3M . . Communication in the law, information on law
S4 . . History of law (general)
S55 . . Relations with other subjects, phase relations

S5A . Jurisprudence, theory of law
S5A 6A . . Historical jurisprudence
. . . * By Period, Place and individual jurists
A . . Philosophical jurisprudence
. . . * Divided as class A/AL Philosophy - e.g. Legal positivism S5A CHP.
N . . Social-political theory & law
S5B P . . Special approaches in jurisprudence
. . . * E.g. comparative law (as a method), analytical jurisprudence.

S5C . . Sources of law
. . . *Operations*
S5C D . . . . Analysis & interpretation... Codification...
U . . . . Unification, harmonization...
S5D . . . Customary law
S5D G . . . . Local custom
S5E . . . . Ethnic law within a jurisdiction
S5F . . . . Religious law within a jurisdiction
S5G D . . . Formal sources
F . . . . Governments... Non-government bodies...
S5H . . . . Treaties, agreements
. . . . . * Special to International and Supranational law.
S5J . . . . Conventions, conferences...
S5M . . . . Legislation, statute law
S5N . . . . Codes
. . . . . * Comprehensive, systematic statements of bodies of law.
S5P . . . . . Delegated legislation, subordinate legislation
S5P W . . . . Precedents... Case law...
. . . . *By other jurisdictions as sources*
S5R . . . . . International law as source

[Law S]
[Jurisprudence S5A]
. [Sources of law S5C]
. . [Formal sources S5GD]
. . . [By other jurisdictions as sources]
. . . . [International law as source S5R]

S5S . . . . Supranational law as source, communities law
S5T A . . . . Other national jurisdictions as source, foreign law as source
. . . . . * For Conflict of laws, see SA.
F . . . Documentary sources... Commentaries...
N . . . Conventional law (of clubs, etc.)

S5U B . Law & society
C . . Human behaviour... Justice... Natural law...
S5V D . . Things, objects of legal rights, Res...
S5W . . Special fields of social action in relation to law
. . . * Divide like whole classification, - e.g. public opinion and law; political parties and the law.

S6 Practice & procedure, administration of justice, procedural law
S69 . Access to the law
S6A . Practice of law
. . * Activities, personnel, etc. in day-to-day running of a law practice or section.
S6A C . . Malpractice... Evaluation of performance...
. . *Agents*
S6B . . . Law practices, law departments...
. . *Operations*
S6B Q . . . Management
. . . . * As TQ Management in general.
S6C . . . Preparation and use of legal documents...
S6C E . . . . Composition... Drafting...
V . . . Advocacy... Briefs...
S6D . . . Legal aid
S6D 38 . . . . Community law services, law centres

S6E . Courts & court procedure
S6E Q . . Management of courts
S6H . . Jurisdiction of courts, powers of courts
S6J . . Court procedure (narrowly)... Rules of court...
S6K B . . Law officers, judicial officers of court
S6N . . . Judges... Court attorneys...
S6V C . . Court officials... Bailiffs... Interpreters

. . *Types of courts*
S7D . . . *By various characteristics*
. . . . * E.g. general/special jurisdiction; first instance/appeal; superior/inferior; common law/equity...
. . . *By hierarchical structure of court system*
S7Q . . . . Supreme courts
. . . . . * As final appeal courts, see Appeals S9H
S7R . . . . Higher courts
S7S . . . . Lower courts

Outline of Law

[Law S]
[Practice & procedure S6]
[Courts & court procedure S6E]
[Types of courts]
. [By hierarchical structure of court system]
. . [Lower courts S7S]

S7T . . . Summary jurisdiction courts
S7U F . . Courts of special function
. . . * See function (e.g. appeal) or subject - e.g. criminal courts, family courts.
R . *By geographical jurisdiction*
. . * For jurisdictions with federal or other decentralized system.
S7V . . States courts... Local courts...
. . . * For federal courts, see S7P.

S8 Actions, lawsuits, suits, litigation, cause
. * Steps taken in initiating and carrying through a legal claim or other proceedings. civil and criminal actions. This class covers actions in general and civil actions; it excludes matters peculiar to criminal law (see SBW).
S8A . Parties to an action
. . *Properties*
S8A C . . . Capacity... Rights & duties...
. . *Operations*
S8B B . . . Services to parties... Legal representation...
S8C . . Plaintiff... Defendant...
S8E M . . Special status parties (children, victims...)
. *General organizational processes*
S8F . . Limitation of actions... Consolidation of actions...
S8F V . . Conduct of proceedings
Y . . . Investigatory systems (general)
. . . . * For accusatorial v. inquisitorial systems, see Criminal proceedings SBW 8FY.
S8L . Preliminary proceedings, pretrial proceedings
S8L N . . Commencing an action... Writs...
S8M U . . Appearance... Discovery & inspection of documents...
S8N . . Pleadings
S8R J . . Issues in action... Interlocutory applications...
S . . . Trial preparation...
W . . Settlement of action... Compromise...
WW . . . Pre-trial settlement...

S8S . Court actions (narrowly), trial proceedings, hearings
S8S T . . Trial procedure
U . . . Trial practice, courtroom procedure...
W . . . Fact & law... Causation...
S8T . . . Evidence, matters of fact
. . . . * Many of the concepts are particular to criminal law; see SBW 8T.

[Law S]
[Practice & procedure S6]
[Courts & court procedure S6E]
[Actions S8]
[Court actions narrowly S8S]
[Trial procedure S8ST]
[Evidence S8T]

S8T V . Admissability... Proof... Fact & opinion...
Y . Elicitation of facts
S8U . . Forensic science & technology
. . . * Divided like whole classification; e.g. physics, chemistry, genetics, anthropometry, medicine, psychiatry, etc. But the notation is amended.
S9A B . Forms of evidence... Sources...
F . . Confessions...
G . . Illegally obtained... Privileged... Real...
R . . Documentary evidence... Recordings...
V . . Witnesses
. . . *Types of witnesses*
S9B H . . . . Personal evidence... Opinion evidence...
S9C Matters of law, questions of law

S9D Judicial decision, deciding conclusion of action
S9D 5US . Public policy, ordre publique
. . * Indefinite moral values (the 'public good') invoked to justify a decision.
H . Judicial discretion
L . Summing up, closing speeches

S9E . Jury trials, juries
S9E FG . . Selection... Performance...
GJ . . Composition...
P . Findings in fact, verdict of jury
S9F . Judgements, awards
S9G . Remedies
S9G I . . Execution of judgement...
L . . . Writs of execution...
Y . . Administrative remedies
S9H . . . Appeals, appellate proceedings
S9H 7 . . . . Appeal courts
S9I . . . . Grounds of appeal... Rights of appeal...
S9K . . . Prerogative writs & orders...
S9K L . . . . Habeas corpus... Certiorari...
S9L . . Civil remedies...
S9M . . . Damages... Injunctions...

Outline of Law

[Law S]
[Practice & procedure S6]
. . [Actions S8]
. . . [Court actions narrowly S8S]
. . . . [Remedies S9G]
. . . . [Civil remedies... S9L]
. . . . [Damages... S9M]

S9Q . . . Dipute resolution other than litigation
. . . . * For Settlement out of court, see S8R W.
S9R . . . . Arbitration
S9R Y . . . Special types of proceedings
S9S F . . . . Government actions, crown proceedings
H . . . . Forms of action
I . . . . . Actions in personum... Actions in rem...
P . . . . . Class actions...Public interest actions...

S9V B Substantive law, subjects of law
H . Rights (substantive law)
J . . Antecedent... Remedial... In personam... In
. . rem...
. *By historical development factors*
P . . Strictum jus, rigor juris...
Q . . Equity (general), aequitas...

. *By relation of jurisdiction to persons*
S9W . . Private law (general)
. . . * As distinct from public law (and sometimes
. . . criminal law).
S9X . . . Civil law in general
. . . . * For civil law systems, see SR.

SA . . . Conflict of laws, private international law
. . . . * That part of a system of private law which must
. . . . be invoked when an issue involves a foreign or
. . . . trans-frontier element so that the rules of the
. . . . foreign system need to be considered also.
SA8 . . . . Actions
SA8 T . . . . . Evidence
TW . . . . . . Proof of foreign law
SA9 FV . . . . . Foreign judgements
R . . . . Arbitration
RF . . . . . Foreign arbitral awards
. . . . *Special concepts in conflict of laws*
SAB . . . . . Jurisdiction... Preliminary questions...
SAD . . . . . Choice of law... Renvoi..

SAP . . . Persons
SAQ . . . . Legal personality
SAT . . . . Capacity
SAV . . . . *Types of persons by various characteristics*
SAX L . . . . . By age: Children...

[Law S]
[Substantive law S9VB]
[By relation of jurisdiction to persons]
[Private law S9W]
[Persons SAP]
. [Types of persons by various characteristics SAV]
. . [By age: Children... SAXL]

SAX V . . By sex: Females...
SAY AB . . By disadvantage: Mentally ill...
. . Insane...
SBC A . . By religion... By ethnic group...
F . Family & kinship law
. . * As Class K Society (KPG/KPY).
FI . . Kin groups, relatives... Affines...
G . . . Children (family law)
HD . . . . Adopted.. Fostered...
K . . Marriage, matrimony
PM . . Sexual relations...
R . . Procreation... Family planning...

TB . Corporate persons (general)
TC . . Unincorporated... Incorporated...
. . . * For company law, see SBO Q.
. . *Types of groups*
WQA . . . Voluntary bodies... Friendly
. . . societies...
X5 . . . Research institutions...
XPF . . . Religious bodies...

SBD Obligations & contract & tort
SBD G . Liability (general)
I . . Formation... Agreement (general)...
M . . Consideration... Intent...
SBE . Contract
SBE I . . Formation
P . . . Terms & conditions...
. . *Types*
X . . . Void & voidable contracts...
SBF B . . . Speciality contracts
BL . . . Contracts uberrimae fidei...
N . Guarantee... Indemnity...
T . Quasi-contract & agency
SBG . Torts, civil wrongs
SBG DG . . Liability
K . . Negligence... Nuisance...
N . . Torts against the person...
. . Defamation...
R . . Abuse of legal process...
TL . . Torts with strict liability
TN . . . Dangerous activities...
U . . Liability for animals, cruelty to
. . animals

[Law S]
[Substantive law S9VB]
[By relation of jurisdiction to persons]
[Private law S9W]
[Obligations & contract & tort SBD]
. [Torts SBG]
. . [Liability for animals SBGU]

SBH Property
SBH G . Torts... Trespass to property
. *Properties & processes*
J . . Ownership & possession
P . . . Transfer of property, transfer of title
R . . . . Sale of property... Transfer inter vivos...
TY . . . . Settlement & trusts...
U . . . . . Trusts & trustees
SBI . . . . Inheritance & succession
SBI N . . . . . Testamentary succession... Wills...
Q . . . . . Intestate succession...
RE . . . Extinction of estates & interests
. *Types of property*
SW . . Family settlement... Alien property...

SBJ . . Real property
. . . Ownership & possession
SBJ HJ . . . . Land tenure
HL . . . . Land titles
HU . . . Trusts & trustees in land
I . . . Inheritance of land
. . . *Types of real property*
. . . . * For real property subjected to regulation under planning law, see SBK.
Q . . . . Freehold... Leasehold interest...
S . . . . Rented property, landlord & tenant

X . . . . Environment, environmental law
. . . . . * Alternative (not recommended) to locating at SBS (for libraries wishing to collocate it with Town & country planning law).

SBK . . . . . Planning & development law, town & country planning law
. . . . . . * See also Environmental law SBS
SBK LG . . . . . . Government regulation & control of real property
LR . . . . Planning procedure... Applications...
MB . . . . Decisions... Appeals...
MF . . . . Enforcement of decisions
MH . . . . Compulsory acquisition...
MI . . . . Compensation...
MJ . . . . Eminent domain...
. . . . *By site initial conditions*
MS . . . . New site planning...
MW . . . . Development planning...

[Private law S9W]
[Property SBH]
. [Types of property]
. . [Real property SBJ]
. . . . . [Planning & development law SBK]
. . . . . . [By site initial conditions]
. . . . [Development planning... SBKMW]

. . . . . . *Objects of planning & control*
SBK NC . . . . Change of use...
NE . . . . Amenity preservation...
O . . . . Land use planning
P . . . . Building law...
QQ . . . . Access to land...
. . . . *By ownership*
QS . . . . Public land use... Private land use...
. . . . *By particular use*
RF . . . . Zoning, regional land use
RH . . . . Agricultural use... Industrial use...
S . . . . Urban development, town planning
ST . . . . Residential zones...
TB . . . . Recreation zones...
TG . . . . Wilderness conservation...
TH . . . . Protection...
TX . . . . Water resources planning
W . . . . Atmosphere control
. . . . * See also Air environmental law SBS V

SBL . . Personal property
SBL J . . . Intellectual & industrial property
K . . . . Copyright... Industrial property...
SBM . . . . Patents law... Trademarks...

SBN Commercial law, mercantile law, economics law, business law
. * Unlike commercial law narrowly, this is not a well established, traditional branch of law. Its location is therefore governed by the general principle in BC2 that the law of a special subject goes with the subject. So this position is an alternative (not recommended) to subordinating to the subject (in class T).
. * Add to SBN letters A/Y following T, with the adjustments indicated.
. * Retroactive synthesis within economics concepts follows the rules in Class T; qualification by legal concepts follows intercalator 9X; e.g. SBN L9X E Labour contract.
SBN 9UC . Regulation of economic & business activities
. . * As distinct from the broader class Economic planning and planning SBN AB.
A . Economic policy... Economic intervention...
DQ . Exchange... Finance... Banking...

Outline of Law

[Law S]
[Substantive law S9VB]
[By relation of jurisdiction to persons]
[Private law S9W]
[Commercial law SBN]
[Exchange... SBNDQ]

SBN G . Credit... Negotiable instruments...
GK . Consumer credit...
GL . Capital investment... Securities... Insurance...
HYY Economic production & distribution
I . Commerce & trade (general)
J . Production & industry (general)
K . Economic resources (general)
L . . Labour law, industrial law (narrowly)
L9X E . . . Contract
L9X FD . . . . Master & servant, contract of service (general)
L9X FG . . . . Independent contractors, contract of work & labour
LC . . . Industrial relations, labour relations
LD . . . . Trades union law, labour union law
LG . . . . Industrial disputes
LO . . . Employment... Unemployment...
M . *Forms of production & sectorial economics*
MB . . Work at home...
N National economy
. * Includes alternative (not recommended) for Public finance, preferred under Public administration SCK.
O International economic relations...
OI . International commerce
OM . . Import trade... Export trade...

Q Business law (narrowly)
QQ . Business management law
. . * As Class TQ Management of enterprises.
T . . Accounting
V . . Production management
W . . Marketing
WL . . . Advertising law
XG . . . Sale of goods, selling
XQ . . . Consumer law... Retailing law...
SBO G . Business enterprises, The Merchant
G9U C . . Regulation of businesses
G9U H . . . Registration...Licensing...

[By relation of jurisdiction to persons]
[Private law S9W]
[Commercial law SBN]
. [Business law narrowly SBNQ]
. . [Business enterprises SBOG]
. . . [Regulation of businesses SBOG9UC]
. . . . [Registration... SBOG9UH]

SBO HB . . . Sectors of economic enterprises
HD . . . . Government reorganization of business
HE . . . . . Economic assistance
I . . . . Public sector... Nationalization...
N . . . . Private sector... Privatization...

. . . *Types of businesses by structure*
P . . . . Partnership...
Q . . . . Corporations, company law
. . . *Types of businesses by product*
SBP . . . . Transport law
SBP 9UC . . . . . Regulation
. . . . . *Agents*
JN . . . . . . Owners... Personnel...
. . . . . *Operations & processes*
LD . . . . . . Traffic... Safety...
QN . . . . . Infrastructure... Vehicles...
TC . . . . . Carriers
U . . . . . . Carriage of goods... Passengers...

SBQ A . . . . . Sea transport, maritime law
C . . . . . Land transport... Road... Railway...
F . . . . . Aviation law... Space law...
L . . . . Communications law
. . . . . * For information sciences and computer law, see SBV 7.
M . . . . . Postal services... Publications... The Press...
Q . . . . . Telecommunications... Broadcasting...
T . . . . Agriculture
U . . . . Technologies, industrial law
. . . . . * As Class U/V Technology.
Y . . . . Other classes of businesses

SBS Environmental law, ecology law, protection of environment
. * See also Town & country planning SBK and the alternative at SBJ X.
. *Operations*
SBS PH . . Control & protection of environment
. *Objects of control*
PN . . Dangerous substances
Q . . Waste control
R . . Pollution control (general)
. . . *By source*
RR . . . . Industrial pollution... Radiation pollution...
. . . *By location*
T . . . . Land pollution... Water... Air, atmosphere...

[By relation of jurisdiction to persons]
[Private law S9W]
[Environmental law SBS]
. [Objects of control]
. . [Pollution control SBSR]
. . . [By location]
. . . . [Land pollution... SBST]

SBS W . . Conservation of natural resources
. . *Resources controlled*
XEH T . . . Wildlife protection & conservation...

SBT A Social law & legislation
. * Law primarily concerned with regulation of a number of basic social conditions and relations.
. * None of these reflect clearly any particular branch of law and few of them feature very prominently in the legal literature. The preferred arrangement is to subordinate them to the subject concerned and the provision here is an alternative (not recommended). If the option is taken, proceed as follows:
. * The order below is the same as in the whole classification, but the notation is amended.
B . Health & medicine law
. . * As in Class H Health and medicine, but with substantial adjustments of notation in the interests of briefer classmarks.
C . . Medical practice
G . . Public health, hygiene & safety
M . . Curative medicine, medical care
NP . . . Treatment, therapy
NQJ H . . . . Euthanasia...
Q . . Disorders... infectious diseases...
X . . Psychiatry, medical psychology
Y . Education law
. . * As Class J Education.
SBU . Social welfare law
. . * As Class Q Social welfare.
SBU F . . Social security

SBV 2 Cultural law
. * Subjects in civil law other than those already provided for. Taken in the order of the whole classification.
4 . Knowledge & research in general...
7 . . Information sciences & technologies... Computers...
AY . Scientific & technological research & development
E . . Biological research... Biotechnology...
K . . Social processes & structures)
. . . * Divided as Class K.
KB . . . Population policy... Customs & observances...
L . . Historical research... Archeology... Sites...
VY . . Recreation... Entertainments...

[Law S]
[Substantive law S9VB]
[By relation of jurisdiction to persons]
[Private law S9W]
. [Cultural law SBV2]
. . [Scientific & technological research & development SBVAY]
. . . [Recreation... SBVVY]

SBV W . . . Arts... Artworks protection... Performing arts...
XL . . . Languages & literatures

SBW Criminal law
. * Sometimes regarded as part of public law; treated here as bridge between private and public law.
SBW 6 . Practice & procedure, administration of justice
6E . . Courts & procedure
7V . . . Magistrates' courts
8 . . . Actions, criminal proceedings, prosecution
. . . . *Organizational processes*
8FV . . . . . Conduct of criminal proceedings
8FY . . . . . . Investigatory systems
8G . . . . Accusatorial systems (general)
8H . . . . Inquisitorial systems (general)
8J . . . . Prosecution procedure
8L . . . . Preliminary proceedings, pre-trial proceedings
8LN . . . . . Criminal investigation, police law
8MB . . . . . Process (narrowly)...
8MP . . . . . . Arrest & charge...
8N . . . . . Preliminary examination... Indictment
8RB . . . . . Remand...
8S . . . . Trials, court actions...
8SE . . . . . Defence proceedings
8T . . . . . Evidence
9D . . . . . Judicial decision
9H . . . . . . Appeal
9PL . . . . . Sentencing
9RC . . . . . . Penalties, punishments
9TV . . . . . Individual trials
. . . . . . * Arrange A/Z.

. *Substantive criminal law*
A . . Conflict of laws criminal law
C . . Criminal offences, crimes
. . . *Elements of crimes*
CE . . . . Commission or omission...
CG . . . . Criminal responsibility...
D . . . Criminals, offenders
DS . . . . Principals in crime... Accessories...
EA . . . . First offenders... Occasional offenders...
. . . *Forms of offences*
EK . . . . Completion & attempt...

[Substantive law S9VB]
[By relation of jurisdiction to persons]
[Criminal law SBW]
. [Substantive criminal law]
. . [Criminal offences SBWC]
. . . [Forms of offences]
. . . . [Completion & attempt... SBWEK]

. . . . *By procedural factor*
SBW EQ . . . . . Non-arrestable & arrestable offences...
. . . . *By structure*
FA . . . . . Compound crimes... Occupational crimes...
FQ . . . . . Organized crime...
. . . . *By scene of crime*
FW . . . . . Street crime... Urban crime...
. . . . *By victim/offender relation*
GP . . . . . Witness intervention... Victimless crime...
. . . . *By legal definition*
HI . . . . . Offences against the State...
I . . . . . Offences against the person... Child abuse...
KX . . . . . . Homicide... Assault... Sexual offences...
R . . . . . Against public order...
UL . . . . . Against property...
. . . . *By special type of offender*
X . . . . . Juvenile criminal law

SBY Public law
SC . Constitutional law
. . * Alternative (not recommended) is to locate with constitutions in R Politics.
SC5 C . . Sources
L . . . Constitutions (making, etc.)
SC9 VB . . Substantive law
. . . * SCA is divided like SBA/SBW so far as applicable.
. . *Subjects special to constitutional law*
. . . *Political processes, properties etc.*
. . . . * Divided like RB/RQ in Politics.
SCC W . . . . Human rights
. . . . *By groups of persons*
SCD ON . . . . . Citizens & citizenship... Nationality...
. . . *Political institutions*
SCE . . . . Government
SCG E . . . . . Powers of government
. . . . . *Branches of government*
SCH . . . . . . Electoral system...
SCI . . . . . . Legislature... Executive...
SCK . . . . . . Public administration
SCK F . . . . Administrative law
F9J . . . . Judicial review in administrative law

[Subjects special to constitutional law]
[Political institutions]
[Government SCE]
[Branches of government]
[Public administration SCK]
. [Administrative law SCKF]
. . [Judicial review in administrative law SCKF9J]

SCK J . Organization of public administration (general)
. . * Most of the literature relates to a specific level; e.g. central, local.

SCL Central government & administration
SCL MF . Treasury, public finance department
MG . Public finance administration
MJ . . Tax law... Non-tax revenue...
MQ . . Public expenditure
N . Other government departments (general)
. . * Prefer law of other public services with subject.
QB . Quasi-government agencies...
QG . Public utilities...
V . National security & defence...
SCM . . Armed services, military law
SCM Y . Law enforcement agencies... Police...
SCO . . Penal law
. . . * Divided as Class QQ.
SCO YC . Other administrative agencies & functions

SCQ Devolved government & administration
SCR . Regional government & administration
SCS . State government & administration
. . * In jurisdictions with a federal structure.
SCT . . *Individual states of the country concerned*
SCU . Local government & administration
SCV . . *Individual local authorities of the country*
SCW . Overseas territories, dependencies
SCX Judiciary
. * Constitutional status; for administration of justice, see S6.
SCY B Ecclesiastical law, secular ecclesiastical law
. * For religious law, see SW.

[Law S]
[Substantive law S9VB]
. . . . [Subjects special to constitutional law]
. . . . . [Political institutions]
. . . . . . [Government SCE]
. . . . [Branches of government]
. . . . [Ecclesiastical law SCYB]

SCY M . . . . . *Constitutional law by type of nation state*
* For example, monarchies.

X Jurisdictions, legal systems
. *By political authority*

SD . . International law

SD2 . . . *Primary materials*
SD2 B . . . . Treaties (texts), conventions (texts), agreements (texts)
F . . . . International conferences
N . . . . Cases in international law (texts)

. . . *Secondary materials*
SD5 A . . . . Jurisprudence
A6A . . . . . Historical jurisprudence
A7C . . . . . . Ancient world... Medieval... Modern...
C . . . . . Sources
GD . . . . . . *Formal sources*
* Normal retroactive synthesis by S5C is interrupted here in order to incorporate Processes of international law; it is resumed at SD5 TK.
GP . . . . . . Processes of international law, regulatory agencies
* Providing codes of practice (usually, if not always, observed) for the self-regulation of inter-national relations and providing mechanisms for the settlement of disputes.
. . . . *Agencies*
GT . . . . Diplomatic missions (general)
H . . . . International agreements, treaties
. . . . *Operations*
HK . . . . Formation (treaty making)...
JB . . . . Enforcement... Termination...
. . . . *Properties*
JP . . . . Application of treaties...
JQ . . . . Duration...
JS . . . . Binding force... Reciprocity...
. . . . *Types*
KE . . . . State agreement forms... Ententes...
KK . . . . Contract treaties... Cultural agreements...

[Secondary materials]
[Jurisprudence SD5A]
. [Sources SD5C]
. . [Processes of international law SD5GP]
. . . [Agencies]
. . . . [International agreements SD5H]
. . . . . . [Contract treaties... SD5KK]

SD5 LC . . . . International conventions, congresses, etc.
LS . . . . International organizations
N . . . . . United Nations
Q . . . . . Regional organizations in international law
* See also Supranational communities law SE
SC . . . . Comitas, international courtesy...
TK . . Other sources
* Normal retroactive synthesis by S5C/S5T is resumed here after its interruption at SD5 GD.

XD . Disputes in international law (general)
* For settlement of disputes threatening peace, see Judicial settlement SDP 6.

Practice & procedure, administration of justice
SD6 A . Judicial settlement, adjudication & arbitration
E . . International courts & procedure
SD8 . . . Actions
. . . Other results of litigation
SD9 Q . . . Compromise... Negotiation...
R . . . Arbitration
UX . Non-peaceful settlement
* See International relations SDP E/SDR

VB Substantive international law
W . Private law
SDA . . International private law
* Alternative (not recommended) to subordinating to private law (conflict of laws) at SA.
SDA P . . International law of persons
SDB H . . International property law
LJ . . . Intellectual & industrial property
LK . . . . International copyright law... Patents
N . . International economics & commercial law
NL . . . International labour law
P . . . International transport law
W . International criminal law
* See also war crimes SDT W
WXJ . . Crimes against humanity

Outline of Law

[Jurisdictions SCYX]
[By political authority]
[International law SD]
[Secondary materials]
[Substantive international law SD9VB]
. [International criminal law SDBW]
. . [Crimes against humanity SDBWXJ]

SDB WY . Public international law
. . * The term International law usually assumes public international law. Use SD for the general class.
X . . Constitutional law
. . . * International law differs from all other jurisdictions in that it has no sovereign lawmaker; the concept of an international constitutional law therefore hardly exists.
. . . * For United Nations, see SD5 N (sources of international law); for other subjects usually associated with constitutional law, see Political process in international law below (SDC A).

Subjects special to international law

SDC A . Political process in international law
. . * Divided like RA/RN, with amendments.
B . . Political control, etc.
W . . . Human rights
SDD L . . Collectivities, groups of persons
SDE . . . World government

SDE M . . . States as international persons
. . . . * As Class R Political science.
. . . . *Special attributes*
SDF . . . . . Sovereignty, independence...
SDF V . . . . . State responsibility, state liability
W . . . . . Jurisdiction of sovereign states
XW . . . . . Changes in sovereignty
SDG . . . . . State succession
SDH L . . . . . Limitations of sovereignty...
M . . . . . . Servitudes...
SDI . . . . . Nationality & citizenship...
. . . . . Aliens...
SDJ Y . . . . State as physical entity
SDK . . . . . National territory...
SDK L . . . . . . Acquistion...
NB . . . . . . Boundaries, frontiers...
UD . . . . . . Adjoining territory...
. . . . . . Neighbouring territory...

. . . *Types of states*
SDL NW . . . . Sovereign states..
NX . . . . Dependent states...
O . . . . Extended sovereign states...
. . . . Imperial systems...
P . . . . . Imperialist systems...
SDM B . International relations

[Law S]
[Jurisdictions SCYX]
[By political authority]
[International law SD]
[Secondary materials]
[Subjects special to international law]
[International relations SDMB]

* As RO/RQ, with adjustments.
Formalized relations
SDM T . Foreign services of states
U . . Diplomacy & diplomatic services
. . . * For diplomatic missions as source of international law, see SD5 GT.
Other forms of international relations
SDN K . International cooperation...
M . International aid...
P . Peacemaking, world peace & international law
V . International security
W . . Arms control...
. . Surveillance...
YC . . Collective security...
. . Alliances...
YY . . Security forces
SDO A . . . National security forces...
. . . . Defence systems...
AY . . . . Armed forces...
Q . . . . Weapons systems, armaments
SN . . . International security forces

SDP . Disputes endangering peace
SDP 6 . . Judicial procedures
. . Other procedures
E . . . Delinquencies...
. . . Measures short of war...
K . . . Sanctions... Hostilities short of war...

SDR . War, law of war
SDR RP . . Participants...
. . Combatants... Non-combatants...
SDS B . . Non-participants...
C . . . Neutrality...
SDT B . . Process of war, belligerency, state of war...
D . . . Declaration of war...
E . . . Invasion...
F . . . Conduct of war

[By political authority]
[International law SD]
. . . [International relations SDMB]
. . . . [Other forms of international relations]
. . . . . [War SDR]
. . . . . . [Process of war SDTB]
. . . . [Conduct of war SDTF]

SDT G . . . . Enemy property...
W . . . . Criminal law in war... War crimes...
SDU E . . . . Cessation of hostilities...
L . . . . Peace settlements... War claims...
SDW D . . . . . . *Forms of warfare*
J . . . . Land war... Sea war...
R . . . . Conventional war... Total war...
T . . . . Prohibited forms of warfare...
SDX B . . . . Guerilla warfare... Civil war...

SE Supranational law
* Body of customary and treaty rules accepted as legally binding between members of a group of nation states.
* Detail based on European Union as a working model of a developed supranational jurisdiction.
* This general class may be amplified like SG so far as applicable.
SF . Preferred community
* This location is reserved for the community of particular relevance to the library concerned.
SFY . European supranational law (general)

SG . . European Union law, EU law
SG2 . . . Primary materials
* As in Auxiliary Schedule S3.
SG2 A . . . . Official publications of the EU
B . . . . . European Parliament... European Council...
F . . . . Treaties of formation
H . . . . Treaties of accession
L . . . . Acts, legislation
P . . . . Court decisions, cases

. . . Secondary materials, works about
SG5 A . . . . Jurisprudence
C . . . . . Sources
CU . . . . . . Approximation of laws, unification of laws
GP . . . . . . Processes
* Divided like International law (SD) so far as applicable.

SG6 . . . . Practice & procedure
SG7 R . . . . . Court of Justice of EU (ECJ)
S . . . . . Court of First Instance (EU)
SG9 VB . . . . Substantive law
SGA . . . . . Conflict of laws
SGN . . . . . Economics & commercial law

[By political authority]
[Supranational law SE]
[European supranational law SFY]
. [European Union law SG]
. . [Secondary materials]
. . . [Substantive law SG9VB]
. . . . [Economics & commercial law SGN]

SGN AB . . . . . Intervention
AGO . . . . . . Economic aid... Grants...
DQ . . . . . Economic exchange
EK . . . . . . Market system
EN . . . . Competition
EP . . . . Restrictive practices
F . . . . . . Financial exchange
FK . . . . Cental banking
FQ . . . . Money, currency
I . . . . . . Commerce & trade
O . . . . . International economic relations
OF . . . . . . European Monetary System
OFT L . . . . . . European Exchange Rate Mechanism
OLC . . . . . . Protection & free trade
Q . . . . . Business law
V . . . . . . Production... Standards...
W . . . . . . Marketing... Advertising...
SGO Y . . . . . Industries & undertakings by product
SGP . . . . . . Transport... Agriculture...
SGS . . . . Environmental law... Social law...

. . . . Constitutional law
* Divided as SC Constitutional law.
SGX . . . . . Organization law
SGX CW . . . . . . Human rights
GQ . . . . . . Institutions of EU
H . . . . Electoral system
I . . . . European Parliament
IU . . . . Council of the EU
J . . . . Commission of the EU
P . . . . Subordinate institutions of EU
* For institutions serving specific subject function, see subject - e.g. investment, atomic energy.
* For EEC, use general class SG.
PE . . . . Economic & Social Committee, ESC
Q . . . . Devolved government in EU
U . . . Relations with member states
* For their role as legal entities within the community.

SGY Y . Other European supranational communities
SHJ C Asian supranational organizations
SHN C Australasian supranational organizations
SHO C African supranational organizations
SHR C American supranational organizations

Outline of Law

[Law S]
[Jurisdictions SCYX]
[By political authority]
[Supranational law SE]
. [American supranational organizations SHRC]

SHX . Non-governmental supranational organizations

SHY National law (general), municipal law (general)
* Each jurisdiction is divided as indicated in Auxiliary Schedule S1. An amplified demonstration of its operation is given at SN (English law) for a unitary state and at SP (USA law) for a federal state.

SI . Ethnolaw, pre-literate societies law, ethnological jurisdictions
* The preferred arrangement is to subordinate an ethnological system operating within a modern national jurisdiction to the latter; but alternatives are provided.
* This location takes general works on an ethnological group which is distributed over several different modern national jurisdictions.
* Divided like Auxiliary Schedule 3A (Ethnic groups) so far as applicable - e.g. Fulani law SIH KH.

. *By broad period & place*
SJA . . Ancient & medieval systems
SJB . . . Ancient law
SJX . . . . Roman law
SKB . . . Medieval Western law
SKC . . . . Germanic law... Celtic law... Slavic law...
SKE . . . . Feudal law... Lubeck law, Lubish law...
SKG . . Modern law (c.1500-)
* General works only. Use S3/SC for subclasses.
SKV . . . Present-day legal systems

SL . . . . Common law systems (general)
* An alternative (not recommended) is to treat the common law as a single system, in which the national jurisdictions are treated as subclasses and cited after the branches of law: this would give, e.g., Common law systems - Contract law - UK. Details of this option are given in Auxiliary Schedule S4.
SM . . . . . Preferred country (common law systems)
* Alternative for libraries wishing to file their home country first.

[By political authority]
[National law SHY]
[By broad period & place]
[Modern law c.1500- SKG]
[Present-day legal systems SKV]
[Common law systems SL]
[Preferred country common law systems SM]

SN England & Wales, English law
* As instructed in Auxiliary Schedule S1.
SN2 . *Primary materials*
SN2 A . . Parliamentary publications
C . . . House of Commons
C8E . . . . Journal... Debates... Bills...
D . . . House of Lords
D8E . . . . Journal... Debates... Bills...
F . . Legislative acts
G . . . Statutes... Subordinate legislation...
JS . . Prerogative instruments
MC . . Administrative & executive publications (general)
N . . Law reports
N8 . . . Digests & abridgements...
. . . *By court*
NF . . . . Common law courts... Equity courts...
PB . . . . Modern period, post-1865
* Divided as SN7.
UB . . . . Administrative decisions

SN3 . Secondary materials, works about
SN6 . . Practice & procedure
SN6 E . . . Courts & court procedure
. . . . *By historical jurisdiction*
SN7 J . . . . . Common law courts... Chancery courts...
. . . . *By status*
. . . . . Supreme court
Q . . . . . . House of Lords
* For House of Lords as an appeal court, see Appeal courts SN9 H7Q.
R . . . . . High courts
RQ . . . . . . High Court of Justice
RS . . . . Divisional courts
RT . . . . Queen's Bench...
RU . . . . Chancery...
RW . . . . Crown courts...
S . . . . . Lower courts
SQ . . . . . . County courts...
T . . . . . . Magistrates' courts...
SN8 . . . . Actions, lawsuits
SN9 H . . . . . Appeals
H7 . . . . . . Courts
H7Q . . . . House of Lords

[Common law systems SL]
[England & Wales SN]
. [Secondary materials SN3]
. . [Practice & procedure SN6]
. . . . . [Appeals SN9H]
. . . . . . [Courts SN9H7]
. . . . [House of Lords SN9H7Q]

SN9 VB . . Substantive law
SNA . . . English conflict of laws
SNA P . . . Persons... Contract & tort...
SNH . . . Property... Economics & commercial
. . . law...
SNS A . . . Social law... Cultural law...
SNW . . . Criminal law
SNX . . . Constitutional law
SNY F . . . . European Union law & English law

SOA . Wales
SOB . Scotland, Scots law
SOB 6 . . Practice & procedure
7 . . . Courts
7R . . . . Higher courts
7RQ . . . . . Court of Session
7S . . . . Lower courts
7SQ . . . . . Sheriff court... Magistrate court...
9H . . . Appeal
9H7 . . . . Courts
. . . . . Supreme court
9H7 Q . . . . . . House of Lords (Scots law)
. . . . . Higher courts
9H7 RQ . . . . . . Court of Session (appeal)
. . . . . Lower courts
9H7 SQ . . . . . . Sheriff Principal
SOC Ireland... Channel Islands...
SOP British Commonwealth (general)
SOS Australia... Canada

SOW North America, Anglo-American law
SP . USA, Anglo-American law
SP6 . . Practice & procedure
SP7 . . . Courts
SP7 P . . . . Federal courts (general)
Q . . . . . Supreme court (general)
. . . . . . * For Appellate jurisdiction, see
. . . . . . SP9 H7Q.
RQ . . . . . District & circuit courts
SP9 VB . . Substantive law
SPX . . . Constitutional law
SPX S . . . . States law
S6 . . . . . Practice & procedure
S7 . . . . . . Courts
S7S . . . . County courts
S7T . . . . Township courts, Justice of the
. . . . Peace courts
T . . . . . *Individual states*

[Present-day legal systems SKV]
[Common law systems SL]
. [North America SOW]
. . . [Substantive law SP9VB]
. . . . [Constitutional law SPX]
. . . . . [States law SPXS]
. . . . . . [Individual states SPXT]

. . . . * As Auxiliary Schedule 2
SQB . Caribbean & Central America (common
. law systems)

SR Civil law systems (general)
SSB . Roman-Dutch law (general)
. . * For individual jurisdictions, use ST/SV.
SSD . Socialist law (general)
. . * For individual jurisdictions, use ST/SV
ST . Favoured country (civil law systems)
. . * That is, the home country of the library using
. . BC2.
SV . Others
. . * Add letters from Auxiliary Schedule 2 for Place
. . - for example:

SVF . . France
SVF 6 . . . Practice & procedure
7 . . . . Courts
. . . . . Supreme court
7Q . . . . . . Cour de Cassation
. . . . . Higher courts
7R . . . . . . Tribunaux de Grande Instance
7RT . . . . . . Tribunaux Civiles
. . . . . Lower courts
7S . . . . . . Tribunaux d'Instance
7ST . . . . Tribunaux de paix

SVG B . . Spain... Italy... Belgium... Netherlands...

SVK A . . Germany
A6 . . . Practice & procedure
A7 . . . . Courts
A7N X . . . . . Ordentliche Gerichte, regular courts
A7Q . . . . . . Supreme courts
A7Q T . . . . Bundesgerichtshof, federal court
A7Q U . . . . Gemeinsamer Senat der Obersten
. . . . Gerichtshofe des Bundes
A7S . . . . . . Lower courts
A7U F . . . . . Courts of special jurisdiction
A7U H . . . . . . Military government courts
. . . . . . (1945/1955)
A7U K . . . . . . Competence conflict courts
A9V B . . . Substantive law
AX . . . . Constitutional law
AXS . . . . . States law
AXS 6 . . . . . . Practice & procedure

[Jurisdictions SCYX]
[By political authority]
. . . . . . [Others SV]
. . . . [Germany SVKA]
. . . . [Constitutional law SVKAX]
. . . . [States law SVKAXS]
. . . . [Practice & procedure SVKAXS6]

. . . . Supreme courts
SVK AXS 7Q . . . . Oberlandesgerichte
AXS 7R . . . . Higher courts
AXS 7RS . . . . Landgerichte, regional courts
AXS 7S . . . . Lower courts
AXS 7T . . . . Amtsgerichte, magistrate courts
AXT . . . . *Individual states*
. . . . * As Auxiliary Schedule 2.
. . . . * See also East Germany SVK B
B . . . . East Germany, German Democratic Republic
H . . . . West Germany
. . . . * Use SVK A.
S . . . . Czechoslovakia... Yugoslavia... Poland...
SVM . . . . Scandinavia... USSR...
SVO H . . . . Turkey... Saudi Arabia...
SVQ A . . . . Pakistan... India...
SVR B . . . . China... Japan...
SVV A . . . . Egypt... Ghana... Nigeria...
Q . . . . South Africa... Zimbabwe...
SVZ B . . . . Mexico... Brazil... Argentina...

By religious system
SWE . Ecclesiastical law, religious legal systems
. . * For ecclesiastical law as an integral part of the constitutional law of a country, see SCY B (& for each country the subclass -YB).
SWE 5A . . Jurisprudence
6 . . Practice & procedure
9VB . . Substantive law
. . . * Divide SWE A like SA/SB - e.g. Marriage law SWE ACK; Property law SWE AH.
. . . *Subjects special to religious law*
. . . . * As Class P Religion.
B . . . . Systematic theology... Doctrines...
D . . . . Practice of religion... Worship...
FB . . . . Ecclesiology... Church government...
G . . . . . Clergy & ecclesiastical offices
M . . . . . Church government
R . . . . Religious orders... Monastic orders...
V . . Sects, etc. within a religion

[Law S]
[Jurisdictions SCYX]
[By religious system]
[Ecclesiastical law SWE]
. [Sects SWEV]

SWF *Particular religious systems*
. * Alternative (not recommended) to locating in Class P Religion (at PFG). See notes at SWF in the full schedule.
. * Any given religion or sect may be divided fully like SWE. Demonstrations of how the detail of SWE may be adjusted and amplified to meet the special needs of the given religion are given at SXJ (Roman Catholic canon law) and at SYB (Islamic law).
SWG F . Pre-literate societies' religious law
J . Ancient religious law
. *Extant religious legal systems*
SWH B . . Oriental systems... Hindu law...
SWU . . Semitic & Western systems
. . . Sources
SWU 5C . . . . The Bible & law
SWW . . . Jewish law

SWX . . . Christian law, canon law, church law
SXB . . . . Patriarchates
SXC . . . . . Eastern churches & sects...
SXJ . . . . . Roman Catholic canon law
SXJ 2 . . . . . . *Primary materials*
29Y . . . . Pre-Corpus juris canonici texts
2A . . . . Corpus juris canonici
2C . . . . Codex juris canonici
2D . . . . Papal documents...
2G . . . . Papal bulls...
2S . . . . Cases
3 . . . . . . *Secondary materials*
6 . . . . Practice & procedure
6KB . . . . Law officers
6TC . . . . Promoters of justice...
7 . . . . Courts
7Q . . . . Papal courts...
9F . . . . Judgements...
9PX . . . . Penalties...
9PY K . . . . Ecclesiastical censure...
9PY P . . . . Excommunication...
9VB . . . . Substantive law
ACK . . . . Marriage & divorce
AH . . . . Property
AW . . . . Criminal law
. . . . *Subjects special to RC Church*
ER . . . . Ritual & liturgy
ERQ . . . . Sacraments (general)
ERU . . . . Repentance... Confession... Absolution...
G . . . . Clergy & offices
K . . . . Pope... Cardinals...
PE . . . . External relations of RC church

[Semitic & Western systems SWU]
[Christian law SWX]
. [Patriarchates SXB]
. . [Roman Catholic canon law SXJ]
. . . [Secondary materials SXJ3]
. . . . [Substantive law SXJ9VB]
. . . . . [External relations of RC church SXJPE]

SXK . Protestant churches...
SXL . . Anglican church...
SXO . . Non-conformist churches...

SYB Islamic law, Shari'a
SYB 2 . *Primary materials*
3 . *Secondary materials*
. . Jurisprudence
5A6 8 . . . Fiqh... Ikhtilaf... Furuq...
5C . . . Sources
5CX . . . . Usul.. Urf, 'Adah...
5F . . . . Qu'ran (works about)... Tafsir...
5GB . . . . Sunna (works about)... Hadith...
5GK . . . . . Athat... Usul al-fiqh...
5GQ . . . . Ijma... Ijtihad...
5PW . . . Precedents
5PW S . . . . Istishab... Fatawa...
. . . *Concepts special to Islamic law*
5UM B . . . . Mubah... Wajib... Makruh... Hisbah...
6 . . Practice & procedure
7 . . . Courts
7P . . . . Mazalim courts... Qadi courts...
9VB . . Substantive law
CK . . . Marriage & divorce
CMW B . . . . Talaq... Khul... Idda... Mut'a...
H . . . Property
. . . . Transfer & settlement
HSV . . . . . Hiba... Sadaqa... Waqf...
N . . . Economic & commercial law
NG . . . . Riba, usury... Salam, salaf...
W . . . Criminal law
W9R C . . . . Punishments
W9R W . . . . . Hadd, hudud... Ta'zir...
. . *Subjects special to Islamic law*
. . . Systematic theology
YBD . . . . Five pillars of Islam...
. . . Worship
YDB . . . . Ibadat...
. . . Ritual observances
YER P . . . . Tahara... Salat...
. . . Pilgrimage
YEX X . . . . Hajj...
YFP E . . . External relations
YFP F . . . . Siyasa shar'iyya...

[Extant religious legal systems]
[Semitic & Western systems SWU]
[Islamic law SYB]
[Secondary materials SYB3]
. [Subjects special to Islamic law]
. . [External relations SYBYFPE]
. . . [Siyasa shar'iyya... SYBYFPF]

SYC B *Schools & sects*
E . Sunnite law
H . . Hanafi law... Maliki law...
SYD B . Shi'ite law
D . . Ismailii law... Wahhabi law...
SYE *Islamic law in specific countries*
. * Alternative (not recommended) to subordinating to
. the country.

S Law

S2 . *Primary materials*
. . * This class is used only under particular jurisdictions;
. . e.g. English law - Primary materials - Statutes
. . SN2 G.
. . * See Auxiliary Schedule S2 for instructions.

. *Common subdivisions*
. . * These conform to the order of classes 2/9 in Auxiliary
. . Schedule 1 but with substantial modifications of
. . notation.
. . * Add to S3 numbers 2/3 in Auxiliary Schedule 1 with
. . the additions shown at S33 Y.
S3 . . General works on the law
S33 B . . Dictionaries, encyclopedias
G . . Journals, periodicals, serials
. . . * For indexing & abstracting journals, see S3WH.
H . . Yearbooks
J . . Directories, law lists
. . . * Primarily for use in qualifying persons,
. . . organizations, etc.
LR . . Conference proceedings
RA . . Literature & the law
. . . * Imaginative literature, etc.
T . . Legal anecdotes, wit & humour in the law
Y4 . . Persons in general
. . . * Use for non-legal personnel, officials, etc.
. . . * Normal synthesis by CSD is interrupted here. It is
. . . resumed at S3M.
Y5 . . Organizations in general, agencies
. . . * Use only if needed to qualify classes preceding S38.

S34 . . Legal profession
. . . * See also Practice of law S6A
S34 6 . . . Reform of legal profession
7 . . . Structure
8 . . . . Divided legal profession, fused legal
. . . . profession
C . . . Ethics, social relations, etc.
. . . . * Add to S34 letters C/F following 4 in Auxiliary
. . . . Schedule 1.
CE . . . . Ethics in the law
DC . . . . Supply & demand (personnel)
DF . . . . . Admission to practice
DG . . . . . . Licensing of practitioners
DK . . . . . . Disbarment from practice
DR . . . . Salaries, remuneration
EV . . . . Customs, etiquette, dress
F . . . Personnel relations in legal profession
FV . . . Professional charges, costs
. . . . * Most of the literature on legal costs relates to the

[Law S]
[Common subdivisions]
[Legal profession S34]
[Professional charges S34FV]

. rulings of courts as to the distribution of costs
. amongst parties; see S9F R Award of costs.
S34 G Study in law, education in law, training in law
. * An alternative (not recommended) is to locate this
. class in J Education.
. * Add to S34G numbers & letters 2/9, A/V following
. J in J2/JV.
GGD . Student bar associations
GGM . Moots
GTC . Law schools (general)
H Research in law
. * For research in the narrow sense of searching the
. legal literature, see S3R D.
. * See also Jurisprudence S5A
. * Add to S34 H numbers 3/9 following K in K3/K9.
H6 . Methodology
H6M . . Models

J Lawyers, attorneys, advocates, practitioners
. * For works on the formal status, etc. of particular
. parties or persons in the legal profession. For works
. on their practical functioning, see Practice of law
. S6A.
. * Theoretically, BC2 subordinates personnel to their
. specific function (e.g. advocacy). But the varied
. nature of the tasks undertaken & the possibilities of
. reorganization which may alter the degree of
. specialization of particular personnel make this hard
. & fast distinction impracticable. Most of the
. literature refers to types of personnel, but this
. should be interpreted as covering their duties as well
. as their office.
. *Properties*
JB . . Psychology of lawyers
JBT . . . Motivation of lawyers
JC . . Effectiveness, competence
. *Types by various non-legal characteristics*
. . * Add to S34J letters GU/U following 4 in
. . Auxiliary Schedule 1 - e.g. Women in the law
. . S34 JN.
. *By role*
UY . . Notaries
S35 . . Solicitors
S36 . . Barristers, counsel, trial lawyers
. . . * For counsel-client relations, see S8B G.
S36 V . . . Leading counsel, senior counsel
W . . . Junior counsel
S37 B . . Private practitioners
D . . Public practitioners, government law
. . officers
. . . * For prosecutors & defenders, see Services of
. . . counsel S8B C.

[Law S]
[Common subdivisions]
[Legal profession S34]
. [Lawyers S34J]
. . [By role]
. . . [Public practitioners S37D]

S37 F . . . . Minister of Justice, head of the Judiciary
G . . . . Chief law officers of the Government
. . . . . * For law officers of the Crown, see English law SN3 7G.
. . . . . * See also Law officers (courts) S6K B
N . . . . *By special function*
Q . . . Legal officers
. . . . * For court officers, see S6K B.
. . . . * For probation officers, see Class QRB WX.
S . . . . Sheriffs
W . . *By specialization*
. . . * Alternative (not recommended) to locating under specialization (if outside the law).
WD . . . Advisory services for lawyers
WR . . . Lawyers in politics
WRU . . . Lawyers in public service
WY . . . Lawyers as writers

S38 Organizations & agencies
. * Use this only when no special provision is made for organizations in the subject.
. * For corporate persons as legal entities, see SBC TB & its notes & subclasses.
S39 . *Operations, processes, parts*
. . * Add to S39 numbers 3/8 following 5 in Auxiliary Schedule 1.
S3A . *Types*
. . * Add to S3 letters A/K following 5 in Auxiliary Schedule 1.
S3D . International organizations
S3J . Government bodies
. . * Use S9T J.
S3J P . Law societies, bar associations
. . * For Inns of Court & Chancery, see English law SN3 KC.
S3M Communication in law, information on law
. * Normal synthesis by CSD is resumed here after its interruption at S34.
. * Add to S3 letters M/W following 5 in Auxiliary Schedule 1.
S3N . Language & law
S3N J . . Technical terms, legal jargon
K . . . Particular words, etc.
N . . Abbreviations
P . . Citation in law
. . . * As a subject. For citation indexes, see S3W J.
R . . Paleography, court hand
S . . Etymology
T . . Bilingualism
. . *Special languages*

[Law S]
[Common subdivisions]
[Communication in law S3M]
. [Language & law S3N]
. . [Special languages]

S3N V . . . Latin in the law
W . . . Other languages
S3P . Data processing, computers
. . * As a process; for the data bases, etc. themselves, see S3X.
S3Q E . Authorship, legal writing
. . * See also Bill drafting S5M R; Law reporting S5Q 3QE
F . . Correspondence
G . . Translation
S3R . Documentation of law
. . * See also Legal documents (preparation & use) S6C
S3R D . . Searching the legal literaturea
S3T . . Publishing in law, bookselling in law
S3U . . Bibliographies
S3W H . . . Abstracts & indexes
J . . . . Citation indexes in law
Y . . Libraries in law
S3X C . . Documentation centres in law
H . . . Automated information systems, databases
J . . . . Named systems
. . . . . * Arrange A/Z.
. . . . . * For example, CELEX (EU law) SG2 3XJ C.
KE . . . . Expert systems
P . . Primary materials in law (as a subject)
. . . * As a subject. Primary materials themselves (statutes, etc.) occur only under specific jurisdictions.
. . . * See also Sources of law S5C
S3Y . *Other agents & processes*
. . * Add to S3Y letters Q/S following 6 in Auxiliary Schedule 1.

S4 History of law
. * General works only, covering jurisprudence, practice & procedure, subjects of law as well as jurisdictions. The history of a specific branch, etc. goes with the latter. For the history of legal systems per se (jurisdictions) see SCY X4.
S47 . *Periods*
. . * General works only on a particular period; periods in a particular country go with the country.
. . * Add to S47 letters C/S from Auxiliary Schedule 4A.
S48 . *Places*
. . * Countries define the primary facet in Law (Jurisdictions by political authority) and are usually cited before everything else.
. . * However, this common facet is needed at a number of points, especially in SD International law & SF Supranational organizations; e.g. SDK 48 Territorial claims - (By country). In all such cases, Place is specified as follows:

[Law S]
[Common subdivisions]
[History of law S4]
. [Places S48]

. . * Add to -4 letters E/Z in Auxiliary Schedule 2.
. . * Sometimes, the resulting class (with its classmark ending with a country classmark drawn from Auxiliary Schedule 2) needs to be qualified by all or some of the legal concepts in Auxiliary Schedule S1. Very occasionally, this calls for the use of a special intercalator; see the notes at SV for how this is done.
. . * Sometimes, having cited a country or other local division from Auxiliary Schedule 2 (e.g. as at SD2 Q International courts) a second country needs to be cited. In such cases, proceed as follows:
. . * Add to -4 (where the hyphen represents the country classmark to be added to) letters E/Z in Auxiliary Schedule 2.
. . * Sometimes, the classmark for a national jurisdiction needs to be qualified by a local division of that country. In such cases, only the letters following that country's classmark (for states, counties, cities, etc.) need be added; e.g. York Court of Quarter Sessions SN7 RV4 PL (in which SN is English law, 7RV is Quarter Sessions courts & PL is for York, from EPL in Auxiliary Schedule 2 - the E for England being dropped since it is implicit in SN.

S52 Biography, lives of legal persons
. * This will usually go under a particular jurisdiction, e.g. English lawyers at SN5 2.
S53 . Collective biography
S54 . Individual biography

S55 Relations with other subjects, phase relations
. * Locate here only when the relationship is too general to warrant subordination to a specific topic (e.g. to sources of law).
. * Add to S55 letters A/Z from whole classification.
S55 P . Religion & law
S56 . Comparison with another subject
. . * For comparisons between branches or systems, see S59.
S57 . View of a subject from another subject
S58 . Influence of another subject
S59 . Relations between branches or system of law, comparisons
. . * See also Relations between subjects of law S9V B59; Relations between jurisdictions SCY X59.
. . * Add to S59 numbers & letters 5/9, A/Y in Auxiliary Schedule S1.

[Law S]
[Common subdivisions]
. [Relations with other subjects S55]
. . [Relations between branches or system of law S59]

S5A Jurisprudence, theory of law
. * The science, philosophy & theory of law. For jurisprudence as the study & knowledge of law in the widest sense, see Study & research S34 H.
S5A 4 . History
. . * Use Historical jurisprudence S5A 6A.
6 . Theory in jurisprudence
. . * The main purpose of this location is to allow qualification of specific topics, - e.g. justice theory S5U E6.
67 . Jurisprudence as theory of law
. . * Science of law in the narrower sense, together with philosophy of law.
68 . . Pure theory of law, fundamental nature of law
689 . . . Basic norms in law
69 . . Other theories

6A . Historical jurisprudence
. . * See note under Philosophical jurisprudence below (S5A A).
. . * This class takes the general writings of individual jurists, each appearing under the relevant place & period. Note that the usual citation order is reversed here and place is subordinated to period.
6D . . *By place*
. . . * Use only for general works on the jurisprudence of a country or other place covering all the periods below. If in doubt, prefer the location for this concept under Modern jurisprudence (S5A 8).
. . . * Add to S5A 6 letter D/Z from Auxiliary Schedule 2.

7C . . Ancient jurisprudence
7D . . . Topics special to the period
7G . . . Eastern jurisprudence (ancient & medieval)
7GD . . . . Topics special to Eastern jurisprudence
7H . . . . *By place*
. . . . . * Add to S5A 7H letters C/O following C in Auxiliary Schedule 2.
7J . . . Western jurisprudence (ancient)
7K . . . . Topics special to the period
7L . . . . Greek ancient jurisprudence
7M . . . . . Special topics
7N . . . . . *Individuals*
. . . . . . * Arrange A/Z.
7P . . . . Roman ancient jurisprudence
7Q . . . . . Special topics
7R . . . . . *Individuals*
. . . . . . * Arrange A/Z.
7S . . . . Other places
. . . . . * Arrange A/Z.

[Law S]
[Jurisprudence S5A]
[Historical jurisprudence S5A6A]
[Ancient jurisprudence S5A7C]
. [Western jurisprudence ancient S5A7J]
. . [Other places S5A7S]

S5A 7T Medieval jurisprudence
. * To c.1500.
7U . *By place*
. . * Use only for general works on a place during the
. . medieval period.
. . * Add to S5A 7U letters D/Z from Auxiliary
. . Schedule 2.
7V . *Special topics*
7W . *Individuals*
. . * Arrange A/Z.

8 Modern jurisprudence
. * Some prominent jurists are enumerated below as
. examples under particular periods & places.
. * Each jurist may be divided, if wished, as indicated
. at SD5 A9.
87 . *By place*
. . * General works on the jurisprudence in a
. . particular place in the modern period. For that
. . place in a particular period see the period.
. . * Add to S5A 87 letters D/Z from Auxiliary
. . Schedule 2.
. *By period*
8A . . *1500-1700*
8B . . . *Special topics*
8C . . . *Individuals*
. . . . * Arrange A/Z.
8CH . . . . Hale M
8CP . . . . Pufendorf S von
8D . . *18th century*
. . . * From the 18th century onwards each period is
. . . given a combined Place and Individual facet. In
. . . each case, proceed as follows (where the hyphen
. . . represents the classmark assigned to the facet):
. . . * Add to - letters D/Z from Schedule 2.
. . . * Under each country, proceed as follows:
. . . Add to - (where the hyphen represents its
. . . classmark)
. . . - 9 Topics special to the period
. . . - A/Z Individuals
8E . . . *Special topics*
8F . . . *By place & individual*
8FE . . . . Great Britain
8FE 9 . . . . . *Topics special to the period*
. . . . . *Individuals*
. . . . . . * Arrange A/Z.
8FE BL . . . . . . Blackstone W
8FE BU . . . . . . Burke E
8FF . . . . France
. . . . . *Individuals*
. . . . . . * Arrange A/Z.

[Jurisprudence S5A]
[Modern jurisprudence S5A8]
[By period]
[18th century S5A8D]
. [By place & individual S5A8F]
. . [France S5A8FF]
. . . [Individuals]

S5A 8FF MO . . . . Montesquieu C L de S
8FF PO . . . . Pothier R J
8FI . . Italy
. . . *Individuals*
. . . . * Arrange A/Z.
8FI VI . . . . Vico G B
8G *19th century*
8H . *Special topics*
8J . *By place & individual*
8JE . . Great Britain
. . . *Individuals*
. . . . * Arrange A/Z.
8JE MA . . . . Maine H J S
8JK . . Germany
. . . *Individuals*
. . . . * Arrange A/Z.
8JK HU . . . . Hugo G von
8JK KO . . . . Kohler J
8JK PU . . . . Puchta G F
8JK SA . . . . Savigny F C von
8JK TH . . . . Thibaut A F J
8JY . . U.S.A.
. . . *Individuals*
. . . . * Arrange A/Z.
8JY CA . . . . Carter I C
8JY FI . . . . Field D D
8K *20th century*
8L . *Special topics*
8M . *By place & individual*
8ME . . Great Britain
. . . *Individuals*
. . . . * Arrange A/Z.
8ME V . . . . Vinogradoff P G

Philosophy of law

[Law S]
[Jurisprudence S5A]
[Historical jurisprudence S5A6A]
. . . . [By place & individual S5A8M]
. . . . . [Great Britain S5A8ME]
. . . . . . [Individuals]
. . . . [Vinogradoff P G S5A8MEV]

S5A A Philosophy of law, philosophical jurisprudence, legal philosophy
. * Theoretically, a distinction can be drawn between Philosophy of law and Philosophical jurisprudence. The former covers theories relating to law propounded by philosophers rather than by jurists; it is characterized by abstractedness & generality. The latter is more like other branches of applied philosophy in that it examines the basic principles & assumptions of law, its nature & purpose (see S5B Q).
. * It is, however, impossible in the literature to distinguish these at the general level. So this classs takes general works on both. But the special detail of the former (Philosophy of law) will be found below in the classes S5AA/S5AL whilst the general writings of the jurists which form a substantial part of the latter (Philosophical jurisprudence) will be found under the relevant period and/or country in Historical jurisprudence (S5A 6A).
. * Add to S5A letters A/L following A in AA/AL.
. * Western philosophy is confounded here with general philosophy. A selection of prominent examples is given below.

BA . *Philosophical doctrines & viewpoints*
CG . . Rationalism
CH . . Empiricism
CHP . . Legal positivism
CL . . Legal realism
CTR . . Structuralism
DA . *Philosophical schools by period & place*
DC . . Ancient Greek
DEJ . . . Plato
DJ . . Medieval
DNH S . . . Aquinas
DO . . Modern
. . . * For Marxist legal theory, see S5B AST.
DUK J . . . Hegel
FAY . *Branches of philosophy*
GG . . Metaphysical jurisprudence
GQF . . Freewill & determination
HK . . Ethics & jurisprudence, moral philosophy
. . . * For Justice, see Law & society, S5U E.
. *By philosophical tradition*
. . Western philosophy of law
. . . * See S5A A.
I . . Eastern philosophy of law
M Special theories
. * E.g., normative theory of criminal law SBW 5AM.

[Law S]
[Jurisprudence S5A]
[Special theories S5AM]

S5A N Social-political theory & law
. * Add to S5A letters O/Q following K9Q and U/X following K9. Some examples of prominent concepts are given below.
O . Reflecting order view of society
Q . Reflecting control view of society
V . Sociological jurisprudence
. . * See also Law & society (i.e. study of the operations of law in a particular context) S5U B.
W . Social anthropology & jurisprudence
Y . Other social theories
. . * For egalitarian justice, see Rule of law S5U V.
. . * Add to S5A Y letters A/R following K.
YFV . . Transactional theory
YHS Q . . Functional jurisprudence
YIC . . Conflict theory & jurisprudence
. . . * Law as system of social control, reflecting social ends.
S5B A . Political theory & jurisprudence
. . * Add to S5B A letters N/T following RA in RAN/RAT.
AN . . Ideologies & jurisprudence
ANS . . Nationalsm & jurisprudence
APB . . Authoritarianism & jurisprudence
AS . . Collectivism & jurisprudence
ASQ . . . Socialist legal theory
. . . . * See also socialist jurisdictions SSD.
AST . . . . Marxist legal theory
. . . . . * See also USSR legal system SVN.

Special approaches in jurisprudence
P . Comparative law
. . * As a method of enquiry. For comparisons of specific aspects of law, see S59 - e.g. comparison of legal systems SCY X59.
Q . Analytical jurisprudence
R . . Classification in law
RF . . Reform of law
. . Special concepts in analytical jurisprudence
. . . * Concepts special to a given branch of law (e.g. person, obligation) are subordinated to that branch. Class here analytical concepts which are too general to be subordinated thus.
S . . . Judicial process
. . . . * As compared with the legislative and administrative process.
T . . . Causation in law
V . . . Certainty in law
W . . . Justiciability
. . . . * Quality of being capable of being considered legally & determined by adjudication. Applies particularly in International law.
X . . . Other special concepts

[Law S]
[Jurisprudence S5A]
[Special approaches in jurisprudence]
. [Analytical jurisprudence S5BQ]
. . [Special concepts in analytical jurisprudence]
. . . [Other special concepts S5BX]

. . . . * Arrange A/Z, e.g. duty S5B XD.

S5B Y Concepts special to a context
. * For example, see Process of war SDT B.

S5C Sources of law, origins of law
. * See also Historical jurisprudence S5A 6A
. *Operations*
S5C D . . Analysis of sources, interpretation & construction
. . . * For interpretation of legal documents, etc. in Practice of law, see S6C F.
H . . Codification
K . . . Official codification
N . . . Non-official codification
U . . Unification of laws, harmonization of laws
. . . * Elimination of inconsistencies (especially national peculiarities) primarily to facilitate use/integration between different jurisdictions.
. . . * For approximation, see EU law SG5 CU.
S5D . Custom, customary law
. . * Customs, usages and practices which are sufficiently fixed and settled over a particular area as to be known, recognized and deemed obligatory as much as written formulations of law. Still widespread (e.g. in Africa, China, etc.) and may equal or exceed in significance legislative or case law.
S5D G . . Local custom
T . . Ethnic law, tribal law
. . . * For Ethnolaw, see SI. This location should be used only when qualifying a jurisdiction or a subject of law to indicate that concepts from an ethnic law are considered in reaching a legal decision.
S5E . . . *By ethnic group*
. . . . * This concept applies only under specific jurisdictions.
. . . . * Add to S5E letters B/Y from Auxiliary Schedule 3A.
S5F . . Religious law
. . . * For ecclesiastical law, see SWE. This location should be used only when qualifying a jurisdiction or a subject of law to indicate that a concept from religious law is considered in reaching a legal decision.
. . . *By religion*
. . . . * This concept applies only under specific jurisdictions.
. . . . * Add to S5F letters W/Y following S in SW/SY.
S5G B . Historical sources
. . * For specific elements under a given system (e.g. law merchant in English law) see the system.
D . Formal sources

[Law S]
[Jurisprudence S5A]
[Sources of law S5C]
[Formal sources S5GD]

* By reason of recognized authority. This class is for these sources as subjects. For primary materials themselves, see -2 under a given jurisdiction - e.g. for Statutes, Codes
Agencies
. * Political authorities responsible, from point of view of their role as sources of law.
S5G E . Lawmaking bodies
F . . Governments
G . . . Administrative sources of law
H . . Non-governmental bodies as sources of law
. . . * Apply mainly to international law.
P Processes
. * Codes of practice observed for self-regulation; see International law SD5 GP

S5H Treaties
. * See International law SD5 H: Supranational law SE5 H.
S5J Conventions, conferences
S5K Common law as source of law
S5L Constitutions
. * This location is primarily for use under Constitutional law RC5 L.
S5M Statute law, legislation (sources of law)
. * For constitutions, see Constitutional law SC5 L.
S5M CD . Interpretation
. . * See also Rights (substantive law) S9V H
CE . . Mischief rule
CF . . Ejusdem generis rule
CG . . Other rules of interpretation
. . . * E.g., golden rule.
P . Preparations of statutes
. . * For the political process of proposing bills, debating them, etc. see Class R.
R . . Drafting bills & legislation
. . . * See also Language of law S3N
T . Retrospective legislation, retroactive legislation, ex post facto legislation, intertemporal law
X . Plebiscites, referenda
S5N Codes
. * Comprehensive, systematic statements of major bodies of law (e.g. civil, criminal) superseding accumulated mixtures of customary and statutory law, decisions, etc.

Sources of law

[Law S]
[Jurisprudence S5A]
[Sources of law S5C]
[Formal sources S5GD]
[Codes S5N]

. * As subject. For particular codes, see under
. jurisdictions SD/SY & under their primary
. materials.

S5P Delegated legislation, subordinate legislation, subsidiary legislation, indirect legislation
. * Administrative rules and regulations, etc.

S5P Q Quasi-legislation
. * Procedural rules, codes of practice, etc.

R . Autonomous law
. . * Rules created by bodies of persons to whom
. . restricted legislative powers have been
. . conferred - e.g. universities, professional
. . bodies, public corporations.

S Proclamations, statutory declarations, charters

T . Local legislation

V Other communications with force of law
. * For example, see Roman law - Senatus
. consultiam SJX 5NV.

W Precedents
. * For specific forms of precedence (e.g. court
. precedence, conveyancing precedence) see the
. context.

X . Judicial precedence
. . * Decisions of superior courts.
. . * For Stare decisis, see Judgementis S9F M.

S5Q . Case law
. . Legal writing

S5Q 3QE . . . Law reporting

P . . Principles
. . . * As central feature of case law.

Other jurisdictions as sources

S5R . International law as source of law
. . * Mainly in the case of supranational law.

S5S . Supranational jurisdictions as source of law
. . * When a national jurisdiction is affected by
. . the decisions of a supranational jurisdiction
. . (e.g. European Union law).
. . * The general class for supranational law is
. . SE. Use this location only when qualifying a
. . jurisdiction or a subject of law to indicate
. . that a supranational law is considered in
. . reaching legal decisions.
. . * For impact of another national jurisdiction
. . in particular decisions, see Conflict of laws,
. . SA.

S5T A . National jurisdictions as source of law, foreign law as source

[Law S]
[Jurisprudence S5A]
[Sources of law S5C]
. [Formal sources S5GD]
. . [Other jurisdictions as sources]
. . . [National jurisdictions as source of law S5TA]

S5T B . . . . *Specific jurisdictions*
. . . . . * For example, Reception of Roman law,
. . . . . SKG 5TB.
. . . . . * See also Conflict of laws SA

F . Documentary sources (general), publicists, jurists

G . . Literary sources
. . . * E.g. treatises.

H . . Commentaries, interpretations
. . . * For interpretation & construction in modern
. . . modern practice, see S5C D.

J . . . Glosses, glossators
. . . . * Of medieval legal scholars.

K . . . Commentators, post-glossators
. . . . * Of medieval legal scholars.

M . Responsa, casuistry
. . * Answers of learned jurists to problems posed.

N . Conventional law
. . * Rules originating in agreement of those subject to
. . them (e.g. members of club).

R . Juristic Act, act in the law
. . * Whereby legal persons create, alter or disturb rights
. . and duties, thereby affecting legal relations between
. . persons. Distinguished from acts of the law, where the
. . law itself affects the rights and duties of persons.

S5U B Law & society
. * See also Sociological jurisprudence S5A V

C . Human behaviour, human conduct

D . Purpose of law

E . Justice
. . * Moral value commonly considered to be the end
. . which law tries to attain.
. . * See also Sacred & temporal law S5U P and S5U Q;
. . Distributive justice S5V L

F . . Standards of justice

G . . Fairness as justice

H . . . Natural justice
. . . . * See also Natural law S5U N

J . . . Relative justice

L . . . Compensatory justice

N . Natural law, law of nature
. . * See also Natural justice S5U H

P . . Sacred law, divine justice
. . . * See also Religious law as a source of law S5F

Q . . Positive law, temporal law
. . . * Laid down by humans, in particular communities.

R . . Higher law

RV . . . Civil disobedience as justifiable conduct

Law & society

[Law S]
[Jurisprudence S5A]
[Law & society S5UB]
[Natural law S5UN]
. [Higher law S5UR]
. . [Civil disobedience as justifiable conduct S5URV]

S5U S . Public policy, ordre publique
. . * Judicial interpretation founded on supposed
. . needs of the community.
T Rule of law, supremacy of law, due process of law
V . Equality before the law, egalitarian justice
. . * See also Discrimination in practice of law S6A D
W . Law as control of conduct
. . * See also Sociological jurisprudence S5A V
X . Law as protector of persons
. . * For Victims in law, see Practice & procedure
. . S8E V.

Y Special relations between law & society
. * For law of persons, see SAP.
. * Add to S5U Y letters A/Y following K so far as
. applicable.
S5V B . Interests
. . * For specific forms of interest, see context
. . - e.g. interest in property SBH 5VB.
D . Things, objects of legal rights, Res
. . * See also Law of property SBH
J . Time as legal factor
. . * See also Limitations S8F
K . Duties & rights
L . . Distributive justice
. . . * Justice in distribution of duties, rights and
. . . privileges.
M . . Duties, obligations, responsibilities
N . . . Accountability
P . . Rights, claims on society
. . . * For specific rights, see Human rights law
. . . SCC W.
. . . * For rights in substantive law, see S9V H.
S . *Principles special to a context*
. . * For an example of this, see SG5 V (EU law).

S5W . Special fields of social action
. . * For general works on the place of the law in these
. . fields and their impact on the law. For the
. . detailed legal relations see the relevant branch of
. . law - e.g. Property, Commercial law, Public
. . performance law.
. . * See also Social-political theory and law S5A N
. . * Add to S5W numbers and letters 3/9, A/Z from
. . the whole classification so far as necesary and
. . excluding classes covered elsewhere in S.
S5W AY . . Sciences & the law
H . . Anthropology & the law
KCQ . . Social progress & reform & the law

[Law S]
[Jurisprudence S5A]
[Law & society S5UB]
[Special relations between law & society S5UY]
[Special fields of social action S5W]
[Social progress & reform & the law S5WKCQ]

S5W KEP Communication media & the law
KEQ H . The Press & the law
KEX H . Publicity on the law
KME P . Public opinion & the law
KRS The law & particular types of societies
KW Custom & folklore & the law
. * See also custom as a source of law S5D
KWM R . Witchcraft & the law
P Religion & the law
Q Social welfare & the law
QGN G . Victimology & the law
QP . Law enforcement & the law, police
. & the law
. . * The main class for law enforcement,
. . police and penology is QP. Locate here
. . only those works in which jurisprudence
. . and legal systems are the focus in the
. . relationship.
. . * See also Administration of justice S6;
. . Police law (constitutional law) SCN A;
. . Police law (criminal investigation)
. . SBW 8LN
QQ . . Penology & the law
R Politics & the law
RHL . Political parties & the law
RHL AWR . . Party policy statements & the law
T Economics & the law
U Technology & the law
W The Arts & the law

S6 Practice & procedure, adjective law, procedural law, administration of justice, judiciary, procedure (widest sense), civil procedure
. * Means whereby rights & duties may be declared, defended, remedied, etc., as contrasted with substantive law (S9V B).
. * Includes works covering both civil & criminal procedure.
. * For the narrower meaning (of the steps taken from the initiating of a claim or other proceeding to the final judgement) see S8 Actions, Legal proceedings.
. * For judiciary as branch of government, see Political science RLY; for judiciary in constitutional law, see SCX; for judicial process in analytical jurisprudence, see S5B S.
. * When building compound classmarks retroactively within the notational classes S6/S9, the first two characters (S6, S7, S8 or S9) within each of the classes S6/S9 can be dropped; e.g. S6NP Lay judges and S6KF Appointment can be combined to give S6N PKF for Appointment of lay judges.

. *Processes*
S69 . . Access to the law
. . . * By the citizen or other party.
S6A . . Practice of law
. . . * For legal profession narrowly, see S34. This class covers the operations found in the day-to-day running of a law practice.
S6A C . . . Malpractice
D . . . . Discrimination in the law
E . . . . . Ethnic discrimination in the law, racial discrimination in the law
F . . . . . Sexist discrimination in the law
H . . . . Bribery in the law, corruption in the law
L . . . Evaluation of legal performance
. . . . * By the citizen; for evaluation as a management procedure, see S6B QVP.
N . . . . Efficiency
P . . . . Effectiveness
R . . . . Complaints, criticism of the law

. *Agents*
S6B . . Law practices, law firms, law departments
S6B Q . . . Management of law practices
. . . . * For legal profession, see S34.
. . . . * Add to S6B letter Q/Y following T in TQ/TY.
SO . . . . Clerical services, office services
. . . . . *Personnel*
SOA C . . . . . . Managing clerks, legal executives
SQ . . . . . Records handling
SQJ . . . . . . Correspondence
S6C . . . Legal documents
S6C D . . . . Preparation & use of legal documents

[Practice & procedure S6]
[Agents]
[Law practices S6B]
. [Legal documents S6C]
. . [Preparation & use of legal documents S6CD]

S6C E . . Composition of legal documents, drafting legal documents
. . . * For bill drafting, see Statutes (sources of law) S5MR.
F . . Interpretation & construction
. . . * See also interpretation of statutes S5M CD
G . . . Analogy (interpretation of texts)
H . . Authentication of legal records
. . *Types of documents*
K . . . Forms
L . . . . Legislative documents

N . Note-taking
. . * See also Judges - Notes S6N CN; Court reporting S6F J
V . Advocacy (general)
. . * See also Oral pleadings S8S U6C V.
W . Preparation of briefs
S6D . Legal aid, legal assistance
. . *Personnel*
S6D 35 . . . Duty solicitors
. . *Organizations*
38 . . . Law centres, community law services, neighbourhood law centres
F . . Financial assistance
G . . . Eligibility for legal aid
N . . Counselling
P . . Advice by way of representation, ABWOR

S6E Courts & court proceedings
. * For structure of courts system, see Types of courts, S78.
S6E 5WK . Sociology
5WK FS . . Interpersonal interaction in court
Q . Management of courts, administration of courts
. . * See also Trial proceedings, S8S
. . * Add to S6E letters Q/V following T in TQ/Y so far as applicable. A selection of commonly relevant concepts is given below.
T . . Financial management of courts
TP . . . Court costs
TT . . . . Fees
TU . . . . . Filing fees in courts
. . *Personnel*
U . . . Court personnel, court administrators, court executives
. . . . * Managing non-judicial operations; for Court officials, see S6V C.
V . . Court buildings & equipment
. . . Courthouses, courtrooms
S6F . . Information systems in courts

Courts & court proceedings

[Practice & procedure S6]
[Agents]
[Courts & court proceedings S6E]
[Management of courts S6EQ]
. [Information systems in courts S6F]

S6F G . . Computers in court information systems
H . . Records handling
J . . Court reporting
. . . * Transcribing legal proceedings.
K . . Communication media & court proceedings
L . . . The Press in court reporting
M . . . Photographing court proceedings
N . . . Broadcasting court proceedings
O . . . . Televising court proceedings
Q . Security in court
R . . Screens, The Dock
S . . Surveillance systems in court
T . . . Equipment
V . . Personnel identification
W . . Protection of persons in court
. . . * For protection of specific types of persons, see person - e.g. witnesses, jury.
. *Special processes & procedures*
S6G . . Court calendar, court dockets, trial dockets
S6G H . . . Terms of court, court recesses, nonterm (USA)
J . . . Cause list, listings of cases
. . . . * List of cases due to be heard by a court.
K . . . . Non-jury list
N . . Court intake
P . . . Case flow management, case scheduling, assignment of cases
Q . . . Congestion in court, delays in court
. . . . * See also Right to speedy trial (criminal law) SBW 8SF P
S . . Summons for direction
. . . * Deciding how action is best heard & disposed of.
Properties & processes & constituents
. * The basic function of the court (to provide a forum for adjudicating between plaintiffs or prosecutors and defendants or accused) is served by a mixture of attributes (powers, etc.), processes (procedures, etc.) & the work of the court personnel who collectively constitute the court.
S6H . Jurisdiction of court, powers of court
. . * See also Conflict of laws SA
S6H J . . Temporal application
K . . . Retroactive laws, intertemporal laws, ex post facto laws
L . . Jurisdiction & venue
P . . Territorial applicability
. . . * For Status of forces agreed, see International law SD6 HQ.
R . . Special topics

[Practice & procedure S6]
[Agents]
[Courts & court proceedings S6E]
[Properties & processes & constituents]
[Jurisdiction of court S6H]
. [Special topics S6HR]

S6J Court procedure (narrowly)
. * For procedure relating to action, see Actions, S8.
S6J K . Legal forms, court forms & precedents
L . Rules of court, procedural rules, conduct of court proceedings
M . . Formal rules of court
. . . * See also Simple forms of actions (USA) SP6 JM
N . . Practice directions
P . . Customary procedure
Q . . Rules special to a specific court or procedure
. . . * E.g. Fitness to plead (criminal trials) SBW 8SD 6JQ.
S . Court decorum
T . Contempt of court
U . . Sub judice
V . . Civil contempt of court
W . . Criminal contempt of court

S6K B Law officers, court officers, judicial officers of court
. * Officers special to a particular court or function go with the court or function (e.g. military prosecutor, juror).
D . *Relations with other law officers*
. . * See use of this class under Juries, S9E 6KD
. *Operations*
F . . Appointment & removal
G . . . Selection or election
H . . . . Determining competence to serve
. . . . . * See also Voir dire (witnesses) S9A VX
K . . . . Retention of office
. . . . . * For example, judges' retention election (USA)
L . . . Installation
M . . . Term of office, tenure
N . . . Termination of appointment
P . . . . Removal from office
Q . . . Succession
R . . Performance evaluation, effectiveness
S . . Misconduct in office
T . . . Disqualification, dismissal
U . . . Judicial corruption
V . . . . Bribery
. *Attributes of officers/office*
S6L B . . Characteristics of the office holder
D . . Role of law officers, function of law officers
E . . Powers of law officers

Law officers

[Practice & procedure S6]
[Agents]
[Courts & court proceedings S6E]
[Properties & processes & constituents]
[Law officers S6KB]
[Attributes of officers/office]
. [Powers of law officers S6LE]

S6L G . Privileges, immunities
J *Special attributes & functions of officer/office*
. * See, for example, under juries S9E G;
. Trustees SBH UL.

S6M *Types of law officers*
. *By non-legal characteristics*
. . * Add to S6M letters G/V following 4 in
. . Auxiliary Schedule 1.
S6M L . . *By ethnic origin*
. . *By sex*
N . . . Women
S6N . Judges, chief justices (USA)
. . *Operations*
S6N CN . . . Judges' notes
. . *Types of judges*
MN . . . Women as judges
P . . . Lay judges, assessors (USA)
Q . . . International judges
. . . . * See International law, SD6 N
R . . . Supranational judges
. . . . * See Supranational law, SE6 N
S . . . National judges
T . . . Subnational judges
V . . . . Local judges
X . . . . . Justices of the Peace, J.P.s'
. . . . . . * If distinguished from
. . . . . . magistrates.
S6P . . . . . Magistrate, U.S.
. . . . . Commissioners
S6P R . . . . . . Clerk to the Justices,
. . . . . . magistrates' clerk
RP . . . . . . Lay magistrate
S6Q . . . . . . Stipendiary magistrate
S6Q T . . . . . . Police magistrate
. . . . * Special to US criminal courts,
. . . . which should be cited first.
S6R . . . . . . Juge d'instruction,
. . . . . . examining magistrate
. . . . * Conducts the investigation
. . . . prior to a criminal trial.
. . . . Special to criminal law (which
. . . . should be cited first).
S6R V . . . Designated judges, specially
. . . appointed judges (USA)
W . . . Other types
. . . . * Arrange A/Z.
. . . . * For example, ordinaries, ordinary
. . . . judges.

[Practice & procedure S6]
[Courts & court proceedings S6E]
[Properties & processes & constituents]
. [Law officers S6KB]
. . [Types of law officers S6M]
. . . [Judges S6N]
. . . . . [Other types S6RW]

S6R X . . . Commissioners
. . . . * If distinguished from judges.
. . . . * For sheriffs, see Practice of law S37 S.
. . *By special function*
S6S . . . Arbitrators
. . . . * See Arbitration S9R 6S
S6S X . . . Masters (court appointees)
. . . . * Delegated to conduct special investgations or
. . . . implement court orders.
S6T . . . *Special to particular jurisdictions*
. . . . For example, advocatus diaboli SXJ 6TF.
S6U . . . Court attorneys (general)
. . . . * For prosecution attorneys, see S8C BC; for
. . . . defence attorneys, see defence counsel S8D BC.
S6U UY . . . . Amicus curie
. . . . . * Counsel permitted by court to present an
. . . . . interest not a party to the case before it but
. . . . . assisting the court to decide the latter.
W . . . . Official solicitor
. . . . . * May be directed by court to act ad litem as the
. . . . . next friend or guardian.
S6V C . Court officials, court auxiliary personnel
E . . Notaries
F . . Marshals
G . . Sheriffs (USA)
H . . Bailiffs, sheriff's officers
J . . Sheriff Principal (USA)
K . . Masters (court appointees - USA)
N . . Official referees
R . . Registrars
S . . Receivers
T . . Clerks of the court, justices' clerks,
. . prothonotaries
V . . Court interpreters
S6W . . Other
. . . * Arrange A/Z.
. . . * For example, associates, ushers, viewers.

Types of courts
. *Properties*

[Practice & procedure S6]
[Agents]
[Courts & court proceedings S6E]
[Types of courts]
[Properties]

S78 . Structure of court system, organization of courts

S79 *By place*

By secondary role

S7D . Court from which an appeal is made
. . * Use only when qualifying courts in S9H Appeal.

By stage in decision process

S7E . Courts of first instance, trial courts, courts of original jurisdiction

S7F . Appeal courts (general)
. . * Alternative (not recommended) to subordinating to Appeal S9H.

By breadth of jurisdiction

S7G . Courts of general jurisdiction (general)
. . * For courts of special jurisdiction, see S7U F.

By historical jurisdiction

S7H . Common law courts (general)

S7I . Equity courts (general)
. . * For Chancery courts, see English law SN7 I.

By general branch of law

S7K . Civil courts (general)

S7L . Criminal courts (general)
. . * Alternative (not recommended) to subordinating to criminal law SW.

S7M . Public law courts (general), constitutional courts (general)
. . * Alternative (not recommended) to subordinating to constitutional law SC.

S7N *Categories special to a jurisdiction*
. * E.g. Courts of Record in English law, SN7 N.

By status in courts hierarchy

S7P . National courts (general), federal courts (general)

S7Q . Supreme courts (general)

S7Q F . . Appellate jurisdiction
. . . * Alternative (not recommended) to subordinating to Appeal S9H.

S7R . Higher courts (general), superior courts (general)

S7S . Lower courts (general), intermediate courts (general), inferior courts

S7T . . Summary jurisdiction courts (general), magistrates' courts (general)

[Practice & procedure S6]
[Agents]
[Courts & court proceedings S6E]
[Types of courts]
. [By status in courts hierarchy]
. . [Lower courts general S7S]
. . . [Summary jurisdiction courts general S7T]

S7U F . . Courts of special jurisdiction
. . . * The preferred arrangement for these is to subordinate them to the subject of law concerned (except that civil courts are combined with those of general jurisdiction).
. . . * An alternative is provided here for libraries wishing to keep together the literature on all types of courts. If this option is taken, proceed as follows:
. . . * Add to S7U P letters A/Y in Auxiliary Schedule S1; e.g. criminal courts S7U PW; family courts S7U PCF.

. *By geographical jurisdiction*
. . * For federal courts, see S7P.

R . . Regional courts

S7V . . States courts
. . . * Applies to jurisdictions with federal or other decentralized system.
. . . * Alternative (not recommended) to subordinating to States SCS

S7W . . Local courts
. . . * Alternative (not recommended) to subordinating to Local government SCU.

S8 Actions, lawsuits, suits, litigation, cause, legal proceedings, process (general)
. * Procedure in the narrower sense - that part of adjective law covering the steps taken in initiating and carrying through a legal claim or other proceeding.
. * Usually implies a court as the agency of decision; but an action may be settled out of court.
. * A sharp distinction is usually made between civil and criminal actions. This class gives what is common to both, plus some matters special to civil law; so it takes both material on actions in general and material on civil actions in general. It excludes matter peculiar to criminal law; for these, see SU8 Criminal proceedings.
. * For specific types of proceedings, see S9S.

. *Agents*

S88 . . Forensic science & technology (qualifier)
. . . * The general class is under Evidence, at S8U. Use this location only to qualify concepts appearing before that stage in proceedings (i.e. classes S8A/S8T).

Actions

[Practice & procedure S6]
[Agents]
[Courts & court proceedings S6E]
[Actions S8]
[Agents]
. [Forensic science & technology qualifier S88]

S8A Parties to an action
. *Properties*
S8A C . . Capacity (of parties)
D . . . Fitness to plead
E . . Anonymity of parties
F . . Attitude of parties to adjudication
. . . * Applies mainly in International law, SD.
G . . Reservations by parties
. . . * Applies mainly to International law, SD.
L . . Rights & duties of parties
. . . * In civil law, rights accrue to both parties; in criminal law, only to the accused. For special rights of the accused on trial, see SBW 8SF.
L6A P . . . Effectiveness of rights
M . . . Statutory rights
N . . . Locus standi
. . . . * Right to bring an action or challenge a decision.
P . . . Rights special to a context
. . . . * For example, see under Evidence of defendant S8T D.
S . . . Suability of foreign states
. . . . * See Conflict of laws SA8 AS
. *Operations*
S8B A . . Choice of law
. . . * See Conflict of laws SA8 BA
B . . Services to parties, assistance to parties
. . . * Applies mainly to criminal proceedings - see SBW 8BB.
C . . . Legal representation, services of counsel
CAL . . . . Rights to legal representation
E . . . . Parties with legal aid
F . . . . . Court-awarded legal fees
G . . . . Counsel & client
J . . . . Systems of services to parties
. . . . . * Agencies providing counsel for indigent parties.
P . . . . . Legal investigations for parties
R . . . Ad litem provisions
. . . . * "For the suit": actions taken to provide legal services in particular circumstances (e.g. to act as next friend).
T . . Joinder of parties
. . . * Combining 2 or more persons (whether as plaintiff or defendant) in a single action.
W . Next friend
. . * Acting for infant, mentally incapacitated person, etc.

[Practice & procedure S6]
[Agents]
[Courts & court proceedings S6E]
[Actions S8]
[Parties to an action S8A]
. [Next friend S8BW]

S8C . Claimant, plaintiff, pursuer (Scot.)
. . * For national & supranational jurisdictions as plaintiff, see SD8 C.
S8C BC . . Prosecution counsel
. . . * For public prosecutor, see SW8 CBK.
BT . . Informers, common informers
S8D . Defendant
. . * The classes below refer mainly to criminal cases.
. . * For national & supranational jurisdictions as defendant, see SD8 D.
S8D BB . . Defence services
BC . . . Defence counsel
BJ . . . . Defender systems
. . . . . * Agencies providing counsel for indigent defendants.
BK . . . . . Public defender
BL . . . . . Dock brief
BP . . . . . Defender legal investigation
. . . . . . * Professionals trained in fact finding.
BS . . Pro se defence
. . . * Acting as one's own defence attorney.
S8E B . Subsequent parties
D . Third parties
. . * For witnesses, see S9A V.
E . . Joinder & severance of parties
. *By special status*
M . . Children & minors (as parties)
V . . Victim as party to action
. . . * Most of the literature relates to criminal cases - see SBW 8EV.

General organizational processes
S8F . Limitation of actions, prescription
S8F J . Consolidation of actions
N . Non-contentious proceedings
V . Conduct of proceedings
Y . . Investigatory systems (general)
. . . * For accusatorial & inquisitorial systems, see Criminal law SBW 8FY.
S8J . . Prosecution procedure (general)
. . . * Applies primarily to criminal cases (SBW 8J) under which more details are given.
S8J X . . . Nolle prosequi
S8K . . Defence procedure (general)

Preliminary proceedings

[Practice & procedure S6]
[Agents]
[Courts & court proceedings S6E]
[Actions S8]
[General organizational processes]
. [Conduct of proceedings S8FV]
. . [Defence procedure general S8K]

S8L Preliminary proceedings, pre-trial proceedings
. * These differ markedly as between civil & criminal actions. Details below are mostly peculiar to civil actions.
. * For preliminary examination in criminal cases, see SBW 8N; for accord & satisfaction, see Discharge of contracts SBE TQ.
S8L M . Pretrial review
MP . Proceedings in chambers
N . Commencing an action
P . . Writs, originating summons
Q . . . Versus defendant
R . . . Versus third party
. . . . * Including to witnesses.
S . . . Service of process
. . . . * In some uses (e.g. Scots law) process includes collection of pleadings & documents to put before the court.
T . . . . Amendment
V . . . . Direct service
W . . . . . Specific forms
X . . . . Substituted service
S8M B . . . . Personal service
C . . . . . Acceptance of service
E . . . . Postal service (writs)
G . . . . Service out of jurisdiction
. . . *Types of writs*
J . . . . Summonses
K . . . . . Writ of summons
M . . . . Motions
N . . . . Petitions
O . . . . Other
. . . . . * Arrange A/Z.
P . . Arrest & charge (general)
. . . * Rarely occurs in civil actions.

T . Acknowledgment of service
U . Notice of intention to defend, appearance
V . Non-appearance in court
W . Discovery & inspection of documents, documentation (preliminary proceedings)
. . * Collecting documents to be put before the court (as with pleadings).
S8N . Pleadings
. . * For oral pleading, see Trial practice - Advocacy S8S U6C V.
. . * For admission, see Evidence S9A E.

[Practice & procedure S6]
[Agents]
[Courts & court proceedings S6E]
[Actions S8]
[Preliminary proceedings S8L]
[Pleadings S8N]

S8N P Amendments of pleas, supplements to pleas
Q New matter
. * See also Appellate procedure S9H
R Particulars
S . Bill of pleadings
T Material facts
V Record (Scot.)
. * Comprises summons, conclusions, condescendence & defence, etc.
W Conclusion
. * That part of a summons stating what remedy is sought from the court.
S8P B Statement of claim, declaration, condescendence (Scot.)
C . Points of claim (common causes)
. . * By plaintiff.
. . * See also Remedies S9G
D . Declaration (pleadings), complaints (pleadings)
. . * See also Declaratory judgements S9F N
E . Accusations
F . . False accusations
W Waiver
. * Abandonment of claim, remedy or immunity.

S8Q Defence, plea, points of defence (common law)
. * For Defence pleas in criminal actions, see SBW 8SD.
. * See also Proof (evidence) S8T W.
S8Q R . Traverse
S . Confession & avoidance
. . * For Admission, see Evidence S9A E.
T . Objections on point of law, demurrer
U . Set off & counterclaim
V . Acquiescence
. . * Failure to object to an infringement of a right.
W . Laches
. . * Unreasonable delay or negligence in pursuing a right.
. *Special defences*
S8R B . . Interpleader
. . . * Usually restricted to property claims.

Preliminary proceedings

[Courts & court proceedings S6E]
[Actions S8]
[Preliminary proceedings S8L]
. [Pleadings S8N]
. . [Defence S8Q]
. . . [Special defences]
. . . . [Interpleader S8RB]

S8R C . . . . Special to a context
. . . . . * E.g. under Tort SBG 8RC.
D . . . . Justification
. . . . . * Special to torts & criminal actions.
E . . . . Disclosure in the public interest

F . . Reply (of plaintiff)
G . . Rejoinder (of defence)
H . . Counterclaim, crossclaim
I . . . Setoff
J . . Issues in action
K . . . General issue
L . . . Joinder of issue, litisconstestation
M . . . . Special issue
. . . . . * See also Instructions to jury S9D S
MV . Payment into court
N . Interlocutory application
P . . Ex-parte
Q . . On notice (interlocutory application)
R . Consolidation of actions
S . Trial preparation
. . * Gathering information & evidence to prove or
. . disprove factual matters submitted to court.
. . * For Pre-trial discovery, see S8M W.
T . . Interrogations
U . . Investigation of disputed facts
W . Settlement of action, transaction (civil law)
. . * See also Dispute resolution S9Q
WT . . Discontinuance
WV . . Compromise (settlement of actions)
WW . . Pretrial settlement

S8S Court actions (narrowly), trial proceedings, hearings
S8S 6EQ . Trial management
. . * See also Court management, S6E Q
T . Trial procedure, courtroom procedure
. . * If this is distinguished from trial proceedings in
. . general. In doubt, prefer latter (S8).
U . . Trial practice, trial strategy, trial tactics
. . . Advocacy
U6C V . . . . Oral pleadings (advocacy)
V . . . Opening statements
. . . . * By plaintiff, prosecutor & defendant.
W . . Fact & law
. . . * Relation between matters of fact & matters of
. . . law.
X . . . Causation

[Agents]
[Courts & court proceedings S6E]
[Actions S8]
[Court actions narrowly S8S]
[Trial procedure S8ST]
[Fact & law S8SW]
. [Causation S8SX]

S8T Evidence, matters of fact, extrinsic evidence, trial evidence
S8T 6JL . Rules
6JQ . . Objections (rules of evidence)
D . Defendant
DAH . . Rights of defendants
. . . * For rights of accused, see Criminal
. . . law SBW 8SF.
DAK . . . Right to give evidence
DAL . . . . Statement of the defendant
DAP . . . Protection from illegally
. . . obtained evidence
DAQ . . . Protection from unfair publicity
. *Properties*
V . . Admissability of evidence
. . . * For admissability of a specific form of
. . . evidence (e.g. hearsay) see the form.
. . . * For illegally obtained evidence, see
. . . S9A G.
V5U S . . . Public policy
VJL . . . Rules
. . . . * For Judges' rules, see Criminal
. . . . proceedings SBW 8TV JL.
W . . Proof
. . . * That which establishes the existence
. . . or non-existence of a fact.
WX . . . Burden of proof, onus of proof
XB . . . Standards of proof
XC . . . . Probability
XD . . . . Reasonable doubt
XE . . . . In doubt for the defendant
. . . . (USA)
XF . . . . Corroboration
XG . . . Presumption
. . . . * Inference drawn from established
. . . . fact.
XI . . . . Irrefutable presumption
XJ . . . . Rebuttable presumption
XK . . . . Presumption of fact
XL . . . Relevancy of evidence
XM . . . Credibility of evidence
XN . . . Weight of evidence
XP . . . Estoppel, res judicata
. . . . * What is already admitted cannot
. . . . be retracted. Adjudication is final &
. . . . may not be reopened by the parties
. . . . concerned.
XS . . Fact & opinion
. . . * See also Expert witnesses S9B P
. *Operations*

[Agents]
[Courts & court proceedings S6E]
[Actions S8]
[Court actions narrowly S8S]
[Trial procedure S8ST]
[Evidence S8T]
[Operations]

S8T XV Presentation of evidence

Y Elicitation of facts, fact-finding, identification of facts

S8U . Forensic science & technology
. . * Application of specialized bodies of knowledge to assist elicitation & interpretation of facts relevant to a case.
. . * Most of the literature refers to criminal cases.

S8U Y . . Technical procedures in forensic science
. . . * Add to S8V letters A/F following HI in Class H. The basic structure of this class is given here, with some examples of prominent techniques.

S8V AMY . . . Safety & hygiene
B . . . Material used (properties, etc.)
BP . . . Equipment
. . . . * For example, electronic equipment S8V CHK; Ultrasonic equipment S8V CHO L.
D . . . Technical operations
DL . . . . Detecting & measuring, identification
DS . . . . Visualization & imaging
EC . . . . *Operations on physical phenomena*
ED . . . . . Timekeeping & measureming
EN . . . . . Radiology
F . . . . *Operations on materials*
FF . . . . . Chemical analysis
FFS . . . . . . Chromatography
FGJ . . . . . . Radiation chemical analysis
FGQ . . . . Spectrometry
FQ . . . . . *Operations on biological materials*

S8W . . Biology in forensic science

[Court actions narrowly S8S]
[Trial procedure S8ST]
[Evidence S8T]
[Operations]
[Elicitation of facts S8TY]
[Forensic science & technology S8U]
[Biology in forensic science S8W]

* As object of investigation.
* Add to S8W letters B/H following E in EB/EH.

S8W D Special physiology
DHU . Bioluminescence

S8X Medical jurisprudence, forensic medicine, legal medicine, human biology
. * See also Forensic psychiatry S8Y IW
. * Add to S8X letters B/Y following H in Class H.

S8X BJ . Physiology
BP . . Biochemistry
DY . Microsystems
E . . Cytology in forensic science
ES . . Histology in forensic science
FM . Physical anthropology in forensic science
FN . . Genetics in forensic science
FNY . . . Genetic profiles, genetic fingerprinting
GHA P . . Anthropometry in forensic science
. . . * General works only; for measurement of specific bodily features, see Parts, organs & systems S8X T/X.
. *Medical actions*
HNG . . Clinical investigation & measuring
HNH . . . Diagnosis
. . Treatments
NV . . . Pharmacotherapy
OL . . . Surgery
. *Processes*
P . . Pathology
PKS . . . Death
PKT . . . . Autopsies
PKU M . . . . Time of death
PKU N . . . . Cause of death
PT . . . Diseases
QX . . . Injuries
SQQ . . . Poisons, toxicology
ST . . . Drug addiction
STJ . . . . Alcoholism

[Evidence S8T]
[Forensic science & technology S8U]
[Biology in forensic science S8W]
. [Medical jurisprudence S8X]
. . [Processes]
. . . . [Drug addiction S8XST]
. . . . . [Alcoholism S8XSTJ]

S8X STJ DL . . . . . . Breathalysers
STL . . . . . Narcotics
STL DL . . . . . . Narcoanalysis
. . *Parts & organs & systems of body*
TF . . . *Regions*
THM . . . . Fingers, fingerprints
TWT . . . . Footprints
. . . *Systems*
UA . . . . Integumentary system
UAT . . . . . Nails
UB . . . . . Hair
UC . . . . . Skin, dermatology
UG . . . . Cardiovascular system
UL . . . . . Blood, haematology
UON . . . . . Blood groups
UR . . . . Nervous system, forensic neurology
VCB . . . . . Sense organs
WGV . . . . . . Voice
WK . . . . Dental system, teeth
WV . . . . Urogenital system
XDU . . . . . Semen
XFF . . . . . Gynaecology

S8Y I . . Psychology, juridical psychology
. . . * Add to S8Y I letters A/Y following I in
. . . Class I.
IHW . . . Hypnotism
. . . . * Hypnotism as investigative technique.
IW . . . Forensic psychiatry
IWU G . . . . Lying
IWU GRL . . . . . Lie detectors, polygraphs

Forensic technology
. * Use class S8U Forensic science & technology for
. general works.
. * Details may be taken from Class U/V
. Technology. Notation below is temporary
K . Communications technology
L . . Recording & listening devices
LW . . . Wiretapping
M . Materials technology
N . Metals technology
NT . . Castings technology
P . Fibres
Q . Glass
S . Explosives

[Actions S8]
[Evidence S8T]
[Operations]
. [Elicitation of facts S8TY]
. . [Forensic science & technology S8U]
. . . [Forensic technology]
. . . . [Explosives S8YS]

S8Y T . . . . Weapons technology
U . . . . . Firearms
UVD . . . . . . Ballistics

S9A B Forms of evidence
. * For police evidence, see Criminal proceedings
. SBW 9AD X.
C . Judicial notice, judicial cognizance
. . * Information assumed to be known; no evidence
. . required.
D . Circumstantial evidence, presumptive
. evidence
DH . Direct evidence
DK . Sources of evidence
DM . . Evidence taken abroad
DP . . View (evidence)
. . . * Inspection by judge or by judge & jury of any
. . . place or thing relevant as evidence.
DR . . Evidence from previous proceedings
DT . . Evidence on commission
DV . . Statutory statement
DX . . Police evidence
. . . * See also Criminal law SBW 9AD X
E . . Admission
. . {*Confession evidence*}
. . . * See Criminal law SBW 9AF
G . . Illegally obtained evidence
GJ . . . Evidence under duress, evidence under
. . . torture
H . . . Unauthorized interception of
. . . communication, eavesdropping
J . . . . Unauthorized listening devices,
. . . . electronic bugging, wiretapping
K . . Privileged communication, confidential
. . communication
. . . * Court cannot require it to be produced.
KN . . . Client/Attorney confidentiality
. . . (evidence)
L . . . Special forms
. . . . * Arrange A/Z.
. . . . * For example, religious confessions.
M . . Prima facie evidence
N . . Real evidence, material facts
. . . * Physical materials & artefacts.
. . . * See also Forensic science & technology S8U
. . . - e.g. medical evidence S8X.
N8V DL . . . Identification & analysis
NP . . . Collection of real evidence
NS . . . . Search & seizure
. . . . . * For operation of searching, see Police QP.

Evidence

[Trial procedure S8ST]
[Evidence S8T]
[Forms of evidence S9AB]
[Sources of evidence S9ADK]
[Real evidence S9AN]
. [Collection of real evidence S9ANP]
. . [Search & seizure S9ANS]

S9A NV	. Preservation of evidence
P	. *Agents*
R	Documentary evidence, written statements
	. * See also Legal documents S6C
RT	. Attestation
RV	. Affidavit, deposition
RW	. Written interrogation
S	. Handwriting, writing
S	. . Identification
ST	. Typewriting
SU	. Computer output
SW	. Letters rogatory
	. . * Evidence requested of another jurisdiction by the court.
	{*Oral evidence*}
	. * See Witnesses S9B F
T	Recordings (evidence)
	. * See also Unauthorized interception of communication S9A H
TV	. Videotaped testimony, filmed testimony
V	Witnesses
V8A L	. Rights of parties
VVT	. Payment of witnesses
VW	. Selection of witnesses, choice of witnesses
VX	. . Voir dire
	. . . * Preliminary examination to determine competence to serve.
WB	. . Lie detectors
WD	. . Oath, affirmation
WE	. Subpoena
WF	. Right to compulsory process
WG	. Right to confront
WH	. Attendance of witnesses
X	. Examination of witnesses
YC	. . Leading questions
YE	. . Examination in chief
YG	. . Cross examination
YJ	. . Re-examination
S9B C	. Testimony (general)
	. . * What a witness perceives through senses.
CAY G	. . Cross-examination
CE	. . Credibility of witnesses
E	. Hearsay
F	. Oral evidence, parol evidence
	. . * For Affidavit evidence, see S9A RV.
	. *Types of witnesses*

[Actions S8]
[Trial procedure S8ST]
[Evidence S8T]
. [Forms of evidence S9AB]
. . [Sources of evidence S9ADK]
. . . [Witnesses S9AV]
. . . . [Types of witnesses]

S9B H	. . . . . Personal evidence (general)
	. . . . . . * For admission, see S9A E; for confession, see Criminal cases SBW 9AF.
H8A	. . . . . . Parties' evidence
H8C	. . . . Plaintiff's evidence
H8D	. . . . Defendant's evidence
J	. . . . . . Eyewitnesses
K	. . . . . . Deathbed declarations, dying declarations
L	. . . . . . Hypnosis induced evidence
O	. . . . . Opinion evidence
P	. . . . . . Expert witnesses
	. . . . * See also Forensic science & technology, S8U
Q	. . . . Special fields of expertise
	. . . . * When not covered by Forensic science & technology.
R	. . . . . . Disposition evidence
	. . . . * Including character evidence if treated together.
RT	. . . . . . Character evidence
S	. . . . . Hostile witnesses
T	. . . . . Children as witnesses
U	. . . . . Victims as witnesses
XC	. . Archaic sources of evidence
XE	. . . Trial by ordeal
XG	. . . Trial by battle
XJ	. . . Compurgation, trial by oath
S9C	Matters of law, questions of law
	. * Dispute as to the relevant rules of law to be applied.
	. * See also Interpretation of documents S6C F

[Practice & procedure S6]
[Agents]
[Courts & court proceedings S6E]
[Actions S8]
[Court actions narrowly S8S]
[Trial procedure S8ST]
[Matters of law S9C]

S9D Judicial decision, deciding (conclusion of action)
. * Reaching a conclusion to a dispute or action.
S9D 5US . Public policy, ordre publique
. . * Indefinite moral value ('the public good') invoked to assist a decision.
E . Judicial error, misconduct of trial
. . * For Misdirection of jury, see S9D SDF.
G . . Special forms
. . . * Arrange A/Z.
H . Judicial discretion
L . Summing up, closing speeches
M . . Order of closing speeches
P . . Prosecution's summing up
Q . . Defence's summing up
S . . Judge's instructions to jury, directions to jury
SDE . . . Judicial error
SDF . . . . Misdirection of jury

S9E . Jury trials, juries
. . *Operations & properties*
. . . * Details here are taken from those for court officers (S6K B).
. . . Relations to other law officers
S9E 6KD C . . . . Attorney-jury relations, counsel-jury relations
6KD J . . . . Judge-jury relations
. . . . . * For judge's instructions to jury, see Summing-up S9D S.
F . . . Appointment & removal
. . . . * Add to S9E F letters F/V following S6K, with the additions indicated.
FG . . . . Selection of jury, summoning of jury
. . . . . * For challenges to composition, see S9E GL.
FGL . . . . . Automated jury selection
FH . . . . . Voir dire (juries)
FJ . . . . . Subpoena (juries)
FR . . . . Performance evaluation of juries
FRU . . . . . Utilization of jury
FS . . . . Misconduct (juries), corruption (juries)

[Actions S8]
[Trial procedure S8ST]
[Judicial decision S9D]
[Jury trials S9E]
. [Operations & properties]
. . [Appointment & removal S9EF]
. . . [Misconduct juries S9EFS]

S9E FT . . . . Disqualification (juries)
G . *Attributes of juries*
. . * Add to S9E G letters C/G following S6L, with the additions indicated below.
GB . . Characteristics of jurors
GD . . Role of jury
GE . . Powers of jury
GG . . Privileges & immunities of juries
GH . . . Conflict of interests (jurors)
GI . . . Exemption (jurors)
GIO . . . . Conscientious objection (jurors)
. *Special attributes*
GJ . . Composition of jury
GL . . . Challenges to composition of jury
GN . . . . Rights of accused (jury composition)
GP . . . Size of jury
GQ . . . . Changes in jury size
J . . . *Types of persons as jurors*
. . . . * Add to S9E J letters G/V following 4 in Auxiliary Schedule 1.
L . Functions & actions of jury
. . * For judge's directions to the jury, see S9D S.
M . . Decision making (juries), verdict finding by jury
. . . * For verdict, see Finding in fact, S9E T.
MQ . . . Quorum rule, majority verdicts
N . . . . Hung juries
NQ . . . Unanimity rule
. *Types of juries*
NV . . Grand jury
NX . . Petit jury
P Findings in fact, verdict of jury
Q Findings in law
. Decisions
R . . General verdict
. . . * For acquittal & conviction, see Criminal law SBW 9ES/U.
VB . . Special verdicts
. . . * Answers to specific questions, for use by judge.
VL . . Degree of guilt or liability (jury decisions)
W . . Penalties (jury decisions)

S9F Judgements, awards (judgements)
. * For judicial error, see S9D E; for awards narrowly, see Arbitration S9R F.
. * See also SA9 FV Foreign judgements (conflict of laws) for recognition & enforcement of foreign

Judicial decision

[Agents]
[Courts & court proceedings S6E]
[Actions S8]
[Court actions narrowly S8S]
[Trial procedure S8ST]
[Judicial decision S9D]
[Judgements S9F]

. judgements.
S9F G . Consistency in judgement, judicial unpredictability
I . Interlocutory judgements
. . * Deciding particular issues in the case.
J . Final judgements
K . Judgements in personam
L . Judgements in rem
M . Stare decisis
. . * Binding precedent on everyone, not only the parties concerned in the one case.
. . * See also Res judicata (evidence), S8T XP
N . Declaratory judgements
P . Judicial opinions
PR . . Ratio decidendi
PS . . Obiter dicta
PT . . Majority opinion
PV . . Dissenting opinion, conflict of judicial opinion
Q . Advisory judgements
. . * Advice on application or legal effect of some rule of law.
. . * For Appeal to Judicial Committee of the Privy Council, see Commonwealth law SOP 9H7 P.
R . Award of costs
RS . . Security for costs
. . . * Requested by defendant.
RT . . Standard costs
RU . . Taxation costs
RV . . Contentious costs
RW . . Non-contentious costs
T . Other judgements
. . * E.g. Default judgements.
. . * Arrange A/Z.
U . . Miscarriage of justice
. . . * See also Types of administrative remedies S9I V/S9J
V Retroactive judicial decisions, intertemporal law
. * See also Retroactive legislation S5M T; Due process of law S5U T
VW . Prospective overruling

[Courts & court proceedings S6E]
[Actions S8]
[Court actions narrowly S8S]
[Trial procedure S8ST]
[Judicial decision S9D]
[Retroactive judicial decisions S9FV]
. [Prospective overruling S9FVW]

S9G Remedies, legal remedies
. * Most civil remedies are subordinated to the substantive law concerned - e.g. matrimonial disputes.
. * See also Rights & remedies S9V K
S9G HE . Exhaustion of remedies
I . Execution of judgement, enforcement of judgement
IT . . Objections by third party
J . . Court orders
K . . . Specific orders
. . . . * When defined by a specific situation, the latter should be cited first: e.g. Guardianship - Orders.
. . . . * Arrange A/Z.
KDI . . . Diligences
KEM . . . Emergency applications (court orders)
L . . Writs of execution
. . . * See also Prerogative orders & writs S9K
M . . . Financial remedies
N . . . . Fines
O . . . . Attachment of earnings
P . . . . Charging orders
Q . . . . Fieri facias
. . . . . * Fi. fa.; a levy on debtor's possessions.
R . . . . Garnishment of debts
S . . . . Sequestration
T . Extraordinary remedies, special proceedings (remedies)
V . General remedies special to a context
. . * For example, local remedies (international law).
Y . Administrative remedies
. . * For post-conviction remedies, see Criminal proceedings SBW 9GY P.
S9H . . Appellate proceedings, appeals
S9H 7 . . . Appeal courts
7D . . . . Court from which appeal made
. . . . . * Add to S9H 7 letters E/W following S7 in S7E/S7W.
I . . . Right of appeal
J . . . Permission to appeal
K . . . Waiver of appeal
L . . . Result of appeal

Remedies

[Court actions narrowly S8S]
[Trial procedure S8ST]
[Judicial decision S9D]
[Remedies S9G]
[Administrative remedies S9GY]
[Appellate proceedings S9H]
. [Result of appeal S9HL]

S9H M . . Affirmation (appeals)
N . . Overruling (appeals)
P . . Reversal (appeals)
S9I . Grounds of appeal, rights of appeal
S9I K . . Fact & law (appeal grounds)
L . . . Fact (appeal on grounds of)
M . . . . New law (appeal grounds)
N . . . Law (appeal on grounds of)
NP . . Writ of error
. . . * Procedure superseded 1907.
NR . . Rehearing (appeals)
. . . * Procedure superseded 1875.
P . . Case stated (appeals)
Q . . Prerogative order (appeals)
. . . * See also Certiorari S9K M
R . . Exceptions (appeals), bill of exceptions (Scot.)
S . . Cassation (civil law)
. . . * See also Judicial review S9J
S7R . . . Court of Cassation
T . . Special grounds
. . . * E.g. Reformatio in pejus (criminal law) SBW 9JT.
Types of administrative remedy
V . Quashing of judgement
X . New trials, retrials
S9J . Judicial review (general)
. . * For judicial review in administrative law, see SCK F9J.

S9K Prerogative writs & orders
. * Issued by high court for supervision of inferior courts, tribunals, etc.
. * For originating writs, see S8L P; for writs of execution, see S9G L.
S9K L . Habeas Corpus
M . Certiorari
N . Mandamus
P . Prohibition order, cease-desist order (USA)
SB . Superseded writs, etc.
SD . . Quo warranto
. . . * Abolished 1938.
SF . . Scire facias
. . . * Abolished in civil proceedings 1947.
T Declaratory judgements

[Actions S8]
[Court actions narrowly S8S]
[Trial procedure S8ST]
[Judicial decision S9D]
[Remedies S9G]
[Administrative remedies S9GY]
. [Declaratory judgements S9KT]

S9L Civil remedies
. *By historical jurisdiction of court*
. . * Remedies restricted to one kind may become applicable to the other - e.g. interpleader (re debts, goods, etc.)
S9L M . . Common law remedies (general)
Q . . Equitable remedies (general), specific relief
S9M . Damages, compensation (damages)
. . * See also Restitution S9M V
S9M N . . Assessment of damages
O . . Remoteness (damages)
P . . General damages
Q . . Special damages
S . . No fault compensation, no fault liability
. . . * See also Workman's compensation SBU FH
TD . . Substantial & nominal damages
TE . . Exemplary damages
TL . . Liquidated & unliquidated damages
TP . . Provisional damages
TQ . . Latent damages
U . Specific performance
UP . . Particular proof
V . Restitution
. . * See also Quasi-contract SBF VE9 M
VR . . Specific restitution
. . . * See also Quasi-contract SBF U
VT . . Restitutis in integrum (civil law)
. . . * See also Quasi-contract SBF U9M VI
VY . Account & enquiry
W . *Special to a context*
. . * For example, replevin (property) SBL 9MW.
YB . Superseded remedies
. . * For example, Detinue SBL 9MY B.

S9N . Injunction
S9N P . . Ex parte injunction
. . . * Granted after hearing only one party.
Q . . Quia timet
. . . * To restrain imminent or irreparable wrong.
R . . Interlocutory injunction
S . . Perpetual injunction

Dispute resolution other than litigation

[Actions S8]
[Court actions narrowly S8S]
. . [Judicial decision S9D]
. . . [Remedies S9G]
. . . . [Civil remedies S9L]
. . . . . [Injunction S9N]
. . . . . . [Perpetual injunction S9NS]

S9N T . . . . . . Mandatory injunction
U . . . . . . Prohibitive injunction, restrictive injunction
V . . . . Mareva injunction
. . . . * Prevents defendant from removing assets abroad.
W . . . . Other orders, A/Z
WA . . . . Anton Piller order
. . . . * Prevents defendant destroying certain evidence.

S9P E . . . . . Interdict (civil law)
G . . . . . Rescission, cancellation
H . . . . . Rectification
J . . . . . Remedies special to a subject
. . . . . . * For example, Recovery (land law)
L . . . . Sentencing
. . . . . * See Criminal proceedings SBW 9PL
X . . . . . Penalties (civil remedies), punishments (civil remedies)
. . . . . . * Rarely arise now in civil law.
. . . . . . * See also Criminal proceedings SBW 9RC
YF . . . . . . Forfeiture
YFL Q . . . . Equitable remedies

S9Q Dispute resolution (other than litigation), alternative dispute resolution
. * Voluntary participation, but with right to go to court if one side remains dissatisfied.
. * For Compromise and settlement of action, see S8R W.
. * See also Composition (settlement of debt) SBN GGY
S9Q R . Negotiation
. . * Applicable mainly in industrial relations and international law; but in principle, applicable to other branches of law.
T . . Conciliation
U . . Mediation
V . Accord & satisfaction, discontinuance
. . * Agreement not to proceed with action.
W . Consent judgement
. . * Terms authorized by court.
X . Contract (settlement of actions), contract between parties
S9R . Arbitration
. . * See also Commercial arbitration SBN F9R; Industrial arbitration SBM GV
. . Personnel
S9R 6S . . . Arbitrators, arbiters, umpires, oversmen (Scot.)

[Practice & procedure S6]
. . [Courts & court proceedings S6E]
. . . [Actions S8]
. . . . [Dispute resolution other than litigation S9Q]
. . . . . [Arbitration S9R]
. . . . . . [Personnel]
. . . . [Arbitrators S9R6S]

. . . . . . Judgements
S9R F . . . . Awards (arbitration)
S . . . . . . Court directed arbitration

Y . . . . Special types of proceedings
. . . . . * For those defined by the branch of substantive law concerned, see branch.
S9S D . . . . . Summary proceedings (general)
. . . . . . * Judge only, no jury. For jury trials, see S9E.
F . . . . . Government actions, Crown proceedings (general)
. . . . . . * Proceedings by or against the government (the Crown in English law). Civil proceedings may be taken against the Crown (Crown Proceedings Act, 1947).
. . . . . . * See also Actions in administrative law SCK 8
H . . . . . Forms of action
. . . . . . * Abolished in English law by 1875 Judicature Act, but still exerts influence in principle.
J . . . . . Actions in personam, personal actions (general)
L . . . . . Actions in rem, real actions
N . . . . . Single form of action (USA)
P . . . . . Class actions (USA), multiple claims actions
. . . . . . * Strategy (e.g. in personal injuries actions) uniting individual plaintiffs (to fight, for example, a powerful corporation).
R . . . . . Citizen suits (USA), public interest actions, popular actions (USA)
T . . . . . *Special to an action*
. . . . . . * For example, Possessory action SBH 9UP.
V . . . . . Individual actions (collections)
. . . . . . * For general collections of civil actions. Actions in specific subject areas go with the subject.

S9T Constitutional law of specific subjects
. * Use this class only for qualifying specific subjects. The primary reason for this provision is to allow qualification of a subject by administrative agencies serving it or regulating it.
. * Add to - (where the hyphen represents the classmark added to) letters AY/O following SC (Constitutional law).
S9T J . Central government department serving the subject
Q . Special committees, etc. concerned with subject

[Constitutional law of specific subjects S9T]
[Special committees S9TQ]

S9U Ecclesiastical law intercalator
* See explanatory note at SWE 9U Ecclesiology of particular subjects.

S9V B Substantive law, subjects of law
. * That part of law concerned with the rights & duties
. of legal persons (individual and corporate) in
. particular circumstances, as distinct from adjective
. law (S6) which is concerned with the machinery by
. which the rights & duties are declared and enforced.

B59 . *Relations between branches of substantive*
. *law*

B5C U . . Substantive unification
. . . * Covers substantive law & conflict of laws. For
. . . the latter alone, see SA.
. . . * For unification proposals regarding a specific
. . . subject, see the subject, e.g. unification of private
. . . law.

H . Rights (substantive law)
. . * For Human rights law in general, see SCC W.

J . . Primary rights, antecedent rights
. . . * To have performance of duties owed by another
. . . or to have freedom from harm or interference
. . . from another.

K . . Secondary rights, remedial rights, rights &
. . remedies
. . . * To have a legal remedy if the primary duty is
. . . not duly implemented.

L . . Rights in personam, personal rights
. . . * Availing only against a definite legal person.

M . . Rights in rem, real rights
. . . * Availing against persons in general.

N . . Vested rights
. . . * Rights accruing to a person, as distinct from
. . . acquired rights.

. *By historical development factors*
. . * The distinction found in English law between
. . common law and equity reflects a situation found in
. . many legal systems - that of a supplementary body
. . of law developing when the existing formal
. . provisions have become inadequate for securing
. . natural justice in some areas of law.

P . . Strictum jus, Rigor juris
. . . * Strict rules of established law.
. . . * See also English common law SN9 VP

Q . . Equity (general), equitable principles,
. . Aequitas
. . . * Application to particular circumstances of what
. . . seems naturally just.
. . . * See also English law of equity SN9 VQ

. *By relation of state or jurisdiction to persons*

S9W . . Private law (general)
. . . * As distinguished from public law (SBY). The
. . . distinction is crucial in civil law systems, but less
. . . so in common law systems.
. . . *Relations with other branches of law*

[Substantive law S9VB]
[By relation of state or jurisdiction to persons]
[Private law general S9W]
[Relations with other branches of law]

S9W 58 . Public law & private law
. . * Including works specifically on the influence of
. . public law on private law. For influence of
. . private law on public law, see latter, SBY.

5CU Unification of private law

5CU 3D International organizations

5CU 3DI . International Institute for Unification of
. Private Law, Rome Institute
. (unification of law)
. . * See also Hague Conference on Private
. . International Law SA5 CU5 LDH; UN
. . International Law Commission SD3 DL

S9X Civil law (private law) in general
. * The term 'civil law' has at least three different
. meanings which are widely used:
. * In Roman law, it referred mainly to the range of
. persons to whom it applied (citizens, non-citizens,
. etc.), but also, eventually, to state law as distinct
. from church law.
. * In modern civil law systems it refers to the law
. applicable to ordinary citizens as distinct from
. commercial law, applicable to merchants, etc.
. * In common law systems, it may refer to the
. regulation of ordinary relations between persons,
. as distinct from those in special areas (criminal
. law, administrative law, military law, ecclesiastical
. law).
. * For civil law systems, see SR.

SA Conflict of laws, international private law,
private international law,
intermunicipal law, diversity of laws
. * A branch of its private law peculiar to each
. jurisdiction - that part which must be invoked
. when an issue involves a foreign or trans-frontier
. element so that the rules of the foreign system
. need to be considered also.
. * The same problem arises within many national
. jurisdictions as a result of the diversity of juridical
. traditions within it - e.g. Islamic law within a
. state with a primarily secular law, or tribal law
. within many African states. The term 'diversity'
. usually signifies this special example of conflict of
. laws.
. * For conflict of laws in a particular jurisdiction,
. see the jurisdiction - e.g.

[Substantive law S9VB]
[By relation of state or jurisdiction to persons]
[Private law general S9W]
[Conflict of laws SA]

English conflict of laws SNA.
* An alternative (not recommended) is to collocate this class with international law (i.e. public international law) at SDA. Note that the latter class has an alternative location in class R Politics. It is recommended that this class (Conflict of laws) should not be located with (public) international law if the latter is located in Class R.

SA5 8	*Relations with other topics*
8BY	. Public law & conflict of laws
8DD	. Sovereignty & conflict of laws
A	Jurisprudence
C	. Sources
	. . * The modification of Formal sources (S5G D/S5T) used in International law (at SD5) is used here.
	. . * Add to SA5 letters GD/T following SD5; e.g. International conferences SA5 LC.
	. Unification
	. . * For unification of conflict rules in specific subjects, see subject. For regional unification, see region - e.g. Latin American Congresses for Unification of Private International Law SVZ A5C 3D.
CU	. . International unification, international approximation
CU5 LC	. . . International conferences
CU5 LDH	. . . . Hague Conference on Private International Law (1893-)
CU5 LDH 27	. . . . . Serials
CU5 LDH 27B	. . . . . Monographs, by date
CU5 LDH R	. . . . . First & subsequent conferences
	. Retrospective laws
MU	. . Intertemporal conflict of laws, retroactive laws (conflict of laws)
TR	. Juristic acts
Y	*By jurisdiction with which in conflict*
	. * Use this class only when qualifying one jurisdiction by a second one.
	. * An alternative (not recommended) is to cite the foreign country before the legal problem. This option is provided at SAN.
	. * Add to SA5 Y letters D/Y following S in SD/SY - e.g. English law - Conflict - Export law - Conflict with French law SNA LNO O5Y VF.
SA6	Practice & procedure
SA6 E	. Courts & court procedure
GX	. . International civil procedure (conflict of laws)

[Substantive law S9VB]
[By relation of state or jurisdiction to persons]
[Private law general S9W]
[Conflict of laws SA]
[Practice & procedure SA6]
[Courts & court procedure SA6E]
. [International civil procedure conflict of laws SA6GX]

SA6 GY	. . Access to foreign courts
H	. Jurisdiction
	. . *Special topics*
HR	. . . Judicial assistance
	. . . . * Enforcement by one country or state of judicial acts of another country or state.
	. . . . * See also Letters rogatory (evidence) SA9 ASW; Execution of foreign judgements SA9 FWE; International judicial assistance in criminal law SBU A6H R
HS	. . . Jurisdiction by consent or submission
SA8	Actions
SA8 A	. Parties to action
AS	. . Suability of foreign states
BA	. . Choice of law by the parties, party autonomy
	. . . * See also Connecting factors SAE
F	. Limitation of actions
	. Stages in action
LS	. . Process & service
N	. . Pleading & motions
QT	. . . Defence objections
QTR	. . . . Exceptions
RH	. . . Counterclaim, crossclaim
S	. . Trials
T	. . . Evidence
TW	. . . . Proof of foreign law
SA9 ASW	. . . . Letters rogatory
F	. . . . Judgements
FS	. . . . . Security for costs
FV	. . . . . Foreign judgements
	. . . . . . * Including foreign judgements and arbitral awards together.
FWB	. . . . . . Recognition of foreign judgements
FWE	. . . . . . Execution of foreign judgements, enforcement of foreign judgements
FWF	. . . . Direct enforcement of foreign judgements
	. . . . * By action in local courts.
FWH	. . . . Enforcement against foreign states
G	. . . Remedies

[Substantive law S9VB]
[Conflict of laws SA]
[Practice & procedure SA6]
. [Actions SA8]
. . [Stages in action]
. . . [Trials SA8S]
. . . . [Remedies SA9G]

SA9 R . . Arbitration
RF . . . Arbitration awards (conflict of laws), foreign arbitral awards
RFG H . . . . Execution
S . . . International arbitration in private cases

Special concepts in conflict of laws
SAB . Jurisdiction (conflict of laws)
. . * General considerations of the jurisdictions of different legal systems (i.e., their wider compatibility and/or comparability).
. . * See also Courts - Jurisdiction SA6 H
SAC . Preliminary question (conflict of laws)
. . * Prior to choice of law.
SAC E . . Classification (conflict of laws), characterization (conflict of laws), qualification (conflict of laws)
SAD . Choice of law (conflict of laws), party autonomy (conflict of laws)
. . * For choice of law by the parties, see parties, SA8 BA.
SAE . . Connecting factors (conflict of laws), points of contact (conflict of laws)
SAF . . . Nationality & domicile
. . . . * See also Renvoi SAG
SAF H . . . . Choice of domicile
J . . . . Citizenship[as point of contact
P . . . Juristic persons (conflict of laws)
. . . . * General works only; specific types should go in Law of persons
Q . . . . Dependant persons (conflict of laws)
R . . . . Corporate persons (conflict of laws)
V . . . Locus regit actum
SAG . . Renvoi
. . . * See also Nationality & domicile SAF.
. . . Theory
SAG 5A6 . . . . Foreign court theory
SAH . . Foreign laws (conflict of laws)
. . . * For proof of foreign laws, see Evidence SA8 TW.
SAJ . . . Limits of application (conflict of laws)
. . . . Public policy
. . . . . * See also Retroactive law S5M T; Vested right S9V N
SAJ L . . . . . Evasion (conflict of laws)
M . . . . Recognition of particular foreign laws
. . . . . * For specific branches involved, see branch; e.g. Criminal law - Conflict of laws SBW AJM; Revenue laws - Conflict of laws SCL MIW AJM.

[Substantive law S9VB]
[Private law general S9W]
[Conflict of laws SA]
. [Special concepts in conflict of laws]
. . . [Foreign laws conflict of laws SAH]
. . . . [Limits of application conflict of laws SAJ]
. . . . . [Recognition of particular foreign laws SAJM]

SAJ R . . . . . . Political laws (conflict of laws)
T . . . . . . Confiscatory laws (conflict of laws)
SAL . *Conflict of laws in special branches of law*
. . * The preferred arrangement is to locate this under the branch.
. . * An alternative is provided here for libraries wishing to keep all Conflict of laws together:
. . * Add to SALA letters P/Y following SA; Add to SAL letters B/U following SB - e.g. Penal laws SAL W9R C; Crimes committed abroad SAL WAJ M.
SAM . *Conflict of laws in particular jurisdictions*
. . * The general rule is to treat conflict of laws in a country or other jurisdiction as a branch of that jurisdiction's law.
. . * This class takes only those works which deal with the general concept of conflict between two or more legal systems which are in force in the same territory; e.g. a secular and a religious system.
SAN . Jurisdiction conflicted with
. . * Alternative (not recommended) to citing the legal problem (SAB/SAL) first & using -5Y to introduce the conflicting jurisdiction.
. . * Add to SAN letters N/V following S in SN/SV; e.g. English law - Conflict of laws - with France - Export law SNA NVF ALN OO. laws - with France SNN OO9 XAN VF.

SAP Law of persons
. * Any entity regarded as capable of suing or being sued.
. * For personal law reflecting the law of a tribe, caste, religious group, etc. as distinct from the territorial law of the country to which the person belongs, see the group concerned; e.g. Tribal law SI; Religious law SWE/SY.
. * For juristic persons, see conflict of laws SAF P.
. * Within the classes SAP/SAY retroactive synthesis is effected as follows (where the hyphen represents the class qualified):
. * Add to - numbers 2/9 and letter A following S; e.g. Insane - Minors SAY EAX M.
. * Add to -B letters B/X following SB so far as applicable.
SAP 5A . Jurisprudence
5TR . . Juristic act, act in the law
. . . * See definition at S5T R.
. *Operations*
R . . Recording & registration of persons
S . . . Vital records
T . . . . Registers of birth

[Substantive law S9VB]
[Private law general S9W]
[Law of persons SAP]
[Operations]
. [Recording & registration of persons SAPR]
. . [Vital records SAPS]
. . . [Registers of birth SAPT]

SAP U . . . Registers of marriage
V . . . Registers of death
Properties
SAQ . Legal personality
. . * Legal attribute of being a person. For corporate
. . personality, see SBC TDA Q.
SAQ S . . Status
. . . * A person's standing in law which determines
. . . their rights & duties in a legal situation.
. . . * For a particular status or characteristic, see
. . . Types of persons defined by these, e.g. married
. . . persons.
T . . . Legal rights & duties
. . . . * See also Rights (substantive law) S9V H;
. . . . Human rights SCC W
U . . . . Legal standards
. . . . . * Criteria by which the observance or
. . . . . contravention of principles or rules may be
. . . . . judged - e.g.reasonable care, prudence (of a
. . . . . trustee).
V . . . . . Standard individual
. . . . . . * Hypothetical person characterized by the
. . . . . . full complement of 'norms' - e.g. a citizen,
. . . . . . of full age, legitimate.
W . . . . Privileges & immunities
. . . . . * May also attach to circumstances - e.g.
. . . . . protecting goods from legal distress.
WX . . . . . Absolute privileges
X . . . . . Conditional privileges
SAR . . . . Liabilities (general), legal
. . . . responsibility (general), legal
. . . . accountability (general)
. . . . . * For liabilities in a specific context, see
. . . . . latter - e.g. Product liability, Parents'
. . . . . liability.
SAS . . . Special status
. . . . * Giving special rights & responsibilities (e.g.
. . . . to ambassadors, trustees). For the special
. . . . rights, etc. attending these, see the holder of
. . . . the office.
SAT . . Capacity
. . . * Legal ability to bear and exercise rights and
. . . liabilities.
SAU A . . . Active capacity
C . . . Passive capacity
. . . . * Capacity to be subject to legal liability (e.g.
. . . . a child is not capable of criminal
. . . . responsibility).
D . . . Full capacity
E . . . Limited capacity

[Substantive law S9VB]
[Private law general S9W]
[Law of persons SAP]
[Properties]
. [Legal personality SAQ]
. . [Capacity SAT]
. . . [Limited capacity SAUE]

SAU G . . . Disability (law), incapacity (law)
. . . . * For particular disabilities, see persons
. . . . characterized by degree of capacity - e.g.
. . . . alien, unborn child.
J . . Absence & presumption of death
. . . * See also probate & wills SBI NL
N . . Personal names
. . . * Including change of name.
P . . Domicile
. . . * See also Conflict of laws SAF H

Types of persons
SAV . Natural persons, individuals
. . * For general works on the status and capacity,
. . etc. of persons in the categories indicated, and for
. . use in qualifying any context in which the
. . capacity of a particular class of person needs to be
. . indicated.
. . * For these persons in special legal contexts, see
. . latter - e.g. social security, husband & wife,
. . children in family law. If in doubt as to whether
. . the specific context is more appropriate, locate in
. . that context -e.g. employees in labour law.
. . * The order of classes is largely that in Class K
. . Society, with the adjustments noted below.

SAW B . . *Properties, attributes*
. . . * These vary with type of person. For specific
. . . attributes, see type of person characterized.
J . . *Operations*
. . . * These vary with types of person; e.g. Tests of
. . . insanity under Insane persons.

MW . . *Persons by social factors*
. . . * Add to SAW letters MW/NI following K in
. . . KMW/KNI.
MWQ . . . Illiterate persons
NAP . . . Royalty
NE . . . Castes (law of persons)
NG . . . Slaves (law of persons)

V . . *Persons by employment factors*
. . . * See also Labour law SBO L
. . . * Add to SAW letters V/YM following TL in
. . . Class TL Labour economics.
VEB . . . Employees (law of persons)
VHO . . . Temporary workers
VHQ . . . . Seasonal workers
VHR . . . Contract workers
VHT . . . Part-time workers

[Substantive law S9VB]
[Private law general S9W]
[Law of persons SAP]
[Types of persons]
[Natural persons SAV]
[Persons by employment factors SAWV]
. [Part-time workers SAWVHT]

SAW VJB . Residential workers
VJH . Expatriate workers
VP . Professionals
XH . Employers
XJ . Managers
XL . Self-employed persons
YB . Involuntary labour, forced labour, tied labour
YM . Illegal workers

SAX B *Persons in public service*
. * For judicial officers, see S6K B.
. * Add to SAX B letters I/Y following SC, with additions indicated.
BI . Legislators
BIS . . Members of lower house
BIV . . Members of upper house
BK . Public services personnel, civil servants
BM . Armed forces personnel
BMM . . Serving personnel
BMX . . Ex-service personnel, veterans
BMY . . Prisoners of war
. . . * For status in international law, see SDR W.
BP . Other persons in public service
. . * Arrange A/Z.
BPD . . Diplomatic personnel
Persons by financial status
CB . Bankrupts
CC . Solvent persons

Persons by age
. * Add to SAX letters L/T following KN in KNL/KNT.
L . Age groups
. . * For completely general works on these classes of persons.
. . * An alternative (not recommended) is to locate all works on children in Family law SBC G.
. . * See also Family law SBC F
M . . Children, minors
MX . . . Unborn persons
N . . . Infants
R . . . Young persons, youth, teenagers
S . . Age of majority, age of consent, adults
T . . . Aged persons, old persons

[Substantive law S9VB]
[Types of persons]
[Natural persons SAV]
[Persons by age]
. [Age groups SAXL]
. . [Age of majority SAXS]
. . . [Aged persons SAXT]

SAX V *Persons by sex*
. * For persons characterized by marital and/or familial status (e.g.married women) see status, SBC N.
. * For sexual behaviour see SBC PM.
. * Add to SAX letters V/X following KN in KNV/KNX.
W . Females, women
X . Males
YC . Transexual persons
. . * Biologically normal persons who consider that they belong to the opposite sex.
YE . . Sex change
YG . Intersexuality
. . * With biological abnormality in sex organs.
YH . . Pseudohermaphroditism

Persons by social/psychological attributes
. * Add to SAY A letters N/W following KOA in KOA N/KOA W.
SAY AB . Disadvantaged persons (general), victims (general)
. . * For victims of crime, see Welfare law SBU JHO.
AN . . Disaster victims
AV . . Economically deprived persons, poor persons, paupers
BA . . Culturally deprived persons
. . . * Add to SAY B letters C/K following KOB so far as applicable.

C . . Mentally disadvantaged persons
. . . * Terminology here is confused and different branches of law may use different terms.
. . . * The content & order of the classes below conform to that in KOBM/KOC, but with notational adjustments to meet the needs of law.
. . . Statutes
C2G . . . . Mental health laws
D . . . Mentally ill persons, mental patients
E . . . . Insane persons
. . . . . * For criminally insane, see SBW DM
EAQ S . . . . . Legal status
. . . . . *Operations*
EAW K . . . . . . Tests of insanity (general)
. . . . * For McNaghten rules, see Criminal law SBW DM8 SJ.
EAW L . . . . . . Commitment & detention
F . . . Mentally handicapped, mentally retarded
H . . Physically handicapped persons
JC . . Deviants (general)

Substantive law

[Substantive law S9VB]
[Law of persons SAP]
[Types of persons]
[Natural persons SAV]
. [Persons by social/psychological attributes]
. . [Disadvantaged persons general SAYAB]
. . . [Deviants general SAYJC]

. . . . * For criminals, see SBW D; for sexual
. . . . deviants, see SBC PMU.
SAY JK . . . Vagrants
P . . . Suicides (persons)
S . . . Addicted persons
V . . . . Drug addicts

. *By citizenship status*
. . * Classes SBB N/SBB P represent the concept of
. . citizens in general. Most of the literature deals
. . with their status in constitutional law - see
. . SCD ON. If in doubt, prefer SCD ON.
. . * Add to SBB letters N/Y following KO in
. . KON/KOY, with the modifications indicated.
. . * Within classes SBB N/SBB Y retroactive
. . synthesis is effected as follows (where the hyphen
. . represents the classmark added to):
. . * Add to - numbers 2/9 and letter A following S.
. . * Add to -B letters N/W following SBB so far as
. . applicable.
. . * Add to -C letters C/Y in Auxiliary Schedule S1
. . so far as applicable.
SBB N . . Citizens, nationals
. . . * Usually assumed. See also Citizens
. . . (constitutional law) SCD ON.
NT . . . Naturalized citizens (law of persons)
NV . . . Dual citizenship holders (law of
. . . persons)
O . . . Indigenous population, aboriginals
PT . . . Aliens
Q . . Minorities (general)
. . . * For ethnic minorities see SBC C.
RB . . Migrants
RH . . . Expatriates
S . . . Immigrants
WN . . . Foreign residents
WP . . . Non-immigrants, tourists, visitors
WR . . . Refugees

Persons by various characteristics
. * Within classes SBC A/SBC Y retroactive
. synthesis is effected as follows (where the hyphen
. represents the classmark added to):
. * Add to - numbers 2/9 and letter A following S.
. * Add to - letters B/C following SB.
. * Add to -D letters D/Y in Auxiliary Schedule S1 so
. far as applicable.
SBC A . *Persons by religion*
. . * Add to SSB CA letters GH/V following P in
. . PGH/PV.

[Substantive law S9VB]
[By relation of state or jurisdiction to persons]
[Private law general S9W]
[Law of persons SAP]
[Types of persons]
[Persons by various characteristics]
[Persons by religion SBCA]

SBC B *Persons by language*
. * Add to SBCB letters D/Y in
. Auxiliary Schedule 3.
Persons by ethnic or racial group
C . Ethnic minorities
. . *Properties & processes*
CG . . . Race relations
CI . . . . Integration (race relations)
CK . . . . Discrimination (race
. . . . relations), racism
CM . . . . Desegregation (race
. . . . relations)
CP . . . . Miscegenation
D . . *Specific ethnic or racial groups*
. . . * Add to SBCD letters B/Z in
. . . Auxiliary Schedule 3A.

Persons by marriage & descent relations
. * The intricate relationships generated
. by kin, the family, marriage and
. sexual relations are scheduled in
. detail at KPG/KRP. Whilst the scope
. of family law as found in most
. Western jurisdictions is somewhat
. narrower, this is not always the case.
. So some slight modifications of the
. schedule in K are made below in order
. to accommodate more accurately the
. terminology of family law in the West
. without diminishing the provision for
. non-Western societies.

F . Family & kinship law
. . * For domestic relations law see
. . SBC J.
. . * Add to SBCF letters G/Y
. . following KP in KPG/KPY.
FH . . Kinship
FI . . Relatives, kin groups
FK . . . Cognates, kindred
FM . . . Descent groups
FO . . . . Cognate descent,
. . . . multilineal descent
FP . . . . Unilineal descent
FS . . . . . Matrilineal descent
FT . . . . . Patrilineal descent,
. . . . . agnates

[Substantive law S9VB]
[Persons by marriage & descent relations]
[Family & kinship law SBCF]
[Relatives SBCFI]
[Descent groups SBCFM]
. [Unilineal descent SBCFP]
. . [Patrilineal descent SBCFT]

SBC FUT Adopted kin (general)
. * Nearly all the literature refers to adopted
. children; see SBC HD.
FUW Guardianship (general)
. * Nearly all the literature refers to children; see
. SBC GPU W.
FV Affines, relations by marriage
. * See also Marriage - Impediments SBC LM
FVX Primary relatives
FW . Parents, legal parentage
FW9 G . . Remedies
FW9 PJ . . . Affiliation
. . . . * Usually an order against the father.
. . . . * See also Illegitimate children SBC GR
FWA QT . . Rights & duties
FWA RS . . . Maintenance of children
FWT . . Unmarried parents
. . . * See also Illegitimate children SBC GR
FX . . Mothers, motherhood
FY . . Fathers, fatherhood
FYL . . . Paternity
FYL AWK . . . . Testing
FYR . . Surrogacy
. . . * E.g. disputes as to who are the 'real'
. . . parents in situations like 'rent-a-womb',
. . . AID, etc.

G . Offspring, children (family law)
. . * Add to SBCG letters P/Y following KQA
. . Add to SBCH letters D/H following KQB
. . with the amendments shown.
. . * For children as legal persons generally see
. . SAX M (under Age groups).
. . * An alternative (not recommended) is to
. . locate here this general material also (instead
. . of at SAX M). See SBC GQ below.

. . Parents
GCF W . . . Parent & child
GPU . . Filiation, acknowledgement (filiation)
. . . * Attachment of child to parents.
GPU V . . Fostering
. . . * Use SBC HF.
GPU W . . Guardianship
GPU X . . . Guardians ad litem
GPV . . Support of children
GPW . . Custody of children, parental custody
. . . * See also divorce SBC MV
GPX . . . Access to children (parental
. . . custody)

[Substantive law S9VB]
[Family & kinship law SBCF]
[Relatives SBCFI]
[Primary relatives SBCFVX]
[Offspring SBCG]
[Custody of children SBCGPW]
. [Access to children parental custody SBCGPX]

SBC GPY C Child minding

Types of children
GQ . *Children by age*
. . * This location is an alternative (not
. . recommended) to SAX M for libraries
. . wishing to keep all material on children
. . under Family law. If this option is taken,
. . proceed as follows:
. . * Add to SBC GQ letters M/R following
. . SAX; e.g. Infants SBC GQN.
. *By other characteristics*
GQY Legitimate children
GR Illegitimate children, illegitimacy,
bastardy
GRP V . Support
. . * For affiliation, see Parents
. . SBC FW9 PH.
GRT . Legitimation of children
GRV . Paternity tests
GV Orphans
HD Adopted children, adoption
HF Foster children, fostering, foster home
HFA YF . Mentally handicapped foster
. children
HFC FW . Parents
HFC FWA PW . . Licensing (foster parents)
HG . Kinship fostering
HH . Short-term fostering, crisis fostering
HJ . Long-term fostering
HN Wardship, wards of court
HP Stepchildren
HPF W Step-parents

HQ Children subject to welfare action
. * For Welfare law in general, see SBU.
. *Agencies*
HR . . Public authorities (children's
. . welfare)
HRT . . Children's homes
. *Operations*
HSD . . Interviewing children (welfare
. . action)

[Substantive law S9VB]
[Persons by marriage & descent relations]
[Family & kinship law SBCF]
. . [Primary relatives SBCFVX]
. . . [Offspring SBCG]
. . . . [Children subject to welfare action SBCHQ]
. . . . . [Operations]
. . . . . . [Interviewing children welfare action SBCHSD]

SBC HSF . . . . . . Safety orders
HT . . . . . Children in care
HV . . . . . Abused children (general)
. . . . . . * Children suffering molestation by parents or others.
. . . . . . * An alternative (not recommended) is to locate legal aspects in the general class in QLL J.
. . . . . . * For specific offences against children, see Criminal law SBW.
HX . . . . . Reasons for welfare concern
. . . . . . * Arrange A/Z.
. . . . . . * Other than those characterized as abuse; e.g. punishment by parents.

. . . . *Other categories of offspring*
. . . . . * Add to SBC IB letters J/L following KQB.
. . . . . * Add to SBC IC letters L/X following KQC.
IBJ . . . . . Daughters
IBL . . . . . Sons
IC . . . . . Siblings
IDB . . . Secondary relatives
. . . . * Add to SBCI letters DD/I following KQ.
IFT . . . Tertiary relatives

J Families & households, domestic relations law
. * Add to SBC J letters J/RX following KQ in KQJ/KQRX.
JBG . Torts
JBG N . . Domestic violence
JMB . Domicile (domestic relations), residence (family law)
JQ . Extended family
JQS . Joint family, undivided family
JRT . One-parent family, single-parent family
JS . Other
. . * Arrange A/Z.
. . * For example, immigrant children.

[Substantive law S9VB]
[Law of persons SAP]
[Types of persons]
[Persons by various characteristics]
[Persons by marriage & descent relations]
[Families & households SBCJ]
. [Other SBCJS]

SBC JW Sexual union, marriage & sexual relations
JX . Sexual union (general)
JY . . Marital union, conjugal union
. . . * Stable union, married or otherwise. Most of the literature refers to marriage as the normal form.
. . . * For cohabitation, see SBC PLK.

K . . . Marriage, matrimony
. . . . * Add to SBCK letters G/T following KQS in KQSG/KQST
. . . . Add to SBCL letters U/Y following KQS in KQSU/KQSY
. . . . False statements, perjury
KBW HJG . . . . . Jactitation of marriage
KHP . . . . Conjugal rights
KHV Q . . . . Brideprice, dowry
. . . . . * See Property relations in marriage SBI TJD (or SBC LQJ D in the alternative below).
KR . . . . Mate selection
KRR . . . . . Marriage brokerage
KTB . . . . Betrothal, promise of marriage, engagement
KTC . . . . . Breach of promise
KTV . . . . Consent to marriage
KTX . . . . Marriage contract
. . . . . * Use SBC LC.
LC . . . . Contract of marriage, antenuptial contract, marriage articles, prenuptial contract
. . . . . * For performance of marriage, see SBC LYD.
LM . . . . . Impediments to marriage
LN . . . . . . Pre-marital examinations, medical examination (marriage)
LP . . . . Prohibitive impediments, prohibited degrees (marriage), affinity (prohibited degrees)
LQ . . . . . Property relations (marriage),
. . . . . . * Alternative (not recommended) to locating under Property law, at SBI T Matrimonial property.

Marriage

[Substantive law S9VB]
[Sexual union SBCJW]
[Sexual union general SBCJX]
[Marital union SBCJY]
[Marriage SBCK]
[Contract of marriage SBCLC]
. [Property relations marriage SBCLQ]

	. . If this option is taken:
	. . * Add to SBC LQ letter J following SBI T; e.g. Dowry SBC LQJ D.
SBC LU	. Religious contract in marriage
LV	. Secular marriage contract, civil marriage contract
LVT	. Marriage by proxy
LW	Solemnization of marriage, weddings, ceremony of marriage
LWA NY	. Marriage license
LYD	Maintenance of marriage, performance of marriage
M	Termination of marriage, dissolution of marriage, divorce (broadly)
	. * Add to SBCM letters Q/Y following KQT in KQTQ/KQTY.
	. * See also Domicile in domestic relations SBC JMB
	. Actions
M8	. . Matrimonial proceedings, matrimonial causes
M8R WV	. . Compromise
M8R X	. . . Conciliation (marriage), counselling (marriage)
M8R X38	. . . . Agencies
MR	. Annulment of marriage
MRV	. . Nullity of marriage
MRW	. . . Void nullity
MRX	. . . Voidable nullity
MS	. Desertion & non-support, abandonment of family
MT	. Marital separation
MTW	. . Legal separation, judicial separation
MV	. Divorce (narrowly)
MV8	. . Actions
MV8 F	. . . Time factor (divorce actions)
MV9 F	. . . Judgements
	. . . . * For custody of children, see Parents & children SBC GPW.
MV9 FR	. . . . Costs in divorce
MV9 G	. . . . Remedies
MV9 PH	. . . Alimony, maintenance of spouse
MV9 PJ	. . . Decree (divorce)
MV9 PK	. . . . Decree nisi
MVT	. . Breakdown of marriage

[Substantive law S9VB]
[Sexual union general SBCJX]
[Marital union SBCJY]
[Marriage SBCK]
[Termination of marriage SBCM]
. [Divorce narrowly SBCMV]
. . [Breakdown of marriage SBCMVT]

SBC MVU	. . . Grounds for divorce, matrimonial offences
	. . . . * See also Alienation of affection (enticement) SBG NT; Seduction SBG PG
MVV	. . . . Special grounds
	. . . . . * Arrange A/Z.
	. . . . . * For example, adultery.
MVW	. . Undefended divorce
MVX	. . Other forms of divorce
	. . . * Arrange A/Z.
MW	Post-dissolution (of marriage)
N	*Persons by marital state*
	. * Add to SBCN letters U/Y following KQ in KQU/KQY
NU	. Unmarried persons, single persons
NV	. Married persons, spouses, husband & wife
NV9 VH	. . Marital rights
	. . . * See also Nationality SCD ON
NW	. . Married women, wives
NWW	. . . Widows
NX	. . Married men, husbands
NXW	. . . Widowers
NYG	. Divorcees
NYH	. Separated persons
O	*Types of marriages*
	. * Add to SBCO letters A/Y following KRA in KRAA/KRAY, with the additions and amendments indicated.
	. * Add to SBCP letters B/L following KR in KRB/KRL.
OAD	. Invalid marriages, voidable marriages
OAE	. Deathbed marriages
OAF	. Posthumous marriages, post-mortem marriages
OGX	. Mixed marriages (general
OPA	. . Interfaith marriage, denominational marriages
OPD	. . Interethnic marriages
OPE	. . Interracial marriages
OUY	. . Cross national marriages
PEA	. Arranged marriages
PHW	. Morganatic marriages
	. . * See also Inheritance law SBI
PJ	. Polygamy
	. . * For illegal multiple marriages see Bigamy SBW PF
PLH	. Common-law marriages, consensual marriages

[Persons by marriage & descent relations]
[Sexual union SBCJW]
[Sexual union general SBCJX]
. [Marital union SBCJY]
. . [Marriage SBCK]
. . . [Types of marriages SBCO]
. . . . [Common-law marriages SBCPLH]

SBC PLK . . . . Cohabitation, unmarried couples
PLN . . . . Concubinage
PLR . . . . Remarriage

PM Sexual relations, sexual conduct
. * For sex education, see Education law SBT YK;
. for sex crimes, see criminal law SBW N.
Q . *Forms of sexual behaviour*
. . * Add to SBC Q letters H/X following KRM. A
. . selection of the forms most prominent in the
. . legal literature are given here for convenience.
QQS . . Marital sex
QRO . . Extramarital sex, adultery
QTQ . . Prostitution, prostitutes
QTR . . . Pimps, living off immoral earnings
QTS . . Pornography, pornographers
QU . . Sexual deviations
QW . . . Incest
QWX . . . Paedophilia
QWY . . Bisexuality
QX . . Homosexuality
QY . . . Male homosexuality
QYS . . . Female homosexuality, lesbianism

R Procreation, reproduction (procreation)
. * Add to SBC R letters S/Y following KRN.
RS . Fertility & infertility
RV . Unborn child, pregnancy
RVQ . Birth, newborn child
. . * For concealment of birth, see criminal law
. . SBW LS.
RVQ APR . . Recording
. . . * For Registration of births, see SAP T.
S . . Birth control, family planning
. . . * Add to SBC S letters S/Y following KRO,
. . . with the modifications indicated.
SU . . . Contraception
SVK . . . Sterilization (birth control), vasectomy
SVL . . . . Involuntary sterilization
SVO . . . Abortion
SVP . . . Infanticide
SW . . Birth promotion

[Substantive law S9VB]
[Types of persons]
[Persons by various characteristics]
. [Persons by marriage & descent relations]
. . . [Procreation SBCR]
. . . . [Birth SBCRVQ]
. . . . . [Birth promotion SBCSW]

SBC SWP . . . . . . Artificial insemination of
. . . . . . humans, in vitro fertilization
SWR . . . . Artificial insemination by
. . . . donor, AID
SWS . . . . . . Embryo transfer
SWT . . . . . . Surrogate motherhood
SWU . . . . . . Other techniques
. . . . * Arrange A/Z

SY . Quasi-family communities
. . * Add to SBC SY letters B/V following KRP -
. . e.g. Clans SBC SYK.

TB Corporate persons, juristic persons,
artificial persons, groups of persons
as legal persons
. * Groups of indivduals deemed to be a single legal
. entity, enjoying perpetual succession, etc.
. * For particular types, see class SBC V/SBC X
. below (except for business enterprises - see
. SBN YI/SBO).
TC . Unincorporated societies (general),
. associations, non-corporate groups
. (general)
. . * Associations with no legal personality distinct
. . from those of its members.
. . * The exact scope of these may vary between
. . legal systems and/or within the same system,
. . (e.g. in the status of trade unions in English law).
. . * For specific types of associations, see SBC
. . V/SBC X below (which does not distinguish
. . incorporated societies from unincorporated ones).
TD . Incorporated bodies
. . * Associations with corporate personality - i.e. a
. . personality distinct from those of its members.
TDA PR . . Incorporation, registration (corporate
. . bodies), charter (corporate persons)
. . . Personality
TDA Q . . . . Corporate personality
TE . . Corporations sole (general)
. . . * Constituted in a single person - e.g. some
. . . ecclesiastical offices.
TG . . Corporations aggregate (general)
TH . . Non-profit corporations, membership
. . corporations
. . . * Incorporated associations other than business
. . . corporations.
. . . * For foundations & endowments, see
. . . SBC WQR.

[Substantive law S9VB]
[Private law general S9W]
[Law of persons SAP]
[Types of persons]
[Corporate persons SBCTB]
[Incorporated bodies SBCTD]
. [Non-profit corporations SBCTH]

Types of groups & organizations
. * See notes above under unincorporated & incorporated associations. The following schedule does not distinguish whether a given type of group belongs technically to one or the other, but this will usually be clear from the work concerned.
. * For business associations, incorporated or unincorporated, see commercial law SBN YI/SBO.
. * Each type of group may be divided as instructed under Types of economic enterprises (immediately following SBN YHW). Proceed as follows (where the hyphen represents the classmark added to):
. * Add to - numbers 2/9, A/P following SBO Q (companies) so far as applicable.

SBC V . *Types by general characteristics*
. . * Mostly abstract categories of groups, lacking clear structure and unlikely to constitute legal persons.
. . * Add to SBCV letters M/Y following KL in KLM/KLY.
. . Add to SBCW letters A/I following KM in KMA/KMI, e.g. Audiences SBC WH.

WIT . . Meetings (corporate persons), conferences (corporate persons)

WJ . *Types of organized groups*
. . * Add to SBCW letters J/S following KM in KMJ/KMS. Some examples of those more likely to occur in the literature are given below, with the additions indicated.

WMS . . Committees (corporate persons)
WPT . . International organizations (as persons)
. . . * For international benevolent associations, see SBC WQY.
WQA . . Voluntary organizations
WQL . . Clubs
. . . * See also Licensing laws SBT KTI H
WQQ . . Charities, charitable institutions
WQR . . Trusts (charities), endowments (charities), foundations (charities)
WQX . . Friendly societies, benevolent societies, benefit societies

[Private law general S9W]
[Law of persons SAP]
[Types of persons]
[Corporate persons SBCTB]
[Types of groups & organizations]
[Types of organized groups SBCWJ]
. [Friendly societies SBCWQX]

. . * Other than insurance businesses.
SBC WQY . . International benevolent societies
. . . * For example, Red Cross.

X *Types by other functions*
. * Use only for corporate bodies not provided for elsewhere, especially under social law (SBT A) and Commercial & economic law SBN Y/SBO.
. * Add to SBCX numbers & letters 3/9, A/Z from the whole classification; e.g.
X5 . Research institutions
. . * Classmark provisional.
XHH . Medical corporations
XHM . Hospitals
XHM Q . Nursing homes
XPF F . Religious trusts

Obligations

SBD Obligations, personal obligations, contract & tort (together)
. * Obligations are created when two persons establish a legal relationship with enforceable rights and duties. In civil law systems they cover all such relationships, whether contractual or arising in particular circumstances by some principle of law. In common law systems, obligations as a general class are not regarded as a distinct branch of law, although the various grounds of obligation (contract, tort, restitution or quasi-contract, etc.) are so regarded.
. * Add to SBD numbers and letters 2/9, A/C in Auxiliary Schedule S1.
. * Add to SBD D letters D/Y in Auxiliary Schedule S1 so far as applicable.
SBD F . Parties
. . * For joint obligations, see SBD UF.
FAT . . Capacity
FG . . *Special parties*
. . . * For example, aliens, minors.
G . Liability (general)
. . * For Civil liability, see Torts SBG DG; for Criminal liability, see Criminal law SBW CG; for Indemnity against liability, see SBD LT.

. *Processes*
. . * Note that all the concepts which follow are repeated under Contract SBE (as creating a specific obligation).
I . . Formation of liability (general)
J . . Agreements (general)
. . . * See also Types of obligations SBD U
JX . . . Offer & acceptance
K . . . . Offer
KM . . . . . Termination of offer
KR . . . . . . Revocation of offer
L . . . . Acceptance
LM . . . . . Communication of acceptance
. . . . . *Types of acceptance*
. . . . . . * For express and implied agreements, see Terms SBE P.
LN . . . . . . Conditional acceptance, acceptance subject to contract
LP . . . . . . Acceptance by compliance
LQ . . . . . . Oral acceptance
LR . . . . . . Written acceptance
LT . . . . . . Indemnity against liability, hold harmless agreement
LV . . . Express & implied agreements
LW . . . . Express agreements
LX . . . . Implied agreements

M . . Consideration, causa
MP . . . Privity of contract
N . . Intent to create legal relations
. . . * For criminal intent, see Criminal law SBW CL.
NN . . . Declaration of intent, expression of intent
NP . . . Formalities (obligations)
. . . . * Evidence of serious intent.

[Obligations SBD]
[Processes]
. [Intent to create legal relations SBDN]
. . [Formalities obligations SBDNP]

SBD NR . . Earnest of intent
P . Terms & conditions
. . * See Contract SBE P
RX . Operation of law (obligations)
. . * Mode by which certain legal consequences follow, as distinct from those willed by parties.
S . Discharge of obligation (general)
Types of obligations
UC . Accessory obligation
. . * Security for fulfilment of primary obligation (Scots law).
. . * See also Accessory contracts SBE WC; Surety & guarantee SBF P
UE . Real obligation
UF . Joint obligation
UG . Promise (obligation)
UH . Natural obligation
UJ . Bond by deed (general)
. . * Usually involving money.
. . * For Performance bonds, see SBD UP.
. . * See also Deeds (contract) SBF B
UM . Express & implied guarantees
UN . . Express guarantees
UP . . Performance bonds, performance guarantees
. . . * When security for performance of a contract.

SBE Contract law, real agreements
. * See also Commercial law SBN; Sale of goods SBN XG
. * Add to SBE numbers and letters 2/9,A/C in Auxiliary Schedule S1.
. * Add to SBE CY letters E/Y in Auxiliary Schedule S1 should the need ever arise.
. * Add to all classes within SBE/SBF letters F/U following SBD (Obligations), with the addition indicated below.
. *Influencing factors*
SBE 58R O . . War & contract law
58T BV . . Economic crisis & contract law
58T PP . . State planning & contract law
F . Contractual parties
. . * For joint obligations, see SBD UF.
. . Capacity
FAT . . . Contractual capacity
FG . . *Special parties*
. . . * For example, aliens, minors.
. *Processes*
G . . Liability in contract
. . . * If considered distinct from general liability at SBD G.
I . . Formation (contract)
. . . Standard clauses & forms

Contract law

[Obligations SBD]
[Contract law SBE]
[Processes]
[Formation contract SBEI]
[Standard clauses & forms]

SBE J Agreement
JX . Offer & acceptance
K . . Offer
KM . . . Termination of offer
KR . . . . Revocation of offer
L . . Acceptance
LM . . . Communication of acceptance
. . . *Types of acceptance*
. . . . * For express & implied agreements, see SBD LV.
LN . . . . Conditional acceptance, acceptance subject to contract
LP . . . . Acceptance by compliance
LQ . . . . Oral acceptance
LR . . . . Written acceptance
LT . . . . Indemnity against liability, hold harmless agreement
M Consideration, causa
MP . Privity of contract
N Intention (contract)
NN . Declaration of intent, expresion of intent
NP . Formalities
. . * Evidence of serious intent.
NR . Earnest of intent

P Terms & conditions of contract, covenants (contract)
PR . Regulation (contract terms)
. . * To ensure fairness between parties.
PS . Certainty of terms
PT . Modus
. . * Modus et conventio vincunt legem.
PU . Uberrimae fidei
PY . Conditions & warranties
Q . . Conditions (contract terms)
. . . * For immoral conditions, see Immoral contracts SBE YC.
QR . . . Precedent conditions, suspensive conditions
QS . . . Subsequent conditions, resolutive condition
QT . . . Protestative conditions
QU . . . Casual conditions
QV . . . Mixed conditions
. . . . * Dependent both on choice and chance.
QW . . . Stipulation, non-functional stipulation, material stipulation
. . . . * Especially in sale of goods.
. . . . * See also Warranties SBE R

[Contract law SBE]
[Processes]
[Formation contract SBEI]
. [Terms & conditions of contract SBEP]
. . [Conditions & warranties SBEPY]
. . . [Conditions contract terms SBEQ]
. . . . [Stipulation SBEQW]

SBE QX . . . . *Special to a context*
. . . . . * For example, Caveat emptor (sale of goods) SBN XGE QX.
R . . . Warranties, fundamental stipulations
RT . . Exclusion clauses, exception clauses
RU . . . Derogation
RV . . Preliminary contracts
RW . . Transfer of rights
. . . * For example, in copyright.

S Discharge of contracts, termination of contracts
. * See also Limitation of action S8F
SW . Waiver (contracts)
TC . Rescission, cancellation, renunciation (contracts)
TD . . Resolution (Roman law), Lex commissoria (rescission), Pactum commissorium
TE . Acceptance breach
TF . Due performance
TG . . Payment (due performance)
TH . . . Special rules
. . . . * For example, gold clause in paying debts.
TJ . . . Time of payment
TK . . Special clauses
. . . * Especially in sale of goods.
TN . Discharge by agreement
TP . . Alteration of contract, novation, replacement of contract
TQ . . Accord & satisfaction
TR . Frustration, impossibility of performance, supervening impossibility
TV . Revocation
TW . Nullity (discharge of contract)
U Obligations in contract
. * Usually, these define types of contract; see SBE WC/SBE WP.

V Breach of contract, non-performance
V8 . Action
V8F . . Limitation of action
V9G . . Remedies
. . . * For Quantum meruit, see Quasi-contract SBF U9M VW.
V9L Q . . . Equitable remedies general
V9M . . . Damages
V9M Q . . . . Unliquidated damages
V9M R . . . . Liquidated damages

[Obligations SBD]
[Contract law SBE]
[Processes]
. [Breach of contract SBEV]
. . [Action SBEV8]
. . . [Remedies SBEV9G]
. . . . [Damages SBEV9M]
. . . . . [Liquidated damages SBEV9MR]

SBE V9M U . . . . Specific performance
V9N . . . . Injunction
VU . . Inducement of breach of contract
VV . . Breach of condition
VVX . . Fundamental breach
VW . . Breach of warranty

Types of contracts
WA . Forms of contract
. . *By obligation*
. . . * Add to SBE W letters C/P following SBD U.
WC . . . Accessory contracts (general)
. . . . * For Guaranty, see SBF P.
WR . . Contracts needing written evidence
WT . . Enforceable contracts, enforceability of contracts
WV . . Unenforceable contracts
. . . * Legal and valid, but unenforceable for some reason.
WW . . Unilateral contracts
WX . . Synallagmatic contracts
X . . Void & voidable contracts, unlawful contracts
. . . Capacity
XAT . . . . Invalid capacity in contracts
YB . . . Contracts against public policy
. . . . * For contracts in restraint of trade, see Commercial law SBN EP.
YC . . . Immoral contracts, unconscionable contracts
YD . . . Contracts lacking authentic consent
YE . . . . Mistakes in contracts
YF . . . . . Rectification of mistakes (contract)
YG . . . . . Mistakes at law (contract)
YH . . . . . Mistakes in equity (contract)
YJ . . . . . Mistakes in identity of parties
YM . . . . Misrepresentation in contracts
YM8 . . . . . Actions
YM9 G . . . . . . Remedies
YM9 PF . . . . Rescission
YN . . . . . . Negligent misrepresentation
YP . . . . . . Innocent misrepresentation
YQ . . . . Duress in contracts, undue influence (contracts)
YR . . . . Fraudulent contracts

[Obligations SBD]
[Contract law SBE]
[Types of contracts]
[Forms of contract SBEWA]
[Void & voidable contracts SBEX]
. [Contracts lacking authentic consent SBEYD]
. . [Fraudulent contracts SBEYR]

SBE YS . . Concealment of facts in contracts, non-disclosure (contracts)
. . . * See also Contracts uberrimae fidei SBF BL; Maintenance & champerty SBG RV; Torts SBG

YT Simple contracts, parol contracts
. * The great majority - not under seal, but orally or in writing.
YV Verbal agreements, statute of frauds
SBF B Specialty contracts, contracts under seal, deeds
. * See also Estoppel S8T XP; Performance bonds (obligations) SBD UP
BH . Delivery of deed
BJ . Escrow
. . * Deeds subject to a particular condition.
BL Contracts uberrimae fidei
. * Requiring disclosure of material facts.
By parties
CC . Subrogation
CE . Assignment (contracts)
CF . Novation
CH . Contracts in favour of third parties
CJ . Joint contracts
CP . Public contracts
CR . Foreign contracts
CT . Government contracts
CV . War contracts
E *Contracts special to a context*
. * Notation here is reserved for use in special contexts; e.g. Bottomry SBQ AFH; Employer & employee (master & servant) SBN L9X FD.
L *By subject*
. * The preferred arrangement is to subordinate these to the subject - e.g. sale of goods SBN XG.
. * An alternative is provided here for libraries wishing to keep together all contract law. If this option is taken, proceed as follows:
. * Add to SBFL letters A following S, and B/C and G/V following SB so far as applicable.

[Obligations SBD]
[Contract law SBE]
. [Types of contracts]
. . [Forms of contract SBEWA]
. . . [By subject SBFL]

SBF N Guarantee & indemnity
P . Guarantee & suretyship, guaranty, principal & surety
. . * An accessory contract.
. . * Add to SBF P letters F/V following SBE, with the additions indicated.
PF . . Parties
PFH . . . Principal debtor
PFJ . . . Surety, guarantor, cautioner (Scot.)
Q . . Security (guaranty), secured transactions
QS . . . Personal security (guaranty)
QT . . . Real security
. . . . * For mortgages, see SBJ N.
QU . . . . Fiducia (Rom.)
QV . . . . Hypothec, hypothecation
. . . . . * See also Liens SBJ N; Accommodation bill (bills of exchange) SBN GJU FP
QW . . . . Pledge
R . . Subrogation
. . . * Surety (e.g. an insurer) is put in the place of the debtor for the purpose of obtaining relief from other parties.
RT . . Delegation (surety)
S . Indemnity
. . * An independent obligation, not an accessory one.
. . * Add to SBF S letters F/V following SBE.

T Quasi-contract & agency
. * Add to SBF T and all its subclasses (SBF U/X) letters F/V following SBE so far as applicable.
U . Quasi-contract, restitution (civil law)
U9G . . Remedies
U9G VT . . . Restitutio in integrum
U9G VU . . . Quantum lucratus
U9G VW . . . Quantum meruit
UY . . Implied contracts, fictional agreements
VB . . Unjust enrichment, unjustified benefits
VD . . . Negotiorum gestio
W . Agency
. . * Relationship between an agent and his/her principal.
XB . . Principal & agent
XD . . Mandate
. . . * Authority given by one person (the mandator) to another to take some course of action.
XF . . Power of attorney
XG . . Agent of necessity
XH . . Negotiorum gestis
XJ . . Special types
. . . * See also Factoring SBN GHF

[Obligations SBD]
[Quasi-contract & agency SBFT]
. [Agency SBFW]
. . [Special types SBFXJ]

SBG Torts, delicts, civil wrongs, wrongful acts
. * A wrong, not arising from a contract, for which there is a remedy by compensation.
. * For criminal wrongs, see Criminal law SBW EH.
. * Add to SBG numbers and letters 2/9, A/F in Auxiliary Schedule S1, with the modifications indicated at SBG DG.
. * Add to SBG G letters G/Y in Auxiliary Schedule S1 should the need ever arise.
SBG 59 . *Relation to other law*
59W . . Crimes & tort
6 . Procedure
8A . . Parties to action
8AC . . . Capacity
8DJ . . . Joint tortfeasors
8DL . . . Concurrent tortfeasors
8Q . . Defences
8RC C . . . Consent
8RC E . . . Self-help
8RC F . . . . Necessity (torts), state of necessity
8RC G . . . . Self defence (torts)
8RC H . . . . Defence of land & goods
8RC J . . . . Lawful discipline or arrest
8RC L . . . Abatement of nuisance
8RC M . . . . Distress damage feasant
. . . . . * Abolished 1971.
8RC N . . . . Reception
8RD . . . Justification
. . . . * E.g., of libel.
9G . . Remedies
. . . * For replevin, see SBL 9MW.
9LQ . . . Equitable remedies
9M . . . Damages
9N . . . Injunction

D . Obligation (torts), duty (torts)
DG . . Liability (torts), accountability (torts), legal responsiblity, civil liability
. . . * For liability for torts, see Parties SBG 8A; for criminal liability, see SBW CG.
DGH . . . Fault or accident, casus fortuitus
DGJ . . . . Proximate cause
DGK . . . . Liability without fault
DGM . . . Malice (liability), error (law)
DGN . . . Negligence (liability)
. . . . * As element in committal of another tort. For negligence as specific tort, see SBG K.
DGP . . . Mistake (liability), error (liability)
DGQ . . . Strict liability (general)
DGR . . . Absolute liability, liability without fault
. . . . * Standard of liability set by statute, regardless of care taken.
DGT . . . Limited liability

[Obligations SBD]
[Torts SBG]
[Obligation torts SBGD]
. [Liability torts SBGDG]
. . [Limited liability SBGDGT]

SBG DGV . . Vicarious liability, vicarious responsibility,
. . liability for torts of others
. . . * For Master & servant (employer & employee)
. . . tort liability, see SBN L9X GG.
DGX . . . Respondeat superior
DH . . Public liability, government liability
DI . . Others with liability for torts of others
. . . * Arrange A/Z.

Particular torts
. * There are close parallels between some sections of
. torts & crimes. These are observed in the order in the
. classes below.
. * Any tort in SBG K/V may be classed at SBW HK
. if treated as a criminal offence.
K . Negligence (tort)
. . * For negligence as a liability, see SBG DGN; for
. . Contributory negligence, see SBG KW.
K8Q . . Defence
KL . . Voluntary assumption of risk
. . *Attributes*
KM . . . Res ipsa loquitur
KN . . . Duty of care
KO . . . . Damnum sine injuria
KP . . . . Limits of duty of care
KQ . . . . . Of particular persons
. . . . . . * For example, occupier's liability.
KR . . . . Standard of care
. . . . . * Degree and seriousness of risk.
KS . . . . Proximate cause, causation (negligence)
KT . . . . Remoteness of damage
. . *Forms of negligence*
. . . * For criminal negligence, see SBW CN; for
. . . liability for condition of land, see Tresspass to
. . . property SBH GP; for negligence resulting in
. . . damage to goods, see Tresspass to goods SBL GP.
KV . . . Comparative negligence
KW . . . Contributory negligence
L . . . Accident liability
LP . . . . *Forms of accident liability*
. . . . . * Add to SBG LP numbers and letters from
. . . . . the whole classification - e.g. School accidents
. . . . . SBG LPJ.
LR . . . Professional liability, professional
. . . malpractice
. . . . * For liability of particular professions, see
. . . . profession.
LS . . . . Specific professions
. . . . . * Arrange A/Z.
. . . . . * Alternative (not recommended) to
. . . . . distributing by profession.
LX . Breach of duty

[Obligations SBD]
[Torts SBG]
[Particular torts]
[Breach of duty SBGLX]

SBG M Nuisance
. * See also Trespass to land SBJ GP
MN . Public nuisance
MP . Private nuisance
MQ . Attractive nuisance
. *Specific nuisances*
MR . . Disturbance
MU . . Noise as nuisance
MV . . . Aircraft noise
MW . . . . Sonic boom damage

N Torts against the person
NQ . Breach of confidence
NR . Privacy infringement
. . * See also Civil rights (Constitutional law)
. . SCD B; Privacy right (intellectual property)
. . SBL PB.
NS . Harassment
NT . Enticement, alienation of affections
. . * For seduction, see Torts SBG PG.
NV . Torts against the reputation
NV . . Defamation, calumny
NV8 Q . . . Defence
NV8 RC . . . . Fair comment
NV8 RE . . . . Innocent dissemination
NV9 G . . . Remedies
NV9 PH . . . . Apology
O . . . Libel
. . . . * See also seditious libel SBW HIS T;
. . . . Criminal libel SBW HO; Blasphemy
. . . . SBW UI; Freedom of expression SCD C
OP . . . Slander
OQ . . . Convicium (Scot.)

PE . Sexual wrongs (tort)
PG . . Seduction
PM . Threats, duress (tort), coercion,
. compulsion (tort)
PP . Deception, deceit, false statements (torts),
. misrepresentation, chicanery
. . * For fraud, see Torts respecting business
. . relations SBG TH; for Malicious falsehood, see
. . SBW HPP.
PYB . . Dolus (Rom.)

Q . Trespass to the person
. . * Alternative (not recommended) is to locate
. . under criminal law at SBW K.
. . * See also Offences against the person SBW I;
. . Negligence SBG K
QR . . Real injuries (torts), personal injuries
. . (torts)
. . . * Deliberate injury other then tresspass.

Torts

[Obligations SBD]
[Torts SBG]
[Particular torts]
[Torts against the person SBGN]
. [Trespass to the person SBGQ]
. . [Real injuries torts SBGQR]

SBG QS . . . Assault & battery (torts)
QT . . Death by wrongful act, fatal injuries
. . (torts)

R Abuse of legal process
RS . Malicious accusation
RT . Malicious prosecution
RU . Malicious actions less than prosecution
RV . Maintenance & champerty
. . * Abolished in UK in 1967.
RX . False imprisonment
S Tresspass respecting property
. * Alternative (not recommended) to locating under
. Property, at SBH GP.
TB Business relations torts
. * Torts which are usually (but not always) associated
. with business.
TE . Procuring breach of contract
TF . . Conspiracy to defraud
. . . * For criminal conspiracy, see SBW FT.
TG . . Intimidation (tort)
TH . . Fraud
. . . * For criminal fraud, see SBW WA.
TL Torts with strict liability
. * Standard of liability is more stringent than with
. ordinary torts.
. * For Environmental damage, Pollution damage, etc.,
. see Environmental law SBS.
TN . Dangerous activities (torts)
TP . . Dangerous machinery
TR . . Fire damage (torts)
TS . . Defective premises
U Liability for animals, cruelty to animals,
protection of animals, animal abuse
V Other torts & torts special to a context
. * For example, see Copyright torts SBL KG.

Property law

SBH Property law
. * Add to SBH (and to all classes in SBH/SBK) as follows:
. * Add to SBH numbers and letters 2/9, A/G in Auxiliary Schedule S1.
. * Add to SBH GY letters L/Y in Auxiliary Schedule S1 should the need arise.
. * Add to SBH letters H/IS in Auxiliary Schedule S1 so far as applicable.
SBH 5A . Jurisprudence
5UN . . Natural law
5US . . . Public policy
5VB . . Theory of interests
. . . * For rights of property specifically, see Ownership SBH K.
5VD . . Things, res
5VE B . . . Corporeal things
5VE C . . . Incorporeal things
5VE E . . . Moveable & immoveable things (general)
. . . . * For moveables, see SBL 5VE; for immoveables, see SBJ 5VE F.
5VE J . . . Mixed things
. . . . * Both real & personal.
5VE K . . . Res communes
5VE L . . . Res extra commercium
. . . . * Not objects of commerce, e.g. sacred things.
5VF . . Time factors in property law, limitations (property law)
5VP . . Rights
. . . * Most of the literature reflects the particular rights implicit in ownership and possession, etc.

6 . Practice & procedure
9G . . Remedies
. . . * For Conversion, see SBH GPV.
. . . Restitution
9MV . . . . Repossession
9MW . . . . Distress
. . . . . * Especially relevant to rented property SBJ SU.
9MY B . . . Superseded remedies
9MY E . . . . Ejectment
. . . . . * See also Adverse possession SBH MS; Land titles SBJ HL
9MY F . . . . Fines & recoveries
. . *Special types of action*
9UP . . . Possessory actions (general)

G . Torts
GP . . Trespass to property
. . . * See also Trespass to land SBJ GP; Trespass to goods SBL GP; Trespass to persons SBG Q
GPV . . . Conversion (property law), trover
GPV 9G . . . . Remedies
. . . . . Superseded remedies

[Property law SBH]
[Torts SBHG]
. [Trespass to property SBHGP]
. . [Conversion property law SBHGPV]
. . . [Remedies SBHGPV9G]
. . . . [Superseded remedies]

SBH GPV 9MY D . . . . . Detinue
GPW . . Reconversion (property law)

I *General operations*
. * Operations citing after the particular properties & processes of property law. For an example of the use of this facet, see SBH PI Registration of title.
Properties & processes
J . Ownership & possession
. . * For tenure, see SBJ P.
K . . Ownership (general)
L . . . Title to ownership
LP . . . Uses (ownership), enjoyment (ownership)
. . . . * See also Trusts SBH U
LR . . . Interests (ownership), fragmentation of ownership
LT . . . Co-ownership (general)
. . . . * Usually implies real property; see Tenancies SBJ WN.
M . . Possession (ownership), occupation (ownership)
MS . . . Adverse possession
. . . . * See also Prescription SBH NT

N . . Acquisition & loss of ownership
. . . * For Treasure trove, see Personal property SBL HOX.
. . . Title
NM . . . . Acquisition of title
NR . . . Original acquisition (general)
NS . . . Derivative acquisition (general)
NT . . . Prescription, immemorial usage, usu capio (Roman law)
. . . . * See also Limitations SBI RL; Adverse possession SBH MS
O . . . Accession, accessio
. . . . * Whatever becomes attached or follows from possession.
. . . . * For Confusion & intermixture, see Personal property SBL HOY.
OQ . . . . Alluvion (Roman law)
OR . . . . Artificial accession, industrial accession
. . . . . * Addition by human action.
OS . . . Accretion
OT . . . Constitutum possessorium
. . . . * See also Fiduciaries SBH UG
OU . . . Occupancy
OV . . . Specificatio

[Property law SBH]
[Properties & processes]
[Ownership & possession SBHJ]
[Acquisition & loss of ownership SBHN]
. [Specificatio SBHOV]

. . * Creating something new from another
. . 10 material (in civil law & Scottish law).

SBH OX . Other forms of acquisition & loss
. . * Arrange A/Z.
. . * For example, bankruptcy.

P Transfer of property rights, transfer of title
. *General operations*
PID . . Registration
. . . * See also Real property SBJ HPI D
PV . Alienation
. . * Voluntary disposal.
. . * See also Family provision SBI DFJ
PVR . . Restrictions on alienation, restraint on
. . alienation
PW . . Assignment
. . . * Total alienation, outright transfer.
. . . Equity
PW9 VQ . . . . Equitable assignment
Q . Bailment
. . * See Personal property SBL HQ
. *Forms of transfer*
R . . Sale of property
. . . * For sale of goods in general, see SBN XG; for
. . . sale of real property, see SBJ HR.
S . . Conveyance (general)
. . . * Usually implies real property; see SBJ HS.
TD . . Transfer inter vivos, vendor & purchaser
. . . * For transfer on death, see Inheritance &
. . . succession SBI; for trusteeship, see SBH U.
TF . . . Gifts & endowments
TH . . . Mortgage (general)
TJ . . Transfer under government action
TL . . . Eminent domain, expropriation
TN . . . Forfeiture
TP . . . . Mortmain
TR . . . Compulsory purchase
TT . . . Privatization

[Property law SBH]
[Properties & processes]
[Ownership & possession SBHJ]
[Transfer of property rights SBHP]
[Forms of transfer]
[Transfer under government action SBHTJ]
. [Privatization SBHTT]

SBH TY Settlement & trusts (general)
. * Disposition of land or other property
. made by deed or will (or, rarely, by
. statute) whereby trusts are constituted to
. regulate the enjoyment of the settled
. property by the person(s) designated by
. the settlor.
. * See also Settlements & trusts for sale
. SBJ HTY

U . Trusts & trustees, trusteeship
. . * Separation of legal ownership from
. . beneficial ownership. Property is legally
. . invested in trustee but held in equity for
. . the beneficiary.
. . * See also Equity S9V Q
U5A . . Jurisprudence
U5U S . . . Public policy
. . . . * See also Unlawful trusts SBH XL
UDF . . Parties
. . . * Use SBH UE; normal retroactive
. . . addition of classes from SBH is
. . . interrupted here to provide notation
. . . for Parties to a trust. It is resumed at
. . . SBH V.
UE . . Parties to a trust
UF . . . Settlor
. . . . * Person creating trust.
UG . . . Fiduciaries (general)
. . . . * Persons in position of trust with
. . . . respect to another & legalLy obliged
. . . . to act in their interest.
UJ . . . Trustees
. . . . * Add to SBH UK letters B/V
. . . . following S6K.
. . . . * Add to SBH UL letters B/J
. . . . following S6L (with additions).
UKF . . . . Appointment
UKP . . . . Removal
ULC . . . . Capacity of trustees
ULE . . . . Powers of trustees
ULK . . . . Rights & duties
ULL . . . . . Liability of trustees
ULN . . . . . . Extent of liability of
. . . . . . trustees
ULP . . . . . . Breach of trust
ULP 9G . . . . Remedies
. . . . *Types*
ULU . . . . . Public trustees
UM . . . Beneficiaries, cestu que trust

[Ownership & possession SBHJ]
[Transfer of property rights SBHP]
[Forms of transfer]
[Settlement & trusts general SBHTY]
[Trusts & trustees SBHU]
[Parties to a trust SBHUE]
. [Beneficiaries SBHUM]

	. . Practice & procedure
SBH UM8 Q	. . . Defence
UM8 QV	. . . . Acquiescence
UM8 QW	. . . . Laches
V	*Other obligations, etc. relating to trusts*
	. * Normal retroactive synthesis is resumed here after its interruption at SBH UE.
	. * Add to SBH V letters DG/HU following SB in SBDG/SBHU so far as applicable.
	Operations
WB	. Creation of trusts
WBA T	. . Capacity (creation of trusts)
	. . . * Very general concept, varying in significance according to legal context.
WD	. . Declaration
	. . . * Inter vivos.
WE	. . Precatory trust
	. . . * Requested in a will.
WF	. . Testamentary trust
	. . . * See also Fidei commissum (Roman law) SJX IPG
WG	. . Voluntary transfer, volunteers
	. . . * No valuable consideration given in return.
WJ	. Variation of trust
	Elements in trusteeship
WM	. Deeds of trust
WN	. Trust funds
WQ	. . Accounts (trust funds)
WR	. . . Taxation (trust funds)
WS	. . . Legal investments
	Types of trusts
	. * See also Fiduciaries SBH UG; Creation of trusts SBH WB; Trusts for sale (real property) SBJ HXO
XD	. Discretionary trusts
XF	. Constructive trusts
XG	. Resulting trusts
XH	. Statutory trusts
XJ	. Secret trusts
XL	. Void trusts, unlawful trusts
XN	. Private trusts (general)
XP	. Public trusts (general)
XQ	. . Charitable trusts & foundations, charities, charitable uses
XQH TP	. . . Mortmain
XR	. . . Special advantage

[Property law SBH]
[Settlement & trusts general SBHTY]
[Trusts & trustees SBHU]
. [Types of trusts]
. . [Public trusts general SBHXP]
. . . [Charitable trusts & foundations SBHXQ]
. . . . [Special advantage SBHXR]

SBH XRT	. . . . . Tax relief
XS	. . . . Cy-pres doctrine
	. . . . . * If intention of gift is clearly charitable, uncertainty re precise object of benefit should not nullify.
	. . . *Types of public trusts*
XT	. . . . Relief of the poor (trusts)
XU	. . . . Advancement of education & learning (trusts)
XV	. . . . Advancement of religion (trusts)
XX	. . . . Other
	. . . . . * Arrange A/Z.
SBI	Inheritance & succession
	. * For synthesis in SBI, see notes at SBH.
SBI DF	. Parties
	. . * For Executors, see Estate administration SBI NKM.
DFG	. . Testator
DFG AT	. . . Capacity
DFG ATU	. . . . Undue influence
DFH	. . . Testamentary freedom
DFJ	. . . . Family provision
DFK	. . Beneficiaries (inheritance)
DFL	. . . Heirs, rules of descent (heirs)
DFM	. . . . Prior rights, decedent's family maintenance
	. . . . . * Right to specific share of estate conferred on certain relatives.
DFM P	. . . . . Lex falcidia
DFM Q	. . . . . Legitim (Scots law)
DFM R	. . . . . Mejora
DFM S	. . . . . Forced heirs
DFM T	. . . . . Widow's share
DFM V	. . . . . Disinheritance
	. . . . . . * See Wills SBI PJ
DFN	. . . . Universal succession
	. . . . . * To totality of another on his or her death.
DFP	. . . . Singular succession
	. . . . . * To one element of property only.
	. . . . *Special categories*
DFQ	. . . . . Heirs of the body
DFR	. . . . . Heir apparent
DFS	. . . . . Heir presumptive
DFT	. . . . . Coheirs
DFV	. . . . . Forced heirs
DFW	. . . . . Illegitimate children (inheritance)
DFX	. . . . . Others
	. . . . . . * Arrange A/Z.

Inheritance & succession

[Settlement & trusts general SBHTY]
[Inheritance & succession SBI]
[Parties SBIDF]
. [Beneficiaries inheritance SBIDFK]
. . [Heirs SBIDFL]
. . . [Special categories]
. . . . [Others SBIDFX]

SBI J Decedent's estate, estate of deceased
K . Administration of estate (inheritance)
. . *Agents*
KM . . . Executors & administrators
. . . . * For executors, see SBI NKM; for
. . . . administrators, see SBI QK.
. . . . * Add to SBI KM letter K/L following S6,
. . . . amplified as shown at SBH UK/L (for
. . . . trustees).
KMK F . . . . Appointment
KML K . . . . Rights & duties
. . *Operations*
L . . . Grant of representation
. . . . * For Probate, see SBI NL; for Letters of
. . . . administration, see SBI QL.
MB . . . Devolution of estates
. . . . * Transmission of interests.
MC . . . Claims against decedent's estate
MD . . . Distribution of decedent's estate
ME . . . . Assents
MF . . . Partition of decedent's estate
MG . . . Separation of patrimony, beneficium
. . . separatonis
MH . . . Sale of decedent's estate
. . *Elements*
MN . . . Inventories of decedent's estate
MP . . . Benefit of inventory
MQ . . . Assets (decedent's estate)
MR . . . Debts (decedent's estate)
. . . . * For death duties, see Taxation SCL MNJ.
MS . . . Residuary estate, residue (inheritance)
MT . . . . Bona vacantia
. . *Types*
MU . . . Unclaimed estates
MV . . . Insane persons' estates
MW . . . Foreign estates
MX . . . Others
. . . . * Arrange A/Z.

N Testamentary succession, testament, testate
succession
NK . Administration of estate (inheritance)
. . *Agents*
NKM . . . Executors
NKN . . . . Personal representatives (executors)
. . *Operations*
. . . Grant of representation
NL . . . . Probate
. . . . . * Certification by court that will is proved &
. . . . . registered.

[Transfer of property rights SBHP]
[Forms of transfer]
. [Settlement & trusts general SBHTY]
. . [Inheritance & succession SBI]
. . . [Testamentary succession SBIN]
. . . . [Administration of estate inheritance SBINK]
. . . . [Probate SBINL]

SBI NLM . . . . Revocation of probate
NLP . . . . Presumption of death (wills)
NLR . . . . Common form of probate
NLS . . . . Solemn form of probate
. . . . * Dispute anticipated.

O . . . . Wills, testaments (wills)
O6C F . . . . . Construction, interpretation
OP . . . . . Formalities
OQ . . . . . . Forms & precedents (wills)
OR . . . . . . Presumption of due execution
OS . . . . . Formation of wills, validity of wills
OU . . . . . Revocation of will
OW . . . . . Election (wills)
. . . . . *Elements of wills*
PC . . . . . . Codicils, alterations in wills
PD . . . . . . Devises, bequests, legacies
PE . . . . General & specific legacies
PF . . . . Demonstrative legacies
. . . . * Payable out of specified sources.
PH . . . . Residues, residual legacies
PJ . . . . . . Disinheritance
PL . . . . . . Donatio mortis causa, gifts, causa
. . . . . . mortis
. . . . * Transfer in contemplation of donor's
. . . . death; not strictly part of will.
. . . . . *Types of wills*
PP . . . . . . Privileged wills, noncupative wills,
. . . . . . oral bequests
PQ . . . . . . Holographic wills
PR . . . . . . Joint wills
PT . . . . . . Military wills

Q . . . Intestate succession
. . . . Administration of estates
. . . . . *Agents*
QK . . . . . . Administrators (estates)
. . . . . *Operations*
. . . . . . Grant of representation
QL . . . . Grant of administration, letters of
. . . . administration
QLM . . . . Revocation (grant of
. . . . administration)
QMY . . . . Partial intestacy
QX Other forms of transfer

[Property law SBH]
[Properties & processes]
. [Ownership & possession SBHJ]
. . [Transfer of property rights SBHP]
. . . [Other forms of transfer SBIQX]

SBI RE . . Extinction of estates & interests, loss of ownership
RG . . . Abandonment of property, bona vacantia, dereliction (civil law)
. . . . * For bona vacantia, see Residue SBI MT.
RL . . . Limitations (property)
SP . Other rights & interests in property
. . * For restrictive covenants, see Real property SBJ LT.

Types of properties
SW . Family settlement
T . . Matrimonial property, married women's property, marital property in settlement
. . . * Add to SBI T letters M/P following SBC so far as applicable.
. . . * Alternative (not recommended) is to locate under Marriage, at SBC LQ.
TJD . . . Dowry
TJG . . . Community property (matrimonial)
TJK . . . Separate (matrimonial) property
TM . . Dissolved marriages (property distribution)
. . . * Use also for divorce specifically.
V . Public property, government property
. . * Most of the literature relates to real property; see SBJ OV.
. . * For church property, see Ecclesiastical law SWE AH.
W . Alien property, foreign property
WAT . . Capacity
. . . * Of aliens, in relation to property.
. . . * See also Acquisition of real property by international organizations SBJ HPI L
WX . . Enemy property
X . Other general types
. . * Apart from real or personal property.

[Property law SBH]
[Types of properties]
[Other general types SBIX]

SBJ Real property, land law
. * For retroactive synthesis in SBJ, follow rules at SBH.
SBJ 5A . Jurisprudence
5VE F . . Immoveable things
G . Torts
. . * See also Trespass to land SBJ GP; Trespass to goods SBL GP
GK . . Negligence
GM . . Nuisance
GMR . . . Disturbance
GP . . Trespass to land
. . . Liability
GPG . . . . Liability for condition & use of land
GPQ . . . Eviction
GPW . . . Waste (real property torts)

. Ownership & possession
HJ . . Land tenure (general)
. . . * See also Agricultural land policy (government regulation) SBK RHL G
HL . . . Land titles
. . . . * For investigation of title, see Conveyancing SBJ HSR.
HLT . . . Co-ownership
. . . . * See SBJ WN
HM . . . Possession
HMS . . . . Adverse possession
HN . . . Acquisition & loss of ownership
HNT . . . . Prescription
HP . . Transfer of rights
HPI D . . . Registration of land, cadasters
HPI F . . . . Torrens system
HPI H . . . . Better title, priorities of title, worthier title
HPI L . . . . International organizations land registration
HPV . . . Alienation
. . . *Forms of transfer*
HR . . . . Sale of land, vendor & purchaser (land)
HRE . . . . . Contract
HRF BJ . . . . . . Escrow
HRT . . . . . Control of land sales

HS . . . . . Conveyances, real estate business
. . . . . . * See also Economics of real estate TKT L
. . . . . . *Agents*
HSK . . . . Estate agents, real estate agents
HSK T . . . . Licensed conveyancers
HSK V . . . . Others
. . . . * Arrange A/Z.
HSL . . . . . . Conveyancing

Real property

[Property law SBH]
[Real property SBJ]
[Ownership & possession]
. . [Forms of transfer]
. . . [Sale of land SBJHR]
. . . . [Conveyances SBJHS]
. . . . . [Conveyancing SBJHSL]

SBJ HSL FBJ . . . . . . Deeds (conveyancing)
HSM . . . . . . Standard conditions of sale
. . . . . . (conveyancing)
HSN . . . . . . Costs of conveyancing
HSO . . . . Solicitors' charges
. . . . (conveyancing)
HSP . . . . Stamp duties (conveyancing)
HSQ . . . . Deposits (conveyancing)
HSR . . . . . . Investigation of title, abstracts of
. . . . . . title, searches (conveyancing)
HST . . . . . . Surveying (conveyancing)
HSV . . . . . . Valuation (conveyancing)
HSW . . . . . . Closing & settlement
. . . . . . (conveyancing), completion
. . . . . . (conveyancing)
HSX C . . . . . Chains (sale of properties)
HSX G . . . . . Gazumping
HSY C . . . Consolidation of holdings
HTD . . . Transfer inter vivos
. . . . * For vendor & purchaser, see Sale of land
. . . . SBJ HR.
HTY . . . Settlements & trusts for sale
. . . . * For settlement & trusts in general, see
. . . . SBH TY.
HU . . . . Trusts & trustees in land
. . . . . * Ony works dealing specifically with land
. . . . . as the object of trust go here.
HXO . . . . . Trusts for sale
I . . . . Inheritance of land

Other rights & interests in real property
. * For joint tenancies, see Landlord & tenant
. SBJ WO.
IS . Legal interest
. . * Recognized in common law courts.
. . * Normal retroactive synthesis by SBI T/X
. . (under Property in general) is interrupted here;
. . it is resumed at SBJ O.
IU . Equitable interest
. . * Recognized in Court of Chancery (English law).
. . * See also specific equitable interests; e.g. Uses
. . SBH LP.
IV . . Escheat & forfeiture
JB . Entailed interest
JD . Life interest (real property), settled land
JF . Future interest (real property), future
. estates
JG . . Rules against remoteness
JH . . . Perpetuities
JI . . . Accumulations

[Property law SBH]
[Types of properties]
[Real property SBJ]
[Other rights & interests in real property]
[Future interest real property SBJJF]
. [Rules against remoteness SBJJG]
. . [Accumulations SBJJI]

SBJ JJ . Reversions (estates)
JK . Remainders (estates)
JL . Executory interest
JM . Expectancies, estates in expectancy
JP Determinable interest
JR Interest upon condition
JT Concurrent interest
. * See also Co-ownership SBJ WN

JX Rights & use & profits of another's land
K . Servitudes, incorporeal hereditiments
. . * See also Estates for life SBJ QV
KM . . Easements, real servitudes
KN . . . Light & air (servitudes)
KP . . . Right of way
. . . . * See also Access to land (planning law)
. . . . SBK QQ
KQ . . . Right of access to neighbouring land
KR . . . Easement of necessity
KT . . . Party walls
KV . . . Other easements
. . . . * Arrange A/Z.
L . . Personal servitudes, estates for life,
. . usufruct
LR . . Rent charges
LT . . Restrictive covenants, real covenants
LU . . Positive covenants
LX . . Profit a prendre
M . . Common lands, enclosures, inclosures
MT . . Tithes & advowsons
. . . * See Ecclesiastical law SXJ NK
MY . Real rights of guaranty on real property
N . . Mortgages (rights of guaranty), liens,
. . land charges
. . . * For mortgages as credit, see SBN GKN;
. . . for ships' mortgages and maritime lien, see
. . . SBQ AFQ.
. . . * See also Building societies (private finance
. . . law) SBN GHW
N6 . . . Practice & procedure
N9G . . . . Remedies
N9G WF . . . . . Foreclosure
NS . . Antichresis (Rom.)
NT Other rights
. * Arrange A/Z.
. * For example, Neighbours' rights.
Elements in land ownership
NV . Boundaries
NW . Riparian rights

Rented property

[Property law SBH]
[Types of properties]
[Real property SBJ]
[Other rights & interests in real property]
. [Elements in land ownership]
. . [Riparian rights SBJNW]

SBJ O *Types of real property by general characteristics*
. * Normal retroactive synthesis by SBI T/X is resumed here after its interruption at SBJ IS.
. * See also Planning law SBK
. * Add to SBJ O letters SW/X following SBI so far as applicable.
OV . Public land
Types of real property by tenure
. * For public land, see SBJ OV.
. Equity
P9V Q . . Equitable interests (real property)
PS . Estates
Q . . Freehold estates
QS . . . Fee simple
QT . . . Fee tail, entail
QV . . . Estates for life, life interest (real property)
. . . . * For servitudes, see SBJ L.
R . . Leasehold interest, chattels real
. . . * See also Landlord & tenant SBJ S
RS . . . Term of years
RV . . Special forms of tenure
. . . * Arrange A/Z.
RVC . . . Copyhold
RVG . . . Gavelkind
RW . . . Special to a jurisdiction
. . . . * Arrange A/Z.
. . . . * For example, Feu in Scots law.

S . Rented property, landlord & tenant, tenancies (broadly)
. . *Elements in landlord/tenant relations*
ST . . . Sanctions (landlord/tenant relations)
SU . . . . Distress
SV . . . . . Bailiffs (landlord/tenant relations)
SW . . . . . Priority of landlord's claims
SX . . . . Eviction, ejectment

T . . . Leases, tenancies (narrowly), letting (rented property)
. . . . * Tenancy for defined period; e.g., agricultural tenancies usually imply a lease.
TE . . . . Contract
TFB . . . . . Covenant (landlord/tenant)
. . . . *Operations*
TU . . . . . Creation of tenancy
TV . . . . . Termination of tenancy
TW . . . . . Enfranchisement of tenancy
UC . . . Security of tenure, protection of tenant rights

[Property law SBH]
[Types of properties]
[Real property SBJ]
[Types of real property by tenure]
[Rented property SBJS]
[Elements in landlord/tenant relations]
. [Security of tenure SBJUC]

SBJ UE . . Continuation of tenancy by relations
UG . Compensation on departure of tenant
UI . . Tied accommodation
UK . Rent (landlord/tenant)
UM . . Review of rents
UN . . Control of rents
UP . . Ground rent
US . . Service charge
VB . Condition of property (landlord/tenant)
VD . . Damage to property (landlord/tenant)
VF . . Repair of rented property, dilapidations
VH . . Improvement of rented property, decoration of rented property
VJ . . Fixtures in rented property
. *Types of landlord*
. . * See Types of tenancy, by landlord SBJ VN/VR

Types of tenancy
. * For farm tenancies, see Agricultural law SBQ TJP.
. * Each type of tenancy may be qualified as follows (where the hyphen represents the classmark added to):
. * Add to - letters S/U following SBJ; e.g. Security of tenure in local authority tenancies SBJ VR UC.
. *By landlord*
VN . . Private landlords, private tenancies
VP . . Housing association tenancies
VR . . Public authority tenancies, local authority tenancies
. *By function of property*
WB . . Housing (tenancies)
WBU C . . . Security of tenure
WD . . . Protected tenancies
. . . . * Replaced in UK law by Assured tenancies.
WE . . . . Controlled tenancies
. . . . . * In UK law, now converted to Regulated tenancies.
WF . . . . Regulated tenancies
WG . . . Statutory tenancies
. . . . * When the former protected tenant continues to live in the property.

Rented property

[Real property SBJ]
[Types of real property by tenure]
. [Rented property SBJS]
. . [Types of tenancy]
. . . [By function of property]
. . . . [Housing tenancies SBJWB]
. . . . . [Statutory tenancies SBJWG]

SBJ WH . . . . . Assured tenancies
. . . . . . * With security of tenure, but at market
. . . . . . rent.
WI . . . . . . Assured shorthold tenancies
WK . . . . Business properties, business tenancies

WN . . . Co-ownership (real property)
WO . . . . Joint tenancy, cotenancy, joint
. . . . property
WOT . . . . Timesharing
WP . . . . Common property (tenancy), tenancy
. . . . in common
. . . . *Other forms of co-partnership*
WPX C . . . . . Coparcenery
. . . . . . * Abolished in UK law, 1925.
WPW E . . . . . Tenancy by entireties
. . . . . . * Abolished in UK law, 1925.
WQ . . . Subleases, subletting
WR . . . Multiple occupation (tenancies)
WS . . . Furnished accommodation
WT . . . Commercial leases, business tenancies
WU . . . Farm tenancies
WV . . . Urban leases
WX *Types of real property by function*
. * Add to SBJ WX letters B/O following SBK Q in
. SBK QB/SBK QQ - e.g. SBJ WXG Condominiums.

SBJ X Environmental law
. * The developing subject of environmental law is not restricted to considerations of land use, although this latter may be regarded as a fundamental element in it. Because of its wider connotation, environmental law is preferred at SBS, whilst that part of it which is more narrowly concerned with land use is preferred here (at SBK).
. * An alternative (not recommended) is to locate environmental law here. If this option is taken proceed as follows:
. * Add to SBJ X letters P/Y following SBS.

SBK . Planning & development law, town & country planning law, regional & city planning law
. . * See note above, under SBJ X.
. . * An alternative (not recommended) is to collocate with Environmental law, at SBS Y.
. . * Add to SBK letters A/J following SB
. . Add to SBK K letters K/R following SB so far as applicable.
. . * Within the class SBK, the 3 initial letters (SBK) can be dropped in retroactive synthesis; e.g., Farm credits SBK RHM P.
. . *Agencies*
SBK LC . . . Land Commission
. . *Operations*
LG . . . Government regulation of development, government control of development, planning control
LI . . . . Registration of title
LJ . . . . Rights of private owners
LK . . . . . Protection of owner's rights
LN . . . . . Land charges
LO . . . . . . Specific classes of charges
. . . . * For example, Classes of charges A/F.

LR . . . Planning procedures
LS . . . . Public participation in planning procedures
LT . . . . Applications
LU . . . . Hearings, enquiries
LV . . . . . Public enquiries, local enquiries
MB . . . . Planning decisions
MC . . . . . Appeals against planning decisions
MD . . . . . Permission to develop
ME . . . . . . Conditions attaching to planning permission
MF . . . . . Enforcement of planning decisions
MG . . . . . . Stop notices
MH . . . . . . Compulsory acquisition, compulsory purchase
. . . . * For compulsory acquisition in housing law, see SBK QD MH.
MI . . . . Compensation
MJ . . . . Eminent domain, expropriation
MK . . . . Nationalization
. . . . * Transfer of rights to state.

[Environmental law SBJX]
[Planning & development law SBK]
[Operations]
. [Planning procedures SBKLR]
. . [Planning decisions SBKMB]
. . . [Enforcement of planning decisions SBKMF]
. . . . . [Eminent domain SBKMJ]
. . . . . . [Nationalization SBKMK]

SBK ML . . . . Land nationalization
MM . . . . . . Other forms of expropriation
MN . . . Development charges, land charges
MNT . . . . Betterment levy
MO . . . Development grants
MP . . . . Credits for development

. *By site initial conditions*
MS . . New site planning
MT . . Replanning, redevelopment
MV . . Improvement planning
MW . . Development planning
MXD . . . Development plans
MXF . . . . Structure plans
MXH . . . . Local plans
MXK . . . . Action area plans
MXN . . . . District plans

Objects of environmental & planning control
NC . Change of use
NE . Amenity preservation & control
NF . . Visual amenity control
NG . . . Advertisement control
NJ . . Nuisance control
NL . . . Noise control
NN . . Amospheric cleanliness control
. . . * Control of smoke, fumes, dust, etc. For Atmospheric pollution (environmental law) see SBS V.
NQ . . Heritage conservation, preservation of social heritage, protection of social heritage
. . . * See also Conservation of wildlife SBS XE; Conservation of wilderness SBK TG
NR . . . Conservation areas
NS . . . Historic remains preservation
. . . . * Alternative (not recommended) is to locate at SBV LES.
NT . . . . Historic monuments & buildings
NU . . . . Historic sites
NV . . . . . Archeological sites
NW . . . . . . Archeological finds
. . . . * See also Treasure trove SBL HOX

[Planning & development law SBK]
[Objects of environmental & planning control]
[Amenity preservation & control SBKNE]
. . [Historic remains preservation SBKNS]
. . . [Historic sites SBKNU]
. . . . [Archeological sites SBKNV]
. . . . . [Archeological finds SBKNW]

SBK NY Environmental use planning
. * Covering land, water & air use together.
O . Land use planning
P . . Buildings law
PE . . . Contract
. . . *Parts & services*
. . . . * For Pipelines & cables, see SBK RM.
PR . . . . Plumbing
PS . . . . Light & heating & ventilation
PSW . . . . . Wiring
PT . . . . Waste disposal
. . . . . * In individual buildings; for waste control at community level, see SBS Q.
PU . . . . . Sewerage
PW . . . . Earthquake resistant elements
. . . *Types*
QB . . . . Private buildings
QC . . . . Public buildings
QD . . . . Residences, dwellings, housing law
. . . . . * For landlord & tenant, see SBJ S.
QE . . . . . Gardens
QF . . . . . Flats, apartments
QG . . . . . Condominiums, horizontal properties, co-operative ownership
QH . . . . . Mobile homes, park homes
. . . . . . * See also Caravanning sites SBK TC
QJ . . . . Offices & shops, commercial properties
QK . . . . . Offices
QL . . . . . Shops
QN . . . . Factories
. . . . . * For Agricultural buildings, see SBK RHP.
QO . . . . . Civil engineering works (general)
. . . . . . * See also specific types, e.g. harbours

. . *Areas*
QQ . . . Access to land
. . . *By ownership*
QS . . . . Public land use
. . . . . * For Parks, see SBK TD.
QSM O . . . . . Land grants (USA), homesteads (USA)
QT . . . . Private land use
QTS . . . . . Estate land use
. . . *By factor used*
QV . . . . Space use
QW . . . . Resource use
QX . . . . . Energy use
RB . . . . . Machinery & equipment

[Planning & development law SBK]
[Environmental use planning SBKNY]
[Land use planning SBKO]
[Areas]
[By factor used]
. [Resource use SBKQW]
. . [Machinery & equipment SBKRB]

. . *Special resources*
SBK RC . . . Chemicals
RD . . . Others
. . . . * Arrange A/Z.
By particular use
RF . Zoning (general), regional land use
RH . Agricultural use
RHL G . . Government regulation, agricultrual land policy
RHP . . Farms buildings
RHR B . . Agricultural machinery
RHR C . . Agricultural chemicals
RHR CS . . . Fertilizers
RHR CT . . . . Particular fertilizers
. . . . . * Arrange A/Z.
RHR CU . . . Pesticides
RHR CV . . . . Particular pesticides
. . . . . * Arrange A/Z.
RHS . . Soil conservation
RHT . . Farm tenancies
RHU . . . Smallholdings
RHU V . . . . Crofts
RHV . . . Agricultural cooperatives
RHW . . . Collective farms
RHX . . . Sharecropping
RHY . . . Allotments
RIC . . Crops
RIM . . . Market gardening
RIN . . . . Nurseries
RIW . . Animals
. . . * For wild animals protection, see SBK TL.
RIX . . . Domestic animals, pets
RJ . . Timber, forestry use, trees

RK . Industrial zones
RL . . Enterprise zones
RLX . . Industrial infrastructure
RM . . . Pipes
RN . . . Electrical supply, cables
. . Special industries
RP . . . Minerals & mining
RQ . . . . Quarries
RR . . . . Coal
RS . . . . Iron
RT . . . . Precious minerals
RU . . . . Radioactive minerals
RV . . . . Oil & gas
RW . . . . Other minerals & mining
RX . . Other industries
. . . * Arrange A/Z.

[Planning & development law SBK]
[Environmental use planning SBKNY]
[Land use planning SBKO]
. [Areas]
. . [By particular use]
. . . [Industrial zones SBKRK]
. . . . [Other industries SBKRX]

SBK S . . . Urban development, town planning
. . . . *Atmospheric control*
SNN . . . . . Smokeless zones
ST . . . . Residential zones, housing
SU . . . . . Slum clearance, city redevelopment, urban renewal, inner city renewal
SV . . . . Non-building zones, green belts
SW . . . . New towns

TB . . . Recreation zones
TC . . . . Camping & caravanning sites
TCV . . . . . Gipsy caravan sites
TD . . . . Parks
TE . . . . . National parks
TG . . . Wilderness conservation
TH . . . . Wildlife protection
. . . . . * Use only if planning considerations narrrowly are the subject. The general class is SBS X Environmental law and when in doubt that should be preferred.
. . . . . * Add to SBK TJ letters D/G following SBS X so far as applicable; e.g. Wild animal protection SBK TJG.

TX Water resources planning
. * See also Water environmental law SBS U; Water transport law SBP X
U . Marine resources planning
. . * For marine installations (harbours, etc.) see Transport law SBQ AQN; for Fisheries law see SBQ BJ.
. . * Add to SBK U letters A/O following SBK.
UP . . Tidal waters planning
UQ . . Non-tidal waters planning, freshwater resources planning
UR . Drainage
US . Irrigation
UV . Water power
UX . Land reclamation

. [Environmental law SBJX]
. . [Planning & development law SBK]
. . . [Objects of environmental & planning control]
. . . . [Environmental use planning SBKNY]
. . . . . [Water resources planning SBKTX]
. . . . . . [Land reclamation SBKUX]

SBK VB . . . . . . Rivers & canals
VC . . . . Rivers
VE . . . . River basins
VG . . . . . . Pools & lakes
VJ . . . . . . Other bodies of water
W . . . . . Atmosphere planning & control
. . . . . . * See also Air environmental law SBS V
. . . . . . * Add to SBKW letters A/O following SBK.
WQ . . . . . . Weather control

. . . *Special facilities controlled*
XP . . . . Transport planning & control
. . . . . * Add to SBK X letters P/Q following SB; e.g.
XPX . . . . . Water transport planning
XQC . . . . . Land transport planning
XQD . . . . . . Roads
XQD QY . . . . Pedestrian facilities
. . . . * Pedestrian crossings, etc.
XQD QUF . . . . Motorways
XQE . . . . . . Railway transport planning
XQF . . . . . Air transport planning

SBL Personal property
. * Add to SBL numbers & letters 2/9, A/I in Auxiliary Schedule S1.
. * Add to SBL IX letters N/Y in Auxiliary Schedule S1 should the need arise.
SBL 5A . Jurisprudence
5VD . . Things
5VE . . . Moveable things, chattels personal
. . . . * For immoveable things, see Real property SBJ 5VE F.
5VF . . . . Choses in possession, things in possession
. . . . . * Tangible things, possessable physically.
5VG . . . . Choses in action, things in action
. . . . . * Intangible things, rights of property enforceable by legal action.
. . . . . * See also Intellectual & industrial property SBL J; Negotiable instruments SBN GJS
5VH . . . . Fungibles, res fungibles
. . . . . * Consumed in use; e.g. food.

Personal property

[Personal property SBL]
[Jurisprudence SBL5A]
. [Things SBL5VD]
. . [Moveable things SBL5VE]
. . . [Fungibles SBL5VH]

SBL 8 Actions & remedies
9G . Remedies
9MV . . Restitution
9MW . . . Replevin
Torts
G . Interference with goods
. . Negligence
GK . . . Damage to goods (result of
. . . negligence)
GP . . Trespass to goods
GPQ . . . Detainer
GPV . . . Conversion of goods
. . . . Superseded remedies
GPV 9MY D . . . . . Detinue

HJ Ownership & possession
HO . Accession
HOX . Finding, discovery, treasure trove
HOY . Confusion & intermixture
HP . Transfer
HPI S . . Declaration of title
HPI U . . Delivery (transfer of movables)
HQ . . Bailment
. . . * Delivery of property to a person (baillee)
. . . under an express or implied contract, to
. . . use in a particular way. Transfer of
. . . possession without transfer of title.
. . . * See also Sale of goods SBN XG
. . . Liability
HQD G . . . . Liability of baillees
. . . . . * See also Innkeeper, hotel-keepers
. . . . . SBT LU
HQS . . . Deposits
HQT . . . Loans
HQU . . . Hire
HR . . Sale of property
. . . * For Carriers, see SBP TC.
HRF Q . . . Secured transactions
HRF QW . . . . Pledges
. . . . . * See also Pawnbrokers SBN GIS P
HRF QX . . . . Liens
. . . . . * See also Retention (Scots law)
. . . . . SOB LHR FQX
HRF QYB . . . . . Legal liens
HRF QYE . . . . . Equitable liens
HRF QYG . . . . . General liens
HRF QYJ . . . . . Particular liens

[Personal property SBL]
[Ownership & possession SBLHJ]
. [Transfer SBLHP]
. . [Sale of property SBLHR]
. . . [Secured transactions SBLHRFQ]
. . . . [Liens SBLHRFQX]
. . . . . [Particular liens SBLHRFQYJ]

Types of personal property
SBL IY . Chattels personal, tangible goods
. . * For chattels real, see Leasehold interest SBJ R.

Intellectual & industrial property together

SBL J Intellectual & industrial property (together), intangible property
* Most of the literature is either on intellectual property (copyright) or on industrial property; there is little on this general class. So a detailed common schedule is given under intellectual property (SBL K/P) & the details in this may be drawn on to qualify both industrial property & this general class (SBL J).
* For business aspects of protection of intellectual property, see TWG P.
* Add to SBL J numbers & letters 2/I in Auxiliary Schedule S1.
* Add to SBL JJ letters J/X in Auxiliary Schedule S1 so far as applicable.
* Add to SBL J letters KQ/P following SBL in SBL KQ/SBL P so far as applicable to general works on intellectual & industrial property together. For example:

J6 . Practice & procedure
JE . Contract law
JKQ . Administrative procedures
JNB . Scope of protection
JPK . *By element or product protected*
. . * See SBL K/SBM Y

K . Copyright, protection of intellectual property, intellectual property in general
. . * The term intellectual property is sometimes used to include industrial property; in such cases, use SBL J.
. . * Major classes in copyright belong strictly to international law & appear there (at SDB LK).
. . * Add to SBL K numbers & letters 2/O in Auxiliary Schedule S1.
. . * Add to SBL KP letters P/X in Auxiliary Schedule S1 so far as applicable.
. . * An alternative (not recommended) is to locate here the materials on international treaties, organizations, etc. on copyright. If this option is taken, proceed as follows:
. . * Add to SBL K numbers 2/5 following SDB LK; e.g. Berne Convention SBL K5L T.

K2 . . *Primary materials*
. . . * Major classes in copyright belong strictly to international law & appear there (at SDB LK2). But see Alternative noted above.

KE . . Contract law
KER W . . . Transfer of rights
. . . *Types of contract*
KFF . . . . Contracts of usage & exploitation
KG . . Torts
. . . Deception
KGP P . . . . Plagiarism
KGV . . . Infringement of copyright
. . . . * For Passing off, see SBL XOU.

[Intellectual & industrial property together SBLJ]
[Copyright SBLK]
[Torts SBLKG]
. [Infringement of copyright SBLKGV]

. . *Permitted acts*
. . . * For acts not permissible, see Scope of protection SBL MB.

SBL KGW B . . . Fair dealing
KGW D . . . Public interest
KGW G . . Contributory infringement of copyright
KGW J . . Secondary infringement of copyright
KGW L . Unauthorized use
KGW P . Unauthorized reproduction
KGW R . Counterfeiting, piracy
KH Property law
KHN . Acquisition of rights
. . * For assertion, see Moral rights SBL NF.
KHO . . Fixation
KHP . Transfer of rights
. . * For Licensing, see Exploitation SBL LR.
KHP W . . Assignment
KHP X . . Succession
KIR E . Loss of rights
KIS P . Renewal of rights

KQ Administration of copyright, protection procedures
. * For transfer & loss of rights, see SBL KHP.
KR . *Agents*
. *Special conditions*
KT . . Wartime measures
. . . * Applicable primarily to industrial property.
. *Formalities*
KV . . Application for copyright
. . . * For acquisition of rights, see SBL KHN.
KW . . . Specification
LB . . Registration of copyright
LD . . Clearance of copyright
LF . . Deposit
. . . * Of designs, etc.
LHB . . Other formalities
LJ . Valuation
LM . Taxation
LO . Exploitation of copyright
LP . . Royalties
LR . . Licensing
LRK R . . . Licensing agencies
LSB . . . Licenses of right
LSD . . . Compulsory licensing
LSF . . . Exclusive licensing
LSH . . . Collective licensing
LSJ . . . Cross licensing
LSL . . . Dependency licensing
LSN . . . Franchising

[Intellectual & industrial property together SBLJ]
[Copyright SBLK]
[Administration of copyright SBLKQ]
. [Exploitation of copyright SBLLO]
. . [Licensing SBLLR]
. . . [Franchising SBLLSN]

Attributes
SBL MC . Protectability, copyrightability
ME . Creativity, authorship, intellectual paternity
. . * For employees' rights, see SBL NK.
MG . . Originality
MJ . Distinctiveness
ML . *Special to a product*
. . * For example, see Validity (patents) SBM ML.

NB Scope of protection, rights, permitted acts
. * For rights special to a product, see latter; e.g.
. Artwork - Droit de suite SBL TPG.
ND . Duration & renewal
NF . Moral rights
NH . . Creators
. . . * Authors, artists, etc.
NI . . Special moral rights
. . . * Arrange A/Z.
. . . * E.g. false attribution, integrity right.
NK . Employees rights

NN . Neighbouring rights, quasi-copyright
. . * General works on these; for those referring to a
. . specific product (e.g. music) see product.
NP . . Remuneration rights
NR . . Rental rights
NT . . Distribution rights
NV . . Reproduction rights, dissemination
NX . . . Copying rights
. . . . *Attributes*
NXM L . . . . . Substantiality
OB . . . Sampling, extraction
OD . . . Recording rights (general)
OF . . . Adaptation
OG . . . Variation & arrangement
OH . . . Translation rights
OJ . . Exhibition rights (general)
OL . . Lending rights (general)
ON . . Performance rights (general)
OP . . . Broadcasting rights (general)
OR . . . Filming & photographing rights
. . . (general)

OT . Unfair competition
. . * Forms of competition from which a right of
. . protection may be sought.
. . * Applicable primarily to industrial property; see
. . SBL XOT for further details.

[Intellectual & industrial property together SBLJ]
[Copyright SBLK]
[Scope of protection SBLNB]
. [Unfair competition SBLOT]

SBL PB . Privacy right
. . * For defamation, see SBG NV Torts against the
. . person; for trespass, see SBH GP.
PC . . Disclosure of private information
. . *By data used*
PDC . . . Name, signature
PDE . . . Portraiture

PF . *Rights special to a medium or product*
. . * For rights special to a product, see the product;
. . e.g. Artwork - Droit de suite SBL TPG.

By element protected
. * These vary according to the product & should be
. subordinated to the product; e.g. Literary works -
. Phrases, words, etc. The following are applicable to
. all or several products.
PK . Idea & title
PM . Fictional characters
PP . *Special to a medium or product*

By product or medium protected
. * For general works on reproduction rights, etc. see
. Scope of protection SBL NB. This facet takes the
. protected works themselves.
QC . Anonymous works
QE . Pseudonymous works
QG . Joint works
QJ . Posthumous works
QL . Unpublished works
QN . Crown copyright
QP . . Parliamentary copyright

R . Publishing, printing
. . * For electronic publishing, see SBL WJ.
. . Contract law
RE . . . Author & publisher contracts
RR . . Books & journals
. . . Lending rights
RRP L . . . . Public lending right
RS . . Manuscripts
RV . . Other physical forms
. . . * Arrange A/Z; e.g. maps.

S . Literary works
. . * For publishing copyright, see SBL R.
. . Scope of protection
SOH . . . Translation rights
. . Elements protected
SOH . . . Titles copyright
. . *Special forms*
ST . . . Private correspondence, letters
SU . . . Articles, journalism

[Intellectual & industrial property together SBLJ]
[Copyright SBLK]
[By product or medium protected]
[Literary works SBLS]
. [Special forms]
. . [Articles SBLSU]

SBL SV . . Plays, drama
SW . . Speeches, public lectures
SX . *Special subjects*
. . * Arrange A/Z.
SXS . . Scientific works

T Artwork, figurative art, graphics
. Scope of protection
TPG . . Droit de suite
. *Special forms of artwork*
TU . . Illustrations, drawings
TV . . Prints, commercial art
TW . . Artistic designs & models
TX . . Photographs
TY . . Others
. . . * Arrange A/Z.

U Performing arts
. *Elements protected*
UPL . . Script writers
UPN . . Directors & producers
UPP . . Performers
UPR . . Costumes

. *Special forms*
UV . . Music copyright
. . . * See also Sound recordings SBL VS
VB . . Theatrical works copyright, plays
VC . . . Drama productions
VE . . . Dance works, choreographic works
VG . . . Shows & spectacles
VJ . . . Other forms
. . . . * E.g. mime productions.
VM . . Motion pictures, films
VP . . Broadcasting productions, radio & television
VQ . . . Special forms
. . . . * Arrange A/Z.
. . . . * E.g. satellite, cable.
VRL . . . Loudspeakers, juke boxes
VS . . Sound recordings
VT . . . Special forms
. . . . * Arrange A/Z.
. . . . * E.g. records, tape recordings, compact disks.
VW . Games

[Intellectual & industrial property together SBLJ]
[Copyright SBLK]
[By product or medium protected]
[Performing arts SBLU]
. [Games SBLVW]

SBL WB Machine-held data, data protection (narrowly)
WC . Computer products
WE . . Computer systems as products
. . . Torts
. . . . Infringement
WEG V . . . . . Hacking
. . . . . . * Unauthorised use of computer system where this gives rise to a tort.
WG . . . Software, computer programs
. . . . * Includes code that is stored in non-volatile memory or embedded in hardware.
WJ . . Computer works, electronic publishing
. . . * Works which run on a computer, whose interpretation is mediated by a computer system and normally require use of a computing device.
WL . . . Multimedia products based on computers
. . . . * Add to SBL WL letters PK/VW following SBL; e.g.
WLV W . . . . Computer games
WN . . . Computer simulation, virtual reality
. . . . * Computer constructed environments which model aspects of reality often with the purpose of allowing the user to be an actor.
WP . . . Databases
WPT . . . Artificial intelligence
WPX . . . Expert systems
WQ . . . Other applications
. . . . * Arrange A/Z; e.g. artificial intelligence.

Other forms of intellectual property
WS . Cultural products & artefacts

Industrial property

[Intellectual & industrial property together SBLJ]
[Copyright SBLK]
. [By product or medium protected]
. . [Other forms of intellectual property]
. . . [Cultural products & artefacts SBLWS]

SBL X Industrial property, industrial intellectual property
. * Add to SBL X numbers & letters 2/P following SBL J so far as applicable, with the additions & modifications indicated below.
XG . Torts
. . * See also Unfair competition (industrial property) SBL XOT
XKQ . Administration
. . *Special operations*
XKT . . . Wartime measures, emergency measures
XKU . . . . Secrecy
XLO . . Exploitation
. . . * For protection of an exclusive right to exploit, see Patents SBM LO.
. Scope of protection
XNK . . Employees' rights

XOT . . Unfair competition
. . . * The general class for unfair competition (including anti-trust law) is SBN EOQ. This class takes only those unfair practices relating to industrial property as a subject for protection.
XOU . . . Passing off
. . . . * Representing marks, packaging, etc. as being those of a competitor, or falsly representing identity or connection with the latter.
XOU 9G . . . . Remedies
XOU 9GV . . . . . Account of profit
XOV B . . . Trade libel
XOV M . . . Misleading trade descriptions
. . . . * See also Consumer law SBN XQ; Product description SBN WGY

. *Elements protected*
. . * For designs as objects of protection, see SBM V; for protection of an exclusive right to exploit, see Patents SBM.
XPK . . Goodwill

SBM . . Patents law
. . . * Patentable things are those elements or products which may be protected by patent in respect of their exclusive exploitation.
. . . * For patents in general, see Science & invention AY.

[Intellectual & industrial property together SBLJ]
[Industrial property SBLX]
[Elements protected]
[Patents law SBM]

* For general works on choses in action, see SBL 5VG.
* Add to SBM numbers & letters 2/Q following SBL K so far as applicable, with the additions & modifications indicated below.

SBM E Contract law
EPU . Disclosure
G Torts
GV . Infringement of patent
H Property law
HN . Acquisition of rights
HP . Transfer of rights
. . * For licensing, see SBM LR.
. *<Assignment>*
HPW . . Assignable rights

KQ Administration
KV . Application
KW . . Specification
KXC . . Grace period
KXE . . Disclosure
KXF . . Examination & search
KXH . . Opposition
KXM . . Amendment
LO . Exploitation
LR . . Licensing of patents
LT . . Foreign licensing agreements

Attributes
MC . Patentability
ML . Validity
MN . . Novelty
MP . . . Prior art
MR . . . Prior use
MT . Industrial applicability
NB Scope of protection

Types of patents

. *By function or attribute*
RD . . Dependent patents
RF . . Process patents
RH . . Improvement patents, added subject matter
RJ . . Repair patents
RL . . Double patents

. *By application*
RP . . Utility models, petty patents
. . . * For Design patents (models patents), see Designs as elements protected SBM VR.
RX . . Inventions
RY . . . Classification of inventions

[Intellectual & industrial property together SBLJ]
[Industrial property SBLX]
[Elements protected]
. . [Types of patents]
. . . [By application]
. . . . [Inventions SBMRX]
. . . . . [Classification of inventions SBMRY]

aSB MS . . . . . *By field of application*
. . . . . . * Add to SBM S numbers & letters from the whole classification; e.g.
SBM SC . . . . . . Chemical patents
SE . . . . . . Microorganisms
SF . . . . . . Plant varieties
. . . . Add to SBM SF letters following F in Class F.
. . . . *Attributes*
SFM J . . . . Distinctiveness
SFM N . . . . Uniformity
SHN X . . . . . . Pharmaceutical patents, drug patents
SHN Y . . . . Specific substances
. . . . * Arrange A/Z.

Other elements protected
. * Each element may be qualified by classes SML/SMP. To qualify by patent (as a particular form of protection) add R; e.g. design patents SBM VR.
SYM . Distinctive marks
T . . Trade marks
. . . Administration
TLB . . . . Registration of trade marks
TLR . . . . Licensing of trade marks
. . . *Attributes*
TMJ . . . . Distinctiveness
TML . . . . . Functionality
TMN . . . . Generic use
TMS . . . . Secondary meaning
. . . *Elements protected*
TPL . . . . Goodwill
TPN . . . . Shape, configuration
TPR . . . . Other elements
. . . . . * Arrange A/Z.
. . . . . * E.g. colour, fragrance.
. . . *Types of trade marks*
TU . . . . *By industry*
. . . . . * Add to SBM T letters U/V in Classes U/V.
TW . . . . . Other industries
. . . . . . * Arrange A/Z.
UB . . . . Service marks
UD . . . . Certification marks
UF . . . . Collective marks
UH . . . . Personal name trademarks
UJ . . . . . Geographical names of origin
UL . . . . . Marks of origin, hallmarks
UN . . . . . Brand names
UP . . . . Signatures, insignia

[Intellectual & industrial property together SBLJ]
[Industrial property SBLX]
[Other elements protected]
[Distinctive marks SBMSYM]
. [Trade marks SBMT]
. . [Types of trade marks]
. . . [Signatures SBMUP]

SBM UR . . . Portraits
UT . . . Logos, signs
UV . . . International trade marks
UX . Other distinctive marks

V Designs (industrial property)
. * Visual features of shape, pattern, ornament, etc. applied to an article.
. Administration
VLB . . Registration of designs
. Scope of protection
. . Patents
VR . . . Design patents, models patents
. *Types of designs*
VX . . Registered designs
VY . . Unregistered designs
WB . . Industrial designs
. . . * If distinguished from the general class.
WD . . Computer generated designs
WE . . Fashion designs
WG . . . Hair style designs
WJ . . Other designs
. . . * Arrange A/Z.
. . . * E.g. recipes.

WP Confidential information
WQ . Breach of confidence
WR . Trade secrets
WS . . Industrial espionage, commercial espionage
WT . . Know-how

SBN Commercial law, mercantile law, economics law
. * In common law systems, commercial law is an indeterminate term covering topics from civil law particularly relevant to business and commerce in the widest sense and often including industrial law. It draws heavily on contract and property law. When a particular transaction or other legal relationship is considered (e.g. bankruptcy) its primary connotation relates to business associations, but includes also individuals.
. * In civil law systems it is usual to treat commercial law as a branch of law distinct from civil law and some concepts (e.g. merchant, commercial transaction) have a particular significance outside civil law.
. * The following schedule follows that in T/TP Economics and TQ/TY Management of economic enterprises, amplified by concepts prominent in the law of some classes, such as company law (SBO Q) and transport law (SBP).
. * For commercial law in the narrow sense of business law (i.e. relating to the administration and management of businesses & their various types) see SBN Q.
. * Add to SBN letters A/Y following T in TA/TY.
. * Compounding of economic and management concepts within classes SBN A/Y follows the normal retroactive rules in class T. These do not allow at the same time the retroactive synthesis of class S (i.e. adding directly letters A/Y from Auxiliary Schedule S1). So number 9 from Auxiliary Schedule S1 has been modified, as indicated below, to accommodate all the legal concepts needed to qualify the economic and commercial classes which follow.
. * Any class in SBN and SBO may, unless otherwise noted, be retroactively qualified as follows (where the hyphen represents the classmark added to):
. * Add to - numbers 2/9T following S in S2/S9T.
. * Add to -9U letters C/S following SBN 9U.
. * Add to -9V letters B/Q following S9V and letters W/X following S9.
. * Add to -9X letters A/Y in Auxiliary Schedule S1 so far as applicable; e.g. SBN I9X FW Commercial agency.
. * Add to -9Y letters U/W following SBN 9Y (for industries) so far as necessary.
. * Add to - letters A/P following SBN (taken from TA/TP & normally only added retroactively).

SBN 9UC . Regulation of economic & business activities
. . * As distinct from the more comprehensive policy of economic planning (see SBN AB). Usually seen in the government regulation or self regulation of enterprises (see SBN QQ) & akin to the administration of the law.
. . * See also Public administration operations SCK KC, with the divisions of which the classes below are consistent.
9UD . . Regulatory agencies, regulatory bodies

[Commercial law SBN]
[Regulation of economic & business activities SBN9UC]
. [Regulatory agencies SBN9UD]

SBN 9UE . . Persons
9UF . . Organizations
. *Operations*
9UH . . Registration, licensing
9UI . . Identification
. . . * For example, in transport undertakings.
. . . * See also Names of businesses SBO F9U I
9UJ . . Inspection
9UK . . Testing
9UL . . Enforcement
9UM . . . Specific measures
. . . . * Arrange A/Z.
9UP . . Government regulation of economic activities
9UQ . . . Particular agencies
9UR . . Self-regulatory agencies
9US . . . Particular agencies

9VH Economic rights
9VO . Economic freedom, right to establish businesses
9VW Private law
9VX . Civil law
9YU *By industry*
. * Industries represent types of businesses defined by product. The general class is at SBOY/SBQ. This location allows qualification of a legal problem (e.g. public health & safety) by industry when this is the preferred arrangement.
. * If qualification by a specific industry or product is needed, proceed as follows (where the hyphen represents the classmark of the industry):
. * Add to -9YU letters A/Y following U
. * Add to -9YV letters A/Y following V
. * Add to -9YW numbers & letters from the whole classification, so far as applicable.

A Economic policy, public policy
AB . Intervention, planning, government intervention
AC . . National economic planning, government economic planning
. . . * For International economic planning, see SDB NAC.
AGP . . Implementation of economic planning
AGR . . . Government grants, grant aid
AGS . . . Compensation in economic planning
AHD . . . Planning controls
AHP . . . . Appeals against planning
AHQ . . . . Inspection, supervision
AJH . . Emergency measures
AJJ . . . Disaster provisions

[Commercial law SBN]
[Economic policy SBNA]
. [Intervention SBNAB]
. . [Emergency measures SBNAJH]
. . . [Disaster provisions SBNAJJ]

SBN B Economic processes
CT . Economic cost
CXL . . Externalities
DQ Economic exchange
. * See also Sale of goods SBN XG
DS . Price determination
DT . . Price regulations, price controls
. . . * For price fixing, see SBN EPR.
DTV . . . Price discrimination
DU . . . Resale price maintenance
EK . Market system
EN . . Competition
EOQ . . . Unfair competition, unfair trade practices
. . . . * For protection against unfair competition see Industrial property law SBL XOT.
EP . . . Restrictive trade practices, restraint of trade
EPR . . . . Price agreements, price rings, price fixing
EQ . . . . Cartels, industrial trusts (Am.), anti-trust law
EV . . . Monopolies, engrossing, forestalling, cornering, combination in restraint of trade
EX . . Barter

F . Finance, financial exchange
FG . . Banking law
FG9 UC . . . Regulation of banking operations
FGS I . . . Electronic banking
FGS J . . . Home banking
FGT . . . Bank accounting
FGV . . . . Security
FHJ J . . . . . Collection of cheques
FHJ P . . . . . Confidentiality, secrecy
FJE . . . . . Bank deposits
FJH . . . Customer services
. . . . * For cheques, see SBN ; for cheque cards, see SBN GKP S; for bank loans & overdrafts, see SBN GJW FG.
FJH Q . . . . Deposit accounts
FJJ . . . . Cheque accounts, checking accounts (Am.)
. . . . . * For bills of exchange in general, see SBN GJU.
FJJ X . . . . Travellers' cheques
FJW . . . Banks of issue
FK . . . Central banking
FMW . . . Clearing houses
FN . . . Commercial banks, joint stock banks
FNW . . . Private banks

[Commercial law SBN]
[Economic exchange SBNDQ]
[Finance SBNF]
[Banking law SBNFG]
. [Private banks SBNFNW]

SBN FNX . Cooperative banks
FOG . Merchant banks
FOS . Savings banks

FQ Money, currency
. * For Forgery, see Criminal law SBW WG. for Foreign exchange, see SBN OF.
FRJ . Mints
FRL . Coinage
FRN . Paper money
. . * See also negotiable instruments SBN GJS
FRN Q . . Banknotes
FRP . Legal tender, fiat money
FXR Near-money, quasi-money (general)
. * See also Credit instruments SBN GIT
FXR W . Postal orders

G Credit, debt, debtor & creditor
GDX . Interest
GDX H . . Usury
GDX J . . Rates of interest
GGP . Collateral, liens, guarantees
GGR . Payment of debt, settlement of debt
GGS . . Composition
GGW . . Moratorium, extension of credit
GHA . . . Extinguishment of debts
. . . . * See also Discharge of contract SBE S
GHB . Non-payment of debt, defaults in payment
GHD . . Recovery of debts, collection of debts
GHF . . . Factoring
GHJ . Bankruptcy (general), insolvency (general)
. . * For business bankruptcy, see SBO QLL.
GHJ R . . Receiver
GHJ V . . Personal bankruptcy
GHS . Credit institutions
. . * For Banks, see SBN FG.
GHW . . Building societies, savings & loan associations
GIE . . Investment institutions
GIG . . . Investment trusts, investment companies
GIH . . . Unit trusts
GIK . . . Other investment institutions
. . . . * Arrange A/Z.
GIM . . Loan societies, loan associations
GIN . . Finance houses, commercial finance companies, credit companies, instalment credit companies
. . . * See also Consumer credit SBN GK
GIQ . . Industrial loan associations (Am.)

[Commercial law SBN]
[Economic exchange SBNDQ]
[Finance SBNF]
[Credit SBNG]
[Credit institutions SBNGHS]
. [Industrial loan associations Am. SBNGIQ]

SBN GIS . Money lenders
GIS P . Pawnbrokers

GIT Credit instruments
GIW . Rollover credits
GJ . Short term loans
GJS . Negotiable instruments, bills of credit, commercial paper
. . * See also Securities SBN GPH; Warehouse receipts SBN XGT P: Choses in action SBL 5VG.
GJS 9XE . . Contract
GJS 9XE M . . . Consideration
GJS M . . Holder in due course
GJS N . . Loss
GJS P . . Protests
GJS Q . . Bearer instruments (general)
GJS R . . . Share warrants payable to bearer
GJS S . . Acceptances
GJS T . . Cheques
GJS U . . . Stamp duties on cheques
GJS V . . . Travellers' cheques
GJT . Promissory notes
. . * For banknotes, see SBN FRN Q.
GJU . . Bills of exchange
. . . * For Acceptances, see SBN GJS S.
. . . Contract
GJU E . . . . Novation & surety
. . . Guarantee & surety
GJU FP . . . . Accommodation bill, accommodation endorsement
. . . Stamp laws
GJV G . . . Document bills & credit
GJV H . . Letters of credit, bills of credit
GJV K . . Drafts, bank drafts
. . . * Orders for payment of money drawn by one person on another.
GJV S . . IOUs
GJV W . . Certificates of deposit
GJW Cash credit
GJW . Cash credit
GJW FG . . Bank loans
GJW FIV . . Overdrafts
GJW P . Personal loans

[Commercial law SBN]
[Economic exchange SBNDQ]
[Finance SBNF]
[Credit SBNG]
. [Cash credit SBNGJW]
. . [Personal loans SBNGJWP]

SBN GK . Consumer credit
GKL . . Instalment credit
GKM . . . Hire purchase
GKN . . Mortgage credit, chattel credit
. . . * See also Mortgages SBJ N
GKO . . Revolving credit, check credit plans (Am.)
GKP . . . Credit cards, charge cards
GKP S . . . Bank cards, cheque cards
GKQ . . Credit accounts, charge accounts, budget accounts

GL Capital investment
GLS . Stocks & shares, bonds (Am.)
. . * Often loosely called securities; see note at SBN GPH below.
GLT . . Acquisition of stocks & shares
. . . * For procedures of issuing new securities, etc., see Capital raising SBO QF.
. . *Agents*
. . . * For investment trusts, etc. see credit institutions SBN GIG.
GLT 38 . . . Investment services
GLT 389 UC . . . . Regulation of operations
GN . . . Stock Exchange, stock market
GNN . . . . Market makers, brokers
GNT . . . . Forward market operations
. . . . . * For futures dealing, see Commodities SBN GYS.
GNU . . . . Stock options
GNV . . . . . Put & call transactions
GNX . . . . . Contango & backwardation
GNX R . . . . . . Hedging
GNY . . . . Arbitrage
GOB . . . . Speculation
GOH . . . . Margins
GON . . . Over the counter markets, OTC markets
GOO . . . Third market
. . . . * Dealing with large blocks of shares (e.g. for institutional investors).

. *Types of investments*
GPH . . Securities
. . . * Investments in respect of which the holder has a claim backed by enforcement rights in security - so exclude stocks & shares.
. . . * For specific types of company stock, see Company law SBO Q.
GPN . . . Unlisted securities

[Commercial law SBN]
[Economic exchange SBNDQ]
[Finance SBNF]
[Capital investment SBNGL]
. [Types of investments]
. . [Securities SBNGPH]
. . . [Unlisted securities SBNGPN]

SBN GPO	. . . Hybrid securities
GQB	. . . Bearer bonds
GRB	. . . Stock
GRD	. . . . Debentures
GRP	. . . . Preference shares
GS	. . . Ordinary shares, equities, common stock (USA)
GTG	. . . Risk capital, venture capital
GTQ	. . . Foreign securities, foreign investments, capital exports
	. . . . * Alternative (not recommended) to locating at SBN OGT Q.
GV	. . . Government securities, public securities (Am.)
GVY	. . . Municipal bonds, local government securities
GY	Commodities dealing
GYS	. Forward markets in commodities
GYT	. . Futures contracts
H	Insurance law
HB	. Risk carriers, insurers
HC	. . Underwriters
HCJ	. . Foreign insurers, overseas insurers
HCT	. Risks
HE	. Policy issuing, covering
HEH	. . Discrimination in insuring, discriminating rates
HEK	. . Policies, insurance contracts
HFB	. . Conditions of policies, clauses
HFD H	. . . Uniform insurance conditions, standard clauses
HFD J	. . . Warranties
HFK	. . . Indemnity principle
HFP	. . . Exclusions
HFS U	. . . . Subrogation
HHF	. Reinsurance
HHX	. Hazards
HIB	. . Negligence
HIE	. . War risks
	. *Branches of insurance*
HJF	. . Persons insured, policy holders, personal insurance (general)
	. . . * For specific forms, see branch; e.g. Accident insurance SBN HN; Life assurance SBN HT.
HJJ	. . . Travellers, holidaymakers
HKB	. . . Group insurance
HKH	. . Property insurance
HKJ	. . . Financial interest insurance, pecuniary loss insurance

[Commercial law SBN]
[Economic exchange SBNDQ]
[Finance SBNF]
[Insurance law SBNH]
[Branches of insurance]
[Property insurance SBNHKH]
. [Financial interest insurance SBNHKJ]

SBN HKK	. Consequential loss
HKS	. Legal costs insurance, litigation insurance
HKU	. Guarantee insurance, surety insurance, title insurance
HKY J	. Mortgage insurance
HLY	. Product insurance
	. . * For Products liability insurance, see SBN HNW L.
HM	. . Specific industries
	. . . * Arrange A/Z.
HMA	. . . Agricultural insurance (general)
	. . . . * For livestock insurance, see SBN HNQ.
HN	Accident insurance, casualty insurance
HNQ	. Livestock insurance
HNW	. Liability insurance, general liability, third party insurance
HNW J	. . Employers' liability insurance
HNW L	. . Products liability insurance
HP	Fire insurance
HPR	. Special perils, extended coverage
	. . * E.g. earthquakes.
HPY	Transport insurance
HQ	. Marine insurance
HQ9 XG	. . Torts
HQ9 XGJ	. . . Proximate cause
HQE K	. . Policies
HQF DH	. . . Standard policies & clauses
HQF DJ	. . . . Seaworthiness clause
HQF E	. . . Average in marine insurance
HQF F	. . . . General average
HQF FB	. . . . Hague Rules
HQF FC	. . . . York-Antwerp Rules
HQH F	. . Reinsurance
HQH X	. . Hazards
HQI E	. . . War risks
	. . . Special
	. . . . Bottomry
HQI Y	. . . . . Ship mortgages insurance, hypothecation insurance
HR	. Aviation insurance, air insurance
HS	. Motor insurance, automobile insurance, car insurance
HSN	. . Traffic accidents
HT	Life assurance, life insurance
HTW L	. Burial insurance

[Commercial law SBN]
[Economic exchange SBNDQ]
. [Finance SBNF]
. . [Insurance law SBNH]
. . . [Branches of insurance]
. . . . [Life assurance SBNHT]
. . . . . [Burial insurance SBNHTWL]

SBN HVN . . . . . Annuities
HW . . . . . Pensions insurance
HX . . . . . Personal sickness & accident insurance, health insurance
HY . . . . Social insurance
. . . . . * Alternative (not recommended) to locating in Class QFB FC.

HYY Economic production & distribution

I . Commerce & trade (general), distributive trades
. . * Legal aspects of economic structure & policy relating to this area. For law relating to the activities of individual firms, see SBN QQ.

. . Agency
I9X FW . . . Commercial agency
I9X FXB . . . . Principal & agent
I9X FYD . . . . Power of attorney
I9X FYJ . . . . *Special types*
IJD . . . . . Merchants
IJF . . . . . Brokers, commission agents, factors
IJH . . . . . Commercial travellers, firms' representatives
IJK . . . . . Tradesmen, dealers
IJM . . . . . Forwarding agents, distributors
IJP . . . . . Middlemen, intermediaries (general)
IJR . . . . Chambers of Commerce

. . *Forms of trade*
. . . * For Market intermediaries (wholesaling & retailing), see SBN XHW.
ILC . . . Illegal trade, black market
IP . . . Home trade
. . . . * For International trade, see SBN OI.

J . Production & industry (general)
. . * Legal aspect of economic structure & policy relating to this area.
. . * For industrial law in the narrow sense of labour law, see SBN L.
. . * For individual industries, see SBN 9Y.
JKL . . Location of industry
. . . * See also Industrial zones (planning law) SBK RK
JL . Wealth & income
JR . . Distribution of wealth
K . Economic resources (general)

[Commercial law SBN]
[Economic production & distribution SBNHYY]
. [Economic resources general SBNK]

SBN KQ . . Conservation of economic resources (general)
KRM . . Exploitatiob of resources (general)
. . . * For Pollution law, see SBS R.
KT . . Land
. . . * See also Real property SBJ
KW . . Capital
. . . * See also Corporation finance SBN TR; Investment SBN GL

L Labour law, industrial law, employment law
. * Compendious term covering employment & the relations between employers & employees & drawing heavily on the law of contract & tort.
. * An alternative (not recommended) is to collocate with Social law at SBU W.
. * For Industrial law (general), see SBQ U.

L9X E . Contract
L9X FD . . Employer & employee contract, master & servant, contract of service (general)
. . . * For specific elements in the contract, see the element - e.g. termination of employment.
L9X FG . . Independent contractors, contract of work & labour
L9X FH . . . Mechanics' liens
L9X FJ . . . Professional services contracts
L9X FK . . . Technical services contracts
L9X GG . Tort liability
L9X GV . . Vicarious liability
L9X HY . . . Tort liability
L9X I . . . Employers' tort liability
. . . . * See also Workmen's compensation SBU FH
L9X J . . . . *Particular types*
. . . . . * Arrange A/Z.

LC . Industrial relations law, labour relations law
LCN . . Government's role
LD . . Trades unions, labour unions
. . . * Please check classmarks here.
LDM RUN . . . Formation of trades unions, registration of trades unions
LDM RUT . . . Responsibilities & immunities
LDM RY . . . Management
LDM T . . . . Funds & accounts
LDM TW . . . . . Subscriptions
LDM TX . . . . . Political funds
LDN G . . . Inter-union relationships
LDN P . . . Membership

[Commercial law SBN]
[Labour law SBNL]
[Industrial relations law SBNLC]
. [Trades unions SBNLD]
. . [Membership SBNLDNP]

. . . * See also Closed shop SBN LLO
SBN LDN R . . . Rules of membership
LDO F . . . Meetings
LDO J . . . Elections
LDP D . . Officials
LDP H . . . Shop stewards
LDQ . . Branches, chapels
LDR R . . Political activities
LDR S . . . Political fund
. . *Types of trades unions*
LDS D . . . Illegal trades unions
LEE . Employers' associations
LF . Worker participation, employee participation, employee representation in management

LG . Industrial disputes, labour conflict
LGH . . Collective bargaining
LGL . . . Grievance procedure
LGP . . . Consultation, joint consultation
LGR . . . Negotiation
LGT . . . . Conciliation, grievance procedure
LGU . . . . . Mediation
LGV . . . Arbitration
. . . . Agencies
LGX . . Unilateral action
LHB . . . Industrial action (general), strikes & lockouts
LHC . . . Sympathetic action
LHE . . . Blacklisting
LHJ . . . Legal action in industrial action
LHK . . . . Injunctions in industrial action
LHM . . . Militant action, intimidation
LI . . Government action in industrial disputes
LIL . . . Industrial courts, labour courts
LIN . . . Industrial tribunals
LJ . . Workers' action in industrial disputes
LJM . . . Unofficial action
LJS . . . Strikes
LJS T . . . . Picketing
LK . . Employers' action
LKT B . . . Lockouts
. . *Subjects of action*
LLL . . . Unfair employment practice
LLN . . . Shop arrangement, union shop (Am.), union security (Am.)
LLO . . . . Closed shop
LM Labour supply, workforce

[Commercial law SBN]
[Labour law SBNL]
[Labour supply SBNLM]

SBN LO Employment (narrowly)
. * For administrative procedures (selection, etc.) see SBN LUO.
LO9 VH . Economic rights
LO9 VO . . Right to work, free choice of employment
LOQ R . Job availability
LOR . Equal job opportunities
LOS . . Job discrimination, preferential employment (Am.)
LP Unemployment
. * For unemployment relief, see social welfare SBU FJS.
LPP . Job creation measures
LPQ . Employment services, labour exchanges, employment agencies
LQP . Retraining schemes, vocational rehabilitation
LRK Labour systems (Am.)
. * Types of employment.
LRL . Apprenticeship
LRO . Temporary employment
LRQ . Seasonal employment
LRR . Contract work
LRT . Part-time employment
LRT U . . Job-sharing
LRT V . Multiple employment, moonlighting

LRY Conditions of work (broadly), factory law (narrowly)
. * Including wages & other rewards of labour.
. * See also note at SBN MD.
LS . Wages & salaries, remuneration
LST . . Administration of wages
LSU J . . . Deductions from pay, attachments from pay
LSV . . Control of wages
LSW C . . . Wages councils
LTB . . Wages structure
LTD T . . . Equal pay
LTI . . . Rates of pay
LTK . . . . Minimum wage
LTR . . . Incentive systems
LTS . . . . Bonus systems
LTV T . . . Payment in kind
LTV V . . . . Truck system
LTW . . Supplementary earnings, perquisites
LTW E . . . Tips
LTW F . . . Travel allowances, company cars
LTX . Social security benefits
LTX P . . Occupational pensions
LTX Y . Non-financial benefits, non-wage payments
LTX YB . . Staff canteens

Commercial law

[Commercial law SBN]
[Labour law SBNL]
[Conditions of work broadly SBNLRY]
. [Non-financial benefits SBNLTXY]
. . [Staff canteens SBNLTXYB]

SBN LUA Working conditions (narrowly)

LUO . Recruitment & selection of personnel
LUO LV . . Qualifications of personnel, certification
LUO NT . . Security risks
LUO Q . . References, testimonials
LUO U . . Appointment of personnel
LUO V . . . Employment contracts, service agreements
LUO VT . . . Probation period
LUO WF . . Rules of employment, discipline
LUO WM . . . Suspension from work
LUO XT . . Job security, tenure
LUO YB . . Sick leave
LUP B . Termination of employment
LUP BV . . Resignation
LUP C . . Dismissal, notice
LUP DC . . . Unfair dismissal, wrongful dismissal
LUP DT . . . Temporary dismissal, suspension
LUP DV . . . Reinstatement
LUP F . . Redundancy
LUP FT . . . Compensation for loss of employment
LUP FV . . . Special reasons for job loss
. . . . * For example, closure of firm.
LUP P . Hours of work
LUR R . . Overtime
LUS . . Shiftwork
LUT . . Rest periods
LUU . . Annual leave
LUW . Physical working conditions
LUX . . Health & safety at work
. . . * See also Workmen's compensation SBU FH
. . . Liability
LUX 9XD G . . . . Employers' liability
LUX NF . . . Hygiene
. . . *Special topics in health & safety*
. . . . * Notation from TLU X is amended slightly here.
. . . . Specific health hazards
LUY . . . . . Dangerous substances
. . . . . . * Arrange A/Z, e.g. asbestos SBN LUY A.
LVA . . . Industrial safety, industrial accidents
LVA V . . . . Fire
LVB . . . . Dangerous machinery
LVC . . . . Industrial injuries
LVD . . . . Industrial diseases

[Commercial law SBN]
[Labour law SBNL]
. [Working conditions narrowly SBNLUA]
. . [Physical working conditions SBNLUW]
. . . [Health & safety at work SBNLUX]
. . . . [Industrial safety SBNLVA]
. . . . . [Industrial diseases SBNLVD]

SBN LVE . Employees, workers
LVJ B . . Residential workers
LWM . . Women workers
LYP . Places of employment, workplaces
LYQ B . . Non-industrial employment
LYQ D . . . Shops
LYQ F . . . Offices
LYQ H . . . Catering establishments, hotels
LYR . . . Other special places of employment
. . . . * Arrange A/Z.
LYS . . Industrial employment
LYT . . . Factories, workshops
LYU . . . Mines, quarries

M *Forms of production & Sectorial economics*
MCO . Domestic work, work at home
MCP . . Cottage industries, village industries
. . . * Production in the home by self-employed workers & family.
MCQ . . Home industries
. . . * Production in the home for an external employer.
MD . Factory production, factories, industrial plant
. . * Factory law is usually synonymous, as is industrial law, with the environment & conditions of work of the labour force, for which see SBN LRY.
. . * This class takes only works concerned with legal aspects of the form of production, the physical plant & product & their potential for pollution & other hazards to persons & environment.
MDJ K . . Location of industry
MDP . . Automated production
MDR . . Industrial robots
MEB . . Mass production
MEL . . Recycling
. . . * See also Environmental law SBS
MEN . . Alternative technology

MG . Enterprises, industries, The firm
. . * See Business enterprises SBO G
MH . Sectors
. . * See Businesses by structure SBO HB

[Commercial law SBN]
[Forms of production & Sectorial economics SBNM]
. [Sectors SBNMH]

SBN N National economy, economic constitution
. * For public administration law, see SCK.
NH . Public finance
. . * Alternative (not recommended) to locating with Constitutional law at SCL MF.
NJ . . Taxation law
. . . * Alternative (not recommended) to locating with Constitutional law at SCL MJ. If this option is taken:
. . . * Add to SBN N letters J/O following SCL M.
NU . Regional economies, subnational economies
NW . Local government economies

O International economic relations
. * As a subject of law in all jurisdictions. For the subject in international law, see SDB N.
OAY . International economic agencies
. . * For agencies serving special functions, see function; e.g. International Monetary Fund SBN OFM (under international finance).
. . * For supranational agencies, see SBN OT.
OF . International finance law, international monetary system
OFE K . . Foreign exchange markets
OFG . . International banking
OFG K . . . Central banks
OFT . . Foreign currency
OFT J . . . Convertibility
OFT K . . . Exchange rate
OFT L . . . . Exchange control
OFT T . . . . Clearing
OGJ E . . . International money market
OGJ X . . . . Eurocurrency market
OGL . . . International investment
OGT Q . . . . Foreign securities
. . . . . * Alternative (not recommended) is to locate at SBN GTQ Securities (general).
OGT SQV . . . . . Syndicated loans
OGY . Commodity exchanges

OI . International trade & commerce, foreign trade
. . * See also Sale of goods SBN XG
OIA HW . . Trade agreements (general), commercial treaties (general)
. . . * See also International trade law SDB NOI
. . Barter
OIE W . . . Countertrade
OJ . . Balance of payments, balance of accounts
OLC . . Protection & free trade
OLI . . . Free ports & zones

[Commercial law SBN]
[International economic relations SBNO]
. [International trade & commerce SBNOI]
. . [Protection & free trade SBNOLC]
. . . [Free ports & zones SBNOLI]

SBN OM . . Import trade
OMQ . . . Import controls
OMR . . . . Non-tariff controls
. . . . . * Licenses, quotas, etc.
ON . . . Tariffs
ONR . . . . Preferential tariffs
ONT . . . . . Most favoured nation clause
OO . . Export trade
OOE NY . . . Dumping
OOQ . . . Export controls
OOS . . . Promotion of exports
OOU . . . . Credits for exports
OOV . . . . Subsidies for exports
OOY . . Particular commodities
. . . * Arrange A/Z.
OP . International aid, foreign aid, economic assistance, development aid
OPQ . . Agencies for international aid
OQH . . . Government foreign aid
. . . . * For Lome conventions, see EU law SGN OI5 LNR Q.
OQL B . . . . UNCTAD
OQS L . . Emergency aid, relief
OQU . . Technical assistance

OT . Trade blocs, economic blocs
. . * See also Supranational organizations SE/SH
P Economic systems (general)

Q Business law (narrowly)
. * An exception is made here to the rule at SNB regarding the use of the intercalator 9X:
. * Add to SBN Q numbers 2/9 in Auxiliary Schedule S1.
Q6 . Practice & procedure
Q9R . . Arbitration
Q9U C . Regulation of businesses
. . * The main application of this class is to particular forms of enterprise (e.g. companies SBO Q).
. Substantive law
. . * Add to SBN Q letters A/N in Auxiliary Schedule S1.
. . * Add to SBN O letters O/Y in Auxiliary Schedule S1 so far as applicable.
. Contract
QE . . Commercial contracts (general)

[Commercial law SBN]
[Business law narrowly SBNQ]
[Contract]
. [Commercial contracts general SBNQE]

SBN QQ Business management law
. * Classes SBN QQ/SBN Y are taken from TQ/TY, with some additions (e.g. under Sale of goods SBN XG).
. * Add to SBN QQ letters A/Z following TQ.
. * Add to SBN letters R/Y following T.
. * For retroactive synthesis of legal concepts, follow the instructions on the use of 9U/9Y at SBN.
. * For retroactive synthesis of business concepts within SBN QQ/SBN Y, follow the rules in TQ/TY. Since these rules relate primarily to the use of intercalators special to the Management class, these are repeated here for convenience (where the hyphen represents the classmark added to, and addition is always retroactive):
. * Add to -A letters A/Y following TQ (here, SBN QQ).
. * Add to -B letters A/Y following TR (here, SBN R).
. * Add to -C letters A/Y following TS (here, SBN S).
. * Add to -CY letters A/Y following TT (here, SBN T).
. * Add to -D letters A/Y following TU (here, SBN U).
. * Add to -E letters A/Y following TV (here, SBN V).
. * Add to -F letters A/Y following TW (here, SBN W).
. * Add to -G letters A/Y following TX (here, SBN X).
. * Add to -H letters A/Y following TY (here, SBN Y).

QQC . Managers
. . * For directors, see Company law SBO QCF B.
S . Information in management
SX . Legal departments in business
T . Accounting
TF . . Auditing
TLI . . Assets
TLU . . Goodwill
TOB . . Financial reports
TOC . . Financial statements

TR . Financial management (general), corporate financing (general)
. . * For company accounts, see SBO QE.
TS . . Financing
TSR . . . Sponsorship, patronage
TV . Formation of businesses, incorporation
. . * See Company law SBO QK
U . Personnel management

[Commercial law SBN]
[Business law narrowly SBNQ]
[Business management law SBNQQ]
[Personnel management SBNU]

. * See Labour law SBN L
SBN V Production management
VF . Procurement, industrial purchasing
VFR . . Leasing of equipment
VJS . Warehousing, storage of goods
VMS . Production standards
VMV . Product safety

W Marketing (general), marketing process
. * Most of the literature relates to the sale of goods; see SBN XG.
W9Y J . *By product or service sold*
WGN . The Product
WGP . . Protection of interest in product
. . . * For patent law, see SBM; for brand names, see SBM UN.
WGP L . . . Licensing
WGY . . Product description, trade description
. . . * See also Misleading trade descriptions (industrial property) SBL XOV M
WGY K . . . Information on product
WGY L . . . Standards
WGY M . . . Weights & measures
WGY Q . . . Composition of product, contents of product
WGY R . . . Fitness for purpose, quality
WGY S . . . . Formal evidence
. . . . . * E.g. qualifications of personnel, hallmarks.
WGY V . . . Performance claims
WH . Packaging
WHL . . Labelling, consumer information
WHP . Pricing
. . * For price-fixing & retail price maintenance, see Restraint of trade SBN EP.
WHU . . Discount pricing
WHW . . . Promotional pricing, loss leaders
WJ . Promotion law
WL . . Advertising law
. . . * See also Consumer protection SBN XRH
WLR Q . . . Fraudulent claims

XFR Q . . Sales, pricecutting

XG . Sale of goods, selling
. . * An exception is made here to the rule at SBN regarding the use of the intercalator 9X, as indicated below. This applies only to the general class SBN XG; if the subclasses (SBN XGR/SBN XGY) are qualified by legal concepts, follow the rules at SBN; e.g. Payments procedure - Contracts SBN XGVQ 9XE
. . * The notation at TXG A/W is amended to allow for this arrangement; see SBN XGV below.

[Commercial law SBN]
[Business law narrowly SBNQ]
[Business management law SBNQQ]
[Marketing general SBNW]
[Sale of goods SBNXG]

* Add to SBN XG numbers and letters 2/9, A/N in Auxiliary Schedule S1.
* Add to SBN XGO letters O/Y in Auxiliary Schedule S1 so far as applicable.

SBN XGE Contract of sale
XGE I . Formation
XGE N . . Intention
XGE NR . . . Earnest
XGE P . . Terms & conditions
XGE Q . . . Conditions
XGE QX . . . . Caveat emptor
XGE R . . . Warranties & guarantees
XGE S . Discharge of contract
XGE TD . . Lex commissorium
XGE TF . . Performance
. . . * For CiF & FoB clauses, see SBN XP 9XFE.
XGE TM . . . Weights & measures stipulation
. *Types of contracts*
XGE YV . . Verbal agreements, statute of frauds
XGF P Guaranty & surety
. Pledge
XGF QW . . Earnest
Liability
XGG G . Products liability
XGH P Transfer of property & title
. * For assignment, see Property law SBH PW.

XGR Sales documents
XGS . Invoices, bills
XGT . Documents of title
. . * See also Negotiable instruments SBN GJS
XGT L . . Bills of lading
XGT N . . Delivery orders
XGT P . . Store warrants, warehouse receipts, dock warrants, mercantile warrants
. . . * See also Negotiable instruments SBN GJS
XGU . . Certificates of deposit

XGV Management of selling
. * The notation at TXG A/W is amended here.
. * Add to SBN XGV letters A/W following TXG.
XGV D . Sales persons, salesforce
XGV N . . Salesmanship
XGV OB . Servicing the customer

[Commercial law SBN]
[Business law narrowly SBNQ]
[Business management law SBNQQ]
[Marketing general SBNW]
[Sale of goods SBNXG]
. [Management of selling SBNXGV]
. . [Servicing the customer SBNXGVOB]

SBN XGV OG . . . After-sales service
XGV PS . . Delivery of goods
XGV PV . . . Stoppage in situ
XGV Q . . Payment procedures

XH Channels
XHW . Market intermediaries, middlemen
XHX . . Resellers, title holders
XI . . Wholesaling law
XJJ . . Agents & brokers
XLP . . Franchise marketing
XM Markets
XO . Foreign marketing, international marketing, import-export selling
XP . . Export sales
XP9 XE . . . Contract
XP9 XFE . . . . Special contracts
XP9 XFF . . . . . CiF clauses
XP9 XFG . . . . . FoB clauses

XQ . Consumer law, consumer market
. . * See also Consumer credit SBN GK
. . * See also specific topics in marketing law; e.g. Product description SBN WGY; After-sales SBN XGV OG.
. . * An exception is made here to the rule at SBN regarding the use of the intercalator 9X:
. . * Add to SBN XQ numbers 2/9 & letters A/N in Auxiliary Schedule S1.
. . * Add to SBN XQO letters O/Y in Auxiliary Schedule S1 so far as applicable.
XQ9 UC . . Regulation
. . . * See also Consumer protection SBN RH
XQE . . Contract
XQG . . Tort
XRH . . Protection of consumers
XRR . . . Complaints by consumers
XT . . Retailing law
XUR . . . Shops & shopping
XVO . . . Self-service retailing
XWQ . . . Auctions
XWS . . . Mail order selling
XXH . . . Direct selling, home selling
XXI . . . . Cold calling
. . . . . * Calling uninvited & obtaining a questionable agreement to purchase.
XXN . . . Markets & fairs
XXQ . . . Vending machine selling

[Commercial law SBN]
[Business law narrowly SBNQ]
. . [Marketing general SBNW]
. . . [Markets SBNXM]
. . . . [Consumer law SBNXQ]
. . . . . [Retailing law SBNXT]
. . . . . . [Vending machine selling SBNXXQ]

. . . . *Other markets*
. . . . . * See also specific products, services, etc.; e.g. investments acquisition SBN GLT.
SBN YB . . . . . Organizational markets, institutional markets
YD . . . . . Government market, government contracting
YD . . . . . . Government contracts
YE . . . . . Second-hand market
YG . . . . . Services market

. . . . *Special legal categories of selling*
. . . . . * The notation at TYI/TYR is amended here; for types of business enterprises, see SBO G et seq.
. . . . . * For conditional sale, see Instalment credit SBN GKL.
YHL . . . . . Sale by description
YHN . . . . . Sale by sample
YHP . . . . . Bulk sales
YHR . . . . . Judicial sale
. . . . . . * See also Foreclosure SBJ O9G WF
YHT . . . . . Tax sales, tax-titles
YHV . . . . . Pre-emption
YHW . . . . . Redemption, repurchase

Types of economic enterprises
. * The classes below (SBO G/SBO X) reflect enterprises defined by structure and by legal characteristics. For enterprises defined by product, see SBP/SBQ.

YI *Types by size, etc.*
. * For Project management, see SBO HX; for Small businesses, see SBO I

YNR *By capital distribution & ownership*
. * The notation from TYNR/TYO is adjusted here; see under Types of enterprise by structure and ownership, at SBO G.

[Commercial law SBN]
[By capital distribution & ownership SBNYNR]

Types of enterprises by structure & ownership

SBO G . Business enterprises, businesses, The Merchant
. . * This class takes works on the legal position of the various types of individual enterprises per se. Do not qualify this general class (SBO G) by classes SBN Q/Y Management (from TQ/TY); the concept of businesses is implicit in those classes.
. . * See also Corporate persons (general) SBC TB
. . * Add to SBO letters G/Y following TM, with the adjustments indicated.
. . * Any given type of enterprise may be qualified, so far as applicable, as follows (where the hyphen represents the classmark of the enterprise):
. . * Add to - numbers 2/9 following SBN & letters A/M following SBO Q (companies)
. . * Add to -N letters D/U following SBO H
. . * An example of the application of these instructions is given at Small businesses SBO I.
G9U C . . Regulation of businesses
. . . Identification
G9U I . . . . Names
. . *Special operations*
. . . * Add to SBO H letters D/U following TMH O (with the amendments indicated).
HD . . . Government reorganization of businesses, setting up businesses by government
. . . . * For company formation, see SBO QK.
HE . . . . Economic assistance to businesses
HF . . . . . Subsidies to businesses, grants to businesses
HH . . . . Enforced closure, enforced contraction
HJ . . . . Compensation for government regulatory measure
HM . . . . . Compulsory sharing of resources
HP . . . . . Restrictions on use of resources
HQ . . . . . . Rationing
HR . . . . . . Substitution of resources
HS . . . . . . Rationalization of resources
HU . . . . Transfer of ownership by government
. . . . . * For Nationalization, see SBO IMU; for privatization, see SBO NMU.

. . *Types by size, etc.*
HX . . . Projects, project management
I . . . Small businesses
IE . . . . Financial management
IN . . . . *Special operations*
INE . . . . . Government assistance
INE 38 . . . . . . Business Expansion Scheme

Types of enterprises by structure & ownership

[Types of enterprises by structure & ownership]
[Business enterprises SBOG]
[Types by size]
. [Small businesses SBOI]
. . [Special operations SBOIN]
. . . [Government assistance SBOINE]
. . . . [Business Expansion Scheme SBOINE38]

Types by sector
SBO J . Public sector undertakings, public service industries, public ownership, state ownership
J9U C . . Regulation
. . Government transfer of ownership
JMU . . . Nationalization
K . . Nationalized industries
M . . Municipal enterprises, local government enterprises

N . Private sector undertakings, private industry, The Firm
N9U C . . Regulation
. . . Government transfer of ownership
NMU . . . . Privatization

NX . . Foreign firms
NY . . Unincorporated firms
. . . * For unincorporated bodies in general, see SBC TC.
O . . Sole owners, one-person companies
P . . Partnerships, companies (Am.)
. . . * For Joint ventures, see SBO UV.
PKP J . . . Articles of partnership
PKP X . . . . Dissolution of partnership
. . . *Parties*
PR . . . . Partners
PS . . . . . Joint partnerships
PT . . . . . Silent partner, sleeping partner
PU . . . . . Partnerships limited by shares
PV . . . . Third parties
PW . . . Limited partnership

[Commercial law SBN]
[Types of enterprises by structure & ownership]
[Business enterprises SBOG]
[Types by sector]
[Private sector undertakings SBON]
[Partnerships SBOP]
. [Limited partnership SBOPW]

SBO Q Company law, corporation law (Am.), incorporated companies, public limited companies, limited liability companies
Q6 . Practice & procedure
Q9U C . Regulation
Q9U I . Name of company
QA . Management
. . * Add to SBO Q intercalators A/H for management aspects, as listed at SBN QQ, with the adjustments indicated below.
QAF B . . Directors, board of directors
QAF BR . . . Duties & responsibilities of directors
QAF BT . . . . Disclosure of interest
QAF BV . . . Remuneration of directors
QAF C . . . Non-executive directors
QAF D . . . Executive directors
QAF DG . . . Company chairman, company president
QAF DS . . . Shadow directors
QAF DW . . . Worker directors
QAF E . . . Chief executive, managing-director
QAF J . . Officers

QCY . . Accounting
. . . * Normal synthesis by Management intercalators A/H is interrupted here; it is resumed at SBO QH.
. . . * Add to SBO QD letters A/Q following SBN T (taken from TT Accounting); e.g. Divisional accounting SBO QDQ Y.
QE . . Financial management
. . . * Add to SBO QE letters A/Y following TTR.
QF . . . Capital raising, acquisition of funds
. . . . * Add to SBO QF letters A/QO following TTS.
QFK . . . . Internal funding, self-financing
QFK N . . . . . Reserves
QFN . . . . External funding
QFO . . . . . Loan capital, debt capital

[Private sector undertakings SBON]
[Company law SBOQ]
[Management SBOQA]
[Financial management SBOQE]
[Capital raising SBOQF]
[External funding SBOQFN]
[Loan capital SBOQFO]

SBO QFQ Securities, shares
QFQ LS . Registration of shares
QFQ LT . Purchase of company shares
QFQ M . Flotation, issuing company shares
QFQ MP . . Allotment of company shares
QFQ MX . Transfer of company shares
QFQ MY . . Transmission of company shares
QFQ NU . Options
QFQ OQ . Investors
. . * Use SBO QG; normal synthesis by TTS Q is interrupted here; it is resumed at SBO QGP.
QG . Shareholders
QGA BT . . Disclosure of interest
QGE . . Meetings of shareholders
QGF . . . Voting of shareholders
QGH . . *Types of shareholders by general characteristics*
. . . * Add to SBO QGH letters W/Y following SA.
. . . * Add to SBO QGI letters B/C following SB.
QGJ . . *Types of shareholders by special characteristics*
. . . * Add to SBO QGJ letters R/X following TGO; e.g. Government as investor SBO QGJ W.
QGK . . . Majority shareholders
QGL . . . Minority shareholders
QGM . . . Nominee shareholders

QGP . *Types of securities*
. . * Normal synthesis by TTS Q is resumed here after its interruption at SBO QFQ OQ.
. . * See also Securities (investment) SBN GPH
. . * Add to SBO QG letters PJ/X following TG.
QGQ B . . Bearer bonds
QGQ Y . . Stocks & share (together)
QGR B . . . Stocks, fixed interest securities
QGR C . . . . Non-voting shares
QGR D . . . . Debentures

[Types of enterprises by structure & ownership]
[Company law SBOQ]
[Management SBOQA]
. [Financial management SBOQE]
. . [Capital raising SBOQF]
. . . [External funding SBOQFN]
. . . . . . [Stocks & share together SBOQGQY]
. . . . [Stocks SBOQGRB]
. . . . [Debentures SBOQGRD]

SBO QGR P . . . . Preference shares, preferred stock (Am.)
QGR PT . . . . Convertible preference shares
QGS . . . . Shares, ordinary shares, equities, common stock (Am.)
QGT M . . . . Scrip, warrant scrip

QH . . . Other sources of funds
. . . . * Nornal synthesis by SBN T (taken from TT) is resumed here after its interruption at SBO QCY.
. . . . * Add to SBO QH letters R/V following TTS; e.g. grants SBO QHR S.
QHS . . . . Leasing
QHV . . . . Franchising
QHV Y . . Use of funds
. . . * Add to SBO QH letters VY/Y following TTS.
QHW . . . Capital expenditure
QI . . . Corporate investment
. . . . * Add to SBO QI letters J/Y following TTT
. . . . * Add to SBO QJ letters J/M following TTU
QJN . . . Distribution of profits
. . . . * Add to SBO QJ letters N/Y following TTU
QJP . . . . Dividends

QK Formation & reorganization of business
. * Add to SBO QK letters D/Y following TTV, with the additions indicated.
QKK . Valuation of businesses
QKP . Incorporation of businesses
. . * Formation of business as a legal entity.
. . *Agents*
QKP 38 . . . Promoters
. . *Elements*
. . . * For Company names, see SBO Q9U I.
QKP J . . . Memorandum of association, articles of association, certificate of incorporation (Am.)
QKP K . . . . Table A
. . . . . * Model articles of association
QKP L . . . . Other tables
QKP M . . . Objects clause
QKP P . . . . Ultra vires
QKP Q . . . De facto incorporation (Am.)
QKP X . Disincorporation

Company law

[Types of enterprises by structure & ownership]
[Business enterprises SBOG]
[Types by sector]
[Private sector undertakings SBON]
[Company law SBOQ]
[Formation & reorganization of business SBOQK]
. [Disincorporation SBOQKPX]

SBO QKQ . Reorganization of companies, corporate reorganization
* This class deals with the operations involved in reorganization, etc. For the types of companies which may result from these, see SBO T/SBO X.
* For nationalization, see SBO IMU.
QKV . . Insider deals
QL . . Combination of businesses
* Add to SBO QL letters C/L following TTW; e.g.
QLE . . . Mergers, amalgamations, amalgamations, consolidation of companies
QLG . . . Takeovers
QLG T . . . . Management buyouts
QLH . . Divestiture, divestment
QLK . Failure of businesses
QLL . . Bankruptcy
QLN . . Winding-up, liquidation, dissolution

QM Special operations
* Add to SBO QM letters D/U following SBO H so far as applicable; e.g.
QMD . Government reorganization of companies

QP Other resources in company management
* Add to SBO QP letters U/YG following T; e.g. Labour force SBO QPU; Production management SBO QPV.

QS *Types of companies*
* For Incorporated companies in general, use SBO Q.
* Add to SBO Q letters U/X following TMQ.
* Add to SBO letters R/X following TM, with the adjustments indicated.
QU . Quoted companies
QW . Registered companies
QX . . Joint-stock companies
* If distinguished from the general class SBO Q.
RB . . Private companies
RD . . . Limited private companies
RF . . . Unlimited private companies

[Types of enterprises by structure & ownership]
[Private sector undertakings SBON]
[Company law SBOQ]
. [Types of companies SBOQS]
. . [Registered companies SBOQW]
. . . [Private companies SBORB]
. . . . [Unlimited private companies SBORF]

SBO RH . . . Close companies
RJ . . . Public companies
RU . . . . Limited by guarantee
RV . . . Unlimited companies
S . . Combines, industrial combinations, cartels, industrial trusts (Am.)
T . . Conglomerate corporations
TX . . Holding companies
UD . . Subsidiary companies
UM . . Consortia, groups of companies
* Temporary groupings to undertake large-scale works.
UV . . Joint ventures
* At least one foreign enterprise combining with a local one.
V . . Multinational companies, international business enterprises (Am.)
VX . . Global companies

W Cooperative societies, cooperatives
* For cooperative ownership of dwellings, see SBK QG.
WU . Industrial & provident societies (general)
WV . Producers' cooperatives, industrial cooperatives
XB . . Marketing boards
XD . . Workers' producer cooperatives, integral cooperatives
XF . . Professional producer cooperatives
XH . . Agricultural cooperatives
XJ . Trading cooperatives
XK . . Wholesale cooperatives
XM . . Retail cooperatives

XR Other private organizations
* Arrange A/Z.

Economic & business enterprises by product
. * The rules for retroactive synthesis given at SBN do
. not apply to particular industries; see the special
. provision made for Transport (SBP) & Agriculture
. (SBQ T).

SBO Y . Transport & communications law

SBP . . Transport law, carriage of goods &
. . passengers
. . . * Nearly all the literature relating to the earlier
. . . facets (i.e. preceding Types of transport)
. . . concerns those facets as found within a particular
. . . type of transport (e.g. sea transport) . The
. . . detailed schedule in SBP is applicable to each
. . . type; see SBQ A Sea transport for an example.
. . . * See also International law of transport SDB P.
. . . * Add to SBP and to all the specific forms of
. . . transport in SBP VY/SBQ I as follows (where
. . . the hyphen represents the classmark added to):
. . . * Add to - numbers 2/9 & letters A/H in
. . . Auxiliary Schedule S1, but including the special
. . . use of 9U given at SBN 9U.
. . . * Add to -I letters I/Y in Auxiliary Schedule S1,
. . . so far as applicable.

SBP 9UC . . . Regulation
9UD . . . . Regulatory agencies
9UE . . . . . Persons
9UF . . . . . Organizations
. . . . *Operations*
9UH . . . . . Registration, licensing
9UI . . . . . Identification (tranport law)
9UJ . . . . . Inspection
. . . . . . * For investigation of accidents, see
. . . . . . SBP PQ.
. . . . . . Personnel
9UJ E . . . . Inspectors
9UK . . . . . Testing
9UL . . . . . Enforcement of transport regulations
9UM S . . . . . Stopping & arrest
9UP . . . . . Government regulation
9UR . . . . . Self-regulation
9UT . . . . . Planning
. . . . . . * Alternative (not recommended) to
. . . . . . treating separately under Planning law
. . . . . . SBK QQ.
. . . . . . * If this option is taken, planning law will
. . . . . . be distributed under the particular forms
. . . . . . of transport; e.g. Railway transport
. . . . . . planning SBQ E9U T.
E . . . Contract
. . . . * For contracts of carriage, see SBP UE.
G . . . Tort
GDG . . . . Liability
. . . . . * For transport accidents, see SBP P.
GN . . . . . Personal injuries (transport liability)
GS . . . . . Damage to property (transport
. . . . . liability)

[Economic & business enterprises by product]
[Transport & communications law SBOY]
[Transport law SBP]
[Tort SBPG]
. [Liability SBPGDG]
. . [Damage to property transport liability SBPGS]

SBP I *Other branches of law in relation to transport*
INH . Insurance
. . * For transport insurance, see SBN HPY.
IX . Constitutional law
IXC W . . Rights of transport personnel
IXK . . Public administration
. . . * For regulation of transport, use SBP 9UC.

Agents of transport operations
. * For vehicles and supporting infrastructure, see
. SBP QN; for forwarding agents, see Carriers
. SBP TR.
JN . Owners
JP . Operators
JT . Others agents
. . * For example, agents ashore (marine transport)
. . SBQ AJT.
KA . Personnel
. . * Add to SBP K letters B/VD following SBN L.
KVW . . *Types by general characteristics*
. . . * Add to SBP KV letters W/Y following
. . . SBN L.
. . *Types special to transport*
KW . . . Drivers, main operators of vehicles
KX . . . Other technical personnel
KY . . . Other personnel

Operations & processes
LB . Routes
LD . Traffic
LD9 UC . . Regulation
. . . * For traffic control, use SBP LE; for traffic
. . . offences, see Operation of vehicle SBP N.
. . . * For regulation as an operation designed to
. . . improve the efficiency of traffic movement, see
. . . Transport technology in Class U/V.
LE . . Traffic control, control of traffic
. . . Codes
LE5 N . . . . Traffic rules
LH . . . Control systems
LJ . . . . Automatic aids
LL . . . . Signalling systems
LN . . . . Warning systems
LQ . . . . Tracking
LX . . . . Special hazards
. . . . . * For example, low-flying aircraft in air
. . . . . transport.

Transport law

[Transport & communications law SBOY]
[Transport law SBP]
[Operations & processes]
. [Traffic SBPLD]
. . [Traffic control SBPLE]
. . . [Control systems SBPLH]
. . . . [Special hazards SBPLX]

SBP M . . Operation of vehicles
. . . * Driving, navigating, etc.
MN . . . Control systems
MO . . . . Automatic aids
NK . . . Speed limits
NP . . . Parking & stopping
NX . . . Other operations
. . . . * Arrange A/Z.
O . . Safety
P . . . Accidents
PQ . . . . Investigation of accidents
PR . . . . Collision
PS . . . . Fire & explosions
PV . . . . Special to particular transport forms
QE . . Environmental effects
QF . . . Pollution by vehicles
QI . Searches of vehicles
QJ . Tolls
QL . Charges, fares

QN Infrastructure & vehicles in general
QO . Design requirements
QR . Transport infrastructure
. . * This is nearly always considered in relation to a particular transport form - e.g. roads in land transport, harbours in sea transport, etc. This class takes only the concepts in general.
. . * See also Traffic control systems SBP LH
QS . . Track
. . . * Roads, railway tracks, airlanes, etc.
QTC . . . Accessories to track
QTE . . . . Bridges
QTG . . . . Tunnels
QTJ . . . . . Other
. . . . . . * See Road transport for an example of special accessories (at SBQ DQT C).
QU . . . *Types of track*
QV . . Stations, terminals
QX . . Accessories special to particular transport forms
. . . * E.g. canal locks.
QY . Users other than vehicles
. . * Notably, pedestrians in road transport (SBQ DQY).
R . Vehicles
RO . . Safety standards
. . *Properties*
RU . . . Condition of vehicle

[Economic & business enterprises by product]
[Transport & communications law SBOY]
[Transport law SBP]
[Infrastructure & vehicles in general SBPQN]
. [Vehicles SBPR]
. . [Properties]
. . . [Condition of vehicle SBPRU]

SBP RV . . . Faulty construction
RX . . . *Special to a particular part/type of vehicle*

. . *Parts of vehicles*
SB . . . Body, hull, etc.
SC . . . Machinery
SD . . . . Electrical equipment
SE . . . . Automatic equipment
SF . . . . *By special function*
. . . . . * Arrange A/Z.
SG . . *Types*
. . . * For goods & passenger vehicles, see SBP UR.
. . . *By ownership*
SH . . . . Private vehicles
SI . . . . Other
. . . . . * Arrange A/Z.
SJ . . . . Nationality of ships
SK . . . *By propulsion method*
SL . . . . Nuclear vehicles
SN . . . *Special to form of transport*
. . . . * E.g. containers (goods vehicles).

Types of transport by contractual characteristics
TC . Carriers
TD . . Common carriers
TF . . Ferries
. . . * See Maritime transport SBQ ATF
TP . . Private carriers
TR . . Forwarding agents

Types of transport by thing carried
TY . Carriage of goods & passengers together
U . . Carriage of goods, goods transport
UQL . . . Charges
UQM . . . . Cash on delivery
UR . . . Vehicles
UU . . . Tare
. . . . * Weight of container or vehicle, as distinct from net weight.
UV . . . Goods
. . . . *Types of goods*
UW . . . . . Dangerous goods
UX . . . . . Animals
UY . . . . . Other transport goods
. . . . . . * Arrange A/Z.

[Transport law SBP]
[Types of transport by thing carried]
. [Carriage of goods & passengers together SBPTY]
. . [Carriage of goods SBPU]
. . . [Goods SBPUV]
. . . . [Types of goods]
. . . . . [Other transport goods SBPUY]

SBP V . . Carriage of passengers, passenger
. . transport law
VV . . . Luggage
VW . . . Passengers
VX . . . *Types of passengers*
. . . . * Arrange A/Z.
VXS . . . Stowaways

Types of transport by medium
. * Each type is divided like SBP Transport in
. general. with the adjustments indicated under
. particular types.
VY . *Mixed medium*
W . . Hovercraft
X . Water transport law
. . * See also Water resources planning SBK TX
Y . . International waters (general)
. . . * See also International law SDB PY

SBQ A . . Maritime law, sea transport law, ocean
. . transport law, shipping law, high
. . seas law
. . . * For law of the sea (international waters, etc.)
. . . see SDB QA; for Rhodian laws, etc. see
. . . SDB QA5 A7U.
. . . * For Admiralty law, see Courts
. . . SBQ A7W 6H.

. . . Codes
A5Q . . . . Maritime laws
. . . . . * For Rhodian laws, etc. see
. . . . . SDB QA5 A7U.
A6E . . . Courts & court procedure
A7W . . . . Admiralty Court
. . . . . Jurisdiction
A7W 6H . . . . . . Admiralty law
A8 . . . Actions
. . . . Actions in rem
A9S L . . . . . Arrest of ships
A9U C . . . Regulation
A9U H . . . . Ships' registration
. . . . . * For flags of convenience, see
. . . . . SBQ ASJ P.
A9U I . . . . Identification
A9U IR . . . . . Ships' papers
A9U IS . . . . . Flags
AFP . . . Guaranty
AFQ V . . . . Hypothecation, ship mortgages
AFQ VS . . . . . Maritime lien
AFQ X . . . . . Bottomry

[Transport law SBP]
[Types of transport by medium]
[Water transport law SBPX]
[Maritime law SBQA]
[Guaranty SBQAFP]
. [Hypothecation SBQAFQV]
. . [Bottomry SBQAFQX]

. . . * Hypothecation of ship itself.
SBQ AFQ Y . . Respondentia
. . . * Hypothecation of cargo alone.
AG Tort
AGD G . Liability
Insurance
AHQ . Maritime insurance, marine insurance
. . * Alternative (not recommended) to locating
. . under insurance law SBN HQ.

Agents of operations
. Owners & operators
AJN . . Shipowners
AJT . . Agents ashore
. Personnel
AKA . . Seamen, merchant seamen
AKD . . . Marine unions
AKU W . . . Conditions of work narrowly
AKU WY . . . . Accommodation on shipboard
. . . . Citizenship rights
AKY PB . . . . Welfare in port

Operations & processes
ALD . Sea traffic
ALE . . Control of sea traffic
. . . Codes
ALF . . . . Rules of the road at sea
ALN . . . Lighthouses & lightships
ALP . . . Pilotage
AM . . Navigation
AMO . . . Automated navigation
AMP . . . . Automatic pilots
AO . . Safety at sea in general
. . . * See also Vessels SBQ ARO
AP . . . Accidents
APR . . . . Collision at sea
APV . . . . Abandonment of ship
APW . . . . Assistance & salvage
APW S . . . . . By ship
APW T . . . . . . Lifeboats
APW V . . . . . Air-sea rescue
AQA . . . . . Salvage
AQB . . . . . . Towage
AQB T . . . . Tugs
AQB V . . . . . . Divers
AQB W . . . . . . Wrecks
AQE . . Environmental effects
AQF . . Pollution by sea transport
AQH . . Searches of ships
. . . * See International law SDB QAQ H

[Transport law SBP]
[Types of transport by medium]
[Water transport law SBPX]
[Maritime law SBQA]
[Operations & processes]
. [Sea traffic SBQALD]
. . [Searches of ships SBQAQH]

SBQ AQN *Infrastructure & vehicles*
AQR . Infrastructure
AQT . . Sea lanes
AQV . . Ports & harbours
AQV S . . . Harbourmasters
AQV T . . . Port charges
AQV U . . . . Tonnage fees
AQV W . . . Docks

AR . Ships, vessels
ARO . . Safety
ARO 9UC . . . Regulation
ARO 9UQ . . . . Maritime Safety Committee of the Intergovernmental Maritime Consultative Organization
. . . Personnel
ARO KA . . . . Manning requirements
ARO P . . . Hazards
ARO PS . . . . Fire & fire prevention
ARO PV . . . . Infestation control
ARO PW . . . . Tonnage measures
ARO PX . . . . Loadline

. . *Parts of vessels*
ASC . . . Machinery & equipment
ASE . . . . Electrical installations
ASF . . . . Automated equipment

. . *Types of vessels*
. . . *By owner*
ASI . . . . State owned vessels
ASJ . . . . . Nationality (ships)
ASJ P . . . . . . Flags of convenience
. . . *By propulsion*
ASL . . . . Nuclear-powered ships
. . . *By special function*
ASN . . . . Submarines
. . . . . * Commercial only; for military submarines see International law SDW NR.
ASO . . . . Offshore support vessels
ASP . . . . Pleasure craft
ASQ . . . . . Yachts

Types of services by contract characteristics
ATD . Common carriers
ATF . . Ferries
ATP . Private carriers
Types of services by thing carried

[Economic & business enterprises by product]
[Transport & communications law SBOY]
[Transport law SBP]
[Types of transport by medium]
[Water transport law SBPX]
[Maritime law SBQA]
[Types of services by thing carried]

SBQ AU Carriage of goods by sea
AUE . Contract
. . * For C.i.f. and F.o.b. clauses, see Sale of goods contracts SBN XP9 XFE; for Maritime liens, see SBQ AFQ VS.
AUF F . . Affreightment
. . . * For Hague rules (1921) and Hamburg rules (1978) see International law SDB QAU FF5.
AUF G . . . Freight
. . . . * Money paid by a charterer or shipper to a shipowner for the use of his ship, or space on it, for the carriage of goods.
AUF H . . . . *Types of freight*
. . . . . * Arrange A/Z.
. . . . . * E.g. dead freight.
AUF I . . . Ocean bills of lading
. . . . * For Hague Rules (1921) see SDB QAU FF5.
AUF J . . . Charter parties
AUF KE . . . . Voyage charter
AUF KG . . . . Time charter
AUF KH . . . . . Lay days, laytime
AUF KJ . . . . . Demurrage
. *Agents*
. . * For Ocean freight forwarders, see Carriers SBQ AUT R.
AUJ YB . . Agents ashore
AUJ YD . . Shipbrokers
AUJ YF . . Transit agents
AUJ YH . . Stevedores
. *By contractual characteristics*
AUT C . . Carriers
. . . Forwarding agents
AUT R . . . . Ocean freight forwarders
. *By goods carried*
AUV . . Cargoes
AUW . . . Dangerous cargoes
AUY . . . *Specific types of goods*
. . . . * Arrange A/Z.
AUY GR . . . . Grain
AUY OI . . . . Oil

[Transport law SBP]
[Types of transport by medium]
[Water transport law SBPX]
. [Maritime law SBQA]
. . [Types of services by thing carried]
. . . [Carriage of goods by sea SBQAU]
. . . . . . [Specific types of goods SBQAUY]
. . . . [Oil SBQAUYOI]

SBQ AUY OIS N . . . . Tankers
AUY TI . . . . Timber cargoes, lumber cargoes
AV . . . Carriage of passengers by sea

. *Other forms of water transport*
BB . . Domestic shipping, coastal shipping
. . . * Includes works covering domestic services using inland waterways as well as sea.
BD . . Inland water transport
BE . . . River & lake transport
BEX . . . . Lake transport
. . . . . * If distinguished from river and lake transport.
BF . . . Canal transport
BH . . . International waterways transport
. . . . * For international status, control, etc., see International law SDB Q; for international waters (general), see SDB QBH.
. . . . * For individual rivers, see the region concerned (in international law) SDK NU.

. *Other water-based business*
BJ . . Fisheries
BK . . . Non-tidal water fisheries, private fisheries
BL . . . Tidal water fisheries, inshore fisheries
BM . . . High seas fisheries
. . . . Personnel
BMK . . . . . Fishermen
. . . . Environmental effects
BMQ E . . . . . Conservation laws for fish
BMR . . . . Fishing boats, factory ships
BP . . . *By type of fish*
. . . . * Arrange A/Z.
BS . . Seabed exploitation

C Land transport, inland transport (general)
CQN . Infrastructure & vehicles
CQP . . Landscape
CQU B . . Bridges
CQU D . . Tunnels
CQU F . . . Underwater tunnels
CR . . Vehicles
. . . * See particular forms of land tranport below.

[Economic & business enterprises by product]
[Transport & communications law SBOY]
[Transport law SBP]
[Types of transport by medium]
[Land transport SBQC]
[Infrastructure & vehicles SBQCQN]
. [Vehicles SBQCR]

SBQ D Road transport law, highway transport law
DKW . Drivers of road vehicles
DKW JP . . Licensing
DKW JT . . Testing
DLD . Road traffic in general, motor traffic
DLH . . Control systems
DLL . . . Signalling
DLM . . . . Road signs
DLN . . . . Traffic lights
DM . . Driving
. . . * For road traffic offences, see SBW UA.
DNK . . . Speed limits
DNP . . . Stopping & parking
DO . . Safety
DP . . . Accidents on road
DQJ . . Tolls

DQR . Infrastructure
DQS . . Roads, highways
DQT C . . . Accessory structures
. . . . * See also Traffic control systems SBQ DLH
. . . . *Special accessories*
DQT L . . . . . Lighting
DQT N . . . . . Verges of roads, sidewalks, pavement
DQT P . . . . . Pedestrian crossings
DQT S . . . . . Road signs
DQT T . . . . . Road works
DQT W . . . . . Traffic wardens
. . . *Types of roads*
DQU B . . . . Private roads
DQU D . . . . Unadopted roads
DQU F . . . . Motorways
. *Users other than vehicles*
DQY . . Pedestrians

DR . Motor vehicles, motor cars, automobiles, private cars
DRJ P . . Licensing
DRJ T . . Testing
. . *Types by contract characteristics*
DTC . . . Common carriers
DTP . . . Private cars
DTT . . . Caravans, trailers
. . *Types by thing carried*
. . . Carriage of goods by road

[Transport law SBP]
[Types of transport by medium]
[Land transport SBQC]
. [Road transport law SBQD]
. . [Motor vehicles SBQDR]
. . . [Types by thing carried]
. . . . [Carriage of goods by road]

SBQ DU . . . . . Road haulage
. . . . . Operators
DUJ WP . . . . . . Hauliers
DUR . . . . . Goods motor vehicles, lorries, trucks
DUS N . . . . . . Light goods vehicles
DUS P . . . . . . Heavy goods vehicles
DUS R . . . . . . Containers (road haulage)
DV . . . . Carriage of passengers by road
. . . . . * For private passenger cars, see SBQ DR.
DVS N . . . . . Buses, coaches
DVS P . . . . . . School buses
DVS Q . . . . . Tramways, street railways
DVS T . . . . . Taxicabs, hired cars

DVS V . . Motorbikes
DVS W . . Bicycles

E . Railway transport law
ELD . . Traffic
ELH . . . Control systems
ELL . . . . Signalling systems
EQR . . Infrastructure
EQS . . . Permanent way
EQW . . . Stations
EQX B . . . Frontier sections of railway lines
. . Vehicles
ER . . . Rolling stock
. . *Types of railways*
ESN . . . Underground railways
ESP . . . Monorail transport

F Air transport law, aviation law
. *Agents*
FJW . . Airlines, commercial aviation
FK . . Personnel
FKW . . . Aircrew, flight crew
FKW R . . . . Pilots
FKX . . . Cabin crew
. *Operations & Processes*
FLD . . Traffic
FLE . . . Air traffic control, flight control
FLR . . . Low-flying aircraft
FQE . . Environmental effects
FQG . . . Vibration
FQH . . . Noise, sonic boom
. . . . * See also Nuisance (torts) SBG MV
FQK . . Charter flights
FQR . Infrastructure
FQS . . Airlanes
FQV . . Airports

[Economic & business enterprises by product]
[Transport & communications law SBOY]
[Transport law SBP]
[Types of transport by medium]
[Air transport law SBQF]
. [Infrastructure SBQFQR]
. . [Airports SBQFQV]

. Vehicles
SBQ FR . . Aircraft
. . . * Includes all types - lighter-than-air as
. . . well as heavier-than-air.
FRO . . . Safety
FRO P . . . . Airworthiness
. . . *Parts*
FSF . . . . Automatic flying aids
. . . *Types*
. . . . * For heavier-than-air craft, use
. . . . SBR FR.
FSN . . . . Lighter-than-air craft
FSP . . . . . Airships, dirigibles
FSQ . . . . . Balloons

G Space law, aerospace law, space flight law
. * See also International law SDK T
. Vehicles
GR . . Spacecraft, space vehicles
. . . *Operations*
GRL P . . . . Tracking spacecraft
. . . *Types*
GSK . . . . Rockets
GSM . . . . Space shuttle
GSN . . . . Artificial satellites
. . . . . * For satellites serving specific
. . . . . functions, see function - e.g.
. . . . . Telecommunications, Environmental
. . . . . survey.
GSS . . . . . Space stations

Other transport forms
H . Local transit (general)
I . Pipelines

[Economic & business enterprises by product]
[Transport & communications law SBOY]
[Transport law SBP]
. [Types of transport by medium]
. . [Other transport forms]
. . . [Pipelines SBQI]

SBQ L Communications law
. * For freedom of expression, censorship, etc., see
. Human rights law SCD C; for intellectual property,
. see SBL K; for Informations sciences & computer
. law, see SBV 7.
. * Add to SBQ L itself and to the specific forms of
. communication in SBQ M/S as follows (where the
. hyphen represents the classmark added to):
. * Add to - numbers & letters 2/9, A/I in Auxiliary
. Schedule S1 but including the special use of 9U given
. at SBN 9U
. * Add to -J letters J/Y in Auxiliary Schedule S1 so far
. as applicable.
M . Postal service, mail
. . * For offences committed through the mail, see
. . Criminal law SBW WN.
. . * See also International law of postal services
. . SDB QM (including Universal Postal Union).
MP . . Rates of postage
. . *Classes of mail*
. . . * For postal orders, etc. see Money SBN FXR W.
MQ . . . Parcel post
MR . . . Foreign mail
MS . . . Surface mail
MT . . . Airmail post
MU . . . Registered post
MV . . . Insured mail
MW . . Non-mailable merchandise
MX . . Private postal services

N . Publications (general), publishing
. . * Communicating & making available to the public.
. . * For copyright, see SBL K; for defamation, see
. . SBG NV and SBW HNV (as criminal offence).
NP . . Right of reply in publications
. . *By medium*
. . . * Each medium may be qualified like SBQ N.
O . . . Mass media (general), media law
ONP . . . . Right of reply
OT . . . Printed matter (general)
OV . . . . Books, bookselling
P . . . . The Press
. . . . . * For freedom of the press, see Human rights
. . . . . SCD C
. . . . . * See also Libel & slander SBG O and
. . . . . SBW HO (as criminal offence); Copyright
. . . . . SBL K; Official secrets SCL VS
PNP . . . . . Right of reply

[Transport & communications law SBOY]
[Communications law SBQL]
[Publications general SBQN]
. [By medium]
. . [Printed matter general SBQOT]
. . . [The Press SBQP]
. . . . [Right of reply SBQPNP]

SBQ PS . . . . Newspapers
. . . . . * Many works treat these as virtually
. . . . . synonymous with the Press in general.
. . . . . Locate here only those which exclude the
. . . . . periodicals press.
PV . . . . Periodicals, magazines, journals
. . . . . * See note under Newspapers above.

Q Telecommunications law
QR . Telegraphy, teletype
QS . . Submarine telegraph, submarine cables
QT . Telephones
QU . . Radio telephones
QV . . Telex
QX . . Fax
QYE . Electronic mail

R . Broadcasting, radio & television
. . * See also Performing arts law SBV WY
RNP . . Right to reply
RNW L . . Advertising
. . Selling time
RNX GT . . . License fees
RNX GV . . . Advertising fees
RS . . Frequencies allocation, wavelengths
. . . *Agencies*
RST . . . . International Frequencies
. . . . Registration Board
RTB . . Broadcasting stations
RTC . . . Receivers
RTE . . . Cable transmission
RTF . . . Satellite transmission
RTP . . Programmes
RTQ . . . *Particular forms or subjects*
. . . . * Arrange A/Z.
. . . . * For example, religious broadcasting.
RV . . Radio broadcasting
RVT B . . . Stations
RVT J . . . . Aeronautical radio stations
RVT L . . . . Mobile radio stations
RVT N . . . . Amateur radio, citizens' band radio,
. . . . CB radio
S . . Television broadcasting
STB . . . Stations
STE . . . . Cable television
STF . . . . Satellite television

[Economic & business enterprises by product]
[Transport & communications law SBOY]
. . [Telecommunications law SBQQ]
. . . [Broadcasting SBQR]
. . . . [Television broadcasting SBQS]
. . . . . [Stations SBQSTB]
. . . . . . [Satellite television SBQSTF]

SBQ SY Agriculture & industry together
. * Add to SBQ SY and to all the specific forms of industry in SBQ T/Y as follows (where the hyphen represents the classmark added to):
. * Add to - numbers & letters 2/9, A/N in Auxiliary Schedule S1.
. * Add to -O letters O/Y in Auxiliary Schedule S1 so far as applicable.

T Agriculture
TE . Contracts
TH . Property
TI . . Inheritance & succession
TJ . . Real property
. . . Tenure
TJH J . . . . Farm tenure (general)
. . . Common land
TJM . . . . Countryside rights of public
TJM P . . . . . Footpath rights
TJQ T . . . Entail
. . . . Leasehold interest
TJR . . . . . Agricultural holdings
TJR T . . . . . . Metayer system
TJR V . . . . . . Emphyteusis

TNA B . Government intervention
TNA GR . . Grants
TNA HD . . Production controls, quotas
TND T . . Price regulation
TND TAI B . . . Price supports
. Credit
TNG . . Agricultural credit
TNG IM . . . Farm loans institutions
TNV . Production management
TNV FR . . Leasing farm equipment
TNW . Marketing
TNW GY . . Product standards, grading products

TO . *Other substantive law in agriculture*
. . * Add to SBQ TO letters O/Y in Auxiliary Schedule S1 so far as applicable.

. *Specific agricultural products*
. . * The notation for these is not yet finalized. Provisional arrangement may be A/Z under the following categories.
TP . . *Crops by product utility*
. . . * E.g. food crops, medicinal, industrial (oil-yielding, etc.).
TQ . . *Crops by quasi-taxonomic categories*

[Economic & business enterprises by product]
. [Agriculture SBQT]
. . [Specific agricultural products]
. . . [Crops by quasi-taxonomic categories SBQTQ]

. . . . * E.g. grain crops, fruit crops, vegetables.
SBQ TR . . . Horticultural products
TS . . . Animal husbandry, livestock farming
TT . . . . *Particular kinds of livestock*
TU . . . Dairy farming
. . . . *Particular products*
TUM . . . . . Milk & milk products
TUP . . . . . Poultry
TUR . . . . . Other
. . . . . . * Arrange A/Z.
TV . Veterinary science
TW . Forestry
TX . Wildlife exploitation, game laws
. . * For Fishing, see SBQ BJ.

Other forms of enterprise by product
. * Each specific industry may be divided analogously to Agriculture SBQ T.
U . Industrial law, technologies
. . * For industrial law in its narrower connotation, see Labour law SBN L.
. . * Add to SBQ letters U/V.
. . * The technology class in BC2 is not yet complete & notation is provisional.
UM . . Energy technology (general)
UMT . . . Alternative energy sources
. . . . * Arrange A/Z.
. . . . * For example, tidal power.
UO . . . Nuclear energy
UP . . . Electronic & electrical energy
VG . . Mining, mineral extraction technology
VGR . . . Concessions
VGS . . . Equipment & use
. . . . * Arrange A/Z.
. . . . * For example, drills.
VGT . . . Prospecting, exploration
VGW . . . Seabed mining
VHB . . . Solid fuels extraction
VHC . . . . Coal mining
VHM . . . Metals mining
VHN . . . . Iron mining
VHP . . . . Non-ferrous metals mining
. . . . . * Arrange A/Z.
VHR . . . . Radioactive metals mining
VHT . . . Non-metals mining
VHU . . . . Quarrying
VHW . . . . Precious stones mining, semi-precious stones mining
VI . . . Oil & gas extraction, petroleum extraction
. . . . * For petroleum refining, etc., see SBQ VK.
VI . . . . Safety
VIG S . . . . Equipment

. . [Other forms of enterprise by product]
. . . [Industrial law SBQU]
. . . . [Mining SBQVG]
. . . . . [Oil & gas extraction SBQVI]
. . . . . . [Equipment SBQVIGS]

SBQ VIG SR . . . . Oilrigs
VIO . . . . . . Offshore oil extraction
VIS . . . . . . Gas extraction
VJ . . . . Process industrial technology, chemical technology
VK . . . . . Petroleum technology
VL . . . . . Polymer technology
VM . . . . . Fuel & explosives technology
VP . . . . . Pharmaceutical technology

W . . . Service industries (general), retail industries
. . . . * For specific services, see function; e.g. Banking services SBN FG.
X . . . . Special services
. . . . . * Arrange A/Z.
. . . . . * Alternative (not recommended) to distributing under function.
Y . . Other forms of enterprises
. . . * Add to SBQ Y numbers & letters 4/9, A/Z from the whole classification.

SBS Environmental law, ecology law, protection of environment
. * Regulation of activities which threaten the quality of the environment (for all forms of life other than pathogenic forms) by excessive exploitation, pollution, etc. In the widest sense, includes town and country planning; but this is preferred with real property law (SBK). This clas takes completely general works (i.e. those dealing with environmental and planning law together).
. * An alternative (not recommended) is provided at SBJ X.
. * See also Town & country planning SBK; public health SBT G; Population policy SBV KB.
. * Add to SBS numbers & letters 2/9, A/N in Auxiliary Schedule S1.
. * Add to SBS O letters O/Y in Auxiliary Schedule so far as applicable.
. *Agents*
SBS PE . . Earth resources survey satellites
. *Operations*
PH . . Control & protection of environment
PI . . . Inspection
Objects of control
PN . Dangerous substances
. . * An alternative (not recommended) is to locate under public health & safety SBT LP.
PQ . . Radioactive substances
PR . . . Nuclear wastes,
PRS . . . . Reprocessing nuclear materials

[Objects of control]
[Dangerous substances SBSPN]
. [Radioactive substances SBSPQ]
. . [Nuclear wastes SBSPR]
. . . [Reprocessing nuclear materials SBSPRS]

SBS PT . Toxic substances
PU . . Specific poisons
. . . * Arrange A/Z.
Q Waste control
QQ . Re-use of wastes, recycling
QS . Sewage
QT . Refuse disposal
QU . . Domestic wastes
QV . . Industrial wastes
QW . Litter

R Pollution control (general)
. * See also Public health hazards SBT J and the note there.
. *By source*
RR . . Industrial pollution control
RS . . Domestic pollution control
RT . . Radiation pollution control
RU . . Chemical pollution control
RV . . . Specific substances
. . . . * Arrange A/Z.
RX . . Smells, odours
S . . Noise pollution control
ST . . . Sonic boom
. *By location*
. . * See also the general class for control of resources in Town & country planning SBK.
T . . Land pollution control, ground pollution control,
U . . Water pollution control
UT . . . Land-based water pollution
UV . . . Sea pollution
V . . Air pollution control, atmosphere pollution control

W Conservation of natural resources
. * Conservation for narrowly economic purposes (e.g. of fisheries stock) goes with the economic activity.
WP . Sustainability of resources
WR . Limitation of use of a resource
WT . Renewal of resources

X *Resources controlled*
. * For conservation of cultural property, see SBV KKT; of archeological and historical sites, etc., see SBK NS.
. * Add to SBSX numbers & letters 3/9, A/Z from the whole classification.
XD . Nature reserves, Sites of Special Scientific Interest, SSSI
XEG O . Ecology
XEH T . Wildlife conservation

[Objects of control]
. [Resources controlled SBSX]
. . [Wildlife conservation SBSXEHT]

SBS XEJ B . . Endangered species
XF . . Plant species conservation
XG . . Animal species conservation

Y . Town & country planning
. . * Alternative (not recommended) to locating with real property law (SBK).

SBT A Social law & legislation, social services law
. * Law primarily concerned with regulation of a number of basic social conditions and relations.
. * The preferred arrangement in BC2 is to subordinate the law of special subjects to those subjects, except where it is part of a long-established branch of law (e.g. law of persons, criminal law). Social law is not so firmly established, reflecting social and technological developments which began on a significant scale only in the 19th century.
. * So the schedule below is only an alternative (not recommended) to distributing the law under the special subjects concerned.
. * Add to SBT A and to the specific services in SBT B/Y as follows, unless otherwise instructed (as e.g. at SBT X Psychiatry). The hyphen represents the classmark added to:
. * Add to - numbers & letters 2/9, A/G in Auxiliary Schedule S1, but including the special use of -9U given at SBN 9U.
. * Add to -H letters H/Y in Auxiliary Schedule S1, except XKK (Actions of administrative agencies) which is provided for by -9U.

A9U C . Regulation of services in social law
. . *Agents*
A9U E . . . Persons
A9U F . . . Organizations
. . *Operations*
A9U H . . . Registration in social services, licensing in social services
A9U J . . . Inspection in social services
A9U K . . . Testing in social services
A9U L . . . Enforcement in social services
A9U M . . . . Special forms of enforcement
A9U P . . . Government regulation of social services
A9U R . . . Self-regulation of social services

B . Health & medicine law
. . * The following schedule follows closely the order of classes in HH/HY Medicine, but with substantial modifications to notation.
. . * For Medical jurisprudence, see S8X.
BJ . . Medical research
. . . * See also Biological research SBV E.

[Social law & legislation SBTA]
[Health & medicine law SBTB]
[Medical research SBTBJ]

SBT BL Medical experiments
BQ Human biology research
BR . Tissue, histology
BS . Embryology
BV . Genetics
. . * See also Genetic engineering SBV GRX F

C . Medical personnel, doctors
. . * Add to SBT D numbers & letters 2/9, A/Y following SBN L.
C34 G . . Training of medical personnel
D Medical practice
D9U C . Regulation
. . Registration
D9U H . . . Right to practice
. Liability torts
DGK . . Negligence
DGL R . . Malpractice in medicine, medical compensation
DHN L . Labour law
. . * For medical personnel, use SBT C.
DQ . Ethics
DT . Medical records

F Preventive medicine, health & safety (general), health, environmental health & safety
G . Public health & hygiene & safety
. . * See also Environmental law & pollution SBS
. . Registration
G9U H . . . Certification
G9U J . . Inspection
G9U L . . Enforcement
G9U P . . Government regulation
GX . . Health promotion, health education
H . . Control measures (public health & safety)
HR . . . Health standards
HT . . . Environmental design & planning (health & safety)
. . . . * Primarily design for safety - see SBT L.
HV . . . Supply of dangerous goods, sale of dangerous goods
. . . . * Most of the literature refers to food & drugs; see SBT K.
HW . . . Control of incidence of hazards
. . . . * E.g. control of outbreak of infections.
HX . . . Zones for health & safety

[Social law & legislation SBTA]
[Health & medicine law SBTB]
[Preventive medicine SBTF]
[Public health & hygiene & safety SBTG]
[Control measures public health & safety SBTH]
. [Zones for health & safety SBTHX]

SBT HY Hazards in public health
. * Factors affecting public health which are susceptible to public regulation.
. * For these hazards in particular types of establishments, etc., see SBT LT; for contagious diseases, see SBT Q.
IB . Sanitation
. . *Particular sources*
ID . . . Heating & ventilation
IDR . . . . Air conditioning
IE . . . Refrigeration systems
IF . . . Water supply
IG . . . Cleansing facilities
. . . . * For Toilet facilities, see SBT KXH.
IJ . . . Vermin (public health)
J . Pollution
. . * Public health regulation only; for pollution in general, see Environmental law SBS R.
. . * An alternative (not recommended) is to locate here those subclasses when they refer narrowly to human health. In this case, proceed as follows:
. . * Add to SBTJ letters P/V following SBS; e.g. Sewage (health hazards) SBT JQS.

K . Food, drink & drug laws
K9U J . . Inspection
KL . . Labelling laws, packaging food (public health)
. . . * See also Consumer law SBN XQ
KM . . Additives in food, preservatives in food
KN . . Adulteration
KP . . Specific foodstuffs
. . . * Arrange A/Z.
KQ . . Drinks, beverages
. . . * For alcohol, see SBT KT.
KS . . Drugs
KT . . . Alcohol, liquor laws
KTI H . . . . Licensing hours
KTL . . . . Public drinking of alcohol
KTM . . . . . Public houses
KU . . . Controlled drugs
. . . . * See also Illicit possession (criminal law) SBW QJ
KV . . . . Specific drugs
. . . . . * Arrange A/Z.
KW . . . Tobacco, smoking
KXC . Cosmetics
KXF . Spitting

[Social law & legislation SBTA]
[Health & medicine law SBTB]
[Preventive medicine SBTF]
. [Public health & hygiene & safety SBTG]
. . [Hazards in public health SBTHY]
. . . [Spitting SBTKXF]

SBT KXH . . . Toilet facilities, public conveniences
KY . . . Disposal of the dead, burial, cremation, cemeteries
KYP . . . . Exhumation

L . Safety, accident prevention
. . * See also Product safety (general) SBN VMV; Industrial safety SBN LVA
LI . . Accidents
LJ . . . *By specific cause*
. . . . * Arrange A/Z.
. . . . * E.g. electrical faults.
LK . . Fire prevention & control
LL . . Explosives regulation
LLW . . . Fireworks regulation
LM . . Firearms regulation, guns regulation, weapons regulation
LN . . Dangerous goods
. . . * For dangerous machinery, see SBN LVB.
LO . . Specific dangerous goods
. . . * Arrange A/Z.
LOT . . . Toys (safety regulation)
LP . . Dangerous substances
. . . * Locate here only works dealing with the public health hazard; the main class for dangerous substances is in Environmental law (SBS PN). If in doubt, prefer the latter.
LQ . . . Radioactive substances
LQT . . . . Nuclear waste
LR . . . Poisons, toxic substances
LS . . . . Specific poisons
. . . . . * Arrange A/Z.

LT . . Establishments
. . . * For public houses, see SBT KTM.
LU . . . Hotels & restaurants, inns, motels
LV . . . Public entertainment establishments
LW . . . . Specific types
. . . . . * Arrange A/Z.
. . . . . * E.g., stadia, theatres.
LX . . . Other establishments
. . . . * Arrange A/Z.
LXS . . . . Slaughterhouses

M Curative medicine, medical care
. * For medical personnel, see SBT D; for general practice, see SBT C.
. * Retroactive synthesis within classes SBT M/W follows that in Class H, using the special Auxiliary

[Social law & legislation SBTA]
[Health & medicine law SBTB]
[Curative medicine SBTM]

. Schedules H1/H3.
. * For qualification by legal concepts, folow the
. Add instructions at SBN; e.g. Regulation of
. nursing care SBT MY9 UC.
SBT MN . Medical services (general)
MO . Hospitals
MP . Sanatoria, nursing homes
MU . Patient care, patients
MUD B . . Patients' records
MUF GN . . Rights of patients
. . . * For Consent to treatment, see SBT NPI T.
MY . . Nursing care
N . Clinical medicine
. . * Investigation, diagnosis, treatment of
. . pathological conditions.
NP . . Medical treatment, therapy
. . . * For treatment of specific disorders or organs,
. . . see disorder or organ.
NPI T . . . Consent to treatment, informed consent
NQJ H . . . Euthanasia, right to die
NQL F . . . Permanent life support, prolongation
. . . of life, vegetative state
NV . . . Drug treatment, chemotherapies
. . . . * For drug addiction, see SBT T.
NVM Q . . . . Prescriptions
NXE R . . . . Proprietary medicines
OA . . . . Specific drugs
. . . . . * Arrange A/Z.
OL . . . Surgery
OQ . . . . Transplant surgery
OQF V . . . . . Donation of organs
OWQ . Alternative medicine
OXC . . Homeopathy

P Death
PQ . Autopsy
PR . Proof of death, certification of death
PS . Causes of death
Specific disorders & diseases
Q . Communicable diseases, infectious
. diseases, notifiable diseases,
. contagious diseases
. . Special regulations
QS . . . Isolation, quarantine
QT . . . Vaccination, immunization
. . Specific communicable diseases
QV . . . Venereal diseases, sexually transmitted
. . . diseases
QW . . . Other communicable diseases
. . . . * Arrange A/Z.
R . Other disorders
. . * Add to SBTR letters A/S & U/X following HS
. . in HSA/HSX.
RY . . Addictive disorders

[Social law & legislation SBTA]
[Health & medicine law SBTB]
. [Specific disorders & diseases]
. . [Other disorders SBTR]
. . . [Addictive disorders SBTRY]

SBT S . . . . Alcoholism
T . . . . Drug dependency
TB . . . . . Specific drugs
. . . . . . * Add to SBT T letters B/X following
. . . . . . IWN in IWNB/IWNX.

U . *Parts of the body*
. . * Add to SBTU letters T/X following H in HT/HX
UUL . . Blood transfusion
UXA . . Reproductive system
. *Types of patients*
. . * Add to SBTV letters D/Y following HX in
. . HXD/HXY.
. . * Add to SBTW letters C/S following HY in
. . HYC/HYS.

X . Psychiatry, medical psychology, mental
. health
. . * Retroactive synthesis within class SBT X
. . follows that within Class I Psychology &
. . psychiatry.
. . * For qualification by legal concepts, follow
. . Add instructions at SBN; e.g. Regulation of
. . psychiatric services SBT X9U C; SBT X9X G
. . Torts & psychiatric service.
XBC . . Psychiatric research
XEP . . Psychiatrists
XMN . . Mental health services
XMO . . . Mental hospitals
XMQ . . . Care of psychiatric patients
XO . . Treatment of mental disorders
XS . . Mental patients, mentally ill patients
. . . * For civil status, see SAY E; for criminal
. . . liability, see SBW DM.
XTS . . . Insane people
. . . . Courts
XTS 7W . . . . . Court of Protection
. . . . . . * Administers property & affairs of the
. . . . . . insane.

Y Education law & legislation
. * Alternative (not recommended) to locating in J. If
. this option is taken, proceed as follows:
. * Add to SBT Y letters A/V following J in JA/JV.
. * Retroactive synthesis within class SBT Y follows
. that within Class J Education.
. * For qualification by legal concepts, follow
. Add instructions at SBN; e.g. Regulation of
. admission to schools SBT YDO 9UC.
YD . Management of schools, government of
. schools
YDG . . School finances

[Social law & legislation SBTA]
[Education law & legislation SBTY]
[Management of schools SBTYD]
. [School finances SBTYDG]

SBT YDG J . . Income
YDG K . . . Government grants
YDG Q . . . Fees
YDO . Admission to schools
YDO R . . Discrimination in schools admission
YDO S . . Segregation in education
YDO T . . . Bussing
YDP Compulsory education
YDU Student welfare
YFR V . Counselling of students
YGB . Student assistance
. . Specific forms of assistance
YGB H . . . Financial aid to students, grants to
. . . students
YGB K . . . Other forms of assistance
. . . . * Arrange A/Z.
. . . . * For example, school meals, SBT YGB KM.

YK Curriculum
YKT P . Religion in schools
YL Schools
. * In the common sense of schools serving children to
. the end of the secondary stage and prior to higher
. education.
YLB D Public education, state education, sate
schools
YLB L . Local authority schools
YLB P Private education
YLC G Denominational schools, church schools
YLN Nursery schools
YM Elementary schools, primary schools
YN Secondary schools
YR Higher education
YT Technical education, vocational education

[Social law & legislation SBTA]
[Education law & legislation SBTY]
. [Technical education SBTYT]

SBU Welfare law, social welfare law, public
welfare law, public relief
. * For labour law, see SBN L.
. * Retroactive synthesis within class SBU follows
. that within Class Q Social welfare.
. * Add to SBU letters A/T following Q in QA/QT.
. * For qualification by legal concepts, follow the
. Add instruction at SBN; e.g. Regulation of
. residential care SBU EL9 UC.
. *General principles*
SBU AGR . . Selectivity & universality
. *Agents*
B . . Social workers
B9X DG . . . Liability
C . . Organizations in welfare, welfare
. . agencies
CJ . . . Government welfare agencies
CM . . . Voluntary welfare agencies
. *Operations & processes*
D . . Social work
DDE LT . . Claims to welfare aid
DDE LV . . Appeals

E . Social services, protective welfare services
EL . . Institutional care, residential care
ELL . . . Almshouses, poor houses, workhouses
EN . . Community care, non-institutional care,
. . non-residential care
ENO . . . Day centres
EO . . . Home care, domiciliary care
. . . . * By social work employees.
ERE MS . . Rest homes
. . . * Implying temporary residence only. For
. . . nursing homes, see medical care SBT MP.

F . . Social security, income maintenance
FBC B . . . Abuse of social welfare, false claims
FBC C . . . Claims
FBC D . . . . Persons on welfare, recipients of
. . . . welfare, welfare claimants
FBC F . . . . Appeals
FBC J . . . Welfare rights
. . . . * Includes rules governing payments.
FBC O . . . Means test
FBC QL . . Domicile rules
FBD G . . . People in need, causes of need
FBD W . . . . Carers, voluntary carers, informal
. . . . carers

[Social law & legislation SBTA]
[Welfare law SBU]
[Social services SBUE]
. [Domicile rules SBUFBCQL]
. . [People in need SBUFBDG]
. . . [Carers SBUFBDW]

SBU FBF C . . Social insurance, national insurance
FBF L . . . Overlapping benefits
FBF P . . . Pensions (general)
FBF V . . Non-means-tested benefits
FBG G . . . Unemployment benefits
FBG HB . . . Disablement benefits
FBG J . . . Widows' benefits
FBG P . . . Sickness benefits, invalidity benefits
FBG R . . . Maternity benefits
FBG T . . . Retirement benefits, old age pension,
. . . old persons' benefits
FBH . . . Workmen's compensation, industrial
. . . injuries compensation
. . . . * See also Health & safety at work SBN LUX
FBJ . . Supplementary benefits, public assistance
FBK B . . Family benefits, chilren's benefits
FBL H . . War pensions, ex-servicemen's benefits,
. . military pensions, veterans' pensions
FMD . . Private social security schemes
FSA . *Other forms of aid*
. . * Arrange A/Z.
FSP . . Fuel allowance
FT . . Shelter
FTW Z . . . Assylums, refuges
FXB . Employment aid
. . * Schemes for helping unemployed to gain
. . employment.
. . * See also Employment & unemployment TLO/Q

Causes of need & persons in need
GN . Disaster relief, emergency relief
GV . Poverty relief, poor law
GXH . Unemployment relief
H . Housing welfare law, accommodation
. . * For types of tenancies, see Landlord & tenant
. . SBJ VN/SBJ W.
HH . . Homelessness
. *Persons in need*
. . * Use this class only for general works on these
. . persons as recipients of special social action. For
. . their legal status within particular branches of
. . law (e.g. adopted children) see the branch
. . concerned. If in doubt, prefer the branch.
IR . . Victims of crime
IR9 M . . . Compensation

[Social law & legislation SBTA]
. [Welfare law SBU]
. . [Causes of need & persons in need]
. . . [Persons in need]
. . . . [Victims of crime SBUIR]
. . . . . [Compensation SBUIR9M]

. . . . . . Government agencies
SBU IR9 M3J . . . . Criminal Injuries Compensation
. . . . Board
P . . . Police law
. . . . * See SCN A

W . Employment law, labour law
. . * Alternative (not recommended) to locating
. . with Economics law, at SBN L. If this option is
. . taken, proceed as follows:
. . * Add to SBUW numbers & letters 2/Y following
. . SBN L.

SBV 2 Cultural law
. * Subjects in private law other than those given
. already in S9W/SBU.
. * The classes below (SBV 4/SBV Z) continue the
. provision of alternatives, begun under Social law,
. for those libraries wishing to keep all law together
. in class S; see the note at SBT A.
. * None of the classes below reflects clearly any
. particular branch of law and few of them feature
. prominently in the legal literature. They are given
. in the order of main-classes in BC2 and are easily
. expanded if need be. They are all alternatives (not
. recommended) to the preferred arrangement in
. BC2, which is to subordinate the law of a special
. subject to the subject
. * Add to SBV numbers 4/9, A/Z from the main
. classification, with the adjustments indicated
. below.
. * Retroactive synthesis within the classes
. SBV 4/SBV X follows that within those classes.
. * For qualification of any given class by legal
. concepts, follow the Add instruction at SBN; e.g.
. Regulation of scientific research SBV AYD 9UC.

4 . Knowledge & research in general
. . * Sciences, humanities and arts together.
. . * Add to SBV numbers 4/9 from the main
. . classification (but the notation is provisional).
6A . . Research in general
6J . . . Innovation & discovery (general)
7 . . Information science & technology
. . (general)
. . . * See also Communications law SBQ L
8 . . . Computers (general)
8D . . . . Software (general)
8F . . . . Data storage & processing
8J . . . . Hardware
8N . . . . Data communication

[Cultural law SBV2]
[Knowledge & research in general SBV4]
. [Information science & technology general SBV7]
. . [Computers general SBV8]
. . . [Data communication SBV8N]

SBV 8P . . . . Networks
8V . . . Applications
. . . . * Arrange A/Z.
9 . . Libraries
9M . . Museums & art galleries
9R . . Public records, public archives
9V . . Other institutions devoted to knowledge & information
. . . * E.g. planetaria.

AY Science & technology together
. * Notation is provisional.
AYD . Scientific & technological research
AYM . Scientific instruments & apparatus
AYX . Natural sciences
DH . . Earth sciences
. . . * See also Environmental law SBS
DJ . . . Geological research
DL . . . Atmosphere research
DN . . . . Meteorological services, weather services
DP . . . Oceanographic research
E . . Biological research
. . . * For veterinary science, see SBQ TV; for conservation of wildlife, see SBS XEH T.
GRX . Applied biology, biotechnology
. . * For health, medicine and psychiatry, see SBT; for agriculture, etc., see SBQ T.
GRX AHK . . Ethics of biotechnology
GRX F . . Genetic engineering
GRX G . . . Genetic recombination

K Social processes & structures
. * This class provides for a number of topics relating to features of society not fully provided for otherwise, either by the traditional branches of law or those collocated under social law (SBT/SBU). In particular, it includes matters of social science research, analogous to the provision for the natural sciences in SBV AY. When in doubt, prefer the provision under the branches or under social law.
. * Add to SBV K letters A/Y following K in KA/KY for classes not otherwise provided for.

KB . Population policy, demography
KKT . Cultural property
KKT T . . Protection of cultural property
. . . * See also Heritage conservation SBK NQ
KWB . Customs & observances
KXJ A . . Celebrations, festivals
KXJ D . . . Legal holidays, national holidays

[Cultural law SBV2]
[Social processes & structures SBVK]
. [Customs & observances SBVKWB]
. . [Celebrations SBVKXJA]
. . . [Legal holidays SBVKXJD]

. . . . * See also Employees' leave SBO LUU
SBV KXJ DJ . . . . Bank holidays
KXJ DK . . . . Holy days, Sundays
KXJ DN . . . Parades, processions
. . . . * See also Public meetings SBC WIT
KXJ FB . . . Official ceremonies
KXJ FC . . . . State visits

L Historical research
LEB . Palaeology & epigraphy
. . * See also Public records SBV 9R
LES . Protection of historical property
. . * Alternative (not recommended) to locating with conservation of social heritage at SBK NS.
. . * If this option is taken:
. . * Add to SBV LE letters S/W following SBK N; e.g. SBV LEV Archeological sites.
VX Recreation & arts
VX9 XNT SR . Sponsorship
VY . Recreation
. . * Notation is provisional.
. . * For holidays, see SBV KXJ D; for Recreation areas, see Planning law SBK TB.
VYG . . Outdoor recreations, sports
VYJ . . . Spectator sports
VYJ L . . . Hunting, blood sports
VYJ M . . . . Specific forms
. . . . . * Arrange A/Z.
. . . . . * For example, badger baiting SBV VYJ MBA.
VYS . . Amusements, entertainments
. . . * For performing arts, see SBV WY.
VYS T . . . Circuses
VYX . . Tourism
VYX P . . . Package holidays
W . Arts, works of art
. . * Notation is provisional.
WBD . . Protection of works of art
. . . * See also Protection of cultural property SBV KKT T; Protection of intellectual property SBL K
WBE . . . Artworks in wartime
WBH . . Reproduction of artworks
. . . * For forgery, see SBW WG; for copyright, see SBL K.
WY . . Performing arts
WYM . . . Theatrical performances
WYP . . . Other performances
XL Language & literature
XN . National languages, official languages

SBW Criminal law
. Information in subject
SBW 3M . . Criminal justice information systems
5A . Jurisprudence
. . * For theory and philosophy of criminology and penology, see QO.
5AA . . Philosophy
5AG QF . . . Free will & determinism & criminal law
5AH K . . . Ethics & criminal law
. . . Special theories [
5AM . . . . Normative theory in criminal law
5UB . . Criminal law & society
5VK . . . Duties & rights
. . . . * Most of the literature concerns the citizen's role in the maintenance of law; see Administration of justice S5V K.
5W . . . *Special fields of social action*
5WH . . . . Human biology
. . . . . * See also Forensic medicine in criminal law SBW 8X
5WI . . . . . Psychology & psychiatry
5WK EP . . . . Communication media
5WQ . . . . Social welfare
5WQ O . . . . . Victims of crime
. . . . . . * See SBU O
5WQ Q . . . . . Criminology & penology
. . . . . . * Alternative (not recommended) to locating in class QQ.
. . . Relations between branches of law
5XB G . . . . Civil wrongs & criminal law

6 . Practice & procedure
. . * The detailed schedule for this is given under the general class, at S6/S9. All of it is available here by normal retroactive synthesis. The only classes enumerated below are those which are particular to criminal law, together with a minimal number of general terms necessary to show the scope & contextual structure of the class.
. . * See also the note at SBW 8L (after which point numerous special adjustments occur).
. . * For enforcement of law by police, etc., see QP.
. . Jurisprudence
65A . . . Theory & philosophy of criminal procedure

6E . . Courts & court procedure
. . . Jurisdiction
6H . . . . Criminal jurisdiction
. . . . . * For crimes committed abroad, see Conflict of laws (criminal) SBW AJM; for crimes on ships, aircraft, etc. see SDB WFT.
6KB . . . Law officers
6N . . . . Judges
6R . . . . . Juge d'instruction (criminal law)
. . . *Types of criminal courts*
. . . . *{Appeal courts}*

[Criminal law SBW]
[Practice & procedure SBW6]
[Courts & court procedure SBW6E]
[Types of criminal courts]
. [{Appeal courts}]

. . * See Appeal SBW 9H
SBW 7E . Courts of first instance
7R . . High Courts
7T . . Summary jurisdiction, magistrates' courts

8 Criminal proceedings, prosecutions, criminal actions
. * For prosecution in the narrow sense of the conduct of the case for the prosecution, see SBW 8J; for private prosecution, see SBW 8JR.
8A . Parties
. . * Use for works on the parties per se, & their 'non-legal' characteristics; e.g. sources of finance. For the prosecution & defence as activities in the proceedings, see SBW 8J.
8AE . . Anonymity of parties in prosecutions
. . . Anonymity until sentenced
8AL . . Rights & duties of parties
8BB . . Services to parties, assistance to parties
. . . * Steps taken to assist victims, witnesses, etc. to overcome nervousness, etc. over their participation in the trial.
8BC . . . Counsel
8C . . Prosecutor
8CB C . . . Prosecution counsel
8CB K . . . Public prosecutor
8D . . Accused, defendant (criminal actions)
. . . * See also Rights of accused at trial SBW 8SF
8DB C . . . Defence counsel
8EV . . Victim as party to action
. . . * If victim has legal status in action.
8EW . . Non-legal representatives (parties to action)
. *Organizational processes*
8FV . . Conduct of the proceedings
8FY . . . Investigatory systems
8G . . . Accusatorial system (general)
. . . . * The accusation (by an individual or official) and the evidence for it is examined by a magistrate or group of individuals (jury) in order to determine its substantiation.
8H . . . Inquisitorial system (general)
. . . . * The examining magistrate or judge undertakes his or her own enquiry, which is not limited to the evidence presented.
. . . . * See also Juge d'instruction, SBW 6R
8J . . Prosecution procedure

Criminal proceedings

[Criminal law SBW]
[Practice & procedure SBW6]
[Courts & court procedure SBW6E]
[Criminal proceedings SBW8]
[Organizational processes]
[Prosecution procedure SBW8J]

. * The process of preparing & presenting a case may begin before preliminary proceedings.
. Models
SBW 8J3 4H6 M . . Prosecution models
8JB C . Counsel
. . * For prosecutor per se, see SBW 8CB C.
8JL . Initiation of prosecution
8JM . . *By authority*
8JN . . . Police prosecution
8JP . . . Public prosecution service
8JR . . Citizen's prosecution, private prosecution
8JS . Prosecutional screening
. . * Evaluation of case by prosecutors to determine whether it should go to trial or be dropped.
8JT . Prosecutional diversion, alternatives to prosecution
. . * Decision to channel alleged offence to counselling treatment, etc. & not file charges.
. . * See also Juvenile court waiver SBW X8J TW
8JU . Prosecutional discretion, decision to prosecute
. . * See also Caution SBW 8LP
8JV . . Plea bargaining, plea negotiation
8JW . . Pleading guilty by post
. . . * In minor offences, this is allowed without the defendant appearing in court. Applies only to summary jurisdiction.
8JX . Nolle prosequi
8K Defence procedure
. * This depends on a plea of not guilty; see SBW 8SE.

[Criminal law SBW]
[Practice & procedure SBW6]
[Courts & court procedure SBW6E]
[Criminal proceedings SBW8]
[Organizational processes]
[Defence procedure SBW8K]

SBW 8L Preliminary proceedings, pre-trial proceedings
. * From this point onwards the procedure in criminal law diverges considerably from that in civil law & notation is adjusted accordingly. In particular, S8L M/S8S for general & civil law is replaced by detail special to ciminal trials in SBW 8LM/SBW 8S.
8LL T . *Technical aids*
. . * The general class for Forensic science & technology is under Evidence, at S8U. But some of its techniques may be applied to earlier stages in the proceedings. The only use of this class should be to qualify such stages if the need arises; e.g. aids to surveillance, SBW 8LO LLT.
. . * Add to SBW 8LL T letters U/Y following S8 in S8U/S8Y.
8LM . Pre-trial review (general)
8LN . Criminal investigation, police law (criminal investigation)
. . * The general class for this is QPE. This class takes only works considering these operations as elements in a prosecution. For police law in general, see Constitutional law SCN A.
. . * The following examples demonstrate some topics prominent in the legal literature.
8LO . . Surveillance of suspects
8LP . . Caution
. . . * See also Prosecutional discretion, SBW 8JU
8LQ . . Interrogation of suspects, questioning of suspects
. . . Technical aids
8LQ LLT . . . . Recording interrogations of suspects
8LR . . . Code of practice (interrogation of suspects), judges' rules
8LS . . Interception of communication (criminal proceedings)
8LT . . Inquest (criminal investigation)

[Practice & procedure SBW6]
[Courts & court procedure SBW6E]
[Criminal proceedings SBW8]
[Organizational processes]
[Preliminary proceedings SBW8L]
[Criminal investigation SBW8LN]
. [Inquest criminal investigation SBW8LT]

SBW 8MB	Process (narrowly)
	. * Bringing in suspects before justices. Often used for the documentation (originating process) by which prodeedings are initiated. It is a civil action in Scotland
8MD	. Search & seizure
8ME	. . Search with warrant, search warrants
8MG	. . Search without warrant
8MJ	. Summons (criminal proceedings), writ of summons
8MP	. Arrest & commitment, arrest & charge
8MQ	. . Arrest with warrant
8MR	. . Arrest without warrant
8MS	. . Charge (summons)
8MT	. Extradition
	. . * See also International law SDB W8M T
8MU	. . Right of assylum from extradition
8MV	. . Special topics
	. . . * Arrange A/Z.
8MW	. . Interstate extradition
	. . . * In federal systems.
8MX	. . *By country from which sought*
	. . . * Add to SBW 8MX letters D/Z in Schedule 2.
8N	Preliminary examination, preliminary hearings, preliminary enquiry
	. * To decide if charges sufficiently well founded as to justify trial.
	. * For Pre-trial review, see SBW 8LM.
	. * Add to SBW 8O letters MT/RW following S8.
8PC	. By police or prosecution [
8PE	. By magistrate, justice, Juge d'instruction [
8PG	. Adjudication (preliminary examination)
	. . * Determination by judge.
8Q	Indictment, levelling charges, committal for trial, accusation (indictment)
8QS	. Counts
	. . * Separate statements in an indictment of two or more offences charged.
8QT	. . Alternative counts, contradictory counts
8RB	. Remand
8RC	. . Remand in custody

[Courts & court procedure SBW6E]
[Criminal proceedings SBW8]
[Organizational processes]
[Preliminary proceedings SBW8L]
. [Indictment SBW8Q]
. . [Remand SBW8RB]
. . . [Remand in custody SBW8RC]

SBW 8RD	. . . Pre-trial release
	. . . . * For home detention, see Juvenile crime SBW X9Q KX
LSB W8R E	. . . . Bail
SBW 8RF	. . . . . Bail bonds
8RG	. . . . . . Bail bondsman
8RH	. . . . . . Bail payment methods
8RJ	. . . . . Jumping bail
8RK	. . . . . Forfeiture of bail collateral
8RL	. . . . . Discrimination (bail)
8RM	. . . . . Review of bail
8RN	. . . . Release on cognizance
8RQ	. . . . . Suspended release
8RR	. . . . . Release on recognizance
	. . . . . . * Guaranteeing appearance in court by signing agreement.
8RS	. . . . . Supervised release, custodial release,
8RV	. . Informations
8RW	. . Defective indictment
8S	Trials (criminal law), trial on indictment
	. * For Summary trials, see SBW 9T.
8S5 U	. Social aspects
8S5 WKE P	. . Pretrial publicity, trial by news media, free press & free trial
8S8	. *Legal proceedings, process generally*
	. . * It is unlikely that court actions will need to be qualified by classes SBW 8A/SBW 8R; but should the need arise, proceed as follows:
	. . * Add to SBW 8S8 letters A/R following SBW 8.
8S9	. Omnibus hearings
	. . * Acceleration of criminal proceedings by broad disclosure of prosecution evidence to the defence & judicial supervision of the issues identified.
8S9 U	. Trial practice
8SB	. . Forensic orations & legal arguments
8SC	. . Arraignment
8SD	. . . Pleas (criminal trials)
	. . . . Rules
8SD 6JQ	. . . . . Fitness to plead
8SD E	. . . . Oral pleading
8SD F	. . . . Stand mute
8SD G	. . . . Denial of court's jurisdiction
8SD H	. . . . Objection on point of law, demur (obsol.)
8SD J	. . . . Autrefois acquit
8SD K	. . . . Autrefois convict

[Criminal proceedings SBW8]
[Organizational processes]
[Trials criminal law SBW8S]
[Trial practice SBW8S9U]
[Arraignment SBW8SC]
. [Pleas criminal trials SBW8SD]
. . [Autrefois convict SBW8SDK]

SBW 8SD L . . Pardon (pleas)
8SD M . . Special liability (pleas)
. . . * Now obsolete.
8SD N . . Guilty plea
. . . * For plea bargaining, see SBW 8JV.
8SD P . . Not guilty plea, general issue

8SE Defence proceedings
8SF . Rights of the accused at trial
. . * For rights relating to specific elements in the proceedings, see element (e.g. evidence, witnesses).
8SF G . . Presumption of innocence
8SF H . . Right to be informed of the charge
8SF J . . Right of silence, right against self-incrimination
8SF K . . Right to legal advice, right to call solicitor
. . . * For right to counsel, see SBW 8SF R.
8SF L . . Right not to be detained
8SF M . . . Habeas corpus
8SF N . . Right to fair trial
8SF P . . Right to speedy trial
. . . * For Congestion in court (court management), see S6G Q.
8SF Q . . Right to prepare defence
8SF R . . Right to counsel
8SF T . . Double jeopardy
. . . * Being tried twice for the same offence.
8SF U . . Ex post facto laws (right against), retroactive application of laws (right against)
. *Types of defence*
. . * For criminal liability in general, see SBW CG.
. . * Add to SBW 8SG letters R/Y following S8Q, and to SBW 8SH letters A/E following S8R so far as applicable.
8SH E . . Disclosure in the public interest
8SH G . . Exemption from liability (criminal law)
8SH I . . . Incapacity defence
. . . . * See also Fitness to plead SBW 8SD 6JQ
8SH J . . . . Infancy defence [
. . . . . * See Juvenile offenders SBW X8S HJ
8SH L . . . . Drug addiction defence
8SH N . . . . . Intoxication defence, drunkenness defence
8SI . . . . Insanity defence, mental derangement defence

[Criminal proceedings SBW8]
[Trials criminal law SBW8S]
[Trial practice SBW8S9U]
. . [Types of defence]
. . . [Exemption from liability criminal law SBW8SHG]
. . . . [Incapacity defence SBW8SHI]
. . . . . [Insanity defence SBW8SI]

. . . . . . * See criminally insane SBW DM
SBW 8SL B . . . . . Automatism defence
8SL D . . . . . Brainwashing defence
. . . . . . * See also Compulsion defence, SBW 8SR
8SL H . . . . . Medical incapacity defence
. . . . . . * Under influence of a particular medical treatment.
8SM . . . . Mistake of fact, ignorance of the law
8SN . . . . Entrapment
. . . . . * Inducement by police, etc. to commit crime.
8SP . . . Justification defence
8SQ . . . . Consent of injured party defence
8SR . . . . Duress & threat defence, compulsion defence, coercive persuasion defence, force & fear defence (Scot.)
. . . . . * See also Brainwashing defence SBW 8SL D
8SS . . . . Necessity defence
8ST . . . . Self-defence (criminal law)
8SU . . . . Superior orders defence
8SV . . . Alibis
8SV W . . . Other defences A/Z

8SW Fact & law

8T Evidence, matters of fact
8TD . Defendant
8TD AH . . Rights of accused
8TD AP . . . Admission (rights of accused), declaration against own interest
8TD AQ . . . Right against self-incrimination
8TD AR . . . Evidence of previous conviction
8TV . Admissability of evidence
. . Rules
8TV JL . . . Judges' rules
. . . . * Governing conduct of police in questioning suspects.
8TW . . Proof
8TY . . Elicitation of facts
8U . . . Forensic science & technology
9AB . Forms of evidence
9AD K . . Sources
9AD X . . . Police evidence
9AE . . . Admission
. . . . * Of facts relevant to establishment of guilt.
9AF . . . Confession (criminal evidence)
. . . . * Admission of whole charge.

[Criminal proceedings SBW8]
[Organizational processes]
[Trials criminal law SBW8S]
[Evidence SBW8T]
. [Forms of evidence SBW9AB]
. . [Sources SBW9ADK]
. . . [Confession criminal evidence SBW9AF]

SBW 9AV . . . Witnesses
9BH 8A . . . . Parties
9BH 8D . . . . . Accused
. . . . . . * For admission & confession, see
. . . . . . SBW 9AE.
9BI D . . . . . . Identification of accused
9BI F . . . . Identification parades
9BI H . . . . Photographs, identikits
9D Judicial decision
9E . Jury trial & juries
9EP . Finding a verdict
9ES . . Not guilty verdict, acquittal
9ET . . Guilty verdict, conviction
9EU . . Not proven (Scot.)
9F . Judgement
9FR . . Award of costs
9FR ES . . . Award of costs on acquittal
9FW . . Mitigation
. . . * Statement after conviction suggesting why
. . . penalty should be moderated.
9G . Remedies
. . * Criminal proceedings do not generally afford
. . remedies to aggrieved individuals.
9GY . . Administrative remedies
9GY P . . . Post-conviction remedies
9H . . . Appeal, appellate procedure
9HI . . . . Right of accused to appeal
. . . . Special grounds
9IT R . . . . . Reformatio in pejus
9IU . . . Prerogative of mercy
9IU R . . . . Reprieve
9IV . . . . Quashing of conviction
9IV P . . . . . Pardon, free pardon
9IV S . . . . . Amnesty
9IV V . . . . . Compensation (miscarriage of
. . . . . justice)
9IV X . . . . Commuting of sentence
9IW . . . . Remission of sentence
9IX . . . Retrial
9IY . Arrest of judgement
. . * Action by accused between conviction &
. . sentence.

[Practice & procedure SBW6]
[Courts & court procedure SBW6E]
[Criminal proceedings SBW8]
[Organizational processes]
[Trials criminal law SBW8S]
[Judicial decision SBW9D]
[Arrest of judgement SBW9IY]

SBW 9PL Sentencing, adjudicating
(sentencing)
9PL 38 . Agencies
9PL 3JL . . Sentencing commissions
9PL 5A6 . Theory of sentencing
. . * Legal considerations only;
. . penology in general as a form of
. . social sanction is at QQ.
. Rights of accused
9PL 8AM . . Rights at sentencing
9PM . Aids to sentencing, guide lines
. in sentencing
9PN . . Pre-sentence investigation
9PP . . Reports on convicted persons
. . (sentencing)
9PQ . . . Medical reports (sentencing)
9PR . . . . Psychiatric reports
. . . . (sentencing)
9PS . . . Social enquiry reports
. . . (sentencing)
9PT . . . Probation reports
. . . (sentencing)
9PU . Special factors in sentencing
. . * See also Plea bargaining, SBW 8JV
9PV . . Effectiveness of sentencing
9PW . . Disparities in sentencing
9PX . . . Geographical variations in
. . . sentencing
9QB . . Judicial discretion, judge
. . sentencing discretion
9QC . . . Modifying factors
. . . (sentencing)
9QE . . Aggravating circumstances
. . (sentencing)
9QF . . . Recidivism, previous
. . . convictions (sentencing)
. . . . * As factor in sentencing policy.
. . . . * For previous convictions as
. . . . factor in the trial, see Evidence
. . . . SBW 8TD AR.
9QG . . Extenuating circumstances
9QG L . . Deferment of sentence
9QH . . Length of sentence
. . . * Refers mainly to custodial
. . . sentences.
9QH P . . . Prescribed maximum length
. . . (sentencing)
9QJ . . Severity of penalties
9QJ R . . . Ratings of penalty severity

Sentencing

[Organizational processes]
[Trials criminal law SBW8S]
[Judicial decision SBW9D]
[Sentencing SBW9PL]
[Special factors in sentencing SBW9PU]
. [Severity of penalties SBW9QJ]
. . [Ratings of penalty severity SBW9QJR]

SBW 9QK . Detention
. . * See Juvenile delinquency SBW X9Q K
Types of sentences
. * Legal aspects only. For penology, see QQQ.
9QL . Court orders, court directions (sentencing)
. . * E.g. care order for juveniles.
9QM . Summary sentences
9QM T . . Automatic sentences
9QN . Presumptive sentences
9QO . Suspended sentences
. . * For probation, see Penology QQL.
9QP . Weekend sentences
9QQ . Indeterminate sentences
. . * See also Parole SBW 9SJ
9QR . Reparative sentencing
9QS . Rehabilitation of offenders
. . * Principle that a convicted person who has not been reconvicted for a certain period should be treated as if they had never been convicted or sentenced.
9QU . Discharge
9QV . . Conditional discharge
. . . * Binding over.
9QW . . Absolute discharge, unconditional discharge

9RC Penalties, punishments, penal law
. * Legal aspects only. For penology, see QQ.
. * For penalties special to a given offence, see the offence (particularly juvenile offences).
9RC BA . Conflict of laws
9RD . Non-custodial treatment
. . * See also Types of sentences; e.g. suspended sentence.
9RE . . Probation
. . . * Legal aspects only. General class is QQF EL.
9RG . . Community service
9RH . . . Community service orders
9RJ . . Other non-custodial treatments
. . . * Arrange A/Z.
. . . * E.g. attainder, infamy.
9RK . Economic sanctions
9RL . . Fines (criminal penalties)
9RM . . Forfeiture of foods or office
9RM P . . Confiscation (penalties)

[Organizational processes]
[Trials criminal law SBW8S]
[Judicial decision SBW9D]
[Sentencing SBW9PL]
[Penalties SBW9RC]
[Economic sanctions SBW9RK]
. [Confiscation penalties SBW9RMP]

SBW 9RN Reparation by offender, restitution by offender
9RP Restoration to victim, compensation to victim
. * As element in legal redress. From viewpoint of victim's welfare, see SBU O.
9RQ . Criminal bankruptcy order
9RR Loss of rights (penalties)
9RS . Supervised liberty
. . * See also probation SBW 9RE
9RT . Restrictions on movement
9RT R . . Exile
9RT S . . Deportation
9RT T . . House arrest
9RT W . . Withholding passport
9RU . Attainder, civil death
. . * Extinction of civil rights & powers.
9RV . Infamia (Roman law)
9RW Retributive punishment, deterrent punishment
9RX . With fixed penalties
9RY . With discretionary penalties
9SB Physical punishment
9SC . Corporal punishment
9SD . Capital punishment, death penalty, execution
9SF Committal to medical treatment
. * See also specific crimes (e.g. sex crimes) for specific treatments
9SH Imprisonment, custodial sentences, confinement
9SJ . Parole
9SK . Hard labour
. . * Abolished in England, 1948.
9SL . Life imprisonment
9SM . Preventive detention
9SN . Short prison sentences
9SP . *By type of prison*
. . * E.g., maximum security prison.

[Criminal law SBW]
[Practice & procedure SBW6]
. . [Criminal proceedings SBW8]
. . . [Organizational processes]
. . . . [Penalties SBW9RC]
. . . . [Imprisonment SBW9SH]
. . . . [By type of prison SBW9SP]

. . . *Special types of proceedings*
SBW 9T . . . . Summary actions
. . . . . * Classmark S9T usually represents the constitutional law of a specific subject; use SBW 9U here.
. . . . . * For Actions on indictment, see SBW 8S
. . . . . * Add to SBW 9T numbers 2/9 following SBW and letters E/V following S9S.
9TV . . . . . Individual trials
. . . . . . * By name of accused
. . . . . . * Arrange A/Z.
9U Constitutional law
. * See note at SBW 9T for the reason for this location.

Substantive law in criminal law
A . Conflict of laws
A6 . . Practice & procedure
. . . Judicial assistance
A6H R . . . . International judicial assistance (criminal law)
. Recognition of foreign laws
AJM . . Crimes committed abroad
B . Other branches of civil law arising in criminal law [
. . * It is unlikely that many of the concepts will apply. If any do, proceed as follows:
. . * Add to SBW B letters B/Y in Auxiliary Schedule S1 so far as applicable.

[Criminal law SBW]
[Substantive law in criminal law]
[Other branches of civil law arising in criminal law [SBWB]

SBW C Criminal offences, crimes, unlawful acts, illegal acts
C5B Q . Analytical jurisprudence
. . Classification
C5B R . . . Codification of offences
C5B X . . . . Decriminalization
. *Elements of crimes*
CD . . Statutory statement of facts (Am.)
CE . . Commission or omission of criminal act
CF . . . Causality (crimes)
CG . . Criminal responsibility, liability of criminal
. . . * For exemption from liability, see Defence SBW 8SH G.
CH . . . Extent of liability (crimes)
. . . . * Factors affecting judgement - e.g. court's competence to deal with case, age & mental capacity of offender.
CJ . . . Culpability, guilt (criminal liability)
CK . . . . Actus reus
. . . . . * The act itself.
CL . . . . Mens rea, criminal intent, pre-meditation
CM . . . . . *Elements of intent*
. . . . . . * Arrange A/Z.
. . . . . . * E.g., recklessness, malice, dishonesty.
CN . . . . Criminal negligence
CP . . . Solicitation (criminal law)
. . . . * Intentionally ifluencing another to commit a crime.
. . . *By person*
CS . . . . Juristic persons (criminal liability)
. . . . . * For individuals, see Offenders SBW D.
CT . . . . . Corporate persons (criminal liability)

D . . Criminals, offenders
. . . *By non-criminal characteristics*
. . . . * For juveniles, see SBW XD.
. . . . * Add to SBW D letters GN/N following Q in QGN/QN and letters P/R following QR in QRP/QRR, with the modifications indicated below. Some classes prominent in the literature are given below as examples.
DGP . . . . Deprived persons as offenders
DJJ . . . . Abused persons as offenders

[Criminal law SBW]
[Substantive law in criminal law]
[Criminal offences SBWC]
[Elements of crimes]
. [Criminals SBWD]
. . [By non-criminal characteristics]
. . . [Abused persons as offenders SBWDJJ]

SBW DJN . . . Female offenders
DJN T . . . Male offenders
. . . . * Usually assumed.
DJO . . . Ethnic group members (offenders)
DJP . . . Racial group members (offenders)
DM . . . Mentally ill persons as offenders, criminally insane
DM8 SG . . . . Exemption from liability
DM8 SI . . . . . Insanity defence, mental derangement defence
DM8 SI8 LM . . . . . . Evidence
DM8 SI8 LMY I . . . . Forensic psychiatry
DM8 SJ . . . . . . M'Naghten rules, MacNaghten rules
DM8 SK . . . . . . Diminished responsibility
DMP . . . Mentally retarded persons as offenders

. . *By crime-defined characteristics*
DS . . . Principals in crime, instigators of crime
DT . . . Accessories to crime, accomplices in crime
DU . . . . Subornation
DV . . . . Accessories before the fact, incitement to crime
DW . . . . Accessories after the fact, aiding & abetting
DX . . . . Conspiracy
EA . . . First offenders
EB . . . Occasional offenders
EC . . . . Persistent offenders, hardened offenders, recidivists
EE . . . . Professional criminals
EF . . . . Petty offenders
. . . . . * See Petty crimes SBW FP

EH *Forms of offences*
. * Each type of offence may be qualified as follows (where the hyphen represents the classmark to be added to):
. * Add to - letters A/E following SBW; e.g. Road traffic offences - Persistent offenders SBW UA EC.
. * Add to -F letters F/W following SBW so far as is applicable; e.g. Offences against public order in rural areas SBW RF GA.
EK . Completion & attempt (crimes)

[Criminal law SBW]
[Substantive law in criminal law]
[Criminal offences SBWC]
[Forms of offences SBWEH]
[Completion & attempt crimes SBWEK]

SBW EL . Preparatory act, preparation to commit offence
EM . Attempt to commit offence
By procedural factors
EQ . Non-arrestable offences, misdemeanours
ER . Arrestable offences, felonies
ES . Summary offences
ET . Indictable offences
EU . Regulatory offences
EX . Index crimes (Am.)
. . * Categories of FBI Uniform Crime Reports.
By structure
FA . Compound crimes, multiplicity of offences, mergers
. . * Violation of several laws at a time or of one law several times.
FC . . Continuous crimes
FD . . Joinder & severance of offences
FG . Occupational crimes
. . * For employee theft, see Business crime SBW GB.
FH . . White collar crime
FJ . . Law enforcement officer crime, police crime
. . . * See also abuse of administrative authority SCK GLD
FK . . . On-duty offences
FL . . . Off-duty offences
FP . Petty crimes
. . * See also Non-arrestable offences SBW EQ
FQ . Organized crime, gangster crime
FR . . Syndicated crime
. . . * Large-scale crime deliberately mixed with legitimate business.
FS . . International crime, transnational crime
. . . * For crime in international law, see SDB W.
FT . Conspiracy, criminal conspiracy

By scene of crime
. * For crimes committed abroad, see Conflict of laws SBW AJM
FV . Crime in residences
. . * For domestic crime, see SBW GV.
FW . Street crime
FX . City crime, urban crime
GA . Rural crime
GB . Business crime
. . Costs
GD . . Criminal infiltration of business
GE . . Employee theft

Criminal offences

[Criminal law SBW]
[Substantive law in criminal law]
[Criminal offences SBWC]
[Forms of offences SBWEH]
[By scene of crime]
. [Business crime SBWGB]
. . [Employee theft SBWGE]

SBW GF . . Bank robberies
GG . . Retail business crime
GH . . . Shoplifting
GK . Disaster-related crime
GL . . Looting

By victim/offender relation
. * For Victimology, see QIR.
GP . Witness intervention in crime
GQ . Victimless crime
. . * Offender is own victim, but unwilling to
. . inform authorities of the offence.
. . * See also Drug abuse SBW QG
GR . Unreported offences
GS . Self-reported offences
. . * Admission of crime by undetected offendera.
GT . Stranger-to-stranger offences
. . * Usually assumed.
GU . Offender known to victim (crimes)
GV . . Domestic crimes, crimes within family
GW . Victim-precipitated crimes
GX . Offences against police

By legal definition
HC . Offences in international law
. . * Alternative (not recommended?) to locating
. . in IL, at SDB W. If this option is taken,
. . proceed as follows:
. . * Add to SBW HC numbers & letters 2/X
. . following SDB W - e.g.International
. . terrorism SBW HCT.
HI . Offences against the State, political
. offences, offences against the
. Crown
HIR . . Treason
HIS . . Subversion, sedition, conspiracy
. . against the state
HIS T . . Seditious libel
HIT . . Espionage, spying, official secrets
. . (offences)
HIW . . Assassination of political persons
HIX . . Defection, desertion (crimes against
. . the state)
HIY . . Others A/Z
HIY S . . Sabotage

[Criminal law SBW]
[Substantive law in criminal law]
[Criminal offences SBWC]
[Forms of offences SBWEH]
[By legal definition]
[Offences against the State SBWHI]
. [Sabotage SBWHIYS]

SBW HJD Crimes against Administration
. * For abuse of administrative authority, see
. Administrative law SCK GD.
HJE . Corruption, bribery
HJF . Crimes against justice
. . * For contempt of court, see S6J T.
HJG . . Perjury
HJG S . . . Subornation of perjury
HJI . . Intimidation of witnesses
HJJ . . Intimidation of jurors

HK Criminal torts, tortious crimes
. * Many torts are also crimes (e.g. assault).
. Some crimes (e.g. recklessness) may give
. rise to an action in tort (if it causes injury
. to another).
. * Add to SBW H letters K/P and R/V
. following SBG so far as applicable; e.g.
. criminal negligence SBW HK.
. * For Trespass to the person, see SBW K.
I Offences against the person
. * See also Torts against the person SBG N
IM . Family offences
J . Offences against children, child
. abuse
. . * For special offences, see below SBW
. . K/SBW Q.
JL . . Neglect, juvenile dependency
. . (child abuse)
JP . Crime passionel, crimes of passion
K . Trespass to person (criminal law)
. . * Alternative (not recommended) to
. . locating with Tort, at SBG Q. If this
. . option is taken:
. . * Add to SBW K letters R/T following
. . SBG Q; e.g. Real injuries SBW KR.
KX . . Homicide
L . . . Murder
. . . . * For assassination, see Offences
. . . . against the State SBW HIW; for
. . . . lynching, see SBW SB.
. . . . Trials
LK . . . . . *By means of murder*
. . . . . . * Arrange A/Z.
. . . . . . * E.g. trials of poisoners.
LL . . . . . *By name of accused*
. . . . . . * Arrange A/Z.
LM . . . Manslaughter

Criminal offences

[Criminal offences SBWC]
[Forms of offences SBWEH]
[By legal definition]
[Offences against the person SBWI]
[Trespass to person criminal law SBWK]
[Homicide SBWKX]
. [Manslaughter SBWLM]

SBW LN . Matricide, patricide, fratricide
LR . . Abortion (infanticide), criminal abortion
LS . . Concealment of birth, concealment of pregnancy (Scot.)
LT . Euthanasia, mercy killing
LU . Suicide
LV . . Aiding & abetting suicided
MA Assault
MB . Battery
MC . Common assault
MD . Aggravated assault
ME . Malicious injury, mayhem, wounding, grievous bodily harm
MF . Kidnapping, abduction
MG . Hostage taking
. . * See also Terrorism SBW T
MH . . Ransom
MJ . Communicating venereal disease (crimes)
MM Affray
MN Duelling
N Sexual offences
. * For seduction, see Torts SBG PG.
. * See also Offences against public morality SBW WO
. Penalties
NP . . Castration
NQ . . . Sterilization
NS . Prostitution
NT . . Procuring of women, pimping
NU . . Immoral earnings
NV . . Brothels
NW . . Soliciting
O . Rape
OR . . Rape in marriage
OS . Indecent assault
OT . . Exhibitionism, indecent exposure
OU . Incest
OV . Unnatural sexual practices
OW . . Buggery, sodomy
OX . . Bestiality
PB . Homosexuality
PC . . Male, pederasty
PD . . Female, lesbianism
PF . Fraudulent marriage, bigamy
PG . Adultery
PK . Obscenity

[Criminal offences SBWC]
[Forms of offences SBWEH]
[By legal definition]
[Offences against the person SBWI]
[Trespass to person criminal law SBWK]
[Sexual offences SBWN]
. [Obscenity SBWPK]

SBW PL . . Pornography
PN . Other sexual offences
. . * Arrange A/Z.
QA Addiction offences, drug & alcohol offences
QC . Drunkenness, alcohol abuse, intoxication
. . * For drunken driving, see SBW UDG.
QG . Drug abuse
QH . . Prohibited drugs
QJ . . . Possession of drugs
QK . . . Trafficking in drugs, supplying drugs
R Offences against public order
RS . Breach of the peace, disorderly conduct
. . * For assault, see SBW MA.
RT . Riot
RU . Violent disorder, unlawful assembly
RV . Civil disobedience
RW . Threatening behaviour
. . * For Affray, see SBW MM.
RX . Suspicious behaviour
SB . Lynching
SC . Feuds, vendettas
SE . Offensive weapons possession
SF . . Firearms possession, explosives possession
T . Terrorism
TV . Obstruction
TW . . Obstructing police
TX . . . Resisting arrest

UA . Road traffic offences, driving offences

UA9 RC . . Penalties
UA9 RJD . . . Disqualification from driving, withdrawal of driving license
UA9 RJE . . . Endorsement of license
UA9 RJF . . . Fixed penalties (traffic offences)
UAD . . Offenders
UAE C . . . Persistent offenders
UAH . . *Offences against administrative measures*
. . . * Add to SBW UA letters H/M following SBP 9U, with the adjustments indicated.

Criminal offences

[Criminal offences SBWC]
[By legal definition]
[Offences against the person SBWI]
[Trespass to person criminal law SBWK]
[Offences against public order SBWR]
. [Road traffic offences SBWUA]
. . [Offences against administrative measures SBWUAH]

SBW UAH . . . Driving license offences
UAH J . . . . Driving while disqualified
UAH L . . . . Driving without insurance
UAK . . . Vehicle testing offences
UB . . Other offences
. . . * Add to SBW UB letters J/V following
. . . SBQ D, with the adjustments indicated.
UBL L . . . Traffic signals offences
UBN K . . . Speeding offences
UBN P . . . Parking & stopping offences
UBQ UF . . . Motorway offences
UBV SV . . . Motorbike offences
. . *Special categories*
. . . * Add to each letters A/D following
. . . SBW U.
UC . . . Causing death by driving
UDD . . . Dangerous driving
UDD C . . . . Causing death
UDG . . Drunken driving
. . . Testing
UDG 9UK . . . . Breathalyzer test
UDK . . Hit & run offences

UG . Vagrancy
UH . Begging
UI . Blasphemy
UIS . Sacrilege
UJ Other offences against public order

UL Offences against property
UM . Theft, stealing
UN . . Burglary, housebreaking, breaking & entering, unlawful entry, criminal trespass
UQ . . . Housebreaking tools possession, equipment for stealing
UR . . . Aggravated burglary
US . . Robbery, armed robbery
UT . . . Bandits, outlaws
UV . . . Mugging, footpads
UW . . Embezzlement
. . . * From 1968, treated as theft in English law.
UX . . Misappropriation
VB . . Larcency
VC . . . Theft by finding
VD . . Handling stolen goods, receiving stolen goods, possession of stolen goods
. . *By thing stolen*

[Criminal law SBW]
[Criminal offences SBWC]
[Forms of offences SBWEH]
. . . [Trespass to person criminal law SBWK]
. . . . [Offences against property SBWUL]
. . . . . [Theft SBWUM]
. . . . . . [By thing stolen]

SBW VE . . . . Poaching
VF . . . . Vehicle theft, car theft
VG . . . . Hijacking
VH . . . . Shoplifting
VJ . . . . Trade secrets, industrial espionage
VK . . . . . . Other forms of theft [
. . . . * Arrange A/Z.
VM . . . . . Malicious damage, vandalism
VN . . . . . . Arson
VO . . . . . . Sabotage
VP . . . . . Financial crimes
VQ . . . . . . Debt default
VR . . . . . . Criminal usury, loan sharks
VS . . . . . . Crimes against public finance
VT . . . . Counterfeiting
VU . . . . Smuggling, customs offences
VV . . . . Excise offences
VW . . . . Tax offences
VX . . . . Social security offences
WA . . . . . Fraud, swindles
. . . . . . * For fraud as a tort, see SBG TH; for
. . . . . . embezzlement, see SBW UW.
WB . . . . . . Confidence tricks
WC . . . . . . Other forms of fraud
. . . . * Arrange A/Z.
WD . . . . . Deception
WE . . . . . . False pretences, imposture
WF . . . . . . False accounting
WG . . . . . . Forgery
WH . . . . . Extortion
WI . . . . . . Blackmail
WJ . . . . . . Protection rackets
WK . . . . . Corruption
WM . . . . . Computer crime
WN . . . . . Postal offences, mail delivery offences
WO . . . . Offences against public morality
. . . . . * For obscenity, see SBW PK.
WQ . . . . . Discrimination
WR . . . . . . Sexual discrimination
WS . . . . . . Racial discrimination
WT . . . . . . Religious discrimination
WV . . . . Offences against animals
WX . . . . . Cruelty to animals
WY Other offences A/Z

Criminal offences

[Criminal law SBW]
[Substantive law in criminal law]
[Criminal offences SBWC]
[Other offences A/Z SBWWY]

By special types of persons

SBW X . Juvenile criminal law, juvenile justice system, age of criminal responsibility
X5A . . Jurisprudence
X5U F . . . Juvenile justice standards
. . Courts & procedure
X6E . . Juvenile courts & procedure, youth courts & procedure, children's courts & procedure
X6G N . . . Intake juvenile courts
X8 . . . Actions
X8J . . . . Conduct of prosecution
X8J T . . . . . Diversion (juvenile courts)
X8J TW . . . . . Waiver (juvenile courts)
. . . . . . * Juvenile transfer to criminal court.
X8N . . . . Preliminary examination
X8N N . . . . . Juvenile adjudication
. . . . . . * Determination by judge of involvement or non-involvement in juvenile crime.
X8Q D . . . . Indictment
. . . . . Pre-trial release
X8R D . . . . . . Supervised release (juvenile crime)
X8S . . . . Trial
X8S E . . . . . Defence
X8S H . . . . . . Incapacity
X8S HJ . . . . Infancy (juvenile crime)
X9P L . . . . . Sentencing
X9Q K . . . . . . Juvenile detention
. . . . * Temporary confinement pending court's decision.
X9Q KX . . . . Home detention (juveniles)
X9R B . . . . . Penalties
. . . . . . * For execution of sentence, see class QTF.
. . . . . . Non-custodial treatment
X9R D . . . . Non-secure detention, juvenile shelter care (Am.)
. . . . * Temporary residential facility as alternative to detention.

X9R Y . . . . Special types of proceedings
X9S D . . . . . Summary proceedings

. . . . *Offences & offenders*
XD . . . . . Juvenile offenders, juvenile delinquents, juvenile status offenders (general)
. . . . . . *By particular characteristics*
XDJ M . . . . Female juvenile delinquents
XDJ N . . . . Male juvenile delinquents
XDM . . . . Emotionally disturbed juvenile delinquents

[Criminal offences SBWC]
[Juvenile courts & procedure SBWX6E]
[Actions SBWX8]
[Offences & offenders]
[Juvenile offenders SBWXD]
. [By particular characteristics]
. . [Emotionally disturbed juvenile delinquents SBWXDM]

Offences
SBW XEJ . Juvenile status offences
. . * Violations of law specific to juveniles & not considered crimes if committed by adults.
. Arrestable offences
XER . . Juvenile designated felonies (Am.)
XN . Sexual offences
XNS . . Juvenile prostitution, child prostitution

SBY Public law

. * That part of law which applies to the State and its relations with ordinary individuals, as distinct from Private law (S9W), which deals with the relations between individuals. It is more developed in civil law systems than in common law systems.

. * Most definitions of public law include within it constitutional, administrative and local government law, revenue law, ecclesiastical & military law. Some add to these parts of social welfare law, especially that of social security. Criminal law is sometimes regarded as a part of public law and sometimes as an independent branch bridging private and public law. BC2 follows the last view.

SC . Constitutional law

. . * Although a general principle in BC2 is that the law of a special subject goes with the subject, the preferred arrangement is to locate constitutional law here, in Class S Law. For reasons, see Introduction (Section 12).

. . * An alternative (not recommended) is to locate it in Class R Politics, at RF. In deciding which alternative to use, it may be noted that locating the class here brings all aspects of constitutional law together (i.e. those relating to the legislature, the executive, electoral law, etc.). In the alternative arrangement these special aspects would be distributed according to the branch of government concerned in RG/RL.

. . * For the constitutional law of a specific country, see the country's jurisdiction (in SI/SV).

. . * For elements of constitutional law (particularly government agencies) relating to a special subject in substantive law, see S9T & the note there.

SC2 . . *Primary materials*

. . . * For collections of constitutions of several countries, see SC5 L2. Primary materials of a given country go with the jurisdiction.

. . *Secondary materials, works about*

SC5 A . . . Jurisprudence

C . . . . Sources

CD . . . . . Analysis, interpretation

L . . . . . Constitutions, written constitutions

L2 . . . . . . *Primary materials*

L27 . . . . Collections of constitutions

. . . . . . *Operations*

. . . . * The making and revision of a constituion is a fundamental political operation and the preferred location for this is in Class R Politics.

. . . . * So the following classes constitute an alternative (not recommended) for libraries wishing to keep

[Public law SBY]
[Constitutional law SC]
[Secondary materials]
[Jurisprudence SC5A]
. [Sources SC5C]
. . [Constitutions SC5L]
. . . [Operations]

. . . . works on the making of a constitution with constitutional law. If this option is taken, proceed as follows:

. . . . * Add to SC5 L letters F/X following REX in REXF/REXX. A selection of major concepts is given here for convenience.

SC5 LF . . . Development of constitutions

LG . . . . Making constitutions

LH . . . . . Constitutional conventions

. . . . . . * For constitutional conventions in the sense of practices of government which are not legally enforceable but are commonly followed, see Conventional law S5T N.

LHV . . . . . Ratification of constitutions

LJ . . . . Revision of constitutions

LK . . . . . Interpretation of constitutions

LL . . . . Amendment of constitutions

LM . . . . . Bill of rights

LN . . . . . Judicial review

LP . . . . Reform of constitutions

LQ . . . Control & regulation of constitutions

LR . . . Constitutional authority

LS . . . Constitutional structure

. . . *Types of constitutions*

. . . . * For written constitutions, use SC5 L.

LX . . . . Unwritten constitutions, uncodified constitutions

. . *Sources other than written constitution*

. . . * Add to SC5 letters M/T following S5 in S5M/S5T.

M . . . Statutes

PS . . . Charters

SC6 Practice & procedure

SC6 E . Courts & procedure

. Actions

SC8 . . Constitutional actions

SC9 VB Substantive law

. * Most of the classes in SC are derived from Class R Politics and compounding of political concepts within class SC follows the rules for retroactive synthesis in class R. To avoid clashes and ambiguities in classmarks, retroactive qualification by legal concepts must follow special intercalators, as in class SBN. The relevant rules for

[Public law SBY]
[Constitutional law SC]
[Secondary materials]
[Substantive law SC9VB]

SBN are repeated here for convenience.
* Any class in SC, unless otherwise instructed, may be qualified retroactively by other legal concepts as follows (where the hyphen represents the classmark added to):
* Add to - numbers 2/9T following S.
* Add to -9V letters W/Y following S9.
* Add to -9X letters A/V in Auxiliary Schedule S1.

SC9 XA *Traditional branches of substantive law*
. * These are unlikely to be required here; some take a special form in public law and these are provided below in those subjects special to constitutional law (e.g. SCD ON Nationality & citizenship).

SCA *Political processes, properties & agents*
. * Most of these imply a central government context.
. See note at SCL Central government.
. * Add to SC letters A/DK following R in RA/RDK with the adjustments indicated. A selection of the more prominent concepts is given below for convenience and to show scope.

SCC T . Rights & duties, immunities in general
W . . Human rights, natural rights
W7 . . . Courts
. . . . * See also regional courts (supranational law)
. . . . - e.g. European Court of Human Rights SFY HXC W7R
. . . *Agencies*
WAW CU . . . . United Nations Commission on Human Rights
WAW DTH . . . . European Commission on Human Rights
WM . . . Performance of human rights
WMN . . . . Constitutional guarantees
X . . . . Abuse of human rights, violation of human rights
XT . . . . . Suspension of human rights
SCD B . . . Civil liberties, civil rights
. . . . * See also Habeus corpus (prerogative writs) S9K L
C . . . . Freedom of expression
. . . . . * Of speech, writing, etc.
DDP . . . . Privacy
E . . . Equal rights, equal opportunity

[Constitutional law SC]
[Secondary materials]
[Substantive law SC9VB]
[Political processes SCA]
. [Rights & duties SCCT]
. . [Human rights SCCW]
. . . [Equal rights SCDE]

. *Particular groups of persons*
. . * Add to SC letters DL/DU following R in RDL/RDU with the adjustments indicated.
SCD NG . . Slaves
ON . . Nationals, citizens
ONN . . . Nationality, citizenship
ONN E . . . . Allegiance
. . . *Special processes & elements*
ONN J . . . . Acquisition of citizenship
ONN L . . . . Patriality, rights of abode
ONN N . . . . Naturalization
ONN P . . . . Denaturalization
ONN Q . . . . Loss of citizenship
ONN S . . . . Passports
. . . *Types of citizen status*
ONT . . . . Naturalized citizens
ONV . . . . Dual citizenship
ONV NNE . . . . . Allegiance
OO . . . . Indigeneous persons, aboriginals
OOY . . . . Stateless persons
OPF TW . . . . Married women
OPQ . . . . Dependent territories citizenship
. . . . *Special to a jurisdiction*
OPT . . Aliens
OQ . . Minorities

ORB . . Migrant groups
ORG . . . Emigrants
ORR . . . Refugees
OS . . . Immigrants & immigration
OSE . . . . Administration of immigration, control of immigration
OSG . . . . . Restriction of immigration
OTC . . . . . . Quotas
OTD . . . . . . Deportation
OTL . . . . . Assistance to immigrants
OU . . . . *Types of immigrants by place of origin*
OVL . . . . *Types of immigrants by general characteristics*
OWL . . . . . Guest workers
Processes of government
. * See SCE.

SCE Government
. * This covers both government in general & central government. See note at SCL.
. * Add to SC letters E/LQ following R in RE/RLQ with the adjustments indicated (especially SCK).

[Public law SBY]
[Constitutional law SC]
[Secondary materials]
[Substantive law SC9VB]
[Government SCE]

SCE CD . Communication
. . * Use SCE D.
D . Communication & information control
DEH . . Openness in government
SCG C . Accountability of government
DJ . Regulation of abuse of government (general)
. . * Most of the literature relates to administrative law (SCK F).
. . * See also Tribunals of enquiry SCK F9T H; Ombudsman SCK F9T U
E . Powers of government
F . . Sovereignty of government
. . . * For sovereignty in international law as a subject of constitutional law, see SCY DF.
FQ . . Limitation of powers of government
G . . Separation of powers
GL . . . Delegation of powers
. . *Types of power*
HR . . . Emergency powers of government
I . . . Immunity
J . . . Prerogative powers of government
K . . Authority of government
KV . . . Civil authority
M . . *Powers special to an office*
MT . . . Treaty-making powers
. *Stages in the life of government*
N . . Establishment of government
NP . . Maintenance of government
O . . Dissolution of authority
PU . . Succession in government

Branches of government
R . Interbranch government relations
V . Representation & elections
SCH . . Electoral systems
SCH H . . . Election procedure
L . . . Political parties
O . . . Electorate & suffrage, votes
S . . . Voting systems
TU . . . *Types of election systems*
VD . . Referendum, plebiscite

SCI . Legislative systems, parliaments, congresses
SCI GE . . Powers
H . . Electoral system
HJ . . . Constituencies, legislative districts
L . . Legislative committees
NB . . Legislative procedure
. . . * For procedures relative to financial affairs, see SCL MGO.

[Public law SBY]
[Constitutional law SC]
[Secondary materials]
[Substantive law SC9VB]
[Branches of government]
[Legislative systems SCI]
. [Legislative procedure SCINB]

SCI OB . Legislative action, enactment of laws
S . Lower house
V . Upper house

SCJ Executive government, administration of government
SCJ GE . Powers
GJ . . Prerogative powers
K . Chief executives
KN . . Heads of state
KR . . . Hereditary heads of state, monarchs
. . . . * See also Monarchies SCY MC
KV . . . Presidents
L . . Heads of government
M . . . Executive presidents
MT . . . Prime ministers, premiers
O . . . Cabinets, councils of ministers
SB . Executive action
V . Interim government

SCK Public administration law (general)
. * Organization & structure of public administration & administrative law together; for the latter alone, see SCK F.
SCK A . *Political processes*
. . * Add to SCK letters A/EC following R in RA/REC with the adjustments indicated below.
CW . . Human rights
E . . Government
ECD . . . Communications
. . . . * Use SCK ED.
ED . . . Communication & information control
EDE H . . . . Openness in public administration
. . . *Other properties & processes of government*
. . . . * For accountability, powers & authority (RGC/RGL), see SCK GC.
. . . . * Add to SCK E letters M/T following RG in RGM/RGT so far as applicable.
ER . . . . *Relations with other branches of government*
ERI . . . . . Legislature's relations with public administration

Administrative law

[Constitutional law SC]
[Public administration law general SCK]
[Political processes SCKA]
. [Government SCKE]
. . [Other properties & processes of government]
. . . [Relations with other branches of government SCKER]
. . . . [Legislature's relations with public administration SCKERI]

SCK ERJ . . . . Executive's relations with public administration

F Administrative law
. * Law regulating the exercise by public authorities of the powers of rule-making & adjudication conferred on them by law.
. * See also Regulation of economic activities & businesses, SBN 9UC.
F2 . *Primary materials*
. . * For statutory instruments & other delegated legislation, see primary materials in general under a given jurisdiction.
F5C . Sources
F5P . . Delegated legislation
F5P R . . . Administrative acts, legislative functions of administrative agencies
F5P S . . . . Revocation of administrative acts
. Practice & procedure
F69 . . Access to law
. . . * To forms of redress versus administrative action.
F6E . . Courts & court procedure
F7V . . . Administrative courts, Conseils d'Etat
. . . . * See also Special agencies of redress SCK F9T B
F7W . . . Administrative tribunals
. . . . * If distinguished from the above.
F8 . . . Actions
F8A . . . . Parties
F8N . . . . . Right to prior hearing
F8P . . . . . Right to appeal
. . . Remedies, forms of redress
. . . . * See also Special agencies of redress SCK F9T B
F9G . . . . Administrative remedies, statutory remedies
F9H . . . . . Appeal
F9I V . . . . . Quashing of orders
F9I W . . . . . Statutory default powers
F9J . . . . Judicial review
F9K . . . . Prerogative writs & orders
F9K K . . . . . Non-statutory remedies
F9K M . . . . . . Certiorari
F9K N . . . . . . Mandamus
F9K P . . . . . . Prohibition
F9K T . . . . Declaratory judgements

[Constitutional law SC]
[Public administration law general SCK]
[Administrative law SCKF]
[Practice & procedure]
. [Courts & court procedure SCKF6E]
. . [Remedies]
. . . [Declaratory judgements SCKF9KT]

SCK F9L . . . Civil remedies
. . . . * Damages, injunctions, etc.
F9R YC . . . *Special types of proceedings*
. . . . * Add to SCK F9S letters S/U following S9; e.g. Summary proceedings SCK F9S SD
F9T B . . . Special agencies of redress
F9T D . . . . Parliamentary select committees
F9T F . . . . Enquiries
F9T H . . . . . Tribunals of enquiry
F9T U . . . . Ombudsman
F9T V . . . . . Local ombudsman

F9V B Substantive law
. *Special subjects of administrative law*
. . *Actions for which redress sought*
. . . * Add to SCK G letters C/L following RG.
GC . . . Acountability
GCN . . . Discretion
GD . . . Abuse of administrative authority
GDP . . . . Ultra vires
GDR . . . . Non-compliance with formal rules
GDT . . . . Action in bad faith
GDV . . . . Maladministration, faulty discretion
GE . . . Powers of administrative agencies
GHR . . . . Emergency powers of administrative authorities
GI . . . . Immunity
GJ . . . . Prerogative powers

. . *Functions of agencies within which action taken*
. . . * For specific function, see latter - e.g. Licensing, Taxation. Those below are too general to be subordinated to a single class.
. . . * For specific agencies, see SCL J/O.
HI . . . Legislative function of administration
. . . . * Making rules with the force of law.
HK . . . Directives of administration
. . . . * As to the actions of individuals.
HN . . . Investigative functions of administration
. . . . * Requesting information, etc.
HQ . . . Quasi-judicial functions of administration
. . . . * Adjudicating in disputes.

Administrative departments

[Constitutional law SC]
[Public administration law general SCK]
[Administrative law SCKF]
. [Substantive law SCKF9VB]
. . [Special subjects of administrative law]
. . . [Functions of agencies within which action taken]
. . . . [Quasi-judicial functions of administration SCKHQ]

SCK I Organization of public administration
. * Add to SCK letter I/Q following RK so far as applicable. Note that most of the literature refers to a particular level of administration (central, local, etc.) - see SCL/SCV.
IQ . Management of public administration
. . Personnel
IU . . . Public service employees
. . . . * For civil service, see SCL IU.
IV . . Resources management
IVF . . . Government purchasing, government procurement

J Administrative departments, executive agencies
. * Including sub-departments, sections, etc.
. * Nearly all the literature refers to those at a particular level (central government, local government, etc.)
. * Any given department, section, etc. may be qualified as follows (where the hyphen repreents the classmark of the department):
. * Add to - numbers & letters 2/K following SCK
. * Add to - letters L/Y for special functions
JV . Advisory services to departments
. . * Often required by statute (e.g. the public accounts committee to a treasury).

General operations
. * Functions defined by the main activities of an agency (public finance, trade & industry, foreign affairs, etc.) are given under those functions under central administration (SCL), with which most of the literature is concerned. The operations below may be directed at the activities within any department (e.g. public health).
. * The division of RKK is amended here so that the operations conform to those for regulating economic activities (at SBN 9U).
. * Add to SCK K letters C/S following SBN 9U.
KC . Regulation or control by administrative agencies
. . *Particular regulatory agencies*
KE . . . Persons
KF . . . Organizations

[Constitutional law SC]
[Substantive law SC9VB]
[Branches of government]
. . [General operations]
. . . [Regulation or control by administrative agencies SCKKC]
. . . . [Particular regulatory agencies]
. . . . . [Organizations SCKKF]

. . . . *Operations*
SCK KH . . . . . Licensing, concessions, certification by administrative agencies, registration by administrative agencies
KI . . . . . Identification
KJ . . . . . Inspection by administrative agencies
KK . . . . . Testing by administrative agencies
KL . . . . . Enforcement by administrative agencies
KM . . . . . . Specific measures
KR . . . Self-regulation
. . . . * Usually responsible ultimately to government.
KT . . . Economic assistance by administrative agencies
KU . . . . Grants-in-aid by administrative agencies

Jurisdictions by level of organization

SCL . Central government administration
. . * Most of the concepts in SCA/SCK and nearly all the literature on them usually imply central government. It would be unhelpful to maintain 2 separate sequences (SCA/SCK for truly general works & SCLA/SCLK for central government). So the arrangement recommended is as follows:
. . * Treat central government narrowly (i.e. excluding administration) as implicit in SCAY/SCK;
. . * For general works on central government alone (i.e. distinguishing it from devolved government) & on central administration alone (i.e. distinguishing it from legislative & executive government narrowly), use SCL.
. . * Works on devolved government & administration should go at SCQ/SCW.
. . * Add to SCL letters A/GR following SC and I/K following SCK.

SCL GR . . Interdepartmental government relations

I . . Organization of central administration
IQ . . . Management
. . . . * Add to SCL letters I/Q following RK so far as applicable (see note at SCK I).
. . . . *Personnel*
IU . . . . . Civil service

Central government administration

[Constitutional law SC]
[Jurisdictions by level of organization]
[Central government administration SCL]
[Organization of central administration SCLI]
. [Management SCLIQ]
. . [Personnel]
. . . [Civil service SCLIU]

SCL IV . . Resources management

J Central government departments, ministries
. * The preferred arrangement is to subordinate specific departments to the subject (education, health, etc.) except in the case of certain departments of central importance, such as the Treasury. An alternative is provided at SCL N/P for keeping all departments in this class.
. * Any given department may be qualified as instructed at SCK J.

General operations

KC . Planning & control

Special spheres of government activity

. *Agents*

MF . . Public finance department, treasury
MFL . . . Special functions
. . . . * See SCL MG/MQ.

MG . Public finance administration
. . * Add to SCL M letters H/S following TN National economics, with the adjustments indicated.
. . * Retroactive synthesis within SCL MH/SCL MS follows that in TNH/TNS.
. . * For retroactive synthesis using classmarks from S2/SCK, proceed as follows (where the hyphen represents the classmark added to):
. . * Add to - numbers 2/9X following SC
. . * Add to -9Y letters A/K following SC.
MGN . . Economic & financial policy
MGO . . Parliamentary procedures in financial administration, control of public expenditure
MGP . . . Financial & accounting principles
. . . . * For example, sums granted are maxima, sums granted for one purpose may not be used for another, surpluses may not be carried forward.
MGQ . . . Departmental estimates
MGR . . . . Supply estimates
MGS . . . . Expenditure committee(s)
. . . . . * For example, Select Committee on Expenditure in UK.
MGT . . . . Public accounts committee(s)
. . . . . * For Financial reporting, see SCL MHD OB.
MGU . . . Appropriations

[Substantive law SC9VB]
[Jurisdictions by level of organization]
[Central government administration SCL]
[Special spheres of government activity]
[Public finance administration SCLMG]
[Parliamentary procedures in financial administration SCLMGO]
. [Appropriations SCLMGU]

SCL MGV . . Interim appropriations
. . . * For example, Consolidated Fund Bill in UK.
MGW . Supplementary estimates
MGX . Forward planning

MHA A Fiscal policy
MHA B Intervention, control & regulation
MHA HE . Review
MHC National accounts, public accounting
. *Accounting procedures*
MHD F . . Audit of national accounts
MHE . Budget
MHQ . Money
MHQ AA . . Monetary policy
MHQ AC . . Interest rates
MHR . . Money supply
MI . National debt, public debt
MIU . Receipts & expenditure
MIW . Public revenue

MJ . . Tax law, taxation
. . . * Alternative (not recommended) is to collocate with Public finance at TNJ P.
. . . * Add to SCL M letters J/P following TN, with the adjustments indicated (e.g. at SCL MKX).
MJ6 E . . . Courts & procedure
MJ7 V . . . . Tax courts
MJ9 G . . . . Remedies
. . . . . * For tax appeals, see SCL MJR T.
MJA . . . Conflict of laws
MJA JM . . . . Recognition of particular foreign laws
MJQ . . . Tax demands, levying of taxes
MJR . . . Assessment of taxes
MJR T . . . . Appeal
MJR V . . . . Treasury liens
. . . . . * Money retained by tax authority until overdue taxes are paid.
MJT W . . . . Tax year, period of assessment
MJU B . . . . Tax returns
MJU D . . . . Self-assessment
MJU F . . . . Forward averaging

[Central government administration SCL]
[Public finance administration SCLMG]
[National accounts SCLMHC]
[Public revenue SCLMIW]
[Tax law SCLMJ]
[Assessment of taxes SCLMJR]
. [Forward averaging SCLMJUF]

SCL MJV Allowances, exemptions, relief
MJV L . Personal allowances
. . * For example, for married persons.
MJV N . Savings
MJV P . Expenses
. . * For example, mortgage allowance.
MJV R . Donations to charities
MJV S . Covenants
MJV U . Loss relief
MJV W . *Special categories*

MJW Tax avoidance, tax advantage, tax planning
MJW L . Splitting incomes
MJW N . Transfer of securities
MJW P . . Special forms
. . . * Arrange A/Z.
. . . * For example, bond washing.
MJW R . Transfer of assets abroad
MJW S . . Tax havens
MJW T . . Offshore funds
MJX Determination of tax due
MK Collection of taxes
. * For PAYE, see SCL MMS E.
MKL . Payment at source, withholding tax
MKN . Distraint
MKO . Overdue taxes
MKP . Overpayment of taxes, refunds
MKR . Tax credits
MKT Evasion of taxes, tax dodging
Properties of taxation
MKW . Incidence of taxes
MKW R . . Double taxation
MKW T . Tax structure
. . * Add to SCL MKW letters WU/Y following TNK; e.g. SCL MKW X Progressive taxation.

MKX *By person &/or activity taxed*
. * See also Corporation tax SCL MNM
. *By activity*
MKX C . . Crossborder transactions
. *By person*
. . * Add to SCL MKX letters WM/Y following SA; e.g. SCL MKX XW Taxation of women.

[Central government administration SCL]
[Public finance administration SCLMG]
[National accounts SCLMHC]
[Public revenue SCLMIW]
[Tax law SCLMJ]
[By person &/or activity taxed SCLMKX]
. [By person]

. . * Add to SCL MKY letters N/Y following SBB
. . * Add to SCL MLA letters A/X following SBC; e.g. Taxation on termination of marriage SCL MLA M.
SCL MLA Y . . Paticular industries
. . . * Arrange A/Z.

Types of taxation
MLB . Tax systems
MLC . . Tax base
MLE . . . Evaluation of tax base, tax value
MLF B . . . Residence
MLF D . . . . Foreign nationals
MLG . . Emergency taxes
MLH . . Direct taxation
MLH 4 . . . History
MLH 4FB . . . . Tallages, tailles
. . . . . * Originally feudal tax on tenancies, etc.
MLM . . . Wealth tax
MLN . . . . Capital gains tax
. . . . . * For capital transfer tax, see SCL MNK T.
MLP . . . Property tax
. . . . * For rating, see Local government SCU LML P.
MLR . . . Land tax, site value tax, real estate tax
MLV . . . Personal property tax
MLX . . . . Intellectual property tax

MM . . . Income tax
MMJ R . . . . Assessment
MMJ V . . . . Allowances
MMJ W . . . . Deductions
MMR S . . . . Gross income
MMR T . . . . Taxable income
MMS B . . . . Earned income tax, wages & salaries
MMS C . . . . . Standard rate of tax
MMS E . . . . . . PAYE, pay as you earn
MMS U . . . . Surtax
MMT . . . . Negative income tax
MMU C . . . . Unearned income tax
MMU E . . . . Capital income tax
MMU G . . . . . Annuities tax
MMU H . . . . . Fixed assets tax
MMU K . . . . . Floating assets tax
MMU M . . . . . . Income from securities

Tax law

[Tax law SCLMJ]
[Tax systems SCLMLB]
[Direct taxation SCLMLH]
. [Income tax SCLMM]
. . [Capital income tax SCLMMUE]
. . . [Floating assets tax SCLMMUK]
. . . . [Income from securities SCLMMUM]

SCL MMU Q . . . . . Dividends tax
MMV T . . . . Excess profits tax
MMW . . Foreign income
MMW X . . Other sources of income
. . . * Arrange A/Z.
. . *By type of persons*
MMX G . . . Pensioners
MNI . Transfer taxes
MNJ . . Estate duties, death duties
MNK . . . Inheritance tax
MNK T . . Capital transfer tax
MNL . . Gift tax

MNM . Corporation tax, business tax, company tax
MNM SV . . Profits tax
MNM SVT . . . Excess profits tax
MNM SVV . . . . Confiscation of illicit profits
MNM SW . . . War profits tax
MNM SX . . Payroll tax, employees tax
MNM SY . . Other corporation taxes
. . . * Arrange A/Z.
MNN . . *By type of corporate body*
. . . * Add to SCL MNN letters G/Y following SBO.
MNN I . . . Public service industries
MNN NX . . . Foreign firms
MNN P . . . Partnerships
MNN Q . . . Public limited companies
MNN T . . . Conglomerates
MNN UM . . . Consortia
MNN V . . . Multinationals
MNN W . . . Cooperative societies
MNO . . . Other corporate bodies
. . . . * Arrange A/Z.
MNO C . . . . Charities
MNP . Persons tax, poll tax

MNS Indirect taxation, expenditure taxation
MNT . Consumption tax, sales tax
MNX . Custom & excise duty
. . Evasion
MNX KT . . . Smuggling
MO . . Customs duties, external tariffs
MOT . . . Specific duties
. . . . * Arrange A/Z.
MOT D . . . . Dumping duties, antidumping duties
MOT F . . . . Duty-free imports, free of duty goods
MOX . . Internal tariffs, excise duties, tolls

[Constitutional law SC]
[Central government administration SCL]
[Special spheres of government activity]
. . [National accounts SCLMHC]
. . . [Public revenue SCLMIW]
. . . . [Tax law SCLMJ]
. . . . . . [Tax systems SCLMLB]
. . . . [Indirect taxation SCLMNS]
. . . . [Internal tariffs SCLMOX]

SCL MPE . . . . Sales tax
MPF . . . . Purchase tax
MPG . . . . Turnover tax
MPH . . . . VAT, value added tax

MPI . . . . Administrative revenues
MPI V . . . . Stamp duties, registration taxes
. . . . *By expenditure on which levied*
MPJ B . . . . Sumptuary taxes
MPJ E . . . . Alcohol tax, drinks tax
MPJ F . . . . Tobacco tax, smoking tax
MPJ H . . . . Gambling tax, betting tax
MPK . . . . Other goods & services taxed
. . . . * Add to SCL MP letters K/O following TNP in TNP K/TNP O; e.g. Taxation of finance houses SCL MPK GIN; Taxation of law practices SCL MPO S6B.
MPO N . . . . Non-tax revenue

MQ . . . Public expenditure
MQA HE . . . . Review, scrutiny
MQA HF . . . . . Public Expenditure Survey Committee
. . . . *Types of public expenditure*
MQJ S . . . . . Supply services
. . . . . . * Annually authorized expenditures.
MQK . . . . . Government assistance, state aid
MQM . . . . . . Subsidies, government grants
. . . . *Objects of public expenditure*
MQN . . . . . Capital expenditure
MQP . . . . . Salaries
MQP S . . . . . Pensions
MQQ . . . . . Transfer payments, social welfare expenditures
MQR . . . . . . Public sector borrowing requirement
MQS . . . . . Public works expenditures
MQX . . . . . Compensatory payments, claims on public expenditure

N Other central government departments
. * For law relating to specific areas of public service, see the apecific service. In particular, see SBS/SBV - e.g. health & medical services SBT B.
. * Qualification of a specific subject in substantive law by its public administration is effected by using the intercalator at S9T (see note there).

[Public law SBY]
[Constitutional law SC]
[Secondary materials]
[Substantive law SC9VB]
[Jurisdictions by level of organization]
[Central government administration SCL]
[Other central government departments SCLN]

. * An alternative (not recommended) is to collect all departments here, at SCL N/P. The following 'Add' instruction includes this alternative.
. * Add to SCL letters N/Q following RL in RLN/RLQ (except RLO PY National security) so far as applicable - e.g. Overseas territories SCL OQQ.

Other administrative agencies & functions
SCL QB . Quasi-government agencies
QC . . Public service corporations
QE . . . Nationalized industries
QG . . . Public utilities
QJ . Quasi-autonomous non-governmental organizations, quangos
QP . Privatized public administrative services, contracting out

V National security, national defence
VS . Official secrets
W . Defence department, war office
X . Civil defence
SCM . Military law, armed services, services law
. . * Regulating the conduct of members of the armed forces.
. . * The armed forces are treated here as a special form of public service.
. . * For military personnel appearing before non- military courts, see general courts.
. . * Add to SCM letters G/I following RK (public administration), with the modifications shown.
SCM 6 . . Practice & procedure
. . . * Most of the literature refers to military criminal law - see SCM R.
6E . . . Courts & court procedure
7V . . . . Courts of chivalry, courts of honour
GCJ . . . Accountability
GD . . . Abuse of government

[Substantive law SC9VB]
[Jurisdictions by level of organization]
[Central government administration SCL]
[National security SCLV]
[Military law SCM]
[Practice & procedure SCM6]
[Abuse of government SCMGD]

SCM GE Powers
. * Within the country itself.
Relations with other branches of government
HI . With legislature
HJ . With executive
HLY . With judiciary

I Organization & administration
IQ . Management
IU . . Personnel
IUE . . . Industrial relations law
IUP . . . Conditions & pay
IUQ R . . . . Bounties
IUS B . . . Recruitment & selection
. . . . * Use SCM J. Normal synthesis from RKI U is interrupted here; it is resumed at SCM N.

J . . . Recruitment & enlistment
K . . . . Conscription, compulsory military service, the Draft
KL . . . . . Deferment & exemption
. . . . . . *Special groups*
KP . . . . Conscientious objectors
KT . . . . . Mobilization
. . . *Other properties & processes*
LTB . . . . Discharge from armed services
LTU . . . . Leave, furlough
LU . . . . Health & safety

LV . . . *Types of personnel by general characteristics*
. . . . * Add to SCM L letters V/W following RKI U.
LWC . . . . Civilians in armed services
. . . . . * Including families of serving personnel.
LWC 6E . . . . . Courts & court procedure
LWC 7V . . . . . . Standing civilian courts
aSC MM . . . . Serving personnel, soldiers, services personnel
. . . . . * Usually assumed.
SCM MCW . . . . . Civil & political rights
MN . . . . . Conscripts
MP . . . . . Career soldiers, regular soldiers

Military law

[Central government administration SCL]
[Military law SCM]
[Practice & procedure SCM6]
. . [Management SCMIQ]
. . . [Personnel SCMIU]
. . . . [Types of personnel by general characteristics SCMLV]
. . . . . [Serving personnel aSCMM]
. . . . . . [Career soldiers SCMMP]

SCM MR . . . . . . Commissioned ranks
MT . . . . . . Non-commissioned ranks
MX . . . . . Ex-services personnel law, veterans law

N . . . Resources management
. . . . * Normal retroactive synthesis from RKI is resumed here after its interruption at SCM IUS B.
. . . . * Add to SCM N letters A/Y following RKI V in RKI VA/RKI VY.
NF . . . . Procurement
NGS . . . . Surplus property disposal
NGX . . . . Requisitioning
OW . . . Marketing, public relations
. . . . * Add to SCM O letters W/X following RKI in RKI W/RKI X.

Subjects special to military law
PC . Military privileges & immunities
PE . Military ceremonies & honour
PF . Decorations
PG . Military discipline
PJ . . Articles of war
PL . . Military necessity
PN . . Due force

. *Branches etc.*
PR . . Military districts
PRS . . . Commanding officer
PS . . Auxiliary services, volunteers, militia, territorials, national Guard
PU . . Intelligence services
PV . . Army, landforces
PW . . Navy
PX . . Airforce
PYM . . Military police

R . Military criminal law
R6 . . Practice & procedure
R6E . . . Courts & court procedure
R6K B . . . . Law officers
R6V . . . . . Judge-Advocates
. . . . . . * Advise courts-martial.
R7W B . . . . Courts-martial, military courts
R7W D . . . . . General court martial
R7W F . . . . . District court martial
R7W H . . . . . Field general court martial

[Constitutional law SC]
[Central government administration SCL]
[National security SCLV]
. [Military law SCM]
. . . [Military criminal law SCMR]
. . . . [Practice & procedure SCMR6]
. . . . . [Courts & court procedure SCMR6E]
. . . . . . [Courts-martial SCMR7WB]
. . . . [Field general court martial SCMR7WH]

SCM R8Q . . . . . . Defence
R8R C . . . . Superior orders
R9R C . . . . . . Penalties
R9S H . . . . Imprisonment
R9T V . . . . . . Individual trials
. . . . * Arrange A/Z.

R9V B . . . . Substantive law
SC . . . . . Civil offences in armed forces
. . . . . . * In principle, works on military personnel appearing before non-military courts go under the latter. Should the need arise to locate such material under military law, proceed as follows:
. . . . . . * Add to SCM S letters E/W following SBW.
TC . . . . . Military criminal offences
TE . . . . . . Insubordination
TG . . . . . . Malingering
TJ . . . . . . Desertion
TL . . . . . . Absence without leave
TN . . . . . . Mutiny
TP . . . . . . Military atrocities
TR . . . . Pillage, plundering, looting
TV . . . . . . Foreign enlistment

U . Martial law

Y Law enforcement agencies, public security agencies

Police law

[Public law SBY]
[Constitutional law SC]
[Secondary materials]
[Substantive law SC9VB]
[Jurisdictions by level of organization]
[Central government administration SCL]
[Law enforcement agencies SCMY]

SCN A Police law, police forces
. * The general class for police is QP; this class takes only works dealing with the status of such forces in constitutional law.
. * Add to SCN letters B/R following QP in QPB/QPR, with the amendments indicated below.
AGE . Powers of the police
B . Personnel, police officers
B . . Discipline
DB . Relations of police with the public
. *Methods & Agents*
DG . . Physical force
DH . . Protective gear
DI . . Weapons, arms (police)
DN . . Motor vehicles
DNT . . Mounted police
. *Operations*
DU . . Pursuit & arrest
DX . . Custody of accused
DXD D . . . Death in custody
E . . Criminal investigation
. . . * For police law in the narrow sense of police acting as elements in a prosecution, see SBW 8LN.
EJ . . . Informers
EY . . . Methods of criminal investigation, evidence gathering
G . . . . Interrogation by police, questioning by police
GK . . . . . Intimidation by police, violence by police
H . . Legal procedure in police work
. . . * Alternative (not recommended) to locating with Practice & procedure at SBW 8LN.
DX . . . Custody of accused
DXD D . . . . Death in custody

[Central government administration SCL]
[Law enforcement agencies SCMY]
[Police law SCNA]
. [Operations]
. . [Legal procedure in police work SCNH]
. . . [Custody of accused SCNDX]
. . . . [Death in custody SCNDXDD]

. *Types of police forces*
SCN JD . . International police
JE . . National police, centralized police forces
JJ . . Local police forces
L . . Paramilitary police forces
LR . . Auxiliary police forces, special constabulary
M . . Private security forces
MP . . . Particular private forces
. . . . * Arrange A/Z.
N . . . Private detectives
NP . . . Voluntary police, vigilantes
O . . . Industrial police, security guards
. *Functions*
U . . Law & order maintenance, public safety
UXB . . . Crowd control, riot control
UXF . . . Demonstrations
UXG . . . Industrial disputes, strikes

SCO Penal law
. * The general class for penology is QQ; this class takes only works dealing with the status of penal actions in constitutional law.
. * Add to SCO letters E/Y following QQ in QQE/QQY.
SCO EN . Non-custodial treatment
FO . . Loss of rights
FR . Physical punishment, corporal punishment
FW . . Capital punishment, death penalty
G . Prisons, custodial punishment
GF . . Security in prisons
GJ . . . Discipline in prisons
GK . . Offences in prison
HR . . Rights & privileges of prisoners
HRR . . . Requests by prisoners
HRT . . . Complaints by prisoners
M . . Parole
N . . Release from prison, discharge from prison
NPV . . . Remission, reduction of prison sentences
P . . Conditions in prisons, welfare of prisoners
Q . . Prison sentences
S . . *Types of prisons*
. . . * Add to SCOS letters K/V following QQS; e.g. remand centres SCO SL.
. . . * Add to SCO SW letters T/Y following QQ; e.g. Rehabilitation centres SCO SWX.
TA . . Offenders, criminals

[Constitutional law SC]
[Jurisdictions by level of organization]
[Central government administration SCL]
. [Law enforcement agencies SCMY]
. . [Penal law SCO]
. . . [Prisons SCOG]
. . . . [Offenders SCOTA]

. . . . . * Add to SCOT letters B/E following QR.
. . . . *Types of offenders*
SCO TF . . . . . Discharged prisoners, ex-prisoners
TG . . . . . . After-care of ex-prisoners
U . . . . . Other
. . . . . . * Add to SCOU letters G/Y following QR in QRR/QRY.
. . . . . . * Add to SCOV letters A/Y following QS in QSA/ASY.
. . . . . . * Add to SCOW letters E/Y following QT in QTE/QTY.

. Other administrative agencies & functions
YC . . Coastguards
YE . . Emergency services (general), rescue services (general)

SCQ Devolved government & administration, decentralized government & administration
. * Add to SCQ letters A/K following SC.
SCQ K . Public administration
KF . . Administrative law
KI . . Organization of public administration
KIQ . . . Management
KJ . . Departments, agencies
KK . . . General operations
M . . . *Specific departments*
. . . . * Add to SCQ letters M/Q following SCL so far as applicable.

SCR . Regional government, regional administration
. . * In non-federal states.
. . * Add to SCR letters A/Q following SCQ.
. . *Types of regions by function*
SCR R . . . Ad hoc regional agencies
. . . . * Arrange A/Z.
. . . . * E.g. Regional Planning Areas.
Y . . . *By geographical region*
. . . . * Use only under specific jurisdictions.
. . . . * Add to SCP Y letters A/Z following classmark of country concerned in Auxiliary Schedule 2.

aSC S . State government & administration
. . * In states with federal structure.
. . * Add to SCS letters A/Q following SCQ.
SCT . . *Individual states*
. . . * Notes under SCR Y apply here also.

[Constitutional law SC]
[Secondary materials]
[Substantive law SC9VB]
[Jurisdictions by level of organization]
[Devolved government & administration SCQ]
[State government & administration aSCS]
. [Individual states SCT]

SCU Local government, local authorities
. * See notes at RLU Local government (general) on its differences from central government structure. Division of SCU is parallel with that in RLU & details from the latter may be added if required.
. * Add to SCU letters A/Q following SCQ.
SCU GC . Accountability
GE . Powers
. Legislature
I . . Local councils
IJ . . . Councillors
IND . . . Meetings of local authorities
J . Executive
JKU . . Mayors
K . Local administration
KIU . . Personnel
KIU X . . . Chief executives
MJ . . Taxation
MLP . . . Rating law
. *Types of authorities*
. . Add to SCU letters S/T following RLU in RLUS/RLUT.
SG . . Single tier local authorities
. . . * With comprehensive authority over most services.
SI . . Multi-tier local authorities
. . . * With limited authority over a number of services.
SU . . Urban council, municipal councils
TJ . . County councils
TR . . Rural councils
TV . . Joint authorities
SCV . *Individual local authorities*
. . * Notes under SCR Y apply here also.

SCW Overseas territories, colonies, dependencies
. * This class takes general works on the constitutional law of empires, colonial systems & other forms of dependencies which a country might possess.
. * For the constitutional law of a particular territory, see the territory (in SL/SV); e.g. SVR EC Hong Kong (at present, 1996, a British possession).
. * Add to SCW letters A/U following SC.

Constitutional law

[Public law SBY]
[Constitutional law SC]
[Secondary materials]
[Substantive law SC9VB]
[Jurisdictions by level of organization]
. [Devolved government & administration SCQ]
. . [Overseas territories SCW]

SCX Judiciary
. * Constitutional status, powers, etc. For particular offices & personnel, see function; e.g. Law officers S6K B.
. * Add to SCX letters A/S following RLY so far as applicable; e.g. SCX J Executive process & the judiciary in constituional law.

SCY B Ecclesiastical law (in national law), secular ecclesiastical law, church & state
. * For ecclesiastical law, see SWE.
B2 . *Primary materials*
. . * These apply only to the ecclesiastical law of a particular state.
. . Treaties
B2M S . . . Concordats
B9V B . Substantive law
. *Subjects special to ecclesiastical law*
BE . . State & church jurisdiction
BES . . . Separation of church & state
BF . . . Autonomy of church
BG . . . Secular courts jurisdiction over church
BJ . . Disestablishment of church
BK . . Religious corporations, religious congregations
BL . . Relations of state to particular religions
. . . * For jurisdiction of a specific religion, see latter in SX.
BM . . . Established church
BP . . . Particular non-established religions
. . . . * Arrange A/Z.

[Constitutional law SC]
[Secondary materials]
[Substantive law SC9VB]
. [Ecclesiastical law in national law SCYB]
. . [Subjects special to ecclesiastical law]
. . . [Relations of state to particular religions SCYBL]
. . . . [Particular non-established religions SCYBP]

SCY D . Foreign relations, international relations
. . * For international relations in international law, see SDM B. This class is concerned mainly with the implications of international relations for the constitutional law of individual jurisdictions.
. . * Add to SCY D numbers & letters 3/9, A/Y following SD so far as applicable.
D3 . . International law & constitutional law
D5G T . . Diplomacy & constitutional law
D5H . . Treaties & constitutional law
D5L S . . International organizations & constitutional law
D5N . . . United Nations & constitutional law
D5S C . . Comitas & constitutional law
D5X D . . International disputes & constitutional law
. . . * See also National security SCL V
. . . * For war, see SCY DR.
DF . . Sovereignty in international relations
DK . . National territory
DR . . War & constitutional law

E Supranational associations & constitutional law
. * Add to SCY letters E/H following S in SE/SH so far as applicable.
F . Preferred supranational association
. . * This is used only under a specific country & will take the appropriate notation from SF/SH; e.g. for members or the European Union it will be SCY F.

J . *By present location of jurisdiction*
. . * For use when an ethnic jurisdiction is applied within separate national jurisdictions. See SI (note 4) for example.

M *Constitutional law of nation states*
. * Add to SCY letters M/N following R in RM/RN, except for RMF/RMH.

. *States by governmental structure*
. . * General works only. Do not compound with individual states (in SL/SV).
MC . . Monarchies
MD . . . Constitutional monarchies
ME . . Republics
MK . . Absolutist states
ML . . Dictatorships
MO . . Oligarchies

[Public law SBY]
[Constitutional law SC]
[Secondary materials]
[Constitutional law of nation states SCYM]
[States by governmental structure]
. [Oligarchies SCYMO]

SCY MOT . . Military governments
MQ . Constitutional democracies
NK . Theocratic states
NV Pluralist states, multiracial states

P . Unitary states, centralized states
Q . Federal states
R . . Confederations

By individual state
. * See SI/SV; the subdivision X under each state
. signifies its constitutional law (see Auxiliary
. Schedule S1).

SCY X Jurisdictions, legal systems
. * MC3
. * This general class should not be qualified by the preceding facets S2/SCW; the concept of a containing legal system is implicit in all of them. Exceptions may occasionally be called for in the case of common subdivisions; e.g. see History SCY X4 below.

X4 . *History*
. . * History of law in general is S4. Locate here only those works which consider the different types of jurisdictions (national, religious, etc.) rather than the processes, subjects of law and jurisdictions together. If in doubt, prefer S4.

X59 . *Relations between systems, comparisons*

. *By political authority*

SD . . International law, law of nations, public international law
. . . * MC3
. . . * The body of customary law and treaty rules accepted as legally binding by nation states in their relations with each other.
. . . * The relations between international law and politics are very close. For those libraries preferring to locate international law in politics, an alternative (not recommended) is provided at ROF.
. . . *Common subdivisions*
. . . . * See works about international law (SD3).

SD2 . . . Primary materials
. . . . * Works of law (texts of treaties, etc.) as distinct from works about the law.
. . . . * The categories of primary materials for national and supranational jurisdictions (given in Auxiliary Schedules S2 & S3) are not appropriate for international law. But the following schedule is consistent with them so far as possible & further details may be drawn from them, as indicated at several points.
. . . . * For classes divided by date, follow the instructions in Auxiliary Schedule S2 (note 8/9); e.g. Treaty of Versailles (1919) SD2 DNU V.
. . . . * For primary materials of a given country relating to its foreign relations, see the constitutional law of that country; e.g. USA - Foreign relations - Legislative documents - Senate SPY D2D.

SD2 2 . . . . *By language*
. . . . . * If necessary, qualify by language as follows:
. . . . . * Add to -2 (where the hyphen represents the subject to to be qualified) letters C/Y in Auxiliary Schedule 3; e.g. Versailles treaty (in French) SD2 DNU V2F.

3 . . . . *Common subdivisions*

3R . . . . . Guides to the documentation

[Jurisdictions SCYX]
[By political authority]
[International law SD]
[Primary materials SD2]
[Common subdivisions SD23]
. [Guides to the documentation SD23R]

SD2 4 *Special subsidiary forms*
. * The notes under 24 in Auxiliary Schedule S2 apply here also. These special forms are used primarily to qualify materials in SD2B/SD2Y; indexes, collections, etc. of a particular kind of material go with the latter; e.g., index to cases of the International Court of Justice SD2 O44.
. * Add to SD2 numbers 4/9 following 2 in Auxiliary Schedule S2. A brief selection of some prominent classes is given below for convenience.

44 . Indexes

5 . Official texts

6 . Non-official texts

7 . Collections serial

7B . Collections monographic

8 . Digests

B Treaties, conventions, agreements
. * Texts only. For treaties, etc. as a subject (their significance, drafting, etc.) see SD5 H.
. * For treaties on a specific subject (e.g. air transport) see subject. But peace treaties are excepted, because of the generality of their subject coverage (see SD2 D).

B7 . Collections general

B75 . . Official series

B75 LE . . . League of Nations treaty series

B75 UN . . . United Nations treaty series
. . . . * E.g. Organization of American states series.

B76 . . Non-official series

B76 HU . . . Hudson's international legislation

BB . Regional organizations international treaties
. . * For treaties between members of one organization, see the organization.
. . * Add to SD2 BB letters F/H following S; e.g. EU treaties with external parties SD2 BBG.

BE . *By country*
. . * Add to SD2 B letters E/Z in Auxiliary Schedule 2.

C . Single multilateral treaties

D . . Peace treaties (texts)
. . . * Arrange by date, then name; e.g.

DNU V . . . Versailles treaty (1919)

E . Single bilateral treaties (texts) [
. . * Arrange by date, then first named country (using Auxiliary Schedule 2).

[Jurisdictions SCYX]
[By political authority]
[International law SD]
[Primary materials SD2]
[Treaties SD2B]
. [Single bilateral treaties texts [SD2E]

SD2 F International conferences, international congresses (international law), international meetings
. * The central role of international conferences is acting as forums for discussion, etc., out of which may develop formal treaties, agreements, etc. The preferred place for them is at SD5 LC.
. * This location is an alternative (not recommended) for libraries wishing to treat the texts of their proceedings, resolutions, etc. as primary materials. If this option is taken, proceed as follows:
. * Add to SD2 F letters D/Q following SD5 L.

K Legislation
. * The classes 2L/2N in Auxiliary Schedule S3 (for Supranational law) generally have no equivalent as yet in International law. Letters K/M are reserved here for the eventuality.
. * For the League of Nations & United Nations, (which give the nearest approach to an equivalent) see SD5 M/N.

L . Official acts & regulations

M . *Other forms of legislation*
. . * Add to SD2M letters B/Y following 2N in Auxiliary Schedule S3; e.g. SD2 MB Directives.

MH . . Codes (international law primary materials)

N Cases in international law (texts), law reports, reports of decisions
. * Completely general collections, etc. only, covering decisions of international courts, regional courts and national courts. Most collections are of the first; see SD2 NC.
. * For caselaw as a subject, see S5Q.
. * For cases, claims, etc. relating to specific areas of law, see latter; e.g., for Alabama case, see War - Maritime - Neutrality - Cases (1871) SDW MSC 2N9 LM.

N7 . General collections

N87 . Digests of cases serial

N87 B . Digests monographic

N9 . Individual cases (by date)
. . * Add to the classmark obtained the name of the case.

[Jurisdictions SCYX]
[By political authority]
[International law SD]
[Primary materials SD2]
[Cases in international law texts SD2N]
[Individual cases by date SD2N9]

By court
. * Each type of court, or individual court, may be qualified by classes 9/P as indicated at 2PB in Auxiliary Schedule S2; e.g SD2 OB International Court of Justice - Court records.

SD2 NC . International court cases
. . * Reports and allied official documents only; for international courts as a subject, see SD7.
. . * For courts concerned with specific topics, see topic (e.g. war crimes).
. . * See also supranational courts; e.g. Court of Justice of the European Union SG7 R.

NE . . Permanent Court of International Justice

NE7 5 . . . Official series, by letter & number

NE7 6 . . . Non-official series
. . . . * Arrange A/Z by name.

NE7 B . . . Collections monographic

O . . International Court of Justice, Permanent Court of the Hague, World Court at the Hague
. . . * Set up by UN in succession to the Permanent Court of International Justice.

O75 . . . Official series
. . . . * Arrange by letter and number.

O76 . . . Non-official series

P . . Other international courts
. . . * Arrange A/Z.

Q . . *By country brought to court*
. . . * Add to SD2 Q letters E/Z in Auxiliary Schedule 2.
. . . * The letter(s) for the country bringing the action may be added to that of the defendant country; see instruction at S48 (note 4).

R . Regional (interstate) courts cases (texts)
. . * When involving states outside the region. For cases of disputes within the region, see the latter.
. . * Add to SD2 R letters G/H following S in SG/SH; e.g. Court of Justice of the European Union SD2 RG.

[Jurisdictions SCYX]
[By political authority]
[International law SD]
[Primary materials SD2]
. [Cases in international law texts SD2N]
. . [By court]
. . . [Regional interstate courts cases texts SD2R]

SD2 S . . . National courts cases
. . . . * Decisions & opinions, etc. involving questions of international law decided by national courts.
SE . . . . *By country*
. . . . . * Add to SD2 S letters E/Z in Auxiliary Schedule 2.
T . . . *By subject*
. . . * Alternative (not recommended) to locating with subject. If this option is taken, proceed as follows:
. . . * Add to SD2 T letters A/Y in Auxiliary Schedule S1.

U . . Arbitration cases, arbitral awards

U75 . . . Official series
U75 U . . . . United Nations Reports of International Arbitral Awards
U9 . . . Individual single cases by date
V . . . Permanent Court of Arbitration, The Hague (cases)
V75 . . . . Official reports & series
V76 . . . . Unofficial collections & series
VG . . . Other permanent/semipermanent arbitral bodies
. . . . * Arrange A/Z.
VM . . . Mixed arbitral tribunals & commissions (cases)
. . . . * Arrange A/Z.

Secondary materials, works about international law

SD3 . International law (works about), law of nations, public international law
. . * Most of the literature calling itself International law deals almost entirely with public international law. Use this class also for works which deal with public and private international law together.
. . * For private international law (conflict of laws) see SA (which has an alternative at SDA).
. . *Common subdivisions*
SD3 3G . . . Journals
. . . . * For journals serving as primary materials, see S28 E.
4 . . . Legal profession
7WD . . . . Advisory services
D . . . Organizations
DC . . . . International Commission of Jurists
DL . . . . International Law Commission (UN)

[By political authority]
[International law SD]
[Secondary materials]
[International law works about SD3]
[Common subdivisions]
. [Organizations SD3D]
. . [International Law Commission UN SD3DL]

SD4 . History & theory of international law
. . * This deals with both theory and practice of international law in the periods and places concerned. For historical jurisprudence alone, see SD5 A6A.
. . * See also Jurisprudence in international law SD5 A
SD5 9 *Relations between systems*
9HY . Municipal law & international law

A Jurisprudence
A67 . Jurisprudence as theory of law
A6A . Historical jurisprudence
. . * The usual treatment of history (division by place then period) is changed here to meet the particular requirements of international law.
. . *By broad period, then country*
. . . * Add to SD5 A numbers 7/8 following S5A in S5A7/S5A8 with the modifications as to special topics and writers indicated below; e.g. 18th century Individual writers - Switzerland - Vattel SD5 A8F JBV.
A7C . . . International law in the Ancient world
A7G . . . . Ancient East international law
A7L . . . . Ancient Greece in international law
. . . . . *Special topics*
A7M B . . . . . . Rhodian laws
A7M C . . . . . . Other
. . . . * Arrange A/Z.
A7P . . . . Ancient Rome in international law
. . . . . *Special topics*
A7Q B . . . . . . Jus feciale
A7Q C . . . . . . Jus gentium
A7Q D . . . . . . Jus sacrum
A7Q E . . . . . . Other
. . . . * Arrange A/Z.
A7S . . . . Other places in the Ancient World
. . . . . * Arrange A/Z.
A7T . . . Medieval international law
. . . . * To c. 1500.
. . . . *Special topics*
A7V B . . . . . Consulate of the sea
A7V C . . . . . Laws of Oleron
A7V D . . . . . Laws of Trani
A7V E . . . . . Other
. . . . . . * Arrange A/Z.
A7V G . . . . Writers & publicists
. . . . . * Arrange A/Z.

[Secondary materials]
[International law works about SD3]
[Jurisprudence SD5A]
[Historical jurisprudence SD5A6A]
[By broad period]
[Medieval international law SD5A7T]
. [Writers & publicists SD5A7VG]

SD5 A8 Modern international law
. * Historical and jurisprudential treatments only.
A87 . *By place*
. . * For general works only on a country in the modern period. For that country in a particular period, see the period.
. . * Add to SD5 A87 letters E/Z in Auxiliary Schedule 2.
A9 . *By period*
. . * The instructions following S5A 8D apply here also.
. . * Each writer within a period may be divided as follows:
. . * Add to - (where the hyphen represents their classmark):
. . - 3 Collections
. . - 37 Selections
. . - 62 Individual works
. . * Use 62/64 for major titles.
. . - 6A Other individual works, A/Z
. . - 89 Biography & criticism
. . - 8M Commentaries & criticism
. . - A/Y Subject of author's work
. . * Alternative (not recommended) for libraries with a special collection on the writer - the A/Y representing letters following S in SA/SY.
A8A . . 1500-1700
A8B . . . *Special topics*
. . . . * Arrange A/Z.
. . . *Writers & publicists*
. . . . * Arrange A/Z.
A8C G . . . . Grotius
. . . . . *Individual works*
A8C G62 . . . . . . De jure belli ac pacis
A8C G6A . . . . . . Other
. . . . * Arrange A/Z.
A8C P . . . . Pufendorf
A8D . . 18th century
A8E . . . *Special topics*
. . . . * Arrange A/Z.
A8F . . . *By place & individual writer*
A8G . . 19th century

[International law works about SD3]
[Jurisprudence SD5A]
[Historical jurisprudence SD5A6A]
. [By broad period]
. . [Modern international law SD5A8]
. . . [By period SD5A9]
. . . . [19th century SD5A8G]

SD5 A8H . . . . . *Special topics*
. . . . . . * Arrange A/Z.
A8J . . . . . *By place & individual writer*
A8K . . . . 20th century
A8L . . . . . *Special topics*
A8M . . . . . *By place & individual writer*
A8N . . . . 21st century
A8O . . . . . *Special topics*
A8P . . . . . *By place & individual writer*

AN Social-political theory
BA . Political theory & international law
BAN S . . Nationalism & international law
BAS T . . Marxism & international law
BP Comparative law
BW Justiciability

C Sources of international law
CH . Codification
. . * See also International Law Commission SD3 DL
CH2 E . . Conferences
CH2 GXP T . . . Hague Codification Conference 1930
D . Custom
GD . Formal sources

GP . Processes of international law, regulatory agencies, law making agencies
. . * Providing codes of practice (which are very often, if not always, observed) for the self-regulation of international relations and providing mechanisms for the settling of disputes.
. . * For practice and procedure in international law, see SD6.
GT . . Diplomacy, diplomatic missions
. . . * The main class for this is in political science (ROT). Class here only those works which consider the role of diplomacy as a source of international law.
. . . * See also Foreign services & diplomacy SDM T

Processes of international law

[International law SD]
[Secondary materials]
[International law works about SD3]
[Jurisprudence SD5A]
[Sources of international law SD5C]
[Processes of international law SD5GP]
[Diplomacy SD5GT]

SD5 H Treaties, international agreements (as subject)-
. * These are called by many different names (agreements, treaties, conventions, pacts, compacts, protocols, charters, statutes, acts, covenants, declarations, regulations, engagements, arrangements, accords, provisions); but many of these terms have other meanings also.
. * The only distinctions made below (apart from general discussions of certain variants) are those between treaties and alliances (associated usually with military agreements) and between treaties, etc. and conferences.
. * This is the main class for international agreements as a subject. For works concerned with agreements as part of the political process of international relations, see politics ROA WO.
. * Treaty law relating to specific subjects goes with the subject in international law (e.g. boundaries, taxation).
. * For the texts of treaties, see Primary materials SD2B.
. * Normal retroactive synthesis by S5H/T is interrupted here in order to incorporate details of treaties as a subject and of other processes of international law. It is resumed at SD5 T.

H3L R . Treaties & conventions
H3L RM . . Vienna Convention on the Law of Treaties 1969
HCD . Interpretation of treaties
. *Special operations*
HK . . Formation of treaties, treaty-making, treaty-conclusion
HL . . . Proposals, drafts
HM . . . Negotiation of treaties
HN . . . Adoption of treaties
HP . . . Consent to be bound (treaties)
HQ . . . Reservations in treaties
HR . . . Ratification of treaties, approval of treaties
HR . . . Registration of treaties

[Jurisprudence SD5A]
[Sources of international law SD5C]
[Processes of international law SD5GP]
[Treaties SD5H]
[Special operations]
. [Formation of treaties SD5HK]
. . [Registration of treaties SD5HR]

SD5 HS . . Acceptance of treaties
HT . . Entry into force of treaties
HV . Implementing of treaties
JB . Enforcement of treaties
. . * For enforcement of judgements by courts, see International courts SD9 GI.
JC . . Compulsory enforcement of treaties
JD . . Adherence to treaties
JE . . Violation of treaties
JF . . Amendment of treaties, revision of treaties
JG . . Renewal of treaties
JH . . Termination of treaties, voidance of treaties, breach of treaties
JJ . . . Suspension of treaties
JK . . . Renunciation of treaties
JL . . . . Rebus sic stantibus
Properties
JP . Application of treaties
. . * Territorial scope, etc.
JQ . . Duration of treaties
JR . Validity of treaties
JS . Binding force of treaties
JT . Obligation in treaties
JU . Reciprocity in treaties
. . * For favoured nation clause, see Commercial law SBN ONT.
JW . Pacta sunt servanda
Elements
KB . Third parties in treaties
Types of agreements
. *By property*
. . * For Invalid treaties, see Validity SD5 JR.
. *By form*
KE . State agreement forms
KF . . Ententes
KG . . Declarations (treaties)
KH . . . Unilateral declarations
KI . . . Mutual support declarations
KJ . . Law-making treaties
KK . . Contract treaties, guaranty treaties
KM . . Multilateral treaties
KO . . Bilateral treaties
KP . . Executive state agreements
. *By subject*
. . * Works on treaties concerned with specific subject of international law go with that subject (e.g.boundaries, arbitration, peace). Those below are too diffuse in subject definition to justify separation.

Processes of international law

[International law works about SD3]
[Jurisprudence SD5A]
[Sources of international law SD5C]
[Processes of international law SD5GP]
[Treaties SD5H]
. [Types of agreements]
. . [By subject]

. . . * For agreements centred on military
. . . cooperation, see Alliances SDN YG.

SD5 KS . . . Cultural agreements
KT . . . Friendship agreements
KV . . . *Special to a subject*
. . . . * For use under a specific topic - e.g. Non-
. . . . agression pacts SDR 5KV.
KY . . *By country*
. . . * Add to SD5 LY letters E/Z in Auxiliary
. . . Schedule 2.

LC International conferences, international congresses, international conventions
. * Establishing rules expressly recognized by the
. contesting states and which are the prime
. source of the law applied by the International
. Court of Justice. The resulting agreements are
. generally contained in treaties (see SD5 H for
. treaties as a subject and SD2 F for their texts
. as primary materials).
. * This class takes all the literature produced by
. and relating to conferences. An alternative (not
. recommended) is provided at SD2 F for the
. texts of acts, proceedings, etc. when regarded as
. primary materials (see notes at SD2 F).
. * Conferences on specific subjects go with the
. subject (e.g. copyright). But peace conferences
. are included here since their role is usually
. wider in scope than the question of a peace
. settlement.

[International law SD]
[Secondary materials]
[International law works about SD3]
[Jurisprudence SD5A]
[Sources of international law SD5C]
[Processes of international law SD5GP]
[International conferences SD5LC]

Individual conferences, etc.
. * Each conference may be divided
. as follows (where the hyphen
. represents the classmark of the
. conference):
. -2 Special forms of publications
. * Add to -2 numbers 2/8
. following 2
. in Auxiliary Schedule S2 so far
. as
. applicable; e.g. Indexes 244.
. -4 History
. -C Proceedings, discussions
. -E Acts, resolutions,
. recommendations, etc.
. * Arrange by date.
. -G Treaties, agreements, etc.
. resulting
. * Alternative (not
. recommended) to
. locating at SD2 B.
. * Arrange by date.
. -J Related treaties, agreements,
. etc.
. * Protocols, amendments, etc.
. * Arrange by date.
. -L Other materials
. * Preliminary correspondence,
. announcements, etc.
. -Q Participating countries
. * Add to Q letters E/Z in
. Auxiliary
. Schedule 2.
. * Under each country, add
. numbers &
. letters 2/L following the hyphen
. above;
. e.g. Participants - Great
. Britain -
. Proceedings -QEC.
. -R Subsequent conferences
. * Use for series of conferences;
. e.g.
. -R First conference, -S Second...

[Secondary materials]
[International law works about SD3]
[Jurisprudence SD5A]
[Sources of international law SD5C]
[Processes of international law SD5GP]
[International conferences SD5LC]
[Individual conferences]

SD5 LD Pre-1899 (by date)
LDH Q . Congress of Vienna 1815
LI Other international congresses, 1899-1919 (by date)
LJ Paris Peace Conference 1919
. * For texts of the treaty, see Treaty of Versailles SD2 DNU V.
LL Other international congresses, 1919-1943 (by date)
. * For United Nations preliminary conferences, see United Nations SD5 N7.
. * For conferences on specific subjects, see subject; e.g. Universal Copyright Convention (1952) SDB LK5 LNQ N.
LN Post-1945
Quasi-conferences
LQ . International meetings & visits, international talks
. . * Add to SD5 LQ letters A/K following ROA VW (Political meetings, etc.).
LQC . . Particular meetings (by date)
. . . * When membership is too general to justify classing below.
LQE . . Summits (international meetings)
. . . * Of heads of governments or other senior members of governments.
LQF . . . Particular summits (by date)
LQG . . Heads of State meetings
LQH . . . Particular heads of state meetings (by date)
LQJ . . Foreign ministers meetings
LQK . . . Particular foreign ministers meetings

[Processes of international law SD5GP]
[International conferences SD5LC]
. [Individual conferences]
. . [Quasi-conferences]
. . . [International meetings & visits SD5LQ]
. . . . [Foreign ministers meetings SD5LQJ]
. . . . . [Particular foreign ministers meetings SD5LQK]

SD5 LS International organizations
. * Bodies set up (by multilateral agreements between states, by resolutions of the United Nations, etc.) for cooperative purposes - peace-keeping, public health, communications, etc. Following from their general function, these organizations are also significant as sources of international law - by sponsoring multilateral treaties, elucidating and developing customary international law by declarations, resolutions and practice, etc.
. * The preferred arrangement is to locate general works on these organizations in Class R Politics (RPF/RPH). Locate here only those works which consider their role in international law narrowly.
. * This class takes organizations which are truly international in scope. For supranational organizations restricted to particular regions of the world, see supranational law SE.
. * For international courts, see SD7.
. * Organizations concerned with a specific problem go with the subject; e.g. World Intellectual Property Organization (WIPO) SDB LJ5 LT.
. * Each organization may be divided as follows (where the hyphen represents the classmark of the organization or its significant part):
. * Add to -2 number 2/8 following 2 in Auxiliary Schedule S2 so far as applicable.
. -4 History
. -B Organization & management of organization
. -F Constitution
. -G Charter
. -H Membership (general)
. * For individual participants, see -X
. -I Governing body
. -K Proceedings, debates
. -M Acts, resolutions, etc.
. -P Special commissions, conferences
. * For those on special subjects, see subject.
. -Q Branches
. -R Local
. -T National
. -V Functional
. -X Participatory nations
. * Add to -X letters E/Z in Auxiliary Schedule 2.
LT . Individual organizations
. . * SD5 LT/SD5 LW may be used for these under a specific subject.

International organizations

[Secondary materials]
[International law works about SD3]
[Jurisprudence SD5A]
[Sources of international law SD5C]
[Processes of international law SD5GP]
[International organizations SD5LS]
[Individual organizations SD5LT]

SD5 M League of Nations
. * The general class for the League is in Politics, at RPF. Locate in Class S only strictly legal material.
. * Add to SD5 M numbers & letters 5/W following RPF so far as applicable; e.g.

ML . Assembly of League of Nations
MM . Council of League of Nations
MN . Secretariat
MRM . Agencies, commissions of the League

N United Nations
. * The general class for UN is in Politics, at RPG. Locate in Class S only strictuly legal material.
. * Add to SD5 N numbers & letters 5/W following RPG; e.g.

N7 . History
N7R . . Dumbarton Oaks Conference (1944)
N7S . . San Francisco Conference (1945)
NL . General Assembly (UN)
NM . Security Council (UN)
NN . Secretariat (UN)
NQ . Judicial institutions of UN
. . * For International Court of Justice, see SD7 N.
NRM . Agencies, commissions of UN
NS . . Economic & Social Committee of UN
NT Specialized agencies of international administration
. * Most of these are affiliated to the UN (which was instrumental in setting many of them up).
. * Agencies with clearly defined and limited application (e.g. IMF, ILO) are subordinated to the subject in in international law; e.g. Trusteeship Council SDL T5N T. Those with less well defined fields of action are located here.
. * An alternative (not recommended) is to locate them at SD5 P below.
NU . Unesco
NVC . Children's Emergency Fund

[International law works about SD3]
[Jurisprudence SD5A]
[Sources of international law SD5C]
[Processes of international law SD5GP]
. [International organizations SD5LS]
. . [Specialized agencies of international administration SD5NT]
. . . [Children's Emergency Fund SD5NVC]

SD5 NVF . . . Food & Agricultural Organization, FAO
NVR . . . Relief & Works Agency (UN)
O . . *By subject*
. . . * General works only on quasi-international organizations set up by multilateral agreements to regulate specific areas of interest; e.g. OPEC for the oil industry.
. . . * An alternative (not recommended) is to locate specific subjects here also. If this option is taken, proceed as follows:
. . . * Add to SD5 P letters A/U following SB in SBA/SBU; e.g. Universal Postal Union SD5 PQM.
Q . . Regional organizations
. . . * For organizations specified by a region which is not in itself a supranational jurisdiction.
. . . * Add to SD5 Q letters G/H following S; e.g. African Postal Union SDB QM5 QHO C.
R . . Non-governmental organizations in international law
. . . * Alternative (not recommended) to locating in the subject; if this option is taken, proceed as follows:
. . . * Add to SD5 R letters A/U following SB in SBA/SBU.

. Other processes in international law
SC . . Comitas, international courtesy
. . . * See also Cooperation in international law SDN K
SD . . . Precedence in international relations

TK Other sources
. * Normal retroactive synthesis by S5H/S5T is resumed here after its interruption at SD5 H.
. * Add to SD5 T letters K/T following S5 so far as applicable (i.e., excluding those concepts at S5H/J already provided for above).
TMT . Retrospective legislation
TN . Codes
TPW . Precedents
TQ . . Case law
. . . * For texts of law reports, see primary materials SD2 N.

[Secondary materials]
[International law works about SD3]
[Jurisprudence SD5A]
. [Sources of international law SD5C]
. . [Other sources SD5TK]
. . . [Precedents SD5TPW]
. . . . [Case law SD5TQ]

SD5 TTF . . . Documentary sources, publicists
. . . . * For individual publicists, see Historical jurisprudence S5A 6A.

UB . International law & society
UN . . Natural law
UT . . Rule of law
VK . . Rights & duties
. . . * For particular rights, see Persons in international law, SDA P.
. . *Special fields of social action*
WQG N . Emergencies
. . * For aid & relief measures in the event of disasters, see QGN.
XD . Disputes in international law (general)
XF . . Settlement of disputes
XP . . . Peaceful settlement of disputes (general)
. . . . * For judicial settlement, see SDP 6; for non-judicial methods of dispute settlement see SDQ/SDR.

Practice & procedure in international law
SD6 A . Judicial settlement, adjudication & arbitration
. . * The distinction between adjudication and arbitration is much less significant in international law than in municipal law and they are usually considered together.
. . * Use this class also for works on adjudication alone. For arbitration treated alone see SD9 R.
E . . Courts & court procedure
. . . * For court decisions, see Primary materials SD2 N.
H . . . Jurisdiction of court
HQ . . . . Status of forces agreed
. . . . . * For example, of friendly armed forces stationed in a foreign country.
KB . . . Law officers
. . . . Judges
N . . . . . International judges
. . . *Types of courts*
. . . . * For courts concerned with specific subjects, see subject (e.g. arbitration, human rights).
SD7 . . . . International courts
SD7 M . . . . . Permanent Court of International Justice, World court
. . . . . . * 1921-1945.
N . . . . . International Court of Justice
. . . . . . * 1945-

[International law works about SD3]
[Practice & procedure in international law]
[Judicial settlement SD6A]
[Courts & court procedure SD6E]
[Types of courts]
. [International courts SD7]
. . [International Court of Justice SD7N]

SD7 W . National courts in international law

SD8 Actions in international law
SD8 A . Parties
AF . . Attitude of parties to adjudication
AG . . Reservations by parties (international courts)
AH . . . Reservations as to time
AI . . . Reciprocity in international law
AJ . . . . Optimal clauses (reciprocity)
C . . Plaintiff
CD . . . *By supranational jurisdiction*
. . . . * Add to SD8 CD letters G/H following S in SG/SH.
CE . . . *By national jurisdiction*
. . . . * Add to SD8 C letters E/Z in Auxiliary Schedule 2.
D . . Defendant
DD . . . *By supranational jurisdiction*
. . . . * Add to SD8 DD letters G/H following S in SG/SH.
DE . . . *By national jurisdiction*
. . . . * Add to SD8 D letters E/Z in Auxiliary Schedule 2.
AG . . Reservations by parties (international courts)
AH . . . As to time
AI . . . Reciprocity in international law
AJ . . . . Optimal clauses (reciprocity)
MV . . Non-appearance in court
SD9 F . Judgement
FG . . Judicial unpredictability
G . Remedies in international law
. . * As a subject; for the judgements themselves, see Primary materials SD2 N Court decisions.
GHE . . Exhaustion of remedies
GI . . Enforcement of judgements
GV . . Local remedies
H . . Appeals
H7 . . . Appeal courts in international law

. *Other results of litigation*
Q . . Compromise
QR . . Negotiation
QRT . . . Good offices in international disputes
QRV . . . Inquiries (settlement of disputes)
QS . . . Conciliation
. . . . * Combines inquiry & mediation.
QT . . . Mediation

Judicial settlement

[Practice & procedure in international law]
[Judicial settlement SD6A]
[Courts & court procedure SD6E]
[Actions in international law SD8]
. [Other results of litigation]
. . [Negotiation SD9QR]
. . . [Mediation SD9QT]

SD9 R . . Arbitration
. . . * See also note at SD6 A
. . . Courts
R7 . . . . Arbitration courts
R7J . . . . . Permanent Court of Arbitration (The Hague), Hague Tribunal
. . . . . . * 1899-
R7K . . . . . Others
. . . . . . * Arrange A/Z.
R7L . . . . *By various characteristics*
. . . . . * It is unlikely the international arbitration courts will need to be specified by these, but the provision is made here for the eventuality.
. . . . . * Add to SD9 R7L letters H/M following S7.
R7U B . . . . International administrative tribunals
. . . . . * Hearing disputes between international organizations and their staff.
R7U F . . . . Claims commissions
R7U G . . . . . Individual courts [
R7U H . . . . Mixed arbitral tribunals
R7U J . . . . . Individual tribunals, A/Z
R7U L . . . Papal arbitration
UX Non-peaceful settlements
. * See International relations (subjects of law) SDPE/SDR.

[International law SD]
[Secondary materials]
[International law works about SD3]
[Practice & procedure in international law]
. [Judicial settlement SD6A]
. . [Courts & court procedure SD6E]
. . . [Non-peaceful settlements SD9UX]

SD9 VB Subjects of international law, substantive international law
. * Add to SD numbers & letters 9VB/B following S.
W . Private law
SDA . . International private law, conflict of laws
. . . * Alternative (not recommended) to locating under private law at SA (see the note there). If this option is taken, proceed as follows:
. . . * Add to SDA letters A/O following SA in SAA/SAO.

. . Persons in international law
SDA P . . . International persons
Q . . . . Personality in international law
QT . . . . . Legal rights
. . . . . . * For international law of human rights see SDB YCW.
V . . . . Individual persons in international law
. . . . . *Special categories of persons*
. . . . . . * For state as person, see SDE M.
SDB BN . . . . . . *By citizenship status*
. . . . * For those categories defined by citizenship status broadly (SBB N/SBB W), see SDD ON Nationals, etc.
BNG . . . . . . Slaves
BNJ . . . . . . White slave traffic
BQ . . . . . . Minorities
BWR . . . . . . Refugees, displaced persons
CTB . . . . Corporate persons

H . . International property law
LJ . . . Intellectual & industrial property
. . . . *International organizations*
LJ5 LT . . . . . World Intellectual Property Organization, WIPO
. . . . . . * Formerly BIRPI (International Bureau for Protection of Intellectual Property)

[International law works about SD3]
[Subjects of international law SD9VB]
[Private law SD9W]
[International property law SDBH]
. [Intellectual & industrial property SDBLJ]
. . [International organizations]
. . . [World Intellectual Property Organization SDBLJ5LT]

SDB LK . . Copyright, protection of intellectual property
LK5 LC . . . International congresses & conferences
LK5 LPQ N . . . . Universal Copyright Convention (1952)
LK5 LS . . . International organizations
LK5 LT . . . . Berne Convention, Bern Union, International Union for Protection of Literary & Artistic Work
LX . . Industrial property
M . . . Patents
MT . . . Trade marks
MV . . . Designs
MWP . . . Confidential information

N International economics law, international commercial law
. * See also general law of international economic relations SBN O
NAC . International economic planning
NF . Finance
NFG . . Banking
NG . . Credit & debt
NGL . . Investment
NH . . Insurance
NHQ . . . Marine insurance
. . . . * For Hague rules & York-Antwerp rules, see SBN HQF E.
NL . International labour law, international industrial law
NL5 LS . . International organizations
NL5 NT . . . International Labour Office

NOI . International trade law
NOI 5LS . . International organizations
NOI 5LT . . . General Agreement on Tariffs & Trade, GATT
NOI 5NT . . . United Nations Conference on Trade & Development, UNCTAD
NON . . Tariffs
NOP . International development & aid
OG . Business enterprises
OS . . Cartels
OY . Transport & communication

[International law SD]
[Secondary materials]
[International law works about SD3]
[Subjects of international law SD9VB]
[Private law SD9W]
[International economics law SDBN]
[Transport & communication SDBOY]

SDB P Transport
PY . International waters
. . * For International waterways, see Inland waters SDB QBH.
QA . International maritime law, shipping, law of the sea
. . * See also Water boundaries SDK NQ
QA5 A7T . . Medieval jurisprudence
QA5 A7U . . . Rhodian law
. . . . * Mediterranean, c. 7th/9th centuries.
QA5 A7V . . . Oleron rules
. . . . * Atlantic coast of Europe, c.11th century.
QA5 A7W . . . Trani laws
. . . . * Mediterranean, 11th century.
QA5 A7X . . . Amalfi laws
. . . . * Mediterranean, 12th century.
QA5 A7Y . . . Consulate of the sea
. . . . * Mediterranean, 15th century.
QA5 A8A . . Modern jurisprudence
QA5 A8G PM . . . Hanseatic law of the sea
. . . . * Northern Europe, 1591.
. . Personnel
QAK A . . . Seamen
QAL E . . Sea traffic control
QAL F . . . Rules of the road at sea
QAM . . International navigation law
QAP . . Accidents
QAP R . . . Collisions at sea
QAQ A . . . Salvage of ships
QAQ BW . . . . Wrecks
QAQ H . . Searches of ships
QAS J . . Nationality of ships
QAS JP . . . Flags of convenience
QAU . . Carriage of goods by sea
QAU FF . . . Affreightment
QAU FF5 TN . . . . Codes
QAU FF5 TNP C . . . . . Hague rules (affreightment) (1921)
QAU FF5 TNR T . . . . . Hamburg rules (1978)
QAV . . . Ships' passengers
QBH . International waterways

Subjects of international law

[International law works about SD3]
[Subjects of international law SD9VB]
[Private law SD9W]
[International economics law SDBN]
. [Transport & communication SDBOY]
. . [Transport SDBP]
. . . [International waterways SDBQBH]

SDB QBJ . . . . Fisheries
. . . . Other sea resources
QBS . . . . . Seabed exploitation

QC . . . Land transport law
QD . . . . Roads
QE . . . . Railways

QF . . . International air law
. . . . * See also Air boundaries SDK S
. . . . Jurisprudence
QF5 BY . . . . . International airspace, freedom of the air
QF5 LS . . . . International organizations
QF5 LT . . . . . International Civil Aviation Organization
QFK . . . . Personnel
QFK W . . . . . Aircrew
. . . . *Operations*
QFL E . . . . . Air traffic regulation
QFL NR . . . . . Right to enter (air law)
QFL NS . . . . . . Overfly
QFL NT . . . . . Non-scheduled flights
QFL NU . . . . . . Charter flights
QFL NV . . . . . Scheduled flights
QFR . . . . Aircraft
QFV . . . . Air passengers

QG . . . Space
. . . . * For extraterrestrial Space, see SDK T

QL . . Communications
QM . . . Postal services
. . . . International organizations
QM5 LS . . . . . Postal unions
QM5 LT . . . . . . Universal Postal Union, UPU
QM5 QHO C . . . . . . African Postal Union
QM5 QHR C . . . . . . Postal Union of the Americas & Spain
. . . . * Previously Pan-American Postal Union.
QQ . . . Telecommunications

S Environment
SP . Dangerous substances international environment law
SR . Pollution
SW . Conservation of resources

[International law SD]
[Secondary materials]
[International law works about SD3]
[Subjects of international law SD9VB]
[Private law SD9W]
. [Environment SDBS]
. . [Conservation of resources SDBSW]

SDB TA . Social law
TB . . International public health law
TKS . . . Drug control
U . . International social welfare law
. . . * For international industrial law, see SDB NL.

W International criminal law
. * An alternative (not recommended) is to collocate with criminal law at SB
. * An alternative (not recommended) is to collocate with criminal law at SBW HC
W8M T . Extradition
W8M X . . *By country from which extradition is sought*
. *Types of crimes*
WFQ . . Organized crime
. . *By scene of crime*
WFT . . . Extraterritorial crimes
WFT S . . . . Ships (international criminal law)
WFT V . . . . Aircraft (international criminal law)
WFT X . . . . Space (international criminal law)
WMG . . Hostage-taking
WT . . Terrorism
WVG . . Highjacking international criminal law
WVP . . Financial crime
WX . . Juvenile crime
. . . * Add to SDB WXA letters A/N following SBW X so far as applicable.
WXI . . International crimes
. . . * For war crimes, see SDT W.
WXJ . . . Crimes against humanity
WXK . . . . Genocide
WXP . . . Piracy
WXR . . . Other
. . . . * Arrange A/Z

WY Public international law
. * Use SD3, & see note there.
X . Constitutional law
. . * This has no real equivalent in international law. Those topics in (national) constitutional law which do arise in international law are treated as concepts under Political processes; see SDC/SDD.

Subjects special to international law

. * These are all taken from class R, with some adjustments. Retroactive synthesis within these political concepts follows the rules in class R; e.g. SDG F State succession and sovereignty.
. * To avoid clashes and ambiguities in classmarks, retroactive qualification by legal concepts must follow special intercalators, as at SBN. The relevant rules from SBN are repeated here for convenience.
. * Any class in SDC/SDX may be qualified retroactively by legal concepts as follows (where the hyphen represents the classmark added to):
. * Add to - numbers 2/9T following SD.
. * Add to -9V letters W/Y following S9.
. * Add to -9X letters A/Y in Auxiliary Schedule S1.

SDC A . Political process
. . * The main class for the political process is Politics (R). Class here only those works which consider political concepts in relation to international law. Where a concept has its special place in international law, recognized by its inclusion in SD (e.g. sovereignty SDF), prefer that place to the location derivable here by synthesis from class R Politics.
. . * Some major concepts from class R are given here for convenience.
. . * Add to SDC A letters A/B following R in RA/RB

AAX P . . Political policies
ABB . . Demographic factors
ABC Y . . Political behaviour
ABJ . . . Political offences
B . . Political control
. . . * Add to SD letters CB/DK following R in RCD/RDK.
F . . . Freedom & repression
T . . . . Rights & duties
W . . . . . Human rights
W5L C . . . . . . Conventions etc.
. . . . * For European Convention on Human Rights (1950), see SFY J5L NQL; for European Commission on Human Rights, see SFY J5L T.
W5N 5R . . . . . . United Nations declarations
W5N 5UB . . . . International Covenant on Civil & Political Rights (1966)
W5N 5UC . . . . International Covenant on Economic and Social and Cultural Rights (1966)
W7 . . . . . . Courts
. . . . * For European Court of Human Rights, see SFY J7R.
X . . . . . . Abuse of human rights

[Subjects special to international law]
[Political process SDCA]
. [Political control SDCB]
. . [Freedom & repression SDCF]
. . . [Rights & duties SDCT]
. . . . [Human rights SDCW]
. . . . . [Abuse of human rights SDCX]

SDD B . . . . . Civil & political rights
E . . . . . Equal rights
F . . . . . Social & economic rights

L Collectivities & groups
. * Persons as individuals go at SDA P/SDB; class here classes of persons regarded only from the viewpoint of their political or constitutional status. If in doubt, prefer here.
. * Add to SD letters DL/DU following R in RDL/RDU.
NG . Slaves
ON . Nationals, citizens
. . *Special processes & elements*
ONN . . . Nationality
ONN E . . . . Allegiance
ONN J . . . Acquisition of nationality
. . . . *Conditions*
ONN JM . . . . . Marriage & nationality acquisition
ONN JP . . . . . Domicile & nationality acquisition
ONN N . . . Naturalization
ONN P . . . Denaturalization, deprivation of naturalization
ONN Q . . . Loss of citizenship
ONN R . . . Expatriation
. . . *Citizens abroad*
ONN S . . . . Passports
ONN SV . . . . Visas
ONN T . . . . Protection of citizens abroad
ONN V . . . . Travellers in foreign countries
. . *Types of nationals, citizenship*
ONU . . . Multiple nationality
ONV . . . . Dual nationality
OO . . . Indigenous population, aboriginals
OOY . . . Stateless persons

OPT . Aliens
OPT 7 . . International courts
OPT 8L . . . Preliminary proceedings
OPT 8QT . . . . Preliminary objections
OPT 9XE . . Contract
. . Responsibilities
OPT CUT . . . State responsibility towards aliens
OPT CUU . . . . Minimum international standards
OPT CUV . . . . Imputability
OPT CW . . Human rights
OPT DDX . . . Assylum
. . . . * Use SDD OPU.

[Subjects special to international law]
[Collectivities & groups SDDL]
. [Aliens SDDOPT]
. . [Human rights SDDOPTCW]
. . . [Assylum SDDOPTDDX]

. . . . * Normal retroactive synthesis by CA/DN following SD is interrupted here to secure a shorter classmark for assylum. It is resumed at SDD OPV.

SDD OPU . . . Assylum
OPU 2N . . . . Cases
. . . . *Reasons*
OPU F . . . . . Political offences
OPU G . . . . . Other
. . . . *Places of assylum*
OPU J . . . . . Legations & assylum rights
OPU K . . . . . Ships & assylum rights
OPU L . . . . . Other
OPV . . . Other rights
. . . . * Normal retroactive synthesis under Aliens is resumed here after its interruption at SDD OPT DDX.
. . . . * Add to SDD OPV letters E/M following RD.
OPV F . . . . Social & economic rights
OPV FT . . . . Right to personal property
. . *Special operations*
OPV Q . . . Extradition
OPV R . . . Provisional arrest
OPV S . . . Arrest & imprisonment
OPV T . . . Expulsion of aliens, deportation
OQ . Minorities
OS . Immigrants

SDE Government
. * Add to SDE letters E/L following R in RE/RL so far as applicable.
SDE E . World government, international government
I . . Legislative process
J . . Executive process
JL . . . Head of government
LY . . Judiciary

[Subjects special to international law]
[Government SDE]
. [World government SDEE]
. . [Judiciary SDELY]

SDE M States as persons
. * See also Sovereign states SDL NW, and the note there.

. *Attributes of states*
SDF . . Sovereignty, independence
. . . * See also Acquisition of territory SDL L
. . . *Operations*
SDF PC . . . . Recognition of sovereignty
PE . . . . Protection of independence, self-preservation & sovereignty
PG . . . . Transfer of sovereignty
. . . . . * See State succession SDG FPG
. . . *Attributes*
PJ . . . . State rights
PL . . . . National honour
PN . . . . Vital interests
. . . *Processes*
PR . . . . Origins of sovereignty
Q . . . . . Self determination & sovereignty
R . . . . . . Plebiscites
. . . *Special conditions*
T . . . . Permanent sovereignty
. . . . . * Over natural resources. Applies primarily to transnational economic relations and cooperation.

V . . State responsibility, state liability, state duties
. . . * E.g., not to pollute other territories.
. . . * For state rights, see Sovereignty SDF PJ.
W . . Jurisdiction of sovereign states, competence (sovereign states)
. . . * For extraterritoriality, see Servitudes SDH R.
. . . * For jurisdiction in particular subjects of international law, see subject (e.g. shipping); for general relations between Municipal law & international law, see SD5 9HY.
. . . * Most of the concepts below refer mainly to criminal law; when they do, class in international criminal law SDB W.
XE . . . Act of State doctrine
XF . . . Territorial principle
XG . . . Nationality principle
XH . . . Protective principle
XJ . . . Universality principle

[Subjects special to international law]
[States as persons SDEM]
[Attributes of states]
[Jurisdiction of sovereign states SDFW]
. [Universality principle SDFXJ]

SDF XK . Immunity from jurisdiction
XL . . Sovereign immunity
XM . . Qualified immunity
. . *Of particular persons, etc.*
. . . * See the person, etc.; e.g. consulates, diplomatic missions.
. *Types of jurisdiction*
. . * For extraterritorial jurisdiction, see Servitudes SDH R.
XQ . . Conventional jurisdiction
XR . . Advisory jurisdiction
XS . . Compulsory jurisdiction
XV . . Voluntary jurisdiction
XW Changes in sovereignty

SDG State succession
. * Effects of succession on specific subjects (e.g. private property) goes with the subject.
SDG 5LC . Conventions
5LP RT . . Vienna Convention on State Succession (1978)
EE . Government
EEQ . . Governments in exile
EES . . Change of head of state
F . Sovereignty
FPG . . Transfer of sovereignty, change of sovereignty
G . Contractual rights (state succession)
SDH Dissolution of state, termination of sovereignty
SDH H . Dismemberment of state
. . * For civil war, see SDX V.
J . New states
JF . . Sovereignty
JFP C . . . Recognition
K . . Mergers of states
L Limitations on sovereignty
M . Servitudes
. . * When territory belonging to one state is used to serve in some way the interests of another state.
. . * See also Armed forces stationed in an ally's territory SDN YW.
N . . Sources of servitudes
P . . . Custom as source of servitudes
Q . . . Treaties as source of servitudes
R . . Extraterritoriality
S . . Concessions, capitulations
T . . Free zones (servitudes)
V . . Demilitarized zones (servitudes), neutral zones (servitudes)

[Subjects special to international law]
[States as persons SDEM]
[Attributes of states]
[Limitations on sovereignty SDHL]
. [Servitudes SDHM]
. . [Demilitarized zones servitudes SDHV]

SDJ Y State as physical entity, state right of domain & property
SDK . National territory, territorial claims
SDK 48 . . *By place*
. . . * Add to SDK 48 letters E/Z in Auxiliary Schedule 2.
. . . * See note at S48 for instructions on how to qualify the first cited country by a second country, should this be called for.
HM . . Servitudes
. . . * See Limitations on sovereignty SDH M
L . . Acquisition of territory
LFV . . . State responsibility

. . . *Processes*
LM . . . . Recognition of territory aacquisition
LN . . . . Acquiescence in territory acquisition
LP . . . . Estoppel by conduct, estoppel in pais
. . . . . * One party, by its explicit or implicit conduct, leads another to believe it will act in a certain way.
LQ . . . . Intertemporal law
LQ2 N . . . . . Cases
LQ2 N9P A . . . . . . Island of Palmas case
. . . *Methods of acquisition*
LS . . . . Discovery (territory acquisition)
LT . . . . Occupation of terra nullius
M . . . . Prescription (territory acquisition)
. . . . . * Occupation of territory belonging to another state.
MP . . . . . Conquest, subjugation
. . . . . . * See also Law of war SDR
MS . . . . . Settlement of territory
MV . . . . . Accretion of territory, operations of nature
MX . . . . . Cession of territory, annexation

NB . . Boundaries, frontiers
ND . . . Disputed boundaries (general)
. . . . * For territorial claims by a particular country, use SDK 48.
NE . . . Open boundaries
NF . . . Natural boundaries
NH . . . . Land boundaries
NJ . . . . . Mountains
NK . . . . . . Individual mountains
. . . . * Arrange A/Z.
NL . . . . . Subsoil & boundaries
NM . . . . . Earth's interior & boundaries
NQ . . . . Water boundaries

[States as persons SDEM]
[Attributes of states]
[State as physical entity SDJY]
[National territory SDK]
. [Boundaries SDKNB]
. . [Natural boundaries SDKNF]
. . . [Water boundaries SDKNQ]

. . . . * For international waters, see SDB PY.
. . . . * See also International maritime law SDB QA
SDK NS . . . . Inland waters, national waters
NT . . . . Rivers
NU . . . . . Individual national rivers
. . . . . . * Arrange A/Z.
NV . . . . . International rivers
NW . . . . . . Individual international rivers
. . . . * Arrange A/Z.
OC . . . . Canals
OE . . . . . International canals, interoceanic canals
OF . . . . . . Individual international canals
. . . . * Arrange A/Z.

OH . . . . Lakes, enclosed waters
OI . . . . . Individual lakes
. . . . . . * Arrange A/Z.
OL . . . . Coastal waters
P . . . . . Territorial waters, maritime belt
PQ . . . . . . Three-mile limit
PR . . . . . . Other limits
PS . . . . . . Continental shelf
QB . . . . Gulfs
QC . . . . . Individual gulfs
. . . . . . * Arrange A/Z.
QF . . . . Straits
QG . . . . . Individual straits
. . . . . . * Arrange A/Z.
QJ . . . . Islands
QL . . . . High seas, open seas
R . . . . Sea-bed

S . . . Air boundaries
. . . . * See also International airspace SDB QF5 BY.
SS . . . . Territorial airspace, national airspaces
T . . . . Extraterrestrial space
. . . . . * For International space law in general, see SDB QG
TT . . . . . Solar system
TU . . . . . . Moon
TV . . . . . Artificial satellites
UA . . Artificial boundaries (air)
UD Adjoining territory, neighbouring territory
UE . Nuisances (adjoining territory)

[Subjects special to international law]
[States as persons SDEM]
[Attributes of states]
. [State as physical entity SDJY]
. . [Adjoining territory SDKUD]
. . . [Nuisances adjoining territory SDKUE]

SDL M *Types of states*
. * General studies only; for individual states, regardless of status, see SI/SV.
. * Add to SDL M letters B/Y following RM in RMB/RMY so far as applicable.
. * Add to SDL N letters B/Y following RN in RNB/RNY so far as applicable.
MG . Federal states
NK . Theocratic states
NR . Collectivist states, communist states
NV . Multiracial states, pluralist states

NW . Sovereign states, nation states, independent states
. . * Usually assumed; use this class only if the nature of the independent sovereign state per se is the subject.
. . * For sovereignty, see SDF.
NWP . . Federations of sovereign states, unions of sovereign states
NWS . . Suzerain states, paramount states

NX . Semi-sovereign states, dependent states, non-self-governing states
. . * For specific forms developed under imperialist and colonial systems, see SDL O.
NXP . . Puppet states, vassal states
NXR . . Leased territories
NXT . Non-state nations
NXU . . Partitioned states
. . . * Once-sovereign states which have been partitioned by political or military action.
NXV . . . Reunification of partitioned states
NYB . Internationalized territories
NYD . . Free cities
NYF . . Neutralized states

O . Extended sovereign states, extranational political systems
. . *Forms of extended political sovereignty*
. . . * Add to SDL O letters MR/O following RQ in RQMR/RQ so far as applicable; e.g. Multipolar international systems SDL OMS.
. . . * Add to SDL letters P/V following RQ in RQP/RQV.
OO . . . Regional political systems
P . . . Imperialist systems, empires
PV . . . . Annexation
Q . . . . Colonies, colonial dependencies
QL . . . . . Colonized peoples
. . . . . *Types of colonies*

[Subjects special to international law]
[States as persons SDEM]
. . [Extended sovereign states SDLO]
. . . [Forms of extended political sovereignty]
. . . . [Imperialist systems SDLP]
. . . . . [Colonies SDLQ]
. . . . . . [Types of colonies]

SDL SK . . . . Colonies of exploitation
T . . . . International trustee territories, trust territories
TR . . . . Mandate territories
TT . . . . Protectorates
. . . . . *Types of imperialiosm*
UJ . . . . . . Neo-imperialism, neo-colonialism
V . . . . National liberation movements, post-colonialism
. . . . . * See also National liberation wars SDX N.

SDM B International relations (narrowly), international politics & international law
. * The following classes follow the order in RO/RQ, with some modifications to meet the special needs of international law.
. * For treaties & agreements and international organizations, etc., see SD5 H.
C . Foreign policies & international law
. . * Add to SDM C letters P/X following ROA X so far as applicable.
. *Formalized relations*
T . . Foreign services & diplomacy in international law
. . . * Add to SDM letters T/Y following RO in ROT/ROY.
. . . * Add to SDN A letters A/V following RPA in RPA A/RPA V so far as applicable.
U . . . Diplomacy in international law
. . . . * For diplomacy regarded as a source of international law, see SD5 GT.
V . . . Consular services in international law
X . . . Foreign services operations
Y . . . . Diplomatic relations (narrowly)
SDN AL . . . . *Forms of diplomacy*

. *Other forms of international relations*
. . * Add to SDN letters J/Y following RP in RPJ/RPY so far as applicable.
K . . International cooperation, intergovernmental cooperation
. . . * See also International organizations SD5 LS
M . . International aid, international assistance
P . . Peacemaking & international law, world peace & international law
P5L C . . . International conferences
P5L H . . . . Hague Conferences (1899-)
P5L I . . . . . Hague Peace Conference (first, 1899)

[Subjects special to international law]
[International relations narrowly SDMB]
[Other forms of international relations]
[Peacemaking & international law SDNP]
. [International conferences SDNP5LC]
. . [Hague Conferences 1899- SDNP5LH]
. . . [Hague Peace Conference first SDNP5LI]

. . . . * For Hague Tribunal, see SD0 R7J.
SDN P5L J . . . Hague Peace Conference (second, 1907)
Q . Peace movement in international law
. . * Most of the literature on the peace movement goes under politics rather than law; see RPQ.
QV . . Other organizations
. . . * For Carnegie Endowment for International Peace see RPQ VOC.

V International security
W . Arms control
. . * See also Forms of warfare by weapon SDW R
WQ . . Surveillance (arms control)
WS . . . Inspection of armaments
WT . . Testing of weapons (arms control)
WU . . . Test bans
WV . . Limitation of armaments
WX . . Reduction in armaments, disarmament
XJ . . *Elements controlled*
. . . * Alternative (not recommended) to locating under the element. If this option is taken, proceed as follows:
. . . * Add to SDN XJ letters B/DJ following RQ; e.g. nuclear arms control SDN XJC; arms trade control SDN XJB CD.

YC . Collective security
. . * See also Neutrality SDS C
. . * Add to SDN Y letters C/W following RPY in RPYC/RPYW.
YG . . Alliances
YQ . . . Protective alliances
YR . . . . Military assistance (alliances)
YS . . . . . Military missions, military advisers
YT . . . . . Arms production agreement alliances
YU . . . . . Loan of military equipment, sale of military equipment
YUV . . . . . Leasing of military equipment
YV . . . . . Military bases
YW . . . . . Peaceful occupation, friendly occupation
. . . . . . * Including stationing of armed forces in friendly territory.

National security forces

[International relations narrowly SDMB]
[International security SDNV]
[Collective security SDNYC]
. [Alliances SDNYG]
. . [Protective alliances SDNYQ]
. . . [Military assistance alliances SDNYR]
. . . . [Peaceful occupation SDNYW]

SDN YY Security forces

SDO A . National security forces, national defence
. . * Add to SDO letters B/P following RQ; The more prominent concepts are given below for convenience.
AY . . Defence systems
B . . . Expenditure on arms, arms budgets
C . . . Production of arms, manufacture of arms, arms industry
CT . . . . Arms trade
E . . . Armed forces, military forces
F . . . . Size of armed forces
. . . . *Types of forces*
GF . . . . . Conscripted armed forces
GH . . . . . Mercenary armed forces
H . . . . . Irregular armed forces, guerilla forces
I . . . . . Intelligence services, secret service
J . . . . . Land forces, armies
K . . . . . . Civil defence systems
L . . . . . Sea power, navies
. . . . . . * See also Maritime war SDV M
P . . . . . Air forces

Q . . . Weapons systems, armaments
. . . . * Add to SDO Q letters R/T following RQB with the modifications indicated at SDO QU.
. . . . *Types of weapons*
QR . . . . . Conventional weapons
QT . . . . . Prohibited weapons, banned weapons
QUC . . . . . Chemical weapons
QUE . . . . . Biological weapons
QUP . . . . . Other
. . . . . . * Arrange A/Z.
. . . . . . * Other than nuclear weapons.
R . . . . . Nuclear weapons, atomic weapons
. . . . . . * Add to SDO R letters P/R following RQC in RQC P/RQC R so far as applicable.
RS . . . . . . *Types*
. . . . * Arrange A/Z.

[International relations narrowly SDMB]
[Other forms of international relations]
. . [Security forces SDNYY]
. . . [National security forces SDOA]
. . . . [Defence systems SDOAY]
. . . . . [Weapons systems SDOQ]
. . . . [Types SDORS]

. . . . . *Defence systems by area of deployment*
. . . . . . * Add to SDO S letters E/Q following RQD in RQD E/RQD M.
SDO SG . . . . . . Outer space defence systems
SH . . . . . . Seabed defence systems
SJ . . . . . . Special regions
SK . . . . Antarctica (defence systems)

SN . . . International security forces
SP . . . . International peacekeeping forces
SQ . . . . International strike forces
. . . . . * Authorized by UN to use all necessary force.

SDP Threats to peace
. * This class modifies the provisions in RQE P (International conflict management) to make them consistent with the classes at S9.
SDP 6 . Judicial procedures
9Q . . Peaceful settlement of international disputes
9QR . . . Negotiation
9QT . . . Conciliation
9QU . . . Mediation
9R . . . Arbitration

. *Other procedures in conflict management*
. . * Add to SDQ letters F/Y following RQG with the additions indicated.
SDQ D . . Delinquencies (general)
F . . Unfriendly measures, measures short of war
N . . . Intervention (sanctions)
P . . . . Political intervention
Q . . . . Subversion abroad, destabilization abroad
R . . . . Military intervention
S . . . Sanctions
SR . . . . Enforcement measures
SS . . . . Self-help sanctions
. . . . . * Other than war.
ST . . . . . Retaliation
SV . . . . . . Retorsion
. . . . * Lawful act but designed to injure wrongdoer.
SX . . . . . . Reprisals, letters of marque
. . . . * Normally illegal acts made legal by prior illegal act of wrongdoer.
TC . . . . Cooperative sanctions
TE . . . . Economic sanctions
TF . . . . . Financial sanctions
U . . . . . Embargo, boycott

[International relations narrowly SDMB]
[Threats to peace SDP]
[Other procedures in conflict management]
[Unfriendly measures SDQF]
. [Sanctions SDQS]
. . [Economic sanctions SDQTE]
. . . [Embargo SDQU]

SDQ V . . . Pacific blockade, economic blockade
. . . . * For blockades enforced by military means,
. . . . see SDU TB
VT . . . Other economic measure
. . . . * Arrange A/Z.
VV . Other measures short of war
VX . . Suspension of diplomatic relations
W . Hostilities short of war, undeclared war
Y . Ultimatum

SDR War, law of war
SDR 5H . Agreements, treaties
5KV . . Non-aggression pacts
5LS . International organizations
5N . United Nations in war
. . * For international peace-keeping forces, see
. . SDO SP.

9VB . International substantive law in wartime
. . * The instructions preceding SDC A are waived
. . here:
. . * Add to SDR letters A/B following SD.
AP . . Persons
. . . * For treatment of persons as combatants, etc.,
. . . see SDR RP/X.
BH . . Property
. . . *Types of property*
BIV . . . . Public property
BIW . . . . Alien property
BIW X . . . . . Enemy property
. . . . . . * For treatment of enemy property as
. . . . . . element in the conduct of war, see
. . . . . . SDT G.
BJ . . . . Real property
BKL G . . . . . Government regulation
BKM H . . . . . . Requisition of property in wartime
BKM I . . . . Compensation
BL . . . . Personal property
. . . . . * For treatment of enemy property, see
. . . . . SDT G.
BN . . Economic & commercial law in war
. . . * For Maritime law in war, see SDW M.
BTA . . Social & cultural law in war
BW . . Criminal law
. . . * For war crimes, see SDT W.

[Subjects special to international law]
[International relations narrowly SDMB]
[Threats to peace SDP]
[Other procedures in conflict management]
[War SDR]
[International substantive law in wartime SDR9VB]
. [Criminal law SDRBW]

Elements in law of war
. * Add to SDR letters R/Y following RQH
. in RQH R/RQH Y RQH R/RQH Y, with
. the modifications indicated.
. * For retroactive synthesis within classes
. SDR RP/SDR X the first 3 letters may
. be dropped; e.g. Prisoners of war SDR W;
. Treatment of prisoners of war SDR WTB.
SDR RP . Participants in war
. . *For belligerent states, see SDT C.

RX . . Persons in war
TB . . . Treatment of persons in war
TD . . . . Safe conduct
TF . . . . Repatriation of persons in war
TH . . . . War relief
. . . . . Organizations
TH5 LU . . . . . . International Red Cross
TJ . . . . Protection of persons in war
TL . . . . . Camps for refugees, housing
. . . . . of refugees
TN . . . . . Hospitals in war
. . . . . . *For hospital ships, see Maritime
. . . . . . war SDV NT.
. . . *Persons by physical state*
UC . . . . Sick & wounded, casualties
UCT B . . . . . Treatment
UD . . . . War dead
UF . . . . Missing persons

V . . . Combatants
VTB . . . . Treatment
. . . . *By rank*
VU . . . . . Officers
VUW . . . . . . Commanding officers
VV . . . . . Other ranks
. . . . *By other characteristics*
VX . . . . . Deserters
W . . . . . Prisoners of war
WTB . . . . . . Treatment
WTE . . . . Repatriation
WTF . . . . Exchange of prisoners
. . . . of war
WTJ . . . . Camps for prisoners of
. . . . war
WTP . . . . Taking of prisoners of war
WTQ . . . . Killing of prisoners of war

[War SDR]
[Elements in law of war]
[Participants in war SDRRP]
. [Persons in war SDRRX]
. . [Combatants SDRV]
. . . [By other characteristics]
. . . . [Prisoners of war SDRW]
. . . . . . [Killing of prisoners of war SDRWTQ]

SDR WV . . . . Hostages
WW . . . . Collaborators
WX . . . . Spies, informers
WY . . . . Other types of combatant
X . . Non-combatants
XTB . . . Treatment
. . . . * Note at SDR UCT B applies here also.
XV . . . Enemy aliens
XW . . . Other types
. . . . * Arrange A/Z; e.g. journalists SDR XWJ.
XX . . . Victims of war
XY . . . . Refugees
. . . . . * For war refugees, see SDB BWR

SDS B Non-participants in war
C . Neutrality
. . States
CLM . . . Neutral states
. . *Operations & processes*
D . . . Assylum (neutral states)
DT . . . . Internment (neutrality)
E . . . Infraction of neutrality, prohibited acts
. . . (neutrality)
. . . . * See also Maritime war SDW M
F . . . . Harbouring of warcraft
. . . . . * For war vessels in neutral ports, see
. . . . . SDW MSD Y.
GE . . . . Servicing of warcraft
GG . . . . . Refuelling of warcraft (neutrality)
GJ . . . . Passage of troops, passage of war
. . . . materials
GL . . . . Trade with belligerents (neutrality)
GN . . . . Export of munitions (neutrality)
GP . . . . Foreign enlistment by neutrals
GR . . . . Hostile military expeditions,
. . . . filibustering (neutrality in war)
H . . . . Other actions
. . . . . * Arrange A/Z.
. . *Types of neutrality*
J . . . Partial neutrality
K . . . Perpetual neutrality
L . . . Armed neutrality
M . . . Friendly neutrality
N . . . Voluntary neutrality, imposed neutrality

[International relations narrowly SDMB]
[War SDR]
[Elements in law of war]
. [Non-participants in war SDSB]
. . [Neutrality SDSC]
. . . [Types of neutrality]
. . . . [Voluntary neutrality SDSN]

SDT B Process of war, belligerency, state of war, warfare proper
. * Add to SDT letters B/Y following RQI in
. RQIB/RQIY with the modifications indicated.
B5A . Jurisprudence
. . Special concepts
B5B YC . . . Legality of war
B5B YE . . . Justification of war
B5B YG . . . . Self-defence
B5B YH . . . . . Anticipatory self-defence
B5B YJ . . . Doctrine of necessity
B5B YL . . . Extraterritorial defence
B5B YP . . . Permissible force
. *Agents*
. . * See also Neutral states SDS CLM
C . . Belligerent states
CV . . Aggressor states
CW . . Allied states (state of war)
CX . . Enemy states

D . Declaration of war
. . * For Hostilities prior to declaration of war, see
. . SDQ W.
DV . . Notification of hostilities
E . Invasion, aggression
F . Conduct of war
. . * See also Casualties SDR UC
. . * For effects of a state of war on substantive law
. . generally, see SDR 9VB.
G . . Enemy property
H . . . Damage to enemy property
I . . . Requisitioning enemy property
L . . . Cultural property
. . . *Property of special value*
LV . . . . Artefacts (enemy property)
M . . . . . Specific types
. . . . . . * Arrange A/Z; e.g. art treasures.
W . . War crimes
. . . * See also specific operations subject to abuse;
. . . e.g. Taking of prisoners SDR WTP.
W8S . . . War crimes trials
WB . . . . *Specific trials*
WC . . . . . Nuremberg trials
WH . . . . . Others, by date
. . . . . . * Other than of named individuals.
WK . . . . . *Of named individuals*
. . . . . . * Arrange A/Z.
. . . *Types of war crimes*
WN . . . . Genocide (war crimes)
WR . . . . Reprisals

[International relations narrowly SDMB]
[War SDR]
[Process of war SDTB]
. [Conduct of war SDTF]
. . [War crimes SDTW]
. . . [Types of war crimes]
. . . . [Reprisals SDTWR]

. . . . . * Retaliation by one belligerent against another
. . . . . by otherwise illegitimate acts of warfare, to
. . . . . compel the latter to comply with the rules of
. . . . . legitimate war. In practice, they are frequently
. . . . . an excuse for illegal acts of war.
SDT WX . . . . Other
. . . . . * Arrange A/Z.

. . *Conduct special to war*
. . . * Add to SDU letters B/T following RQJ, with the
. . . additions indicated below.
SDU B . . . Acquisition of territory in war
C . . . . Occupation, occupied territory
DB . . . Sieges, blockades
DD . . . Hot pursuit
DF . . . Capture in war
. . . . * For prisoners of war, see SDR W.

E Cessation of hostilities, termination of war
FB . Truce (warfare)
FD . . Flag of truce
FF . Ceasefire
FH . Armistice
FJ . . Violation of armistice
FL . . Special arrangements in armistice
G . Capitulation, surrender
GV . . Peace terms
. . . * For peace settlement, see SDU L.
GW . . Conditional surrender
GX . . Unconditional surrender

L Peace settlements, peace treaties (subject)
. * For specific peace treaties, see SD2 D.
M . War claims, post-war measures
N . . War reparations, compensation, indemnities
PV . . Restitution
PW . . Prizes
. . . * See also Sea warfare, SDW NH
Q . . Occupation of territory
R . . . Military government of occupied territory
S . . . Civil government of occupied territoy
T . . Partition of states

[International relations narrowly SDMB]
[Threats to peace SDP]
[Other procedures in conflict management]
[War SDR]
[Peace settlements SDUL]
. [War claims SDUM]
. . [Partition of states SDUT]

SDW D *Forms of warfare*
. * Add to SDW letters D/Y following RQK so
. far as applicable.
. * Add to SDX letters B/V following RQL so
. far as applicable.
. *By degree of involvement*
E . . Proxy wars
. *By geographic scale*
G . . Local wars, limited wars
H . . World wars
. *By defence system involved*
J . . Land warfare
L . . Sea warfare
M . . . Maritime war
MSC . . . . Neutrality
MSC 2N . . . . . Cases
MSC 2N9 LM . . . . . . Alabama case (1871)
MSD Y . . . . . War vessels in neutral ports
MUD B . . . . Blockade maritime war
MUD C . . . . . Right of visit & search
MUD H . . . . . Contraband (blockades)
NB . . . . Innocent passage
ND . . . . Continuous voyage doctrine
NF . . . . Capture of vessels
NH . . . . Prize law
NH6 E . . . . . Prize courts
NJ . . . . Mines
. . . . *Types of vessels*
NM . . . . . Privateers
NN . . . . . Armed merchant ships
NP . . . . . Converted merchant ships
NR . . . . . Submarines
NT . . . . . Hospital ships
P . . Air warfare

. *By weaponry*
. . * See also Regulation of weapon systems
. . SDO Q
R . . Conventional warfare, restricted
. . warfare
RT . . Total war, unrestricted warfare
T . . Prohibited forms of warfare
V . . Chemical warfare, poison gas
. . warfare
W . . Biological warfare
X . . Nuclear war, atomic war

War

[International relations narrowly SDMB]
[Threats to peace SDP]
[Other procedures in conflict management]
[War SDR]
[Forms of warfare SDWD]
[By weaponry]
. [Nuclear war SDWX]

By tactics
SDX B . Guerilla warfare
By objectives
D . Defensive war
F . Ideological war
N . . National liberation wars
. . . * For national liberation movements in
. . . general, see SDL V.
V . . Civil war, non-international
. . armed conflict

Supranational law

SE Supranational law, extranational law, supranational communities & organizations

. * Bodies of customary and treaty rules accepted as legally binding between members of a group of nation states or on organizations set up by a group of nations.

. * Bodies restricted to clearly defined subject fields are subordinated to those subjects in substantive law; e.g. European Central Inland Transport Organization.

. * See also supranational groupings in political science, RQW B.

. * Add to this general class SE numbers & letters 2/9, A/Y following SG so far as applicable.

SE2 . *Primary materials*

. . * Add to SE2 numbers & letters 2/X in Auxiliary Schedule S3.

. . * This class applies only to particular supranational communities, etc. For a demonstration of its application, see SG European Union law.

SE5 A . Jurisprudence

C . . Sources

. . . * The schedule at SE5 C/SE5 T is amended to conform to that in International law at SD5 C/SD5 T. For a demonstration of this, see SG5 C/SG5 T.

. . . * Add to SE5 letters C/T following SD.

SE6 . Practice & procedure

SE9 VB . Substantive law

. *Supranational organizations by region*

. . * Individual organizations are subordinated to the broad region within which they operate. They are specified by the year of origin, obtained from Auxiliary Schedule 4C (see instruction in note 9 under Primary materials in Auxiliary Schedule S2).

. . * Each region (except Europe SFY H) is assigned a 3-letter classmark (e.g. Africa SHO); the letter C is added to this to take general works covering several or all of the individual organizations. The letters D/Y are then used for the latter (with the exception of the European Union, at SG).

. . * Classes representing a region in general (e.g. Europe SFY H, South America SHW) do not represent jurisdictions in the strict sense and it would be unhelpful to divide them like particular organizations (e.g. the EU) which do constitute jurisdictions. So although they may be qualified by preceding facets (by adding 2/9, A/B following S) this will not usually be necessary. In particular, treaties, conventions, etc., which are sources of international law, are preferred in the latter; e.g. African Postal Union is SDB QM5 QHO, not SHO BQM 5LT.

[Supranational law SE]
[Supranational organizations by region]

SF Preferred community

. * This location is reserved for the particular body of supranational law of particular relevance to the jurisdiction within which the library finds itself.

. * Add to SF numbers & letters 2/Y following SG so far as applicable.

SFY H European supranational law (general), European regional organizations (general)

H5L C . International conventions

. . * For Conference on Security & Cooperation in Europe (CSCE), see RRO XAW CCS.

HXC W . Human rights

. . * Use SFY J; normal synthesis by Auxiliary Schedule S1 is interrupted here and is resumed at SFY K.

J . Human rights (European supranational law)

. . * Add to SFY J letters A/M folowing SCC W and X/Y following SCC.

J5L C . . Conventions

J5L N . . . Post-1945

J5L NQL . . . . European Convention on Human Rights

. . . . . * 1950.

J5L NQO . . . . European Convention for the Protection of Human Rights

. . . . . * 1953.

. . Individual organizations

J5L T . . . European Commission on Human Rights

J6E . . Courts

J7R . . . European Court of Human Rights

K . *Other constitutional subjects*

. . * Normal synthesis by Auxiliary Schedule S1 is resumed here after its interruption at SFY HXC W.

. . * Add to SFY K letters D/YF following SC.

. *Particular regional organizations, by date*

. . * Add to SFY letters representing date of origin taken from Auxiliary Schedule 4C, except for EU (see SG).

. . * Each organization below may be qualified in the same way as the EU (at SG), with any modifications which may be necessary. Usually, this will entail only a relatively small selection of the classes provided for the EU. Proceed as follows:

. . * Add to - (where the hyphen represents the classmark of the organization) numbers & letters 2/9, A/Y following SG in SG2/SGY so far as applicable.

[Supranational law SE]
[Supranational organizations by region]
[European supranational law general SFYH]
[Particular regional organizations]

SFY QJ . Organization for European Economic Cooperation, OEEC
. . * 1948; replaced in 1961 by OECD (SFY RC).
QK . Council of Europe (1949)
. . International agreements
QK2 JT . . . European conventions (general)
. . . . * Specific conventions go with the subject (e.g. human rights).
QKX I . . Consultative Assembly
QKX IU . . Committee of Ministers
. . . * For Council of Ministers of the EU, see European Council SG5 LQF.
QKX JM . . Other Committees, etc. A/Z
QL . European Payments Union (1950)
. . * Succeeded by European Fund (OECD).
QQ . European Fund (1955)
. . * Succeeded EPU.
RC . Organization for Economic Cooperation & Development (1961), OECD
. . * Up to 1961 called Organization for European Economic Cooperation.

SG European Union law
. * European Union (formerly European Community, or EC) is a collective term for what was originally three bodies: EEC (European Economic Community) ECSC (European Coal & Steel Community) and Euratom (European Atomic Energy Commission). These bodies share four basic institutions: the Council of Ministers, the European Parliamentary Assembly, the European Commission and the European Court of Justice. A number of other institutions, closely connected with the EU, have also developed and contribute to its overall system within specific fields (e.g. cultural cooperation, human rights).
. * European Union law is a legal system quite distinct from the municipal law of its member states. But it binds not only those states but also their individual citizens immediately and directly.
. * This class takes only the law of the EU; for its role as a political entity, see RRP; for its role as a trade bloc, see TOV.

SG2 . *Primary materials*
. . * For institutions or publications on a specific subject, see subject; e.g. European Investment Bank SGN GL9 TQ.
. . * Add to SG2 numbers & letters 2/9, A/X in Auxiliary Schedule S3.
SG2 2 . . *By language*

[Supranational law SE]
[Supranational organizations by region]
[European supranational law general SFYH]
[European Union law SG]
[Primary materials SG2]
[By language SG22]

. * For qualification of specific categories of primary materials.
SG2 3 *Common subdivisions*
. * When applicable to primary materials; e.g SG2 3R Guides to the documentation of EU.
3XJ . Computerized data banks
. . * Arrange A/Z.
3XJ C . . CELEX
4 *Special subsidiary forms*
. * For example, Indexes to the official acts SG2 L44.
A Official documents, Publications of the EU
. * For works about the institutions of the EU, see SGX Organization law of EU.
B . European Parliament, European Assembly
BD . . Debates, proceedings
BH . . Working papers
BJ . . Resolutions, opinions
BM . . Committees, A/Z
C . Council of Ministers of the EU
CMP . . Committee of Permanent Representatives (EU) (texts)
. . . * Administrative organ of the Council.
D . European Commission
. . * For publications on a specific subject, see subject.
D76 C . . COM documents
D76 S . . SEC documents
ED . Economic & Social Committee of EU
EDJ . . Opinions
EF . Court of Auditors of EU
EH . Other institutions of the EU (A/Z)

F Treaties of formation
. * For treaties of EU with external parties, see International law SD2 BBG (or its alternative at SG2 JT).
. * See also Constitution of the EU, SGX
G . *Individual treaties*

GQM . . ECSC treaty of formation (1951), Treaty of Paris (1951)

[Supranational organizations by region]
[European supranational law general SFYH]
[European Union law SG]
[Primary materials SG2]
[Treaties of formation SG2F]
. [Individual treaties SG2G]
. . [ECSC treaty of formation 1951 SG2GQM]

SG2 GQS . . EEC treaty of formation (1957), Treaty of Rome (EEC)
GQS T . . Euratom treaty of formation (1957), Treaty of Rome (Euratom)
GRG . . EC Merger treaty of EC (1965)
. . . * Instituting single Council & Commission of European Communities.
GRL . . Treaty of Luxembourg (1970)
. . . * First budgetary treaty of EC.
GRQ . . Amending treaty of EC (1975)
. . . * Second budgetary treaty of EC.
GSH . . Single European Act (1986), SEA
H Treaties of accession
. *Individual treaties*
HRN . . EC Association treaty (1972), Treaty of Brussels (1972)
. . . * On accession of Denmark, Ireland, Norway & UK.
HRU . . Greece accession treaty (1979)
HSG . . Spain & Portugal accession treaty (1985)
JT International treaties
. * Alternative (not recommended) to locating in International law SD2 BBG.

L Legislation of EU, Acts of the European Union
L44 . Indexes & tables
L7 . Collections
L8E 5 . Official journal of EU texts
L8F C . . C Section
. . . * Proposed legislation.
L8F L . . L Section
. . . * Adopted secondary legislation.
L8H . . Other series
M . Official acts & regulations
NB . Directives
ND . Decisions
NJ . Secondary legislation of EU
NK . . Recommendations
NM . . Opinions
NP . . Other measures, A/Z
. . . * Declarations, Action programmes, etc.
NX . National legislation applying EU (texts)
. . * Collections only; for legislation of individual member states, see state.
NY . . *By country*

[Supranational organizations by region]
[European supranational law general SFYH]
[European Union law SG]
[Primary materials SG2]
. [Legislation of EU SG2L]
. . [National legislation applying EU texts SG2NX]
. . . [By country SG2NY]

. . . . * Alternative (not recommended) to locating with the country. If this option is taken proceed as follows:
. . . . * Add to SG2 O letters E/Z in Auxiliary Schedule 2.

SG2 P . Court decisions of EU, cases, law reports
. . * For reports of courts on specific subjects, see subject; e.g. Human rights SGX CW.
P8 . . Digests
P85 . . . Official
P86 . . . Non-official
R . . Court of Justice of the EU, European Court of Justice
R7 . . . General collections
. . . . Official series
R75 . . . . . European Court reports
. . . . Non-official series
R76 . . . . . Common Market law reports
R8 . . . . Digests
R85 . . . . . Official
R86 . . . . . Non-official
S . . Court of First Instance (EU)
V . . Decisions of national courts in EU
. . . * Collections only; for decisions of courts in the individual states, see the state.

Secondary materials
. * Works about EU.
. * As Auxiliary Schedule S1, with amendments under some subjects to meet special requirements of EU law.
SG3 . *Common subdivisions*
SG3 M . . Communication
N . . . Language in EU
XD . . . European Documentation Centres (EU)
XE . . . European Information Centres (EU)
XH . . . Automated information systems
XJ . . . . Databases
. . . . . * For works about these; databases consisting of official texts are classed under primary materials; see SG2 33X J.
. . . . . * Arrange A/Z.

SG5 A . Jurisprudence
. . Special theories
AMD . . . Duality doctrine
AMM . . . Monist doctrine (EU)
C . . Sources
. . . Unification

[Supranational organizations by region]
[European supranational law general SFYH]
[European Union law SG]
[Secondary materials]
[Jurisprudence SG5A]
[Sources SG5C]
. [Unification]

SG5 CU . . Approximation of laws (EU)
. . . *Properties*
CV . . . Effectivess of integration (EU laws)
GP . Processes
. . * See note at SD5 GP (International law).
. . * A number of concepts from International law are applicable here also, arising from the status of extranational jurisdictions (between International and Municipal law).
. . * Normal synthesis by S5 is interrupted here; it is resumed at SG5 T.
. . * Add to SG5 letters GP/S following SD5.
H . . Agreements, treaties
JB . . . Enforcement
LC . . International conventions, congresses
LQ . . International meetings, talks, etc.
LQE . . . Summits
LQF . . . . European Council
. . . . . * See also Council of Europe SGX IU
LS . . International organizations
N . . . United Nations (sources of EU law)
T . *Other sources*
. . * Normal synthesis by S5 is resumed here after its interruption at SG5 GP.
. . * Add to SG5 T letters K/T following S5.
TPW . . Precedents in EU law
TR . . International law as source of EU law
TTA . . National law as souce of EU law
. . . * For conflict of laws, see SGA.
TTA 5BR F . . . Reform of members' law

UB EU law & the Community
. Special principles of EU law
VS . . Supremacy of EU law
VST . . . Direct applicability principle
VSV . . . Direct effect principle
. . . . * Provisions giving rise to rights or obligations which individuals may rely on before their national courts.
VSX . . Vertical & horizontal direct effects
. . . * Obligations fall on member states only or on individuals.

[European supranational law general SFYH]
[European Union law SG]
[Secondary materials]
[Jurisprudence SG5A]
. [EU law & the Community SG5UB]
. . [Special principles of EU law]
. . . [Vertical & horizontal direct effects SG5VSX]

SG5 VU . . . Subsidiarity
. . . . * Decisions should be taken at the most suitable level.
. . . . * See also Separation of powers SGX GG
VV . . . Proportionality
. . . . * Constraints on public authorities to ensure that they do not impose obligations beyond what is needed to achieve the aim sought.
. . . . * See also Administrative law SGX KF

SG6 Practice & procedure
SG6 E . Courts & court proceedings
. . * For courts relating to special subjects, see subject; e.g. European Court of Human Rights SGX CW7 Q.
. . Relations with national courts
SG7 R . . Court of Justice of EU (works about)
S . . Court of First Instance
SG8 LS . Service of process
SG9 F . Judgement
GI . . Enforcement
T Constitutional law relating to specific subjects
. * Use this position only when qualifying a specific subject filing before SGX (the normal class for constitutional law of EU). See note at S9T.
. * Add to SG9 T letters A/O following SGX.
TQ . Special committees, etc. concerned with the subject
. . * E.g. Committee of Governors of Central Banks SGN FK9 TQ.

VB *Substantive law of the EU*
. * See also substantive law under each of the member states.
. * Add to SG number 9 & letters A/XO in Auxiliary Schedule S1. From SGX P onwards (for constitutional law) the application of Auxiliary Schedule S1 is modified somewhat.
W . Private law general
X . Civil law general
SGA . Conflict of laws
SGA P . Persons
SGD . Obligations, Contracts, Torts
SGE . . Contract
SGE Q . . . Conditions
RT . . . . Exception clauses, exclusion clauses
RU . . . . . Derogation
SGH . Property law
SGL J . . Intellectual & industrial property

Economics law of EU

[Supranational organizations by region]
[European supranational law general SFYH]
[European Union law SG]
[Secondary materials]
[Substantive law of the EU SG9VB]
[Property law SGH]
. [Intellectual & industrial property SGLJ]

SGN Economics law of EU
. * Add to SG letters N/P following SB in
. SBN/SBP.
. * The instructions for retroactive synthesis
. within the class SBN/SBO given at SBN
. apply here also. The main ones are
. repeated here for convenience:
. * Add to - (where the hyphen represents
. the classmark added to) as follows:
. * Add to -9X letters A/Y in Auxiliary
. Schedule S1 so far as applicable.
. * Add to -9Y letters U/W following
. SBN 9Y.
. * Add to - letters A/P following SBN
. (taken from TA/TP).
SGN 9UC . Regulation of economic & business
. activities
AB . Intervention
AC . . National planning
AD . . Economic planning
AGH . . . Objectives
AGO . . . Aid, assistance
. . . . * For aid to non-member countries,
. . . . see SGO P.
AGQ . . . Incentives
AGR . . . Grants, subsidies
AGS . . . Compensation
AGT . . . Loans
AGU . . . Other aid media, A/Z
. . . . * For example, Ortoli facility.

DQ . Economic exchange
DR . . Price mechanism
DT . . . Price controls, regulation of prices
EK . . Market system
EMN . . . Entry conditions to market
EMO . . . . Barriers to entry to market
. . . . . * For example, patents, etc.
EMQ . . . . Concentration of market (EU)
EMS . . . . Market power (EU)
EMT . . . . . Dominance (market power in
. . . . . EU)
EMV . . . . Relevant product market (EU)
EMW . . . . Relevant geographical market
. . . . (EU)

[European Union law SG]
[Substantive law of the EU SG9VB]
[Economics law of EU SGN]
[Economic exchange SGNDQ]
. [Market system SGNEK]
. . [Entry conditions to market SGNEMN]
. . . [Relevant geographical market EU SGNEMW]

SGN EN . . Competition
. . . * See also EU and international trade, SGN OI
ENU . . . Free market (EU), Free competition
. . . (EU)
ENV . . . Agreements affecting competititon
. . . (EU)
ENW . . . . Concerted practice (EU competition)
. . . . . * Restricting competition, but falling short
. . . . . of illegality by EU standards.
ENW R . . . . . Rule of reason (EC competition),
. . . . . Cassis principle (EU)
ENX . . . . . Exemptions (EU competition)
ENX R . . . . . . Block exemptions (EU
. . . . . . competition)
EO . . . Imperfect competition
EOQ . . . . Unfair competition
EP . . . Restrictive practices
EPR . . . . Price agreements
EQ . . . . Cartels
EV . . . . Combination in restraint of trade,
. . . . monopolies
EW . . . . . State monopolies (EU)
. . . . . . * When these operate commercially.
EX . . Barter

F . Financial exchange
FG . . Banking
FK . . . Central banking
FK9 TQ . . . . Committee of governors of central
. . . . banks
FQ . . Money, currency EU law
. . . * See also European Monetary System SGN OF
FQ9 TQ . . . Monetary Committee (EU)
FQ9 TR . . . European monetary cooperation fund
FR . . . European currency unit
G . . Credit
GHS . . . Credit institutions
GJS . . . Negotiable instruments
GK . . . Consumer credit
GL . . . Investment
. . . . Investment institutions
GL9 TQ . . . . . European Investment Bank
H . . Insurance, etc.

HYY Economic production & distribution
I . Commerce & trade, intracommunity trade
. . * See also International commerce & trade
. . SGP OI
IM . . Wholesale trade
IN . . Retail trade

Economics law of EU

[European Union law SG]
[Secondary materials]
[Substantive law of the EU SG9VB]
[Economics law of EU SGN]
[Economic production & distribution SGNHYY]
. [Commerce & trade SGNI]
. . [Retail trade SGNIN]

SGN J	Production & industry general
L	Employment & labour law
LC	. Industrial relations
LD	. . Trade unions
LM	. Labour supply, workforce
LMO	. . Free movement of workers (EU)
LMP	. . Right of entry & residence (EU)
LMQ	. . . Work permits (EU)
LNF	. . Mobility of labour
LO	. Employment
LOR	. . Equal job opportunities
LOS	. . . Job discrimination
LP	. Unemployment
	. *Types of employment*
LRO	. . Temporary employment
LRQ	. . . Seasonal employment
LRT	. . Part-time employment
LS	. Remuneration, wages
LUA	. Working conditions
LVE	. *Types of workers*
LVJ F	. . Itinerant worker
LWG	. . *By nationality*
LWO	. . Young workers
LXC	. . Professional workers
O	International economic relations
OF	. European Monetary System
	. . * See also European Currency Unit SGN FR
OFT L	. . European Exchange Rate Mechanism, ERM
OI	. International trade & commerce
OI5 LC	. . Internationl conventions
OI5 LNR Q	. . . Lome conventions (1975)
OJ	. . Balance of payments
OK	. . . Capital transfer, free movement of capital (EU law)-
OLC	. . Protection & free trade
OLF	. . . Free movement of goods (EU)
OLL	. . . . Protection
OLP	. . . . . Customs duties
OLQ	. . . . . . Customs Union
OM	. . Import trade
OML L	. . . Protection
OMR	. . . . Non-tariff controls
OMS	. . . . . Import licenses
OMU	. . . . . Import quotas
OMY	. . . . . Charges having an equivalent effect (EU), disguised charges (EU tariffs)

[European Union law SG]
[Economics law of EU SGN]
[International economic relations SGNO]
. [International trade & commerce SGNOI]
. . [Import trade SGNOM]
. . . [Protection SGNOMLL]
. . . . [Non-tariff controls SGNOMR]
. . . . . [Charges having an equivalent effect EU SGNOMY]

SGN ON	. . . . Tariffs
	. . . . . Preferential
ONR	. . . . . . Generalized system of preferences (EU)
ONX	. . . . . Common customs tariff (EU), CCT, Common external tariff (EU), CET
OO	. . Export trade
OOE NY	. . . Dumping
OOV	. . . Subsidies for exports
OP	. International aid by EU, development aid by EU
OPQ	. . European Development Fund
Q	Business law
T	. Accounting
TF	. . Auditing
	. . . * See also Court of Auditors, SGX PH
V	. Production management
VMS	. . Standards in production (EU)
VT	. . Quality control in production (EU)
W	. Marketing
WL	. . Advertising
XG	. . Sale of goods
XM	. . . *Types of markets*
XQ	. . . . Consumer market, consumer law
	Enterprises by size
YJ	. Small businesses (EU)
	Enterprises by structure & ownership
SGO G	. Business enterprises, The Merchant, undertakings EU
G9U C	. . Regulation of businesses EU
G9Y HT	. . Right to establish businesses (EU), right to provide services (EU)
HD	. . . Government reorganization of businesses EU
HH	. . . . Enforced closure of businesses EU
I	. . Public sector enterprises
N	. . Private sector enterprises
Q	. . . Corporation law
QK	. . . . Formation & reorganization of companies
QL	. . . . . Combination
QLE	. . . . . . Mergers
V	. . . . Multinational companies
W	. . . Cooperative societies

[European Union law SG]
[Substantive law of the EU SG9VB]
[Economics law of EU SGN]
. [Enterprises by structure & ownership]
. . [Business enterprises SGOG]
. . . [Private sector enterprises SGON]
. . . . [Cooperative societies SGOW]

SGO Y . *Industries & undertakings by product*
SGP . . Transport law
SGQ A . . . Maritime law, Sea transport law
BJ . . Fisheries
T . . Agriculture
T9T Q . . . Agricultural Advisory Committee of EU
. . . Economic policy
TNA . . . . Common Market agricultural policy, CAP
TNA B . . . Intervention
TNA GR . . . . Grants
TNA GS . . . . Compensation
TNF . . . Financial policy
. . . Currency
TNF Q . . . . Green currency (EU)
TRE . . . *By product*

TW . . Service industries general

SGS Environmental law
SGT A Social law
. * For legislations, etc. on a specific field, see latter - e.g. SGN L Labour & employment law.
A2N J . Secondary legislation
A2N P . . Declarations
A2N PSK . . . Social charter (EU 1989)
B . Health & medicine
Y . Education
SGU . Welfare & social security
SGU AG . . Social administration EU
. . . *General principles*
AGG . . . . Applicability of welfare law
AGH . . . . . Lex laboris (EU)
. . . . . . * When the law of the state of employment applies.
AGJ . . . . . Single state principle
AGL . . . . Social advantage, social assistance
AGR . . . . Selectivity & universalism
AGS . . . . Non-discrimination by nationality (EU)
AGT . . . . Payment regardless of residence
AGU . . . . Aggregation of employments (EU)
AGV . . . . Subrogation
DD . . Users of social welfare (EU)
DDE LM . . . Take-up rate
FBF K . . Social security benefits
FBF L . . . Overlapping benefits
SGV 2 Cultural law
SGW Criminal law

[Supranational law SE]
[Supranational organizations by region]
[European supranational law general SFYH]
[European Union law SG]
[Secondary materials]
[Substantive law of the EU SG9VB]
[Criminal law SGW]

SGW Y Public law

. Constitutional law
SGX . . Organization law (EU)
. . . * Constitutional law of the EU itself.
. . . * For treaties of formation, see SG2 GQM; for sources of EU law, see SG5 C.
. . . * Some modifications have been made to the general class for constitutional law (mainly to SCP/SCY), reflecting the differences in structure between the EU and any sovereign state, unitary or federal.
. . . * Add to SGX numbers 6/9 and letters A/O following SC in SC6/SCO.
SGX CT . . . Rights & duties
CW . . . . Human rights
. . . . . * For the European Convention & Commission & Court of Human Rights, see SFY HXC W.
CW2 . . . . . *Primary materials*
CW2 S . . . . . . Cases on human rights
CW5 C . . . . . Sources
CW5 LC . . . . . . Conventions
CW6 . . . . . Courts
. . . . . . * For European Court of Human Rights, see SFY J7R.

E . . . Government
ECD . . . . Communication & information control
GE . . . . Powers
GF . . . . . Sovereignty
GG . . . . . Separation of powers
GGL . . . . . . Delegation of powers
. . . . * For Subsidiarity, see SG5 VU.
GI . . . . . Immunity
GMT . . . . . Treaty-making powers
GMU . . . . . . Express powers
GMV . . . . . . Implied powers
GPV . . . Accession of new member states (EU), adhesion (EU)

[European Union law SG]
[Secondary materials]
[Substantive law of the EU SG9VB]
[Public law SGWY]
[Constitutional law]
[Organization law EU SGX]
[Accession of new member states EU SGXGPV]

. * For treaties of accession, see
. SG2 H; for individual states, see
. SGX U.

SGX GQ Institutions of EU
. * These are only approximately
. equivalent to the recognized branches
. of government in sovereign states.
GR . Relations between branches of EU government
H . Electoral system
. Legislature
I . . European parliament
IGE . . . Powers
II . . . Membership
IL . . . Committees
ILW . . . . Council of Europe joint meetings with EU
INB . . . Legislative procedures
IU . . Council of the EU, Council of Ministers (EU)
. . . * For the European Council, see
. . . Summit meetings SG5 LQF.
. . . * Add to SGX IU letters K/S
. . . following SCJ (Executive
. . . government) so far as applicable.
IUK V . . . President
IUO . . . Committee of Permanent Representatives
IUQ L . . . Committees other than COROPER CPR
. Executive
J . . Commission of the EU
JGE . . . Powers
JM . . Committees of the EU
K . . Administration
KF . . . Administrative law
KJ . . . Executive agencies
. . . . *General functions*
KKC . . . . . Regulation & control
KKH . . . . . . Licensing
KKJ . . . . . . Inspection
KKK . . . . . . Testing
KL . . . . . . Enforcement
L . . . Central administration of EU
LIU . . . . Personnel
LMF . . . . Financial administration of EU
LMI W . . . . . Revenue

[European Union law SG]
[Organization law EU SGX]
[Institutions of EU SGXGQ]
. . [Administration SGXK]
. . . [Central administration of EU SGXL]
. . . . [Financial administration of EU SGXLMF]
. . . . . [Revenue SGXLMIW]

SGX LMJ . . . . . . Taxation
LMN X . . . . Custom & exercise duty
LMP R . . . . . . Members' contribution (EU finances)
LMQ . . . . . Expenditure

LN . . . *Special administrative agencies*
. . . . * In Class SC, the constitutional law provides
. . . . at this point for armed services, police, etc. As
. . . . yet, such agencies do not exist in the EU; but
. . . . provision is made here for the eventuality.
. . . . * Add to SGX letters LV/O following SC in
. . . . SCL V/SCO.

Other institutions of the EU
. * For institutions serving specific functions for its
. members, see the subject. To qualify a specific
. subject by EU institutions, use intercalator 9T; e.g.
. European Investment Bank SGN GL9 TQ.
. * For EEC, use the general class (SG); for the courts
. of the EU, see SG7.
PE . Economic & Social Committee of EU
PEI L . . Consultative Committee of the ESC
PF . European Research & Development Committee
PG . . Statistical Office of the EU, Eurostat
PH . Court of Auditors of the EU
PN . European Coal & Steel Commission
PP . European Atomic Energy Commission, Euratom

Q Devolved government in EU
. * For general works on the relations of EU with the
. various devolved levels of government in its member
. states. For the relations of EU with specific regions
. & localities within these states, see under SGX V
. Individual countries; for other regions, see SGX W.
. * See also Subsidiarity SG5 VU
. * Application of Auxiliary Schedule S1 is modified in
. SGX R/SGX YJ.
R . Regional government
T . Local government
U Relations with member states
V . *By country*
. . * Alternative (not recommended) to locating
. . relations with an individual state under

Organization law EU

[European Union law SG]
[Substantive law of the EU SG9VB]
[Public law SGWY]
[Constitutional law]
[Organization law EU SGX]
[Relations with member states SGXU]
. [By country SGXV]

. . the state. If this option is taken:
. . * Add to SGX V letters E/N in
. . Auxiliary Schedule 2.

SGX WA . *By region within EU*
. . * Add to SGXW letters B/V following
. . RRQ.

WP . . Balkans

SGY D International relations of EU
. * Add to SGY D numbers & letters 2/9,
. A/Y following SD so far as applicable.

D2B . Treaties, etc.

D2B B . . Regional treaties, etc.
. . . * For Lome convention, see
. . . SGN OI5 LNR Q.

D5L T . International organizations

D5N . . United Nations & EU

E . Relations with other supranational
. organizations

F . . *By organization*
. . . * Add to SGY F letters A/Y following
. . . SH; e.g SGY FRM K Relations with
. . . Organization of American States.

G . Relations with groupings of states
. . * Add to SGY G letters W/Y following
. . RQ.
. . * Add to SGY H letters A/W following
. . RR; e.g.

HAV . . Relations with Islamic countries

HK . . Relations with Third World
. . . * For Lome Conventions, see
. . . SGN OI5 LNR Q.

HW . . Relations with Non-state nations

J . Relations with non-member
. sovereign states
. . * Add to SGY K letters E/N in
. . Auxiliary Schedule 2.

[Supranational law SE]
[Supranational organizations by region]
[European supranational law general SFYH]
. . . . . [Constitutional law]
. . . . . . [Organization law EU SGX]
. . . . [International relations of EU SGYD]
. . . . [Relations with non-member sovereign states SGYJ]

SGY Y Other European supranational organizations
. * For European supranational organizations covering
. several or all regions (e.g. Council of Europe), see
. SFY H; for European Union (EU), see SG.
. * Each region is assigned a 3-letter classmark (e.g.
. Western Europe SHB); for the method of its division,
. see notes under Supranational organizations by region,
. following SE9 VB.
. * Each organization may be subdivided like the EU, as
. follows:
. * Add to the organization's classmark numbers & letters
. 2/Y following SG so far as applicable.

SHA C . Northern European supranational
. organizations

QN . . Nordic Council (1952)

SHB C . Western European supranational organizations

QJ . . Western European Union (1948)

QT . . Benelux Economic Union (1958)

R . . European Free Trade Association (1960),
. . EFTA (1960)

SHC C . Central European supranational organizations

QJ . . Danube Commission (1948)

SHD C . Eastern Europe supranational organizations

QK . . Council for Mutual Economic Assistance
. . (1949), Comecon

SHE C . . Balkans supranational organizations

SHF C . Southern Europe supranational organizations

Other supranational organizations
. * The instructions in the second and subsequent notes
. under SGY Y above apply to all the regions given
. below.

SHG C . Mediterranean supranational organizations

[Supranational law SE]
[Supranational organizations by region]
[Other supranational organizations]
[Mediterranean supranational organizations SHGC]

SHH C Afro-Asia supranational organizations
SHI C Middle East supranational organizations, Arabic supranational organizations
CQG . Arab League (1945)
CQU . Central Treaty Organization, Cento, Baghdad Pact (1959)

SHJ C Asian supranational organizations
SHK C Far East supranational organizations
SHL C South-east Asia supranational organizations, South Asia supranational organizations
QL . Colombo Plan (1950)
QP . South-Eastern Asian Treaty Organization, SEATO (1954)
RI . Association of South East Asian Nations (1967), ASEAN

SHM C Pacific supranational organizations, Oceanian supranational organizations
SHN C Australasian supranational organizations
SHO C African supranational organizations
RE . Organization of African Unity (1963)
SHP C . North Africa & Sub-Sahara supranational organizations
SHQ C . Central Africa supranational organizations
E . . Organisation Commune Africaine et Malgache de Cooperation Economique (1965), OCAM (1965)

SHR C American supranational organizations
MK . Organisation of American States, OAS
* 1889-
MK2 F . . Treaties of formation
MK2 GMK . . . Inter-American Conferences
* 1889-
MK2 GQJ . . . Charter (1948)
MK5 CU . . Unification of laws
MK5 CU9 TQ . . . Inter-American Council of Jurists
MK5 LQA . . Meetings of ministers
MKX IU . . Council

[Supranational law SE]
[Supranational organizations by region]
. [Other supranational organizations]
. . [American supranational organizations SHRC]
. . . [Organisation of American States SHRMK]
. . . . [Council SHRMKXIU]

SHR MKX J . . . . Pan-American Union
* Became Secretariat for OAS in 1948.
MKX PE . . . . . Inter-American Economic & Social Council
MKX PF . . . . Inter-American Development Bank
MKX PQ . . . . . Inter-American Cultural Council
MKX Q . . . . Committees (OAS)

SHS C . . . North American supranational organizations
SHT C . . . Latin American supranational organizations
RB . . . . Latin American Free Trade Association (1960)
SHU C . . . Central Amrican supranational organizations
QM . . . . Organization of Central American states (1951)
SHV C . . . Caribbean supranational organizations
RJ . . . . Caribbean Free Trade Area (1968), Caribbean Community (1968)
SHW C . . . South American supranational organizations
CR . . . . Southern Core common market, Mercosur (1995)
* Argentina, Brazil, Paraguay, Uruguay.

SHX Non-governmental supranational organizations
* For specific organizations, see subject; e.g. Inter-Parliamentary Union RIA VOI; International Civil Aviation Organization (1944) SDB QF5 LT.

SHY National law, state law, municipal law
. * General works only; do not qualify SHY by S3/SC unless subject is municipal law, per se, in general.
. * Each jurisdiction may be qualified by all classes S2/SC, as instructed in Auxiliary Schedule S1.
. * An alternative (not recommended) for libraries concerned primarily with comparative law is to cite national jurisdictions AFTER substantive law, practice and procedure and jurisprudence. If this option is taken:
. * Use Auxiliary Schedule S1 as the basic notation for the whole collection. Locate general works on a specific jurisdiction at S4 (e.g. S4E English law). Use 4 to qualify specific classes in S5/SY by jurisdiction; e.g. Criminal law - English SW4 E, Criminal law - French SW4 F; Family law - Courts - USA SCF 74Y.
. * A further alternative (not recommended) for small libraries is to follow the above procedure but treating all works as though they relate solely or primarily to the home country (the jurisdiction under which the library operates). So 4 would not be added for the home country; e.g. SE would be used both for a general study on contract law and for the home country's law of contract. National place classmarks would be added only for countries other than the preferred (home) country; e.g. in an English library French contract law would be SE4 F whereas English law of contract would be simply SE.

SHY 4 . History of national legal systems
. . * The history of law in general goes at S4. Locate here only those works which deal with the history of national legal systems per se. If in doubt, prefer S4.

SI . Ethnolaw, ethnological jurisdictions, non-literate societies law, tribal law, pre-literate societies law, primitive law
. . * This class takes the literature on ethnological jurisdictions as they operated (and perhaps still operate) independently of the context of a modern national jurisdiction (under which virtually all such ethnological groups now live).
. . * Class here also works on the law of an ethnological group which is distributed over several different modern national jurisdictions.
. . * Works on the present operation of these ethnological jurisdictions within a particular modern nation state should go with the latter. The class -XQ (under the constitutional law of the state concerned) should be used to locate them (see Auxiliary Schedule S1)
. . * An alternative (not recommended) is to locate here all works on these jurisdictions, including those which operate entirely within a particular nation state. In this case, the class -YJ is added to the classes in Auxiliary Schedule S1 and used to qualify the ethnic jurisdiction by its present country location(s); e.g. Fulani law - in Nigeria SIH KHY JVV H.

[National law SHY]
[Ethnolaw SI]

. * See also KSH O (Ethnolaw as a social norm).
. * Add to SI letters B/Y from Auxiliary Schedule 3A (Ethnic groups) so far as applicable. A number of prominent exanples is given below to demonstrate scope and arrangement.

SIG . American aboriginal law
SIG EJ . . Choctaw law
G . . Iroquoian law
GP . . Cherokee law
KY . . Zuni law
LN . . Mayan law
MW . . Aztec law
MX . . Nahuat law
V . . Inca law
SIH . African native law
SIH KH . . Fulani law

SJA Ancient & medieval law
. * Systems originating in these periods and which are not clearly or solely identified with any single modern nation state.
. * The normal arrangement whereby place is cited before period is modified here. Division is first by broad period (giving Ancient, Medieval and Modern) and only within these is place cited before (specific) period.
. * Each system may be qualified by all preceding facets (S2/SC) as instructed in Auxiliary Schedule S1.

SJB . Ancient law
SJC A . . Ancient Oriental law (general)
. . . * For this law in specific place, see those places under modern jurisdictions and the period subclass under the place as indicated in S47.

B . . Ancient Near East & Africa & Europe
. . . * Before c. 54O B.C.
. . . * Add to SJ letters C/LL and M/W following C in Auxiliary Schedule 2. A selection of the more prominent societies is given below for convenience & to show scope.

H . . . Sumerian law
I . . . . Cuneiform inscribed law
W . . . Semitic law (general)
SJD A . . . Babylonian-Assyrian law
C . . . . Babylonian law
D . . . . . Code of Hammurabi
R . . . . Assyrian law
SJE D . . . Medean law
E . . . Persian law
K . . . Hittite law
SJG . . . Phoenecian law
SJN . . . Ancient Egyptian law
SJQ X . . . Pre-Hellenic law
Y . . . Classical antiquity law
SJR . . . . Hellenistic law, Ancient Greek law
. . . . . * Eastern Mediterranean, c. 450/150 BC.

[National law SHY]
[Ancient & medieval law SJA]
[Ancient law SJB]
[Ancient Near East & Africa & Europe SJCB]
[Classical antiquity law SJQY]
[Hellenistic law SJR]

SJR L Rhodian law
. * See also International maritime law
. SDB QA5 A7U

SJX Roman law, Civil law (Roman law)
. * See also Byzantine law SKA; Civil law
. systems SR; Roman-Dutch law SSB
SJX 2 . Primary materials
2H . . Codes
2HB . . . Ius Papirianum, Leges regiae
2HC . . . Twelve tables (Roman law)
. . . . * c. 450 BC.
2HE . . . Lex Aebutia
. . . . * c. 150 BC.
2HG . . . Gaius (codes of law)
. . . . * c. 115-180 AD.
2HJ . . . Constitutio Antoninianus
. . . . * 212 AD.
2HK . . . Constitutiones principum
. . . . * Includes edicta, scripta & leges.
2HL . . . Codex Gregorianus
. . . . * 291 AD.
2HN . . . Codex Hermogenianus
. . . . * c. 295 AD.
2HP . . . Codex Theodosianus (c. 439 AD)
. . . . * See SKA 2QD

3 . *Secondary materials*
3N . . Language
3NK . . . Addicere (the word)
56 . . Influences
. . . * For reception, see SKG 5TB.
5C . . Sources
5D . . . Jus non-scriptum
5GD . . . Formal sources
5GE . . . . Jus scriptum
5GF . . . . Senatus consultiam
. . . . {*Concilium plebis*}
. . . . . * See Ancient Rome SJY
5N . . . Codes
. . . . * For texts of the codes themselves,
. . . . see Primary materials SJX 2H.
5NQ . . . . Jus gentium
5NS . . . . Jus civile
5NV . . . . Later Western texts
. . . . . * A/Z by author.
5TH . . . Commentaries

[Ancient & medieval law SJA]
[Ancient Near East & Africa & Europe SJCB]
[Classical antiquity law SJQY]
[Roman law SJX]
[Secondary materials SJX3]
[Sources SJX5C]
. [Commentaries SJX5TH]

SJX 5TJ . . Glosses, glossators
5TK . . Commentators, post-glossators

Law & society
5UN . Jus naturale (general)
5UQ . Jus civile
. . * When it is treated as distinct from jus
. . naturale.
6 Practice & procedure
6E . Courts
7N . . Forum (Roman law)
. . . * Use of any place as a court.
Subjects of law
E . Contract law
. . Damages
EV9 M . . . Universitas
G . Tort
G5M . . Lex Aquila
. . . * Liability for damages to persons or
. . . property.
H . Property law
. . Conveyance
HS . . . Fiducia
I . . Inheritance & succession
IO . . . Wills
IPG . . . . Fidei commissum
Jurisdictions
SJY . Ancient Rome (Roman law
. narrowly)
SJY 5C . . Sources
5GE . . . Lawmaking bodies
5GF . . . . Imperium
. . . . . * Supreme military and judicial
. . . . . power.
5GH . . . . Concilium plebis, Tribunus
. . . . plebis
6E . . Courts & procedure
6KB . . . Law officers, court officials
6NW . . . . Legates
6NX . . . . Procurators (Ancient Rome)
6PB . . . . Praetor
6PC . . . . . Praetor urbanus, praefectus
. . . . . urbi
6PD . . . . . Praetor peregrinus
6PE . . . . Aediles
6PF . . . . Lictors
6PG . . . . Praefectus praetorio
7 . . . Courts
7N . . . . Quaestiones, jury courts
. . . . (Ancient Rome)

Ancient & medieval law

[National law SHY]
[Ancient & medieval law SJA]
[Ancient law SJB]
. . [Classical antiquity law SJQY]
. . . [Roman law SJX]
. . . . [Courts SJY7]
. . . . [Quaestiones SJY7N]

SKA . . . Byzantine law, Graeco-Roman law
. . . . * Roman law as developed in Eastern Europe, c. 600/1453 AD.
. . . . * See also Canon law - Eastern Churches - Collections - Nomocanones SXC 27
SKA 2 . . . . *Primary materials*
2HD . . . . . Codex Theodosianus (AD 439)
. . . . . . * Superseded by Justinian code.
2HF . . . . . Codex Constitutionum (AD 529), Justinian code
2HH . . . . . . Quinquaginta deisiones
2HJ . . . . . . Corpus juris civilis
2HK . . . . Digesta (Corpus juris civilis), Pandectsa (AD 533)
2HN . . . . Institutiones (Justinian), Institutes of Justinian
2HP . . . . Codex repetitae praefectionis
2HR . . . . Novellae constitutiones post codicim
2HS . . . . . Ecloga (AD 726)
2HV . . . . . Basilica (c.AD 900)
2HW . . . . . Hexabiblos
9VB . . . . *Substantive law*
QA . . . . . Sea law
. . . . . . * For Rhodian sea law see Maritime law SDB QA5 A7U.
YP . . . Post Justinian period law

SKB Medieval Western law
. * c. 400-1500
SKB 5C . *Sources*
5TB . . Roman law in the Middle Ages
. . . * See also Reception SKG 5TB
5TC . . Arabic law & medieval law
. *Systems of medieval law*
Y . . Early medieval law
. . . * To c. 1000.
SKC . . . Germanic law
. . . . * Law of the German peoples from their first contact with Roman law until the development of their own territorial law.
SKC 2 . . . . *Primary materials*
. . . . . * The main sources are collections of written laws rather than legislation or comprehensive codes. But these sources are treated here as primary materials.

[National law SHY]
[Ancient & medieval law SJA]
[Medieval Western law SKB]
[Systems of medieval law]
[Early medieval law SKBY]
. [Germanic law SKC]
. . [Primary materials SKC2]

. . . Codes
SKC 2H . . . . Leges Barbarorum
2HF D . . . . . Leges Romanae Barbarorum
SKD A . . Gothic law
B . . . Ostrogothic law
C . . . Visigothic law
D . . . Burgundian law
F . . Frankish law, Frankonian law
G . . . Salic law, Lex Salica
H . . . . Lex Thuringorum
I . . . . Lex Francorum Chamavorum
J . . . . Lex Ribuaria (741-747), Ripuarian law
K . . Bavarian law (c.750)
L . . Lombard law, Leges Langobardicae
L2H FD . . . Liber edictus, Edictus Langobardorum
L2H FJ . . . Liber Papiensis
L2H FL . . . Walcausina (1019-37)
M . . Saxon law
. . . * See also Magdeburg law SKF M
NB . . . Lex Saxorum
NF . . . Lex Frisionum, Friesian law
NK . . . Angli & Warni law
P . . Swabian law
P2H FG . . . Alamannia code (c.725), Lex Alamannorum (c.725)
P6 . . . Practice & procedure
P9G . . . . Remedies
P9G U . . . . . Wergild
P9G V . . . . . Bot
Q . . Scandinavian law, North Germanic law
. . . * See also modern Scandinavian law SVM
R . . Norman law
S . Celtic law
. . * See also Irish law SOC; Welsh law SOA
T . . Brehon laws
. . . * Alternative (not recommended) to locating under Irish law, SOC 47B.
V . Slavic law
Y Later medieval law, pre-modern law
. * c. 1000-1500.
Y47 . *Particular periods*
. . * Add to SKD Y47 letters FH/GY in Auxiliary Schedule 4A.
SKE . Feudal law, droit feodal
SKE 7 . . Courts
7N . . . Manorial courts
J . . Land law

[National law SHY]
[Ancient & medieval law SJA]
. [Medieval Western law SKB]
. . [Systems of medieval law]
. . . [Later medieval law SKDY]
. . . . [Feudal law SKE]
. . . . . [Land law SKEJ]

SKE JP . . . . . . Feudal tenure
JPQ . . . . . . Homage
. . . . * Acknowledgement of bond of tenure.
JQ . . . . . . Allodium, allodial tenure
X . . . . . Constitutional law
. . . . . . Duties
XCU . . . . Scutage, Escuage, Shield money
. . . . * Payment in lieu of military service.
XCU W . . . . . . Immunity (feudal law)
. . . . * Freedom from the power of another.
YDR . . . . . . War
YDR RP . . . . Truce of God
. . . . * Prohibition of fighting on certain
. . . . days by decree of the Church.
YDR RQ . . . . Landfriede, Landpeace
SKF H . . . . Holy Roman Empire law
. . . . . * C. 800-1800.
L . . . . Lubeck law, Lubish law
. . . . . * Lubeck was a leading member of the
. . . . . Hanseatic League.
. . . . . * See also Hanseatic law of the sea
. . . . . SDB QA5 A8G PM
M . . . . Magdeburg law

SKG Modern law, modern legal systems, modern jurisdictions
. * c. 1500 to date.
. * General works only, dealing specifically with the
. modern period.
. * See also Contemporary period SKV and the note
. there.
SKG 5C . *Sources*
5TA . . Ancient law & modern law
5TB . . . Roman law & modern law, Reception
. . . . * Process whereby Roman law (and to a lesser
. . . . degree canon law and feudal law) was taken
. . . . into European legal systems (especially of
. . . . the Germanic countries) c. 1400-1700.
. *Specific periods*
. . * Add to SK letters H/U in Auxiliary Schedule
. . 4A.
SKH . . 15-16th century
SKJ . . 16-17th century
SKL . . 17-18th century
SKN . . 18-19th century
SKQ . . 19-20th century
SKS . . 20-21st century

[National law SHY]
[Modern law SKG]
[Specific periods]
. [20-21st century SKS]

SKV Present-day legal systems, contemporary systems
. * General works only, distinguishing contemporary
. systems from earlier modern systems. If in doubt, prefer
. SKG.
SKW . Civil law & common law systems
. . * When treated together, as systems per se.
. . * For common law systems, see SL; for civil law
. . systems, see SR.

SL . Common law systems
. . * Legal systems founded mainly on the common law of
. . England, as distinct from civil law systems (see SR).
. . * The preferred arrangement is to treat each national
. . jurisdiction separately and to locate here only
. . general works on common law.
. . * An alternative (not recommended) is to treat
. . common law as one integral system, in which the
. . individual jurisdictions based on it are treated as
. . subclasses. So, for example, English contract law,
. . U.S.A. contract law, Australian contract law, etc.
. . would all go under Common law system - Contract.
. . If this option is taken, see Auxiliary Schedule S4 for
. . instructions.

SM . . Preferred country (common law systems)
. . . * Alternative for any library wishing to locate first
. . . the jurisdiction of the country in which it is itself
. . . located.

SN . . England & Wales (jurisdictions), English law
. . . * Including British Isles as a whole, United
. . . Kingdom as a whole, Great Britain as a whole.
. . . * This schedule demonstrates the use of Auxiliary
. . . Schedule S1 in qualifying any given non-federal
. . . jurisdiction (with minor adjustments).
. . . * See also Anglo-American law, SOW
SN2 . . . *Primary materials*
. . . . * As Auxiliary Schedule S2, with some
. . . . adjustments.
SN2 8B5 . . . . Official gazettes
8E . . . . Journals
. . . . . * See note at 28E in Auxiliary Schedule S2.
A . . . . Parliamentary publications
B . . . . . General
. . . . . . * For works covering both Houses.
C . . . . . House of Commons (parliamentary publications)
C8E . . . . . . Journal
CC . . . . . . General papers
. . . . . . Debates

[Present-day legal systems SKV]
[Common law systems SL]
[England & Wales jurisdictions SN]
[Primary materials SN2]
[Parliamentary publications SN2A]
. [House of Commons parliamentary publications SN2C]
. . [Debates]

SN2 CD . . . Hansard (House of Commons)
CG . . Bills
CM . . Committees
D . House of Lords (parliamentary publications)
. . * As for SN2 C House of Commons.
DT . Command papers (UK law)
. . * Alternative (not recommended) to subordinating to subject.
. . * If option taken, arrange as series.

F Legislative acts, legislation texts of acts
G . Statutes texts
G44 . . Indexes, tables, guides to the statutes
. . Early series non-official
GE7 6 . . . Statutes at large
. . . . * Arrange by editor A/Z (e.g. Barker SN2 GE7 6B).
GJ . . Modern series
GJ7 5 . . . Statutes revised
GJ7 58 . . . Sessional volumes
GJ7 6 . . . Non-official editions
. . . . * Arrange by editor, A/Z - e.g. Chitty's statutes
GS . . . Private acts, local acts, personal acts
. . . . * For local legislation, see SN2 L.
GU . . . War legislation, emergency legislation
H . Codes
. . * Codes on special subjects (e.g. sale of goods) go with the subject.
J Subsidiary legislation texts, subordinate legislations texts
JM . Statutory instruments
JM4 4 . . Indexes, tables
JM7 5 . . Revised editions by date
JM7 58 . . Annual volumes
JM7 6 . . Non-official editions
. . . * Arrange by editor, A/Z - e.g. Halsbury SN2 JM7 6H.
JM7 K . . Tables of statutory instrument effects
JP . Other
. . * E.g. special procedure orders (provisional orders). For local authority by-laws, etc. see SN2 L.
JS Prerogative instruments
JT . Royal proclamations & instructions

[Modern law SKG]
[Present-day legal systems SKV]
[Common law systems SL]
[England & Wales jurisdictions SN]
[Primary materials SN2]
[Prerogative instruments SN2JS]
. [Royal proclamations & instructions SN2JT]

SN2 JU . Orders in Council
. . * Made by Privy Council without concurrence of the monarch.
JV . Letters patent
JW . Other
L Local legislation texts, by-laws texts
LP . *By county*
. . * Add to SN2 LP letters following E in Auxiliary Schedule 2.
LR . *By city, municipality etc*
. . * Arrange A/Z.

MC Administrative publications texts, executive publications texts
. * General collections, etc. only. Those on specific subjects go with the subject.
MH . Attorney-General publications (texts), law officers' publications (texts)
MJ . Government department publications texts
. . * Arrange A/Z by name of department.
ML . Royal Commissions (texts)
. . * Arrange A/Z by title.
MP . Other
. . * Inter-departmental & other ad hoc bodies.

N Law reports (English law), cases in English law
N8 . Digests & abridgments general
. . * Digests of a given report series go with the latter - e.g. Law reports digest SN2 PB7 6L8.

N9 . Individual cases
. . * Arrange by date, then name; each case may be subdivided as instructed in Auxiliary Schedule S2. For example, Pleadings in the case of Brown v. Jones (1992) SN2 N9 SNB RJD.

NE . Cases pre-1865
NE7 6 . . Non-official series
. . . *Particular series*
NE7 6E . . . English reports
NE7 6R . . . Revised reports
NE7 8 . . Individual reporters
. . . * Arrange A/Z.
NE8 . . Digests

[Present-day legal systems SKV]
[Common law systems SL]
[England & Wales jurisdictions SN]
[Primary materials SN2]
[Law reports English law SN2N]
[Cases pre-1865 SN2NE]
[Digests SN2NE8]

SN2 NE8 76	. Non-official series
	. . * Arrange A/Z by editor - e.g.
	. . Bacon's Abridgment.
NE8 G	Yearbooks
	. * Arrange by editor or series, A/Z -
	. e.g. Maynard.
	By court
	. * Synthesis by S7 is replaced here by
	. enumeration, to meet the special
	. needs of English case law.
NF	. Common law courts (pre-1875)
NH	. . Court rolls (general)
	. . . * Rolls of particular courts go
	. . . with the court - e.g. Curia Regis.
NJ	. . . Specific rolls
	. . . . * If not classifiable by court; e.g.
	. . . . Pipe rolls.
	. . . . * Arrange A/Z.
NK	. . King's Bench cases, Queen's
	. . Bench cases
NK4 4	. . . Indexes
NK8	. . . Digests
NL	. . . Pre-Yearbooks (c. 1280)
NM	. . . Yearbooks (1280-1535)
NN	. . . Private reports
	. . . . * Arrange by date and name;
	. . . . e.g. SN2 NNG ONC for Coke
	. . . . (1572).
NP	. . . *Individual courts, A/Z*
NPB	. . . . Bail Court (1830-54)
NQ	. . Court of Common Pleas
NR	. . Court of Exchequer (common
	. . law cases)
NS	. . Curia Regis
NT	. . Manorial courts (by date)
NU	. . Nisi Prius (circuit) courts
NV	. . County courts (pre-1846)
OE	. Equity courts (pre-1875)
OF	. . Court of Chancery
OG	. . . Vice-Chancellor's court
OH	. . Court of Exchequer (equity
	. . cases)
OJ	. . Master of the Rolls cases
OK	. . Court of Request cases
OM	. Admiralty & Ecclesiastical
	. precedents
	. . * Combined reports.
ON	. . Admiralty reports

[Common law systems SL]
[Primary materials SN2]
[Law reports English law SN2N]
[Cases pre-1865 SN2NE]
. [By court]
. . [Admiralty & Ecclesiastical precedents SN2OM]
. . . [Admiralty reports SN2ON]

SN2 OP	. . . Ecclesiastical reports
	. . . . * Alternative (not recommended) to locating
	. . . . with ecclesiastical law, SW.
OR	. . Privy Council cases (pre-1865)
PB	Cases post-1865
PB7 6	. Non-official series
PB7 6B	. . Law journal reports (1823-1949)
PB7 6D	. . All England law reports reprint (1843-
	. . 1935)
PB7 6E	. . All England law reports (1936-)
PB7 6G	. . Law times reports (1843-1947)
PB7 6H	. . Weekly reporter (1853-1906)
PB7 6L	. . The Law reports (1865-) (texts)
PB7 6L4 4	. . . Index to the Law reports & Weekly
	. . . law reports
PB7 6L8	. . . Law reports digest
PB7 6M	. . . Weekly law reports
PB7 6N	. . . Appellate series
PB7 6P	. . . Common law series
PB7 6Q	. . . Chancery & Equity series
PB7 6R	. . . Probate, Divorce & Admiralty series
PB7 6T	. . Weekly notes (1866-1952)
PB7 6V	. . Times law reports (1884-1952)
PB7 7	. . Other non-official series, A/Z
PB8	. Digests
PD	. *By court*
	. . * Add to SN2 PD letter D/W following SN7 in
	. . SN7 D/SN7 W so far as applicable.
UB	. . Administrative decisions
UB7 6	. . . Non-official series
UD	. . . *By Ministry, department, etc. A/Z*
WT	. State trials (texts)
	. . * Arrange by editor, A/Z; e.g. Howell's state
	. . trials
X	. Modern series by subject
	. . * Alternative (not recommended) to
	. . subordinating to subject. If this option is taken,
	. . proceed as follows:
	. . * Add to SN2X letters A/Y in Auxiliary
	. . Schedule S1; e.g. Cox's criminal cases (1844-
	. . 1941) SN2 XW

[Present-day legal systems SKV]
[Common law systems SL]
[England & Wales jurisdictions SN]
[Primary materials SN2]
. [Law reports English law SN2N]
. . [Cases post-1865 SN2PB]
. . . [Modern series by subject SN2X]

SN3 *Secondary materials, works about English law*
. * See Auxiliary Schedule S1 for guide to the qualification of English law by S3/SC.
. * Below are given only those classes from S3/SC which generate a terminology peculiar to English law, or whose structure calls for some adjustment to the situation in English law. A minimal number of general terms has been added to show the general structure within which the modifications are to be seen.
. *Common subdivisions*
SN3 4J . . Lawyers
5 . . . Solicitors
6 . . . Barristers
. . . . Leading counsel
6V . . . . Queen's Counsel, QCs, King's Counsel, KCs
. . . Minister of Justice
7F . . . . Lord Chancellor
7G . . . Law officers of the Crown
. . . . * For law lords, see Judges SN6 TB.
7H . . . . Lord Chief Justice
7J . . . . Attorney-General
. . . . . * Principal legal advisor to the government.
7K . . . . Solicitor-General
. . . . . * For Director of Public Prosecutions, see Criminal law SNW 37L.
8 . . Organizations in the subject
JP . . . Law societies
KC . . . . Inns of Court
KG . . . . . Grays Inn
KI . . . . . Inner Temple
KL . . . . . Lincolns Inn
KM . . . . . Middle Temple
KN . . . . Inns of Chancery

SN5 A . Jurisprudence
. . * Only if it concerns specifically English law.
C . . Sources
. . . Supranational jurrisdictions
S . . . . EU law in English law
SN6 . Practice & procedure
SN6 A . . Practice of law
E . . Courts & court proceedings
KB . . . Law officers
. . . . * See also Law officers of the Crown SN3 7G

[Present-day legal systems SKV]
[Common law systems SL]
[England & Wales jurisdictions SN]
[Secondary materials SN3]
[Practice & procedure SN6]
[Courts & court proceedings SN6E]
[Law officers SN6KB]

. History
SN6 KB4 7FB . . Medieval
KB4 7FB J . . . Justiciars
. . . . * 1066-1232.
N . Judges, justices
. . *By special function*
. . . * For coroners in general, see SN7 HDC 6N.
. . . * See also Law officers of the Crown SN3 7G
TB . . . Law lords
. . . . * In British House of Lords or (narrowly) Lords of Appeal in Ordinary.

Types of courts
. *By historical jurisdiction*
SN7 H . . Common law courts
HDC . . . Coroner's court
HDC 6N . . . . Coroners
. . Equity courts
I . . . Chancery courts, Equity courts
. *By special status*
N . . Courts of record, courts not of record
. *By structure of courts system*
. . Supreme courts
Q . . . House of Lords (supreme courts)
. . . . * For appellate function, see SN9 H7Q.
. . High courts
R . . . Supreme Court of Judicature (general)
. . . . * For Court of Appeal (high courts) see Appeal SN9 H7R.
RQ . . . . High Court of Justice, high Court
RR . . . . . Assize courts
. . . . . . * Abolished 1972; civil cases transferred to High Court, criminal to Crown Court.
RS . . . . . Divisional courts
RT . . . . . . Queen's Bench Division
. . . . * Mostly common law cases.
RU . . . . . . Chancery Division
. . . . * Mostly trusts & wills.

Common law systems

[Common law systems SL]
[Courts & court proceedings SN6E]
[Types of courts]
. [By structure of courts system]
. . [High courts]
. . . . . [Divisional courts SN7RS]
. . . . . . [Chancery Division SN7RU]

SN7 RV . . . . . . Quarter sessions
. . . . * Abolished 1971; cases transferred to crown courts.
RW . . . . . . Crown courts
. . . . * Mostly criminal cases.
S . . Lower courts
SQ . . . County courts
T . . . Magistrates' courts
. . . . * Mostly criminal cases.
UF . . Courts of special jurisdiction
. . . * The preferred arrangement is to subordinate to subject - e.g. family courts SNC F7.
. . . * An alternative (not recommended) is to keep them together here. If this option is taken, proceed as follows:
. . . * Add to SN7 V letters A/Y in Auxiliary Schedule S3.

SN8 Actions, lawsuits, cause lawsuits
SN8 L . Preliminary proceedings, pre-trial proceedings
. . * See also proceedings special to criminal law.
S . Trial proceedings, hearings
SN9 G . . Remedies
GY . . . Administrative remedies
H . . . . Appeals, appellate proceedings
H7 . . . . . Courts of appeal
. . . . . . * For Judicial Committee of the Privy Council see SOP 9H7 P.
. . . . . . History
H74 . . . . Court of Appeal in Chancery
. . . . * 1851-1875.
H7D . . . . . . *Court from which appeal made*
. . . . * Use -7D only to qualify a particular appeal court. See note at S7D.
. . . . . . Supreme court
H7Q . . . . House of Lords (court of appeal)
. . . . . . High courts
H7R . . . . Court of Appeal (English law)
. . . . * Includes Civil Division as well as general works.
. . . . * See also Criminal Division, SNW 9H7 R.
K . . . . Prerogative orders & writs
KL . . . . . Habeas corpus
Other results of litigation
Q . Compromise, settlement out of court

[Common law systems SL]
[England & Wales jurisdictions SN]
[Secondary materials SN3]
[Practice & procedure SN6]
. [Courts & court proceedings SN6E]
. . [Other results of litigation]
. . . [Compromise SN9Q]

SN9 R . . . Arbitration
R7 . . . . Courts
R7V . . . . . Small claims court

VB Substantive law, subjects of law
. *By historical development*
. . Strictum jus
VP . . . Common law subjects in English law
. . Equity general
VQ . . . Equity subjects in English law
. . . . * See also special subjects in which the equitable principle applies; e.g. Trusts & trustees SNH U; Remedies SN9 G.
. . . . * Alternative (not recommended) for libraries wishing to keep together works on equity. If this option is taken, proceed as follows:
. . . . * Add to SN9 VQ numbers & letters 2/9,A/Y in Auxiliary Schedule S1; e.g. Equitable remedies SN9 VQ9 G; Trusts & trustees SN9 VQH U.

W . Private law
. . Conflict of laws
SNA . . . English conflict of laws
SNA 2 . . . . *Primary materials*
2MS . . . . . Treaties & international agreements
5Y . . . . *By jurisdiction with which in conflict*
P . . Law of persons
SNC F . . . Family law
SNE . . Contract
SNG . . Tort
SNH . . Property
SNH P . . . Transfer of property rights
U . . . . Trusts & trustees
SNJ . . . Real property
SNL . . . Personal property
SNN . . Economics & commercial law
SNN Q . . . Business law
SNP . . . Transport law
SNT A . . Social law & legislations
SNV 2 . . Cultural law

SNW . . Criminal law
SNW 37G . . . Law officers
37L . . . . Director of Public Prosecutions
6E . . . Courts & procedure
7RT . . . . Divisional Court of Queen's Bench
7RW . . . . Crown courts
7T . . . . Magistrates' courts
7TS . . . . . Stipendiary magistrates' courts

Common law systems

[Common law systems SL]
[Substantive law SN9VB]
[Private law SN9W]
. [Criminal law SNW]
. . [Courts & procedure SNW6E]
. . . [Magistrates' courts SNW7T]
. . . . [Stipendiary magistrates' courts SNW7TS]

SNW 8JP . . . Crown Prosecution Service
9D . . Judicial decision
9H . . . Appeals
9H7 . . . . Appeal courts
9H7 Q . . . . . House of Lords (criminal appeals)
9H7 R . . . . . Court of Appeal (Criminal Division)

Y Public law

SNX . Constitutional law
SNX CW . . Human rights
E . . Government
GV . . . Representation & elections
I . . . Legislature, Parliament
J . . . Executive, The Crown
JKR . . . . Monarch
JMT . . . . Prime minister
JO . . . . Cabinet
JOR . . . . Privy Council
K . . . Public administration
KF . . . . Administrative law
L . . . Central government & administration
M . . . . National security, military law
MY . . . . Law enforcement & police
Q . . . Devolved government
U . . . . Local government & administration
W . . . . Overseas territories
X . . . Judiciary
. . . . * Constitutional status, etc. For administration of justice, see SN6.
SNY B . . Ecclesiastical law, Church & state
. . . * Today, ecclesiastical law in England is concerned only with the constitution and property of the established church (the Church of England).
. . . * For canon law (Church of England), see SXM.
BM . . . Church of England (ecclesiastical law)
D . . International relations
D5H . . . Treaties & constitutional law
F . . European Union & English law
. . . * For EU law as a source of English law, see SN5 S.

[National law SHY]
[Common law systems SL]
[England & Wales jurisdictions SN]
. . [Substantive law SN9VB]
. . . [Public law SNWY]
. . . . [Constitutional law SNX]
. . . . . [European Union & English law SNYF]

SOA Wales

SOB Scotland, Scots law
SOB 6 . Practice & procedure
7 . . Courts
7R . . . Superior courts
7RQ . . . . Court of Session
7RR . . . . . Inner House
. . . . . . * Mainly for appeals; see also SOB 9H7 RR.
7RS . . . . . . First Division
7RT . . . . . . Second division
7RV . . . . . Outer House
7S . . . Inferior courts
7SQ . . . . Sheriff court
7T . . . . Magistrate court
7UF . . . Special courts
. . . . * See subject - e.g. Scottish Land court SOB JS.
9H . . Appeal
9H7 . . . Courts
. . . . Supreme court
9H7 Q . . . . . House of Lords (Scottish law)
9H7 R . . . . Superior courts
9H7 RQ . . . . . Court of Session (appeal)
9H7 RR . . . . . . Inner House appeal
9H7 S . . . . Inferior courts
9H7 SQ . . . . . Sheriff Principal

9VB . *Substantive law*
. . Contract
E . . . Transactions (Scots law)
. . . . * Any agreement tending to the settlement of doubtful claims.
L . . Personal property
LHQ . . . Bailment
. . . . Liens
LHR FQX . . . . . Retention (Scots law)
W . . Criminal law
W7R . . . Superior courts
W7R W . . . . High Court of Justiciary
W7R X . . . . Lords Commissioners
W7S . . . Inferior courts
W7S Q . . . . Sheriff Principal
W7T . . . . Magistrate court, district court
W9H . . . Appeal
W9H 7 . . . . Courts
W9H 7R . . . . . Court of Criminal Appeal
W9H 7RY . . . . . High Court of Justiciary

[National law SHY]
[Common law systems SL]
[Scotland SOB]
. . [Criminal law SOBW]
. . . [Appeal SOBW9H]
. . . . [Courts SOBW9H7]
. . . . . [High Court of Justiciary SOBW9H7RY]

SOC Ireland
. * General works only, for Ireland as a whole.
SOC 47 . History
. . Medieval period
47B . . . Brehon laws, Feinechus
. . . . * Applied in Ireland prior to the Norman invasion and outside the Pale until 17th century.
. . . . * Alternative (not recommended) is to subordinate to Celtic law at SKD T.
47B 5C . . . . Sources
47B 5TE . . . . . Senchus Mor
47B 5TF . . . . . Book of Aieill
SOE . Northern Ireland
SOF . Republic of Ireland, Eire, Irish law
SOG Isle of Man
SOH Channel Islands
SOJ . Jersey
SOK . Guernsey
SOL . Alderney
SOM . Sark
SOP Commonwealth (general), British Commonwealth
SOP 6 . Practice & procedure
9H . . Appeal
9H7 . . . Courts
9H7 Q . . . . Judicial Committee of the Privy Council
SOR Australasia
SOS . Australia
. . * For individual Dependencies, see under specific territory in SV.
SOT . New Zealand
. . * For individual Dependencies, see under specific territory in SV.

SOV America
SOW . North America, Anglo-American law
SOX . . Canada
SOX XS . . . Provinces law

SP . . United States of America law, USA law, American law (USA)
. . . * This schedule demonstrates the use of Auxiliary Schedule S1 in qualifying a state with a federal structure (with minor adjustments).
SP2 . . . *Primary materials*
. . . . * From Auxiliary Schedule S2, with adjustments.

[Modern law SKG]
[Present-day legal systems SKV]
[Common law systems SL]
[America SOV]
[North America SOW]
[United States of America law SP]
[Primary materials SP2]

SP2 B Congressional publications
. * Class SP2 B takes material on both Houses.
. Debates
. . Non-official series
BD7 6 . . . Congressional record
BG . Bills of both Houses
BM . Committees of both Houses
C . House of Representatives
CD . . Debates
CD7 6 . . . Journal of the House
. . . . * See also Congressional record SP2 BD7 6
CG . . Bills
D . Senate
D8J . . Calendars
D8J D . . . Executive calendar
D8J E . . . Calendar of business
DD . . Debates
DD7 6 . . . Journal of the Senate
. . . . * See also Congressional record SP2 BD7 6
DD7 644 . . . . History of the Bills
. . . . . * Index to the Journal.
DG . . Bills

E Constitution & amendments
E75 . Official editions by date
E76 . Non-official editions
. . * By editor or title.

F Legislative Acts, legislation
FE . Early legislative materials
. . * Pre-1776.
G . Statutes
GJ . . Modern period
GJ7 5 . . . Official compilations & revisions
. . . . * By date.
GJ7 58 . . . Sessional volumes
GJ7 6 . . . Non-official compilations & revisions
. . . . * A/Z by editor or title.
GJ7 H . . . Citations
. . . . * Arrange by editor A/Z. For example, Shepard SP2 GJ7 HS.

[Common law systems SL]
[United States of America law SP]
[Primary materials SP2]
[Legislative Acts SP2F]
. [Statutes SP2G]
. . [Modern period SP2GJ]
. . . [Citations SP2GJ7H]

SP2 J Secondary legislation
JM . Administrative rules & regulations
JM7 K . . Federal Register
JMH . . Code of Federal Regulations
JMP . . Proclamations & executive orders
. . . * By date.
L . Local legislation
. . * This relative position is not used here; it is only used under individual States in SPX T (see notes there).
MC Administrative & Executive publications
MG . Department of Justice
MJ . Other government departments
. . * Arrange A/Z.
ML . Special commissions, committees, etc.
. . * Alternative (not recommended) to locating under subject.

N Law reports, cases
. * Until the mid-19th century reports were known by the reporters name; since then they have been known primarily by jurisdiction.

N8 . Digests etc.
. . * General only; digests of a particular series of reports go with the reports.

NE . Early reports (pre-1776)
NE8 . . Digests
PB . Modern reports
PB8 . . Digests
. . . * For example, American jurisprudence SP2 PB8 A; Corpus Juris SP2 PB8 C

. *By court*
PC . . Federal & State Courts reports together
PC7 6 . . . Non-official series
PC7 6E . . . . National Reporter System
. . . . . * For Federal cases, see SP2 PP 76H; for Supreme Court Reporter, see SP2 Q78.
PC7 6G . . . . . Atlantic Reporter
PC7 6J . . . . . California Reporter
PC7 6L . . . . . New York Supplement
PC7 6N . . . . . Northeastern Reporter
PC7 6P . . . . . Northwestern Reporter
PC7 6R . . . . . Pacific Reporter
PC7 6T . . . . . Southeastern Reporter
PC7 6V . . . . . Southwestern Reporter
PC7 7 . . . . Other general series (A/Z)

[Common law systems SL]
[Primary materials SP2]
[Law reports SP2N]
[By court]
[Federal & State Courts reports together SP2PC]
[Non-official series SP2PC76]
. [Other general series A/Z SP2PC77]

SP2 PC7 7A . . American Law Reports
PC7 7L . . Law Reports Annotated
PC7 8 . Specialized series (A/Z)
PD *By court*
. * Should this be required; only works covering both federal and state court systems should go here.
PP Reports of Federal Courts
. * Reports restricted to one Court go with the Court.
PP7 6 . Non-official series
PP7 6G . . National Reporter System (Federal Courts)
PP7 6H . . . Federal Cases
PP7 6J . . . Federal Reporter
PP7 6K . . . Federal Supplement
PP7 6L . . . Federal Rules Decisions
PP7 7 . . Other series A/Z
PP7 H . Citations
PP8 . Digests
PP9 . Individual cases

Q . Supreme Court
. . * For appellate function, see SP9 H7Q.
Q75 . . Official edition
Q76 . . Non-official editions A/Z
Q77 . . . Lawyers' edition
Q78 . . Supreme Court Reporter
Q7H . . Citations
Q8 . . Digests
Q9 . . Individual cases (by date then name)
. Higher courts
. . * For Court of Appeals and Circuit Court of Appeals, see Appeal SP9 H7R.
R . . Circuit courts
RT . . . Particular courts
. . . . * Arrange A/Z.
. Intermediate courts
S . . District courts
ST . . . Particular courts
. . . . * Arrange A/Z.
SV . Other Federal Courts

[Common law systems SL]
[United States of America law SP]
[Primary materials SP2]
. . [By court]
. . . [Federal & State Courts reports together SP2PC]
. . . . [Reports of Federal Courts SP2PP]
. . . . . [Other Federal Courts SP2SV]

SP2 UB . . . . Administrative decisions
UD . . . . . Special, by Department
. . . . . . * Arrange A/Z.

SP3 *Secondary materials*
SP6 . Practice & procedure
SP7 . . Courts
. . . * Civil & criminal jurisdiction is commonly vested in the same court.
SP7 P . . . Federal courts general
. . . . * For State courts, see SPX S7.
Q . . . . Supreme court
Q52 . . . . . Biography
. . . . . . * Lives of Supreme Court justices.
QE . . . . . Original jurisdiction
. . . . . . * For appellate jurisdiction, see SP9 H7Q.
R . . . . Superior courts
RQ . . . . . District & circuit courts
UF . . . . Courts of special jurisdiction
. . . . . * See subject - e.g. Customs court.
X . . . Federal & state courts compared
SP9 H . . Appeal
H7 . . . Courts
H7Q . . . . Supreme court appellate
. . . . Higher courts
H7R . . . . . Circuit courts of appeal, intermediate appellate courts
H7R T . . . . . District courts appellate

VB . Substantive law
SPW . . Criminal law
SPX . . Constitutional law
SPX Q . . . Ethnological law

S . . . States law
. . . . * Works on a specific state go under the state (SPX T).
S2 . . . . *Primary materials*
S3 . . . . *Secondary materials*
S7 . . . . . Courts
S7Q . . . . . . Supreme court
S7R Q . . . . . . District & circuit courts
S7S . . . . . . County courts
S7T . . . . Town courts, township courts, justice of the peace courts

[Common law systems SL]
[America SOV]
[North America SOW]
. . . . . [States law SPXS]
. . . . . . [Secondary materials SPXS3]
. . . . [County courts SPXS7S]
. . . . [Town courts SPXS7T]

SPX T . . . . . . *Individual states*
. . . . * Add to SPX T letters AK/Y following Y in Auxiliary Schedule 2. Use XY for Hawai.
. . . . * Each state may be divided as for USA in general.

SQB Caribbean & Central America
SQC E . British Honduras
F . Bermudas
H . British West Indies
K . . Federation of the West Indies
. . . * 1958-1962.
P . . Bahamas
SQD . . Jamaica
SQE . . Leeward Islands
. . . * Add to SQ letters F/O following ZH in Auxiliary Schedule 2.
SQF . . . British Virgin Islands
SQL . . . St.Kitts, St.Christophers, Nevis
SQM . . . Antigua & Barbuda
SQN . . . Montserrat
SQO . . . Dominica
SQR A . . Windward Islands
L . . . St.Lucia
N . . . St.Vincent
P . . . Barbados
T . . . Grenada
SQT . . . Trinidad & Tobago
SQU Guyana
. * Formerly British Guiana.

[National law SHY]
[Modern law SKG]
[Present-day legal systems SKV]
[Common law systems SL]
. [America SOV]
. . [Guyana SQU]

SR Civil law systems
. * Legal systems, mainly in Western Europe originally, in which principles and concepts from Roman law and the French codification of the 19th century have had great influence.

SSB . Roman-Dutch law
. . * System produced by fusion of medieval Dutch law (mainly of Germanic origin) and of the Roman law accepted in the Reception. Applied to Holland in the 16th/18th centuries and carried to various Dutch colonies in that period.
. . * See also jurisdictions of Netherlands (SVJ U); Ceylon (SVQ W); Surinam (SVZ N); Guiana (SVZ O); South Africa (SVV Q)
. . * For civil law systems in general, see SR.

SSB 2 . . *Primary materials*
2H . . . Codes
2HG . . . . Grotius (Roman-Dutch law)
2HL . . . . Van Leeuwen
2HN . . . . Voet
. . . . . *Individual texts*
2HN 9C . . . . . . Commentarius ad Pandectus
2HN 9E . . . . . . Institutes (Voet)
2HP . . . . Bynkershoeka, Bijnkershoek
2HV . . . . *Others*
. . . . . * Arrange A/Z.
3 . . *Secondary materials*
E . . . Contract law
W . . . Criminal law

SSD . Socialist law
. . * General term for the law of Soviet Russia (1917-c. 1991), of the people's republics of Eastern Europe and of similar regimes in other parts of the world. Based on Romano-Germanic principles modified by Marxist-Leninist ideology. The latter modifies significantly a number of concepts - e.g. contract, property, trade union, liberty.
. . * For law of specific socialist countries, see country, e.g. SVN (USSR).

ST . Favoured country
. . * Alternative for country in which library is located.

SU . Second favoured country or collection of countries
. . * For country, or collection of countries, having a particularly close connection juridically with the favoured jurisdiction.

[National law SHY]
[Modern law SKG]
[Present-day legal systems SKV]
[Civil law systems SR]
[Second favoured country or collection of countries SU]

SV Other countries
. * Add to SV letters F/Z in Auxiliary Schedule 2 so far as applicable (i.e. those not already given in SM/SU). A selection of jurisdictions is given to reflect a wide range of jurisdictional systems.
. * The classmark for an individual jurisdiction must allow direct qualification by A/Y as indicated in Auxiliary Schedule S4. In some cases, the notation in Auxiliary Schedule 2 must be adjusted in order to allow this. For example, using K for Germany as a whole would not allow such qualification, since some of the notational subclasses of K represent other distinct jurisdictions (e.g. KB East Germany, KS Czechoslovakia).
. * In such cases, another letter (usually 'A') should be added, so that direct qualification of A/Z from Auxiliary Schedule S4 does not conflict with the classmarks for other national jurisdictions; so Germany as a whole, for example, should be KA. The number of cases where such adjustment is necessary has increased a little with the fragmentation of nation states which has occurred since 1990. So the selection below includes a number of examples of such adjustment.
. * Note that it is only the occurrence of other nation states as notational 'subclasses' of a nation's classmark which calls for this adjustment. Local divisions of a country (states, cities, etc.) may be ignored, since these are introduced by -XT and -XV in Auxiliary Schedule S4. For example, the new state of Khazakstan will be SVN W; although it has notational sudivisions D/W (i.e. NWD/NWW in Auxiliary Schedule 2) all these are likely to be local divisions of the independent state and would be accommodated at SVN WXT (individual states or regions of Khazakstan).

SVF France
SVF 6 . Practice & procedure
7 . . Courts
7N . . . Historical courts
7NE . . . . Justices seigneuriales, Manorial courts
7NP . . . . Parlement de Paris, Sovereign court of Paris
7NR . . . . Tribunaux Revolutionaires

[Present-day legal systems SKV]
[Civil law systems SR]
[France SVF]
[Practice & procedure SVF6]
. [Courts SVF7]
. . [Historical courts SVF7N]
. . . [Tribunaux Revolutionaires SVF7NR]

	. . Supreme courts
	. . . * For Conseil d'Etat, see Administrative courts SVF XKF 7QR.
SVF 7Q	. . . Cour de Cassation
7Q6 B	. . . . Law officers
7Q6 TM	. . . . . Ministere Public a la Cour de Cassation
7Q6 TP	. . . . . Procureur-General a la Cour de Cassation
7QR	. . . . Chambre des Requetes
	. . . . . * Division of preliminary examination.
7QT	. . . . Chambres Civiles
	. . Higher courts
7R	. . . Tribunaux de Grande Instance
7R6 B	. . . . Law officers
7R6 TP	. . . . . Procureur de la Republique
7RT	. . . Tribunaux Civiles
	. . Lower courts
7S	. . . Tribunaux d'Instance
7ST	. . . . Tribunaux de paix, Cantonal courts
	. . . . . * Justice of the Peace courts.
7UF	. . Courts of special jurisdiction
	. . . * For jurisdiction in specific fields, see subject; e.g. Tribunaux de Commerce.
7UH	. . . Tribunaux des Conflits, Competence Conflict courts
	. . . . * See also Administrative law SVF XKF.
9H	. Appeal
	. . Supreme courts
9H7 Q	. . . Cour de Cassation (appeal)
	. . Higher courts
9H7 R	. . . Cours d'Appel
9VB	Substantive law
9W	. Private law
9X	. . Civil law
	. . . * For Labour law, See SVF NL.
9X2 H	. . . Codes
9X2 HHF	. . . . Code Napoleon (1804)
N	. . Commercial law
W	. Criminal law
W6	. . Practice & procedure
W7R	. . . Higher courts
W7R S	. . . . Courts of Assize
W7R U	. . . . Correctional courts
W7S	. . . Lower courts
W7S T	. . . . Tribunaux de Police
X	. Constitutional law
XI	. . Legislature
XIO K	. . . Conseil d'Etat

[National law SHY]
[Civil law systems SR]
[France SVF]
. [Substantive law SVF9VB]
. . [Constitutional law SVFX]
. . . [Legislature SVFXI]
. . . . [Conseil d'Etat SVFXIOK]

	. . . . . * Advises government on drafting of bills, etc.
SVF XKF	. . . Administrative law
XKF 7Q	. . . . Supreme court
XKF 7QR	. . . . . Conseil d'Etat (administrative courts)
SVG B	Spain
P	Portugal
SVI	Italy
SVJ P	Belgium
U	Netherlands
SVK A	Germany
A2	. *Primary materials*
A2N	. . Court decisions, cases
	. . . *By court*
A2U R	. . . . Regional courts
A2U RN	. . . . . Allied Occupation courts
A2U RP	. . . . . . Vereinigtes Wirtschaftsgebier
	. . . . * Bizonal courts.
A2U RQ	. . . . . . British zone courts
A2U RR	. . . . . . French zone courts
A2U RS	. . . . . . Russian zone courts
A2U RT	. . . . . . American zone courts
A47	. History of German civil law
A47 RNU	. . 1945/1990
	. . . * For the legal system of Eastern Germany during this period, see German Democratic Republic SVK Q.
A6	. Practice & procedure
	. . Courts
A7	. . . Gerichtsverfassung
	. . . . * For criminal courts, see SVK AW7; for States courts, see SVK AXS 7.
A7N X	. . . . Ordentliche Gerichte, Regular courts
A7Q	. . . . . Supreme courts
A7Q R	. . . . . . Reichsoberhandelsgericht (1869-79)
A7Q S	. . . . . . Reichsgericht, Imperial Court (1879-1945)
A7Q T	. . . . . . Bundesgerichtshof, Federal Court
A7Q U	. . . . . . Gemeinsamer Senat der Obersten Gerichtshofe des Bundes

[Civil law systems SR]
[Germany SVKA]
[Practice & procedure SVKA6]
. . [Gerichtsverfassung SVKA7]
. . . [Ordentliche Gerichte SVKA7NX]
. . . . [Supreme courts SVKA7Q]
. . . . . [Gemeinsamer Senat der Obersten Gerichtshofe des Bundes SVKA7QU]

. . . . . . * Joint senate of the federal supreme courts.

SVK A7S . . . . Lower courts
. . . . . * For Amtsgerichte see SVK AXS 7T.
A7U F . . . Courts of special juridiction
. . . . * Courts concerned with special branches of law go under the subject; e.g. Federal Labour Court (Bundesarbeitsgericht) SVK AOL 7P.
A7U H . . . . Military government courts (Germany 1945-55)
. . . . . * Including other temporary courts under the Allied occupation.
A7U H5A . . . . . Jurisprudence
A7U H5A MG . . . . . . Self-government principle, Gerichtliche
A7U I . . . . . Individual courts, A/Z
A7U K . . . . Competence conflict courts
A7U M . . . . Courts of honour, Ehrengerichtsbarkeit

A9V B Substantive law
A9X . Civil law
AN . Commercial law
AW . Criminal law
AW6 . . Practice & procedure
. . . Supreme courts
AW7 Q . . . . Bundesgerichshof (criminal)
AW7 R . . . Higher courts
AW7 RS . . . . Schoffengerichte (court of assizes)
AW7 RT . . . . Schwurgerichte (with jury)
AW7 S . . . Lower courts
AW7 T . . . . Amtsgerichte

AX . Constitutional law
AX5 C . . Sources
AX5 L . . . Constitutions
AX5 LY . . . . *Individual constitutions. by date*
. . . . . * For example, Weimar constitution (1919), Constitution of the Federal Republic (1949)
AX6 . . Practice & procedure
. . . Supreme courts
AX7 Q . . . . Bundesverfassungsgericht
. . Substantive law

[National law SHY]
[Present-day legal systems SKV]
[Civil law systems SR]
[Germany SVKA]
. [Substantive law SVKA9VB]
. . [Constitutional law SVKAX]
. . . [Substantive law]

SVK AXK F . . . . Administrative law
AXK F7Q . . . . . Supreme courts
AXK F7Q P . . . . . . Bundesverwaltungsgericht
. . . . * Federal administrative court.
AXR . . . Regional law
. . . . * See States law SVK AXS
AXS . . . States law
AXS 6 . . . . Practice & procedure
. . . . . Supreme courts
AXS 7Q . . . . . . Oberlandesgerichte
AXS 7R . . . . . Higher courts
AXS 7RS . . . . . . Landgerichte (regional courts)
. . . . * State district courts with general and first instance jurisdiction.
. . . . * For appellate jurisdiction, see SVK AXS 9H.
AXS 7RT . . . . Kammer fur Handelssachen
AXS 7S . . . . . Lower courts
AXS 7T . . . . . . Amtsgerichte
AXT . . . . *Individual states*
. . . . . * As Auxiliary Schedule 2.
B East Germany (GDR)
. * For German Democratic Republic (1945/1990) see SVK Q
H West Germany (1945/1990)
. * Use SVK A.
Q German Democratic Republic (1945/1990)
S Czechoslovakia
TA Czech Republic
. * For Bohemia, use SKT B.
VA Slovak Republic
. * For Slovakia, use SKV B.
SVL F Yugoslavia
G Slovenia
H Croatia
K Bosnia
N Serbia
Y Poland
SVM Scandinavia
SVN A Russia (to 1917)
B USSR
C Russia (1991-)
W Khazakstan

[National law SHY]
[Modern law SKG]
[Present-day legal systems SKV]
[Civil law systems SR]
[Khazakstan SVNW]

SVO H	Turkey
O	Syria
P	Israel
S	Saudi Arabia
V	Iraq
SVP A	Iran
SVQ A	Pakistan
E	India
W	Sri Lanka, Ceylon
SVR B	China
SVS	Japan
SVT K	Indonesia
SVV A	Egypt
AS	Sudan
D	Algeria
GT	Ghana
H	Nigeria
Q	South Africa
RR	Zimbabwe
SVZ B	Mexico
L	Venezuela
N	Surinam
O	Guiana
P	Brazil
T	Argentina
U	Chile

Jurisdictions by religious authority

SWE . Ecclesiastical law, religious law, religious legal systems

* All the law relating to a church or other religious institution, whether derived from state law, divine law, natural law or the rules of any given society.
* The literature is concerned almost entirely with the ecclesiastical law relating to particular religions; this class is for completely general works only.
* For ecclesiastical law as part of the constitutional law of a national jurisdiction (especially when it features an established church) see SCY B.

SWE 2 . . *Primary materials*

* This concept applies only to particular religions.
* Each religion or sect may be qualified by 22/28 in Auxiliary Schedule S2; e.g. Collections of Jewish law primary materials SWW 27.
* Under each religious jurisdiction, the divisions 2A/2X in Auxiliary Schedule S2 are replaced by a substantiallly modified version of them, or by a completely new set.
* Each of these divisions 2A/2X may be qualified by 2/8 following 2 in Auxiliary Schedule S2; e.g. Index to the Talmud SWW 2L44.
* Where the divisions 2A/2X represent a completely new set, each of these may be qualified as follows (where the hyphen represents the classmark to be qualified):
* Add to -9 letters A/X following 2 in Auxiliary Schedule S2.

3 . . *Secondary materials. works about ecclesiastical law*

. . . History

47 . . . . *By period*

48 . . . . *By place*

* For religious law of a particular religion in a particular place, see the Place facet under that religion; e.g. Roman Catholic law by country, SXJ 48.
* This general location (SWE 48) takes only studies of a given country in which a variety of religious legal systems operates.
* An alternative (not recommended) is provided at W/X at the end of each religion for libraries wishing to cite the country first (within the religion); e.g. SXJ XGB Roman Catholic church in Spain.
* A further alternative (not recommended) is to locate the ecclesiastical law of a country under the constitutional law of that country, using -YB in Auxiliary Schedule S1.

[Jurisdictions by religious authority]
[Ecclesiastical law SWE]
[Secondary materials SWE3]
[History]
. [By place SWE48]

SWE 5A Jurisprudence

5C . Sources

5F . . Sacred works

6 Practice & procedure

7 . Ecclesiastical courts (general)

9U *Ecclesiology of particular subjects*

* Use this position only to qualify classes which precede SWE F (Ecclesiology).
* Add to SWE 9U letters F/N following SWE; e.g. Fasting - Dispensation SWE ECJ 9UI N.

9VB *Subjects of law*

* Add to SWE A letters A/Y in Auxiliary Schedule S1.

ACK . Marriage

AH . Property

AW . Criminal law

AX . Constitutional law

Subjects special to ecclesiastical law

* Taken from class PB/PF Religion, with some additions & modifications for some religious systems. Note that the letter A is used above (under SWE 9VB) as an intercalator to introduce substantive law concepts in general, not the classes at PA (which have no applicability to law).
* Add to SWE letters B/E following P in PB/PE.

B . Systematic theology

* Including worship, devotions, rites, etc.

BO . . Doctrines

C . . Moral theology, ethics

D . Practice of religion

* Including worship, devotions, rites, etc.

EC . . Holy days

ECJ . . . Fasting

FB . Ecclesiology

* Class PF has been amended here in order to accommodate all the institutional features relevant to ecclesiastical law.
* Nearly all the literature relates to particular religions and only the barest outline is given here, to show the general structure. Further details may be taken from SWX Christian religion (and particularly from SXJ Roman Catholic Church).

FC . . Powers of the church (general)

FH . . Church property & artefacts

FR . . Persons in a religion

FV . . . *Attributes*

* Holy relics, etc.

FW . . . Founder of a religion

FX . . . Saints, Martyrs

Ecclesiastical law

[Jurisdictions by religious authority]
[Ecclesiastical law SWE]
[Secondary materials SWE3]
[Subjects special to ecclesiastical law]
. [Ecclesiology SWEFB]
. . [Persons in a religion SWEFR]
. . . [Saints SWEFX]

SWE G . . . Priesthood & ecclesiastical offices, ministry, clergy
I . . Discipline
IN . . . Dispensation
M . . Church organization & government, church constitution
MN . . . Unity (church government)
MO . . Ecumenical movement, oecumenical movement
NF . . . Finances (church government)
PE . . External relations
PF . . . Church & state
PG . . . . Establishment, state churches, national churches, state religions
PH . . . . . Disestablishment
PI . . . . State legislation relating to church
. . . . . * See also Sources SWE 5C
PJ . . . Relations with other states
PU . . . Relations with other churches

Subsystems of the religion
R . Religious orders, monastic orders
V . Sects within a religion

W *By country*
* Alternative (not recommended) for libraries wishing to cite country first (instead of using -4 within the religion). If this option is taken, proceed as follows: If this option is taken, proceed as follows:
* Add to SWE X letters E/Z in Auxiliary Schedule 2.

SWF *Particular religious legal systems*
* The preferred arrangement in BC2 is to locate the law of a religion with that religion in class P. This class is an alternative (not recommended) for libraries wishing to keep all legal systems together under law.
* Usually, the detailed vocabulary of a class which is provided with an alternative is given under the preferred location. Because class P was published before a detailed Law schedule had been developed, the detailed vocabulary is

[Jurisdictions by religious authority]
[Ecclesiastical law SWE]
[Secondary materials SWE3]
[Particular religious legal systems SWF]

given here, although it is not the preferred location for the class.
* A further alternative (not recommended) is to subordinate the ecclesiastical law of an established religion (one which is recognized as the official religion of the state) to the state jurisdiction concerned. In such a case, the ecclesiastical law is collocated with the constitutional law of that state, at -YB following the country's classmark (see Auxiliary Schedule S1).
* This location (SWF) may be used for works dealing with the concept of religious legal systems per se.
* For all religions other than Islam (see SYB 9VB) each religion, and any sect within it, may be divided fully as follows:
* Add to - (where the hyphen represents the classmark of the religion or its sect) numbers and letters 2/9,A/W following SWE, amplified where necessary by the detail shown under SXJ (Roman Catholic church).

SWG *By various characteristics*
. * Add to SW letters G/H following P in PG/PH.
SWG F . Pre-literate society religions, primitive religions (legal systems)
J . Ancient religions (legal systems)

. Extant religious legal systems

SWH B . . Oriental religions (legal systems), Eastern religions (legal systems)
. . . * For Semitic (Mosaic) religions, see SWU.
. . . * Add to SWH letters B/Y following PH. A selection of the major ones is given below.
. . . * From SWI onwards the order (but not the notation) is the same as that of the religions in PH/PV.
R . . . Tao law
T . . . Confucian law
W . . . Shinto law

SWI . . . Hindu law, Indian law in general
SWI 2 . . . . *Primary materials*
27 . . . . . Collections general
2D . . . . . Vedas
2E . . . . . . Vedangas, Smritri
2F . . . . Manu code
2G . . . . Yajnavalkya code
2H . . . . Navada code
2J . . . . Others, by author A/Z
2M . . . . . Commentaries & digests

[Ecclesiastical law SWE]
[By various characteristics SWG]
[Extant religious legal systems]
[Oriental religions legal systems SWHB]
[Hindu law SWI]
[Primary materials SWI2]
. [Commentaries & digests SWI2M]

	. . * By author, A/Z.
SWI 3	*Secondary materials*
48	. *By country*
5A	. Jurisprudence
5C	. . Sources
5CH	. . . Codification
5D	. . . Customary law
6	. Practice & procedure
9VB	. Subjects of law
AAP	. . Persons
AAW N	. . . Caste (Hindu law)
ACF	. . . Family law
ACG	. . . . Children
ACH D	. . . . Adoption
ACJ Q	. . . . Support in domestic relations, extended family
ACJ X	. . . . Sexual union
ACK	. . . . . Marriage & divorce
AE	. . Contract
AEF G	. . . Third parties
AFF	. . . Benami transactions, Namartham
	. . . . * See also Trusts & trustees SWI AHU; Fraudulent conveyance SWI AJH
AH	. . Property
AHU	. . . Trust & trustees
AHX Q	. . . . Charities & religious endowments
AI	. . . Succession & inheritance
AJ	. . . Real property
AJH S	. . . . Conveyance
AJH SEY R	. . . . . Fraudulent conveyance
AL	. . . Personal property
AXK F	. . Administrative law
AXL MJ	. . . Taxation
	. . Special to Hinduism
B	. . . Dhama (Hindu law), dharmasastra (Hindu law)
H	. *Other subjects of Hindu law*
	. . * Add to SWI letters H/V following PI so far as applicable.
T	*Schools & sects in Hinduism*
	. * Arrange A/Z.
TD	. Dayabhaga (Bengal Hindu law)
TM	. Mitakshara (Hindu law)

[Ecclesiastical law SWE]
[By various characteristics SWG]
[Extant religious legal systems]
[Oriental religions legal systems SWHB]
. [Hindu law SWI]
. . [Schools & sects in Hinduism SWIT]
. . . [Mitakshara Hindu law SWITM]

SWI V	. Jain law
W	. Sikh law
SWJ	. Buddhist law
SWJ U	. . Burmese Buddhist law
V	. . Tibetan Buddhist law, Lamaism (Buddhist law)
Y	. Parsee law
SWU	Semitic & Western religions (law)
	. * For Mosaic law narrowly, see Torah SWW 2E.
	. Sources
SWU 5C	. . Bible & law
	. . . * For Biblical law, see Jewish law SWW; for Canon law, see Christian law SWX.
SWW	. Jewish law, Hebrew law, Halakha, Biblical law, Judaism (law)
SWW 2	. . *Primary materials*
27	. . . Collections
2D	. . . Commandments, six hundred & thirteen commandments, mizwahs
2E	. . . Torah, Mosaic law
2F	. . . . Pentateuch
2G	. . . . Prophetic books (Mosaic law)
2H	. . . . Hagiographa, Midrash
2J	. . . . Other early texts
2L	. . . Talmud
2L2 7K	. . . . Commentaries
	. . . . . * General only; for specific historical commentaries, see SWW 2N.
2L2 N	. . . . Cases, opinions
2L2 NC	. . . . . Responsa, jus respondendi
	. . . . . . * For individual books, add letters for date to SWW 2L9 NC.
2ND	. . . . Mishna
	. . . . . * c.200 AD
2NG	. . . . Gemara
2NJ	. . . . . Palestinian Gemara, Jerusalem Talmud
2NL	. . . . . Babylonian Gemara
2NN	. . . . . Apocryphal books
2NP	. . . . Mishna Torah
	. . . . . * Of Maimonides, 12th century AD.
2NR	. . . . Tur
	. . . . . * Of Jacob ben Asher, 14th century.
2NS	. . . . Shulhan Aruk
	. . . . . * Of Josef Qaro, 16th century.
2NV	. . . . Midrash
2NX	. . . . Other books
	. . . . . * Arrange by date.

[Ecclesiastical law SWE]
[Extant religious legal systems]
[Semitic & Western religions law SWU]
[Jewish law SWW]
. [Primary materials SWW2]
. . [Talmud SWW2L]
. . . [Other books SWW2NX]

SWW 3 . *Secondary materials*
5A . . Jurisprudence
5CD . . Interpretations & constructions
6 . . Practice & procedure
7 . . . Rabbinical courts
A . . *Subjects of law*
AE . . . Contract
AG . . . Tort
AW . . . Criminal law
. . *Subjects special to Jewish law*
D . . . Devotional
ECF . . . . Sabbath (Jewish law)
ECF R . . . . . Eruv, Erub
. . . Clergy & offices
H . . . . Rabbis
. . . . . Ordination
IU . . . . . . Semikha

SWX Christian law, canon law, church law, public law
* Body of law constituted by ecclesiastical authority for the organization and government of the Christian church.
* Canon law applies preeminently to Roman Catholic law. The Reformation resulted in the removal of the Church in many countries from the jurisdiction of the canon law of the Catholic Church of Rome. But the canon law prior to this remains historically as part of the source of ecclesiastical law in these other churches also.
* These pre-Reformation sources are enumerated under the Roman Catholic Church, but are available for use under the other churches where applicable.
* Analogously, the detailed vocabulary for the legal topics (Practice & procedure, etc.) is given under the Roman Catholic Church but is available for use under Canon law in general as well as under other churches where applicable.

SWX 2 . *Primary materials*

3 . *Secondary materials*
. . * Nearly all the legal literature relates to particular branches of the church (see notes above under SWX).
. . * To avoid an unhelpful fragmentation of the vocabulary and the duplication of parts of it the arrangement adopted here is to give a full schedule (itself a modified extraction from Class P Religion) under one branch (the Roman Catholic church) at SXJ. The detail there is available for the qualification of the Christian church as a whole (here, at SWX) and to all its other branches. The only divisions enumerated here, or under these other branches, are those peculiar to them, or more appropriate to them (e.g. Ecumenical movement under Christian church in general), or those needed to make the hierarchy clear.
* Add to SWX numbers & letters 3/X following SXJ (Roman Catholic church) so far as applicable.

[Secondary materials SWE3]
[Particular religious legal systems SWF]
[By various characteristics SWG]
[Extant religious legal systems]
[Semitic & Western religions law SWU]
[Christian law SWX]
[Secondary materials SWX3]

SWX 48 *By country*
. * For general works on the Christian law of a country, regardless of particular branches or sects. For law of a particular sect in a given country, see the sect.

A *Substantive law in canon law*

Subjects special to canon law
BO . Doctrines
D . Religious practice, devotional practice
. Ecclesiology
FB . . Church property
FH . . Clergy & ecclesiastical offices
G
M . Church government & organization
. . Unity, cooperation within the church
MO . . . Ecumenical movement

[Semitic & Western religions law SWU]
[Christian law SWX]
[Secondary materials SWX3]
[Subjects special to canon law]
. [Church government & organization SWXM]
. . [Unity]
. . . [Ecumenical movement SWXMO]

SWX MP . . . Simultaneum, simultaneous churches
. . . . * In Europe, use of churches, etc. for exercise
. . . . of religion by different creeds.
MQ . . . . Intercommunion
MR . . . . Communicatio in sacris
MS . . . Ecumenical council & synod (Christian
. . . church)
MT . . . . *Particular councils, etc., by date*
MTL K . . . . . Vatican Council 1869-70
NF . . Finances of the church

. *Parts of church organization*
. . * See also Offices & persons SWX G
NS . . Synods & councils
. . *By area of jurisdiction*
O . . . Dioceses, bishoprics, sees
O48 . . . . *By local place*
. *Activities of the church*
PE . . External relations of the church
PF . . . Church & state (Christian church)
PG . . . . Establishment, national churches,
. . . . state churches
PU . . Relations with other churches

. *Subsystems within the system*
R . . Monasticism & religious orders
V . . Sects
SXA Christian churches & sects
SXB . Patriarchates
SXC . . Eastern churches, Oriental churches,
. . Eastern canon law
SXC 2 . . . *Primary materials*
. . . . Collections
27 . . . . . Nomocanones
3 . . . *Secondary materials*
R . . . . Monastic & religious orders

SXD . . . Orthodox church, Eastern Orthodox
. . . church
SXD D . . . . Religious practice
. . . . . Rites
ER . . . . . . Oriental rites, Greek rites
R . . . . Monastic & religious orders
. . . . *By church*
Y . . . . . Slavonic churches
SXE . . . . . . Russian Orthodox church
SXF . . . . . Greek Orthodox church
SXG . . . . . . Others, [

[Christian law SWX]
[Patriarchates SXB]
[Eastern churches SXC]
. [Orthodox church SXD]
. . [By church]
. . . [Greek Orthodox church SXF]
. . . . [Others SXG]

SXH B . Separated Eastern churches
E . . Nestorian church
G . . Monophysite churches

K . Uniate churches, Eastern Catholic church
N . . Nestorian Uniate church
P . . Monophysite Uniate church
SXI Western churches (general)

SXJ . Roman Catholic church, Catholic church
SXJ 2 . . *Primary materials*
27 . . . Collections
29Y . . . Pre-Corpus juris canonici texts
2A . . . Corpus juris canonici
2AG . . . . Gratian's Decree, Decretum Gratiani
2AJ . . . . Decretals of Gregoru IX
2AL . . . . Liber sextus of Boniface VIII
2AN . . . . Constitutions of Clement V
2AP . . . . Extravagantes of John XXII
2AR . . . . Extravagantes communes
2B . . . Later corpus juris canonici, pre-Codex
. . . juris canonici texts
2C . . . Codex juris canonici
2CG . . . . Book I (general canons)
2CJ . . . . Book II (Persons)
2CM . . . . Book III (Things)
2CP . . . . Book IV (Procedure)
2CR . . . . Book V (Crimes & penalties)
2D . . . Papal documents
2E . . . . Acta apostolicae sedis
2F . . . . Papal letters, decretals (papal
. . . . documents)
2G . . . . Papal bulls, bullaria
2GN . . . . . In Coena Domini bulls
2GR . . . . . Crusade bulls
2H . . . . Papal constitutions, apostolic
. . . . constitutions
2J . . . . Papal briefs, breves (papal briefs)
2K . . . . Papal rescripts
2L . . . . Encyclical letters
2M . . . . Papal decrees
2N . . . Papal index
. . . Reports of cases
2R . . . . General collections
2S . . . . Papal court cases
2T . . . . Other courts

[Christian law SWX]
[Patriarchates SXB]
[Western churches general SXI]
[Roman Catholic church SXJ]
[Primary materials SXJ2]
. [Reports of cases]
. . [Other courts SXJ2T]

SXJ 2V	. . *By country*
3	*Secondary materials*
3N	. Language
3NK	. . Particular words
5A	. Jurisprudence
5C	. . Sources
5CD	. . . Analysis & interpretation of canon law
6	. Practice & procedure
	. . Analysis & interpretation
65C D	. . . Epikeia
6E	. . Courts & procedure
6H	. . . Jurisdiction of courts
6KB	. . . Law officers, etc.
6TC	. . . . Promoters of justice
6TD	. . . . Defenders of the marriage bond
6TF	. . . . Advocatus diaboli
7	. . . Ecclesiastical courts, church courts, court Christian, ecclesiastical tribunals
7Q	. . . . Papal courts
7UF	. . . . Other courts [
8	. . . Actions
	. . . . Prosecution counsel
8CB K	. . . . . Public prosecutors (RC church)
8N	. . . . Pleas
9F	. . . Judgements
	. . . . Judicial opinions
9FP	. . . . . Responsa
9G	. . . Remedies
9H	. . . . Appeals
9IT	. . . . . Appeal as from an abuse
9PX	. . . . Penalties
9PY K	. . . . . Punishment
9PY L	. . . . . Ecclesiastical censure
9PY M	. . . . . Deprivation
9PY N	. . . . . Interdict
9PY P	. . . . . Excommunication, anathema
9PY Q	. . . . . Canonical precept, praeceptium extra judicium, papal precept
9PY R	. . . . . Denunciation, denuntiate judicatis, evangelical denunciation

[Christian law SWX]
[Secondary materials SXJ3]
[Practice & procedure SXJ6]
. [Courts & procedure SXJ6E]
. . [Remedies SXJ9G]
. . . [Penalties SXJ9PX]
. . . . [Denunciation SXJ9PYR]

SXJ 9PY S	. . . . Prohibiton of books
9PY T	. . . . . Index librorum prohibitorum, Index expurgatorium
9VB	*Subjects of law*
AA	. Conflict of laws
AAP	. Persons
ABC A	. . Dissenters, non-conformists
ACF	. . Family law
ACK	. . . Marriage & divorce
ACL M	. . . . Impediments to marriage
ACL P	. . . . . Diriment impediments
ACL PS	. . . . . Consanguinity
AE	. Contract law
AEQ	. . Conditions
AEQ X	. . . Impediments
AH	. Property
	. . Real property
AJR W	. . . Mortmain (church lands)
AJR X	. . . Public land (church lands)
AW	. Criminal law
AW8 SD	. . Pleas
AW8 SDM	. . . Benefit of clergy, privilegium fori, privilege of clergy
	. . Offences
AWU I	. . . Blasphemy
AWU IR	. . . Desecration of churches
AWU IS	. . . Sacrilege
AWU J	. . . Simony
AWU K	. . . Apostacy
AX	. Constitutional law
AXC T	. . Rights & duties of persons
AXC UW	. . . Ecclesiastical privileges & immunities
AXD DG	. . . Religious liberty
AXD DX	. . . Rights of assylum, sanctuary
AXK	. . Public administration law
	. . . Taxation
AXL MJ	. . . . Church tax
	Subjects special to canon law
B	. Systematic theology
BO	. . Doctrines
	. . . *Special doctrines*
BVT	. . . . Infallibility
C	. . Moral theology

Christian law

[Christian law SWX]
[Western churches general SXI]
[Roman Catholic church SXJ]
[Secondary materials SXJ3]
[Subjects special to canon law]
[Systematic theology SXJB]
. [Moral theology SXJC]

SXJ CNK	. . Conscience
CNK P	. . . Manifestation of conscience, ratio conscientiae
CNK Q	. . . Casuistry, cases of conscience
D	Religious practice, devotional religion
DEV	. Sacred places
DEY	. . Cemeteries, graves, burial grounds
DS	. Religious art & literature
DT	. . Church music
DXG	. . Prayer books
DXH	. . Creeds, Articles
DXJ	. . Catechism, Catachetics
EC	. Holy days
ECF	. . Sabbath
	. . . Legislation
ECF 5M	. . . . Sunday legislation
ECJ	. . Fasts, fasting
ECJ 9UI N	. . . Dispensation
EDY	. Formal devotional activities
EQU	. . Dedication
ER	. . Ritual & liturgy, rites of the church
ERN	. . . Annointing, unction
ERQ	. . . Sacraments (general)
ERR	. . . Baptism
ERS	. . . Confirmation
ERT	. . . Eucharist, holy communion, lord's supper, last supper, sacrament of the altar
ERU	. . . Repentance, penance
ERU K	. . . . Confession
ERU L	. . . . . Penitentials, penitential books
ERU M	. . . . . Seal of confession
ERU N	. . . . Absolution, reserved cases
ERU P	. . . . Indulgences, jubilee indulgences
ERV	. . . Extreme unction
ESD	. . . Divine service
ESP	. . . Preaching
EWY	. . Submissions
EXL	. . . Holy orders, ordination
EXM	. . . . Vows
EXN	. . . . . Profession of faith
EXO	. . . Obedience
EXT	. . . Renunciation

[Christian law SWX]
[Secondary materials SXJ3]
[Subjects special to canon law]
[Religious practice SXJD]
. [Formal devotional activities SXJEDY]
. . [Submissions SXJEWY]
. . . [Renunciation SXJEXT]

SXJ FB	Ecclesiology
FC	. Powers of the church (general)
FH	. Church property & artefacts
FJ	. . Church lands, glebes
FJN V	. . . Boundaries of church property
	. . . *Processes special to church property*
FJO C	. . . . Maintenance & repair (church property), fabrica ecclesiae
FJO D	. . . . . Dilapidations
FJO F	. . . . . Faculties, canonical faculties
FJO K	. . . . Land grants
FJO M	. . . . Taxation (church property)
	. . . *Types of real property*
FJX	. . . *Types special to church property*
FK	. . . Planning & development law
FKN C	. . . . Change of use
FKN D	. . . . . Secularization of church property
FL	. . Personal property
FLI Y	. . . Chattels personal, tangible goods
FLJ	. . . Intellectual & industrial property
FP	. . . Tangible property
FQF	. . . . Church furniture
FQH	. . . . . Pews & pew rights
FQP	. . . . Altars
FQR	. . . . Relics & reliquaries
FQT	. . . . Bishop's ring, pastoral ring
FQU	. . . . . Pontifical ring
FQW	. . . . Other
FR	. Persons in the religion
G	. . Clergy & ecclesiastical offices, ministry
GH	. . . Ecclesiastical corporations, religious corporations
GP	. . . . Patronage
GQ	. . . . . Benefices, expectative graces, livings
GR	. . . . . . Annates, first fruits
GS	. . . . . . Jus primarium precursium
H	. . . Clergy, priests
	. . . . Buildings
HFJ	. . . . . Residences (clergy)
HGP	. . . . Patronage
HH	. . . . Appointment
HP	. . . . . Confirmation of appointment
HQ	. . . . . . Investiture
HR	. . . . . Deposition (appointment of clergy)
HS	. . . . Remuneration
HT	. . . . Pensions

Christian law

[Christian law SWX]
[Subjects special to canon law]
[Ecclesiology SXJFB]
[Persons in the religion SXJFR]
[Clergy & ecclesiastical offices SXJG]
[Clergy SXJH]
. [Pensions SXJHT]

SXJ HU . Tenure
I . Discipline of clergy
IL . . Indulgencies
IN . . Dispensation
IP . . Profession of faith
IT . Education & training
IU . Ordination
IV . . Vows
JB . Excardination
JC . Incardination
JD . Irregularities
. *Special properties & processes*
JG . . Privileges & immunities (clergy)
JJ . . Powers (clergy)
JK . . . Delegation of powers of clergy
JL . . . Primacy (powers of clergy), supremacy (powers of clergy)
JM . . . Temporal powers (clergy)
JP . . Confidential communications (clergy)
JQ . . Apostolic succession
JR . . Celibacy

Types of clergy/office
. *By special characteristics*
JW . . Women in the church
JX . . Other non-ecclesiastical types
K . Pope, Holy See
KBO . . Doctrines
KBV T . . . Infallibility of the Pope
. . Practice
KEX T . . . Renunciation
KHH . . Appoinment
KHJ . . . Election of Pope, papal conclaves
KHK . . . . Right of exclusion (papal elections), exclusiva, jus exclusivae
KHL . . . . Veto (papal elections)
KHM . . . Vacancy of the Holy See
KIR . . Powers
KP . Apostolic administrators
KQ . Vicars apostolic, prefects apostolic
KR . Cardinals
KS . Archbishops, metropolitans
KT . Bishops, dioceses
KV . Vicars capitular

[Christian law SWX]
[Subjects special to canon law]
[Ecclesiology SXJFB]
[Persons in the religion SXJFR]
. [Clergy & ecclesiastical offices SXJG]
. . [Types of clergy/office]
. . . [Vicars capitular SXJKV]

SXJ KW . . . Vicar-General, general vicars
LC . . . Diocesan chancellors
LE . . . Notaries
LG . . . Rural bishops, chorepiscopoi
LJ . . . Chapters, cathedral chapters, collegiate chapters
LM . . . . Deans
LP . . . . Canons
LQ . . . . . Minor canons, choral vicars, priest vicars
LR . . . Ministers, presbyters, priests, pastors, parochial vicars, parish priests
LT . . . Deacons

M Church organization & government, public law
NF . Finances of church
NG . . Revenue
NHE . . . Ecclesiastical fees
NHM . . . Mass stipends
NI . . . Endowments (church finance)
NJ . . . Taxation by church
NK . . . . Tithes
NL . . . Other sources
NN . . . Expenditure

. *Parts of church organization*
NS . . Synods & councils
NT . . . Plenary councils & synods, church assemblies
NV . . . Church councils, church conferences
. . *By area of jurisdiction*
NW . . . Provinces (church government), archbishoprics
NWN S . . . . Provincial councils & synods
O . . . Dioceses, bishoprics, sees
ON . . . . Diocesan councils & synods
ONN . . . . . Diocesan consultors
OR . . . Parishes (church government)
OT . . Congregations
OV . . . Church attendance
OX . . Church societies

[Christian law SWX]
[Secondary materials SXJ3]
[Subjects special to canon law]
[Ecclesiology SXJFB]
. [Church organization & government SXJM]
. . [Parts of church organization]
. . . [Church societies SXJOX]

	. *Activities of the RC church*
SXJ PC	. . Legitimate ecclesiastical acts, legal ecclesiastical acts, actus legitimi ecclesiastici, authorized ecclesiastical acts
PE	. . External relations of church
PF	. . . Church & state
	. . . *Relations with other states*
PJ	. . . . Foreign relations, diplomatic relations
PK	. . . . . Concordats
PL	. . . . . . Concordat of Worms 1122
PM	. . . . . . Concordat of Vienna 1448
PN	. . . . . . Other, by date [
PO	. . . . . Treaties
PP	. . . . . . *By country*
PQ	. . . . . Diplomatic services
PR	. . . . . . Papal nuncio
PS	. . . . . . Papal legatees
PU	. . . Relations with other churches
PV	. . . Relations with community & society
PX	. . . . Pastoral work (RC church)
Q	. . . . . Educational work (RC church)
QR	. . . . . . Teaching office of the RC church
QT	. . . . . . Theological seminaries
QV	. . . . . . Denominational schools (RC church), diocesan schools (RC church), parochial schools (RC church)
QX	. . . . Missions (RC church)
	Subsystems of the RC church
R	. Monasticism & religious orders, monastic orders
RFH	. . Church property & artefacts
RFJ XJ	. . . Cloisters, enclosures (RC church)
RG	. . Clergy & offices
RLQ	. . . Abbots
RLR	. . . . Abbots nullius
RLS	. . . . Postulancy, postulants
RLT	. . . . . Novitiate, novices

[Christian law SWX]
[Christian churches & sects SXA]
[Patriarchates SXB]
. . . . . [Subsystems of the RC church]
. . . . . . [Monasticism & religious orders SXJR]
. . . . [Clergy & offices SXJRG]
. . . . [Novitiate SXJRLT]

SXJ RLU	. . . . Master of novices
RM	. . . . Organization
RNF	. . . . Finances
RNI	. . . . Dowry (monastic orders)
RS	. . . . Ancient church orders
RT	. . . . Monasticism for women, religious orders for women
RV	. . . . Confraternities
RW	. . . . Secular institutions (RC church)
SH	. . . . Heresies
T	. . . . Non-conformity
TV	. . . . Penal laws against non-conformists
W	. . . . RC Church in specific countries
SXK	Protestant churches
SXL	. Anglican church
SXL R	. . Monasticism & religious orders
SXM	. . Church of England, Episcopal church (C. of E.)
SXM 2	. . . *Primary materials*
27	. . . . Collections
2F	. . . . Legislation of the Church of England
2GE	. . . . . Pre-1603, by date
2GF	. . . . . Canons of 1603
2GG	. . . . . Canons of 1640
2GG T	. . . . . Later amendments, by date
2J	. . . . General Synod measures, General Asssembly measures
2J5 5	. . . . . Revised editions, by date
2J7 58	. . . . . Annual volumes
2JK	. . . . . Individual measures, by date
2K	. . . . Parliamentary legislation affecting the church
2K7 5	. . . . . Collections, by date
2KL	. . . . . Individual Acts, by date
2N	. . . . Reports of cases
2N7 5	. . . . . Series, by title A/Z
2N8 R	. . . . . Individual reporters, A/Z
2N9	. . . . . Individual cases, by date
3	. . . *Secondary materials, works about*
5C	. . . . Sources
5XL	. . . . . Common law & canon law
5XX J	. . . . . Roman Catholic law in Church of England
6	. . . . Practice & procedure

[Christian law SWX]
[Christian churches & sects SXA]
[Protestant churches SXK]
[Anglican church SXL]
. [Church of England SXM]
. . [Secondary materials SXM3]
. . . [Practice & procedure SXM6]

SXM 7 . . . . Courts
7P . . . . . Provincial courts (Church of England)
7Q . . . . . . Court of Arches
7R . . . . . . Court of Faculties
7S . . . . . . Chancery court of York
7V . . . . . Diocesan courts, consistory courts
7X . . . . . Court of Ecclesiastical Causes Reserved
F . . . Ecclesiology
MC . . . . Government
MCN . . . . . Oath of allegiance
MCP . . . . . Conventicle acts
MCR . . . . . Royal supremacy (Church of England)
MCS . . . . . . Acts of supremacy (Church of England)
PE . . . . . External relations
PF . . . . . . Church & state

Y . . . *Church of England in specific countries*
SXN C . . . . Church of England in Wales
E . . . . Episcopalian Church in Scotland, Anglican Church in Scotland
G . . . . Church of England in Ireland, Church of Ireland, Episcopalian Church in Ireland
I . . . . Anglican Church in India
N . . . . Anglican Church in Canada
P . . . . Protestant Episcopal Church in USA, Episcopal Church in USA
R . . . . *Church of England in other countries*

SXO Non-conformist churches, free churches
SXP . Lutheran church
SXQ . Presbyterian church
SXQ BO . . Doctrines
. . . Special doctrines
BVT . . . . Confession of faith
SXR . . Presbyterian Church of England

[Ecclesiastical law SWE]
[Semitic & Western religions law SWU]
[Christian law SWX]
. . . [Protestant churches SXK]
. . . . [Non-conformist churches SXO]
. . . . . [Presbyterian church SXQ]
. . . . . . [Presbyterian Church of England SXR]

SXS . . . . . . Church of Scotand
SXT . . . . . Congregational church
SXU . . . . . . Unitarian church
SXV . . . . . Methodist church
SXW . . . . . Baptist church

SYB Islamic law, Arabic law, Mohammedan law, Shari'a
SYB 2 . *Primary materials*
5A . Jurisprudence
5A6 8 . . Fiqh
5BQ . . Analytical jurisprudence
. . . *Special concepts*
5BY D . . . . Ikhtilaf
5BY F . . . . Furuq
5BY H . . . . Hiyal
5C . . Sources
5CX . . . Usul
5D . . . . Urf, 'Adah
5DM . . . . . Amal

5F . . . . Qu'ran, Koran
5FT . . . . . Tafsir (general)
5GB . . . . Sunna, Hadith, Traditions (Islamic law)
5GJ . . . . . Hadith (oral traditions)
5GK . . . . . Athat
5GL . . . . . Usul al-fiqh
5GM . . . . . Taqlid
5GN . . . . . Isnad
5GP . . . . . Other bodies of traditions, collections, etc.
5GQ . . . . Ijma
5GR . . . . Ijtihad
5GS . . . . . Illa
5GT . . . . . Qiyas, Kiyas
5GU . . . . . . Istihsan
5GV . . . . . . Ra'y
5GW . . . . Iztihsan
5HB . . . Formal sources
5PW . . . Precedents
5PW S . . . . Istishab
5PX . . . . Fatwa, Fatawa (pl.)
5TF . . . . Shurut
5TF 7 . . . . . Tabaqat
5TH . . . . . Commentaries
5TI . . . . . Individual jurists, A/Z
5UB . . Law & society
5UE . . . Justice
. . . . *Special moral dimensions in Islamic law*

[Ecclesiastical law SWE]
[Semitic & Western religions law SWU]
[Islamic law SYB]
[Jurisprudence SYB5A]
. [Law & society SYB5UB]
. . [Justice SYB5UE]
. . . [Special moral dimensions in Islamic law]

SYB 5UM B	. . . . Mubah
5UM D	. . . . . Mandub
5UM F	. . . . Wajib
5UM H	. . . . Makruh
5UM K	. . . . Haram
5UM L	. . . . Hisbah
5US	. . . Istislah
6	Practice & procedure
7	. Courts
7P	. . Mazalim courts
7Q	. . Qadi courts
7W	. . Nizamiyya courts, secular courts (Islamic law)
8T	. Evidence
9AV	. . Witnesses
9CE	. . . Adl
	Substantive law
9VB	. Mu'amalat
	. . Jurisprudence
9VB 5A	. . . Furu al-fiqh
AP	. Persons
AWN G	. . Slaves
BF	. . Women
BFG	. . . Dress of women (Islamic law), purdah, viel (Islamic law)
BPT	. . Aliens
CF	. . Family
CFU W	. . . Guardian & ward
	. . Marriage
CK	. . . Nikah (Islamic law)
CKS HV	. . . Dower, Mahr
CMV	. . . Divorce
	. . . . Compensation
CMV W	. . . . . Mut'a (divorce)
CMW B	. . . . Talaq, repudiation (Islamic law)
CMW C	. . . . . Taliq at-talaq
CMW D	. . . . . Tafwid at-talaq
CMW E	. . . . . Talaq as-sunna
CMW F	. . . . . Talaq al-bid'a, Talaq al-bain
CMW G	. . . . Khul
CMW H	. . . . Tal
CMW L	. . . . Li'an
CMW N	. . . Idda
CO	. . . *Types of marriage*
COV	. . . . Mut'a
CPJ	. . . . Polygamy (Islamic law)

[Ecclesiastical law SWE]
[Islamic law SYB]
[Substantive law]
. [Persons SYBAP]
. . [Marriage]
. . . [Types of marriage SYBCO]
. . . . [Polygamy Islamic law SYBCPJ]

SYB D	. Obligations & contracts
	. . Codes
D5Q	. . . Majalla, mejelle
E	. . Mu'amalat, transactions (Islamic law)
	. . . Formation of contract
EI	. . . . Aqd
GN	. Torts versus person
	. . Defamation
GNV	. . . Qadhf
H	. Property
HP	. . Transfer of property
HSV	. . . Hiba, Gift
HSX	. . . Sadaqa
HTQ	. . . Ariyya
HTY	. . Settlement & trusts
.	. . . *Types special to Islamic law*
HYF	. . . . Waqf
HYG	. . . . . Waqif
HYH	. . . . . Objects of waqf
HYJ	. . . . . Beneficiaries of waqf
	. . Inheritance & succession
I	. . . Ilm al-fam'id
	. . . . Legal cause
IDF X	. . . . . Wala, patronage (Islamic succession)
N	. Commercial law
NG	. . Credit
NGD X	. . . Riba, usury
NXG	. . Sale of goods
NXG W	. . . Salam, salaf
W	. Criminal law
W9R C	. . Punishments
	. . . Retributive
W9R W	. . . . Hadd, hudud
W9R Y	. . . Ta'zir
WQC	. . Wine drinking, muskir
X	. Constitutional law
	. . Aliens
XDO PT	. . . Non-Muslims, dhimmis
	Subjects special to ecclesiastical law
SYC B	. Systematic theology
BD	. . Five pillars of Islam
D	. Practice of religion
	. . Worship
DB	. . . Ibadat
DEV	. . . Sacred places
EC	. . Holy days
	. . . Fasting
ECJ	. . . . Sawm
EQL	. . Confession of the faith

[Ecclesiastical law SWE]
[Extant religious legal systems]
[Semitic & Western religions law SWU]
[Islamic law SYB]
[Subjects special to ecclesiastical law]
. [Practice of religion SYCD]
. . [Confession of the faith SYCEQL]

SYC ER . . Ritual observances
. . . Ritual purity
ERP . . . . Tahara
. . . Ritual prayer
ET . . . . Salat
. . Pilgrimage
EXX . . . Hajj
. . Legal alms
EYB . . . Zakat

FB . Ecclesiology

FEV . . Apostacy
FPE . . External relations
. . . With the State
FPF . . . . Siyasa shar'iyya

FTB Schools & sects (Islamic law)
FTG . Fiqh i-Jami
FTJ . . Iktilaf al-faqaha

SYD E . Sunnite law
H . . Hanafi law
J . . Hanbali law
M . . Maliki law, Malaki law
S . . Shafi'i law
SYE B . Shi'ite law
D . . Ismailii
F . . . Fatimids
H . . . Khojas (Eastern)
K . . . Khojas
M . . . Bohoras
P . . Ithna Ashari
R . . Zaydi
T . . Wahhabi
V . . Abadi

SYF . *Islamic law in specific countries*

Auxiliary schedule S1

. Guide to the subdivision of any national
. jurisdiction
. . * Each jurisdiction may be qualified by the entire vocabulary of Class S other than that of the Jurisdictions facet itself (i.e. by classes 2/9,A/C). But in order to secure briefer classmarks, the simple adjustments indicated below are made.
. . * Further simple adjustments are made for subdividing supranational jurisdictions; see SG (European Union law) for a full demonstration of these.
. . * Slightly different adjustments are made for the subdivision of international law; see SD for these.
. . * Add to - (where the hyphen represents the classmark of the jurisdiction) numbers & letters 2/9,A/Y below.

2 *Primary materials, works of law*
. * Add to 2 numbers & letters 3/Z in Auxiliary Schedule S2.
. * For a detailed example of how adjustments may be made to meet the special needs of a given jurisdiction, see SN2 (English law) for countries with a unitary structure and SP2 (USA law) for countries with a federal structure. Examples of its application to civil law systems will be found at SVF (France) & SVK A (Germany).

Secondary materials, works about the law
3 . *Common subdivisions*
. . * Add to - numbers 3/59 following S in S3/S59.
5A . Jurisprudence
. . * Add to -5 letters A/Y following S5 in S5A/S5Y.
6 . Practice & procedure, procedural law
. . * Add to - numbers 6/9U following S in S6/S9U.
9VB . Substantive law, Subject of law
. . * Add to - numbers & letters 9VB/A following S in S9V B/SA and letters B/W following SB in SBB/SBW - e.g.
9VH . . Rights (substantive law)
9W . . Private law (general)
9X . . . Civil law (general)
A . . . Conflict of laws, International private law
AP . . . Persons
BB . . . . Citizens, nationals
CF . . . . Family & kinship
D . . . Obligations, contract & tort (together)
DG . . . . Liability
E . . . . Contract
FW . . . . Agency
G . . . . Torts
H . . . Property
I . . . . Inheritance & succession
J . . . . Real property
JX . . . . . Environmental law
. . . . . . * Alternative; preferred at S.
K . . . . . . Planning & development law
L . . . . Personal property
LJ . . . . . Intellectual & industrial property
M . . . . . . Patents
N . . . Commercial & economic law

[Secondary materials]
[Substantive law 9VB]
[Private law general 9W]
. [Commercial & economic law N]

NF . . Finance... Banking... Credit...
NH . . . Insurance
NL . . Labour law, industrial law
NO . . International economic relations & trade
NQ . . Business law
NXG . . . Sale of goods... Consumer law
OQ . . . Company law, corporation law
P . . Transport law
QSY . . Agriculture & industry
S . Environmental law... Pollution...
TA . Social law
TB . . Health & medicine law... Education law...
U . . Welfare law
V2 . Cultural law... knowledge & research...
VVX . . Recreation & arts...
W Criminal law
WY Public law
X . Constitutional law
. . * Add to -X numbers & letters 2/9,A/X following SC in SC2/SCX.
. . * Add to -Y letters B/F following SCY in SCY B/SCY F. Some major classes are given below as examples.
XCW . . Human rights
XE . . Government... Legislature... Executive
XK . . . Administrative law...
XL . . . Central government & administration
XP . . . Devolved government & administration
XQ . . . . Ethnological law
XS . . . . State government & administration
XU . . . . Local government
XW . . . . Overseas territories
XX . . . Judiciary (general)
YB . . . Secular ecclesiastical law...
YJ . . . Ethnolaw of a modern country
. . . . * Alternative; preferred under the country.

[Secondary materials]
. [Substantive law 9VB]
. . [Public law WY]
. . . [Constitutional law X]
. . . . [Government... Legislature... Executive XE]
. . . . . [Ethnolaw of a modern country YJ]

Auxiliary schedule S2

. Primary materials under a national jurisdiction

. . * Primary materials may be described as being works of law, as distinct from works about the law.
. . * This schedule is for use under any national jurisdiction; for primary materials of a supranational jurisdiction (e.g. the European Community) see Auxiliary Schedule S3; for primary materials in international law, see SD2.
. . * For official documents reporting the political processes whereby policies are determined and legislation enacted, see RE5 in Class R Politics.
. . * This schedule gives in one consolidated sequence classes appropriate to all kinds of national jurisdictions, whether based on civil law or common law systems (or mixtures of these) or whether the state has a unitary or federal structure.
. . * This means that no given jurisdiction will use all the classes provided - only those appropriate to it.
. . * Demonstrations of how this selection is effected can be seen at English law SN (for a unitary state) & at U.S.A. law SP (for a federal structure) and at SVF French law (for a civil law system).
. . * Add to - (where the hyphen represents the classmark of the country) 23/29,2A/2Y below so far as applicable to that country - e.g. SN2 G English law - Statutes; SVF 9X2 H French law - Civil - Code (where SVF 9X is French civil law).
. . * For classes divided by date, proceed as follows:
. . * Add to - (where the hyphen represents the classmark to be qualified) letters DF/Y from Auxiliary Schedule 4C; For example, the date 1804 is built by (1) taking the starting date of the 2-decade period containing it; here, it is 1800, signified by -H); (2) adding to this a letter signifying the individual year in a period; here, it is the 4th year, signified by -F. So the classmark for the Code Napoleon is SVF X2H HF (where SVF is French law, X is Constitutional law from Auxiliary Schedule S1, 2H is Codes from this Auxiliary Schedule S2, and HF is the date of its publication, 1804).

22 . *By language*
. . * When this needs to be distinguished.
. . * Add to -2 (where the hyphen represents the material to be qualified) letters C/Y in Auxiliary Schedule 3.

[Auxiliary schedule S2]
[By language 22]

23 *Common subdivisions*
. * Very few of these are applicable to primary materials, except for those given below as special forms.
. * Add to 23 numbers 2/9 in Auxiliary Schedule 1 so far as applicable.
235 R . Guides to the documentation
U . Bibliographies of primary materials

24 *Special subsidiary forms*
. * The following classes are used primarily to qualify materials in -2B/2Y. Indexes, collections, etc. of specific kinds of materials go with that material; e.g. Official gazettes - Index (serial) is -28B 44.
. * The numbers 3/9 following 2 in 23/29 may be added to all subsequent categories of materials; e.g. -2F46 Legislative acts - Indexes (monographic).
. * In certain cases, some of the forms below are replaced by special enumerations; e.g. official & non-official editions of statutes; collections of law reports.

244 . Indexes (serial)
. . * By date.
246 . Indexes (monographic)
. . * By date.
248 . Special indexes
. . * See German law SVK for an example.

25 . Official texts, unannotated texts
26 . Non-official texts, annotated texts

27 . Collections (serial)
275 . . Official series
275 8 . . . Annual series, etc.
. . . . * For example, sessional volumes under Official documents, 2B/2D.
A . . . Particular series
. . . . * Arrange A/Z, i.e., 275A/275Z.
276 . . Non-official series
276 A . . . Particular series, by title
. . . . * Arrange A/Z, i.e., 276A/276Z.
278 . . By editor, reporter, etc.
27B . Collections (monographic)
27D . Collections for special groups of users
. . * Arrange A/Z.
. . * For example, for police.
27F . Selections
27H . Citations
27K . Other compilations
. . * For example, tables of effects, commentaries on texts.
28 . Digests, abridgements, summaries
287 . . Serial
287 B . . Monographic
28B . Gazettes
28B 5 . . Official gazettes
28C . . Individual gazettes

[Auxiliary schedule S2]
[Special subsidiary forms 24]
. [Gazettes 28B]
. . [Individual gazettes 28C]

. . . * Arrange A/Z.

28E . Journals
. . * If distinguished from gazettes; in particular, if
. . containing details of current law (texts of legislation,
. . decisions of courts, etc.).
28E 5 . . Official
6 . . Non-official
28G . Yearbooks, etc.
28J . Calendars

2A Legislative & executive documents, official documents, parliamentary papers
. * Published under the authority of parliament or congress,
. etc.
. * Alternative (not recommended) to locating in Politics, at
. RI. If this option is taken, use 2B/2D below.
2B . General
. . * Covering both houses in bicameral legislatures.
. . * For statutes, etc., see 2G.
2B8 E . . Journal
J . . Calendars, order of business, etc.
2BC . . General papers
2BD . . Debates (legislative), proceedings (legislative)
2BG . . Bills
2BM . . Committees (legislative)
. . . * Arrange A/Z.
2BQ . . Other documents
2C . Lower house (official documents)
. . * Add to 2C numbers 3/8 following 2 in 23/28 & letters
. . C/Q following 2B in 2BC/2BQ.
2D . Upper house (official documents)
. . * Add to 2D numbers & letters 3/8,C/Q as for 2C.

2E Constitution & amendments
. * Alternative (not recommended) to locating under
. constitutional law of country.
2E5 . Official editions, by date
2E6 . Non-official editions, by date

2F Legislation, legislative acts
. *Statutes, laws, acts*
. . * For works covering individual statutes and codes.
. . Jurisdictions which generally dispense with codes should
. . use 2G for statutes; e.g. English statutes SN2 G.

2G . . Statutes, Public acts, Public general acts
. . . * Generally uncodified & published in various series
. . . particular to the jurisdiction.
. . . Comprehensive collections
2G7 5 . . . . Official series
6 . . . . Non-official series
H . . . Citations

[Auxiliary schedule S2]
[Legislation 2F]
[Statutes]
[Statutes 2G]
. [Citations 2G7H]

. . * Arrange A/Z by editor.
2GE . Early period
2GE 75 . . Official series
76 . . Non-official series
. . . * Arrange A/Z by editor.
7B . . Monographic collections
7F . . Selections
7H . . Citations
. . . * Arrange A/Z by editor.

2GJ . Modern period, current period
2GJ 75 . . Official series
758 . . . Sessional volumes
. . . . * Arrange by date.
76 . . Non-official series
7B5 . . Official monographs
7B6 . . Non-official monographs

2GS . Private acts (statutes), personal acts
. (statutes)
. . * For local legislations, see 2L.
2GU . Emergency legislation (statutes), war
. legislation (statutes)
2GW . Statutes revision commission reports

2H Codes, codifications
. * Comprehensive & systematic statement of a body
. of law, usually of a particular branch or subject of
. law. Codes on particular branches or subjects go
. with the latter - e.g. Civil law - Codes.
2H4 L . Comprehensive collections
. . * Covering private & public law.
2HD F . Individual codes (by date)
. . * This class will usually apply only to specific
. . branches or subjects of law.
. . * Each code may be divided as follows:
. . * Add to - (where the hyphen represents the
. . classmark

[Auxiliary schedule S2]
[Legislation 2F]
[Statutes]
. [Codes 2H]
. . [Individual codes by date 2HDF]

. . . of the code) letters F/R below:
. . . - F Amendments (by date), amendatory laws
. . . - B (Legislative & executive papers)
. . . - G Bills (texts, by date)
. . . * Records of proceedings, minutes
. . . of
. . . evidence, etc.
. . . - H Drafts, criticisms, etc.
. . . - J Code commission documents (by date)
. . . - K Code revision commission documents
. . . * Arrange by date.
. . . - M Official reports (by date)
. . . * Of code & revision commissions,
. . . federal & state bodies, etc.
. . . - P Commentaries on code (general)
. . . * Including those with court
. . . decisions.
. . . - R Associated legislation,
. . . * E.g. Introductory acts to the code.
. . . * E.g. France - Civil law - Code Napoleon (1804)
. . . - Bills SVF 9X2 HHF G (where SVF 9X is
. . . French civil law, 2H is Code, HF is 1804 in Auxiliary
. . . Schedule 4C and G is Bills).

2HT . . *Codes by subject*
. . . * Alternative (not recommended) to subordinating to
. . . subject. If this option is taken:
. . . * Add to 2HT letter A following S and letters B/W
. . . following SB.

2J Secondary legislation, subordinate legislation, subsidiary legislation, statutory orders, delegated legislation
. * Often made under powers conferred through parliament
. (e.g., by an enabling statute) to supplement ordinary
. statutes by prescribing detailed rules required by their
. operation.
. * See also Administrative publications 2MC

2J7 5 . Official series by date
58 . Sessional volumes, Annual volumes
6 . Non-official series by editor, A/Z
K . Other compilations
. . * E.g. tables of effects.
2JH . Codes
2JK . Individual orders or sets of orders
. . * When not part of a regular series.
. *Types of delegated legislation*
. . * If these are distinguished.
2JM . . Statutory instruments
2JP . . Special orders, A/Z
. . . * Provisional orders, etc.
2JR . . Emergency legislation
2JS Prerogative instruments

[Auxiliary schedule S2]
[Legislation 2F]
. [Prerogative instruments 2JS]

. . * See SN English law for examples.

2K . State legislation (texts)
. . * Alternative (not recommended) to locating under State
. . government SCS. If this option is taken, proceed as
. . follows:
2KM . . *By state*
. . . * Add to 2KM letters following country's classmark in
. . . Auxiliary Schedule 2.
. . . * Add to - (where the hyphen represents the classmark
. . . of the state) letters F/J following 2 in 2F/2J.
2L . Local legislation (texts), bye-laws
. . * Alternative (not recommended) to locating under local
. . government law RCU. If this option is taken, proceed as
. . follows:
2LP . . *By county*
. . . * Add to 2LP letters following country's classmark in
. . . Auxiliary Schedule 2.
. . . * Alternatively, when the Schedule 2 enumeration is
. . . insufficient, arrange A/Z.
. . . * Add to - (where the hyphen represents the classmark
. . . of the county) letters F/J following 2 in 2F/2J.
2LR . . *By city, municipality...*
. . . * Arrange A/Z.
. . . * Add to 2LR as for 2LP.
. . . * Last note under 2LP above applies here also.

2MC Administrative publications (texts), executive publications (texts)
. * General collections, etc. only. Those on specific subjects
. go with the subject.
. * See also Secondary legislation 2J
2ME . Special constitutional councils' publications
. . * For example, Conseil d'Etat in French law.
2MG . Department of Justice publications (texts)
2MJ . Other government departments, A/Z
2ML . Special commissions, etc.
. . * Alternative (not recommended) to subordinating to
. . subject. Arrange A/Z by name or title by which known.
2MP . Other administrative agency publications
. . * Inter-departmental & ad hoc bodies.

2MS Treaties (internal law)
. * Use only for situations in which this form occurs in
. internal affairs (e.g. concordats with a church, etc.). For
. international treaties, see SD2 B; for supranational
. treaties, see SE2 F.
2MT Treaties (international law)
. * The preferred place for these is in international law (SD).
. This class is an alternative (not recommended) in which
. treaties are treated as a special form of legislation, defining
. certain areas of jurisdiction. It takes general treaties only;
. treaties on a special subject go with the subject.
2MU . Multilateral treaties (by date)

[Auxiliary schedule S2]
[Treaties international law 2MT]
. [Multilateral treaties by date 2MU]

2MW . Bilateral treaties (by date)

2N Court decisions, law reports, cases
. * For any series of reports assigned its own classmark, qualification as follows may be made so far as applicable (in addition, of course, to the usual qualification by 3/9 following 2):
- C Citators
- E Main series
- G Supplements
- J Other materials
. * E.g. American law reports - Citator SP2

2N7 . Collections serial
. . * Covering all or several periods & all or several types of courts.

2N7 B . Collections monographic
. . * Covering all or several periods & all or several types of courts.

2N8 . Digests, abridgements, summaries
. . * Covering all or several periods & all or several types of courts.
. . * Digests of a given report series go with the series.

2N9 . Individual cases
. . * Individual cases reported from a specific court or type of court go with the court; see instructions at 2PB). This class takes cases in which the material covers different courts &/or periods.
. . * Arrange by date, then by name. Each case may be divided as follows:
. . * Add to - (where the hyphen represents the classmark of the case)
- B Briefs
- D Pleadings
- F Decision
- H Appeal
- K Other documents on the case

2NB . *Reports & cases by court*
. . * General collections only, covering all or several periods.
. . * See note below (preceding 2NC) regarding division by period. If no period divisions are thought necessary, 2N will replace this class as the general one for all or several courts together.
. . * Add to 2NB letters C/W following 7 in S7C/S7W (as modified for the jurisdiction concerned) so far as applicable.
. . * Any given court may be qualified as instructed for modern courts at 2PB.

[Auxiliary schedule S2]
[Court decisions 2N]
[Reports & cases by court 2NB]

Reports & cases by period
. * For use in jurisdictions in which the court system in earlier periods differed so radically from the present system that it is more helpful to keep separate files for the courts in the earlier period or periods.
. * In this case, 2NC & 2NE will take all kinds of courts within the period concerned.

2NC . Earliest period
. . * This will vary with the jurisdiction.

2ND . . *By court*
. . . * Add to 2ND letters C/W following S7C in S7C/S7W so far as applicable.
. . . * Note 2 under 2NF below applies here also.

2NE . Major subsequent earlier period
. . * This will vary with the jurisdiction.

2NF . . *By court*
. . . * Notes 3 & 4 under 2NB above apply here also.
. . . * Divide like modern period only if appropriate; but usually this will call for an enumeration reflecting the courts of the period; see English law for an example of this (at SN2 NF).

2NG . . . Individual courts
. . . . * Arrange A/Z.
. . . . * If applicable.

2PB . Modern & current period
. . * See note preceding 2NC above regarding the applicability of division by period. If periods are not distinguished, the classes 2PB/2PW below will be the only location for division of cases by court.
. . * The pattern of courts varies greatly from one country to another. Liberal allowance has been made in notation to allow the insertion (if necessary) of courts peculiar to a given jurisdiction.
. . * The order of courts is that under Practice & & procedure (at S7) but with some adjustment of notation.
. . * See also general collections which include, as part of the integral series, cases from particular courts; e.g. Chancery & Equity series in the (English) Law reports.

. . *Reports & cases by court*
. . . * Each type of court, or individual court, may be qualified as follows (in addition to 3/9 following 2):

[Auxiliary schedule S2]
[Court decisions 2N]
[Reports & cases by period]
[Modern & current period 2PB]
[Reports & cases by court]

. - 9 Individual cases, A/Z
. * Each case may be divided as
. instructed at 2N9.
. - B Court records, briefs, etc
. - E Original jurisdiction, First instance
. * If applicable.
. - F Appellate jurisdiction
. * If applicable.
. * Alternative (not recommended)
. to subordinating to
. Appeals S9H.
. - H Common law jurisdiction
. - I Equitable jurisdiction
. - K Civil jurisdiction
. - L Criminal jurisdiction *
. Alternative (not recommended) to
. subordinating to criminal law
. SBW.
. - M Public law jurisdiction
. - N Special tribunals, etc. within the court
. - P Particular courts within the class
. * For example, Supreme court - Original (first
. instance) juridiction 2QE.

2PC Federal & State courts together (reports & cases)
. * For countries with a federal structure; countries with a unitary structure should use 2PL for general works covering all or several kinds of national court.

2PD . *Types of courts*
. . * Use only for works covering both federal & state courts.
. . * Add to 2PD letters D/W following 7 in S7D/S7W so far as applicable.

2PP . National courts (reports), Federal courts (reports)

. . *By characteristics other than hierarchical*
. . . * Add to 2PP letters D/N following S7 in S7D/S7N so far as applicable:

2PP E . . . First instance courts (general)
F . . . Appeal courts (general)
. . . . * Alternative (not recommended) to locating with appeals (S9H).
H . . . Common law courts (general)
I . . . Equity courts (general)
K . . . Civil courts (general)

[Auxiliary schedule S2]
[Reports & cases by period]
[Modern & current period 2PB]
[Federal & State courts together reports & cases 2PC]
[National courts reports 2PP]
. [By characteristics other than hierarchical]
. . [Civil courts general 2PPK]

2PP L . . Criminal courts (general)
. . . * Alternative (not recommende) to subordinating to criminal law SBW.

2Q . Supreme court (reports & cases)
2QE . . First instance & general jurisdiction
2QF . . Appellate jurisdiction
. . . * Alternative (not recommended) to locating under Appeals S9H.
2QL . . Criminal jurisdiction
. . . * Alternative (not recommended) to locating under Criminal law SBW.
2QN . . Special tribunals, etc. within the court
2QR . . Particular courts

2R . High courts (reports), superior courts (reports)

2S . Intermediate & lower courts (reports & cases)

2T . Summary jurisdiction courts (reports & cases), magistrate courts (reports & cases)

2UB National administrative agencies' decisions
. * General collections, etc. only; for decisions of particular agencies, see subject.
2UD . *By department*
. . * Arrange A/Z.
. . * When department's subject jurisdiction is general in scope.
2UF Special jurisdiction courts (reports & cases)
. * Alternative (not recommended) to locating with subject - e.g. consular courts.
2UP . Particular courts (by subject)

2UR Regional courts (reports & cases)
. * For countries with a unitary structure. For state courts, see 2V.

2V State courts (reports & cases)
. * For countries with a federal structure.
. * Alternative (not recommended) to locating under state government (SCS). If this option

[Auxiliary schedule S2]
[Court decisions 2N]
. [Reports & cases by period]
. . [Modern & current period 2PB]
. . . [Federal & State courts together reports & cases 2PC]
. . . . [State courts reports & cases 2V]

. . . . . is taken, proceed as follows:
. . . . . * Add to 2V letters NC/UR following 2 above, so
. . . . . far as applicable - e.g. State supreme court -2VQ.
2VW . . . . . Individual states
. . . . . . * Add to 2VW letters following the country's
. . . . . . classmark in Auxiliary Schedule 2.

2WB . . . . Local courts (reports & cases)
. . . . . * Alternative (not recommended) to locating under
. . . . . local governmen (SCU). If this option is taken,
. . . . . proceed as follows:
. . . . . * Add to 2WB letters C/U following 2V above.
2WC . . . . . Counties (courts)
2WD . . . . . . Individual counties
2WE . . . . . Towns (courts), townships (courts),
. . . . . municipal authorities (courts)
. . . . . . * In some jurisdictions, includes justices of the
. . . . . . peace courts.
2WF . . . . . . Individual towns
. . . . * Arrange A/Z.

2WJ . Trials (law reports)
. . * Alternative (not recommended) to locating under
. . subject. If this option is taken, proceed as follows:
2WK . . Civil trials
2WL . . . Individual cases
. . . . * Arrange A/Z by plaintiff.
2WN . . Criminal trials
2WP . . . *By offence*
. . . . * Arrange A/Z.
2WR . . . Individual cases
. . . . * Arrange A/Z by defendant.

2WT . . Reports of special types of trials
. . . * For example, State trials in English law.

2X . *Reports by subject*
. . * Alternative (not recommended) to locating with subject.
. . If this option is taken, proceed as follows:
. . * Add to 2X letter A following S and letters B/W
. . following SB - e.g. criminal reports -2XW.

2Y *By language*
. * Alternative (not recommended) to 22 for libraries wishing
. to keep parallel sequences of all primary materials in
. different languages. If this option is taken:

[Auxiliary schedule S2]
[By language 2Y]

* Add to 2Y letters G/Y in Auxiliary Schedule 3.
* Add to the resulting classmark numbers & letters 3/9,A/X following 2. In those rare cases where such direct qualification of a specific language (as distinct from a class representing a group of languages) would result in ambiguity, use 2 as an intercalator to introduce 3/9,A/X. For example, 2YQ Russian would need a 2 following it to distinguish its subclasses from (say) 2YQS Polish.

[Auxiliary schedule S2]
. [By language 2Y]
. . [Reports by subject 2X]

Auxiliary Schedule S3

. Primary materials under a supranational jurisdiction

* The notes under Auxiliary Schedule S2 apply here also, except that those relating exclusively to national jurisdictions are replaced below by similar ones relating to supranational jurisdictions.
* This schedule gives in one sequence classes appropriate to all kinds of supranational jurisdictions. However, it is based on the requirements of the European Union (by far the most developed example of a supranational community) so the detail is greater than is likely to be required under less formally organized bodies or those of more restricted scope.
* This means that most jurisdictions will not use all (or even many) classes provided - only those appropriate to it. A demonstration of its full use will be found under the law of the European Union, at SG.
* Add to - (where the hyphen represents the classmark of the jurisdiction) 23/29,2A/2Y below, so far as applicable; e.g. SG2 P European Union - Court decisions.

22 . *By language*
* If necessary, any category of material may be qualified by language as follows:
* Add to -2 (where the hyphen represents the material to be qualified) letters C/Y in Auxiliary Schedule 3; e.g. SG2 882 F European Unoion - Official gazette - in French.

23 . *Common subdivisions*
* Very few of these are applicable to primary materials except for those given below as special forms.
* Add to 23 numbers & letters 2/9, A/Y following S3 so far as applicable; e.g. 23R Guides to the documentation.

24 . *Special subsidiary forms*
* Notes under Auxiliary Schedule S2 apply here also. These special forms are used primarily to qualify materials in 2A/2Y: indexes, collections, etc. of specific kinds of materials go with the latter.
* Add to 2- (where the hyphen represents the specific category of material to be qualified) numbers 4/9 following 2 in Auxiliary Schedule S2; e.g. SG2 M46 European Union - Legislation, official acts - Indexes (monographic).
* A selection of the major forms is given here for convenience & to demonstrate their scope.

244 . . Indexes
25 . . Official texts
26 . . Non-official texts
27 . . Collections serial
27B . . Collections monographic

[Auxiliary Schedule S3]
[Special subsidiary forms 24]
. [Collections monographic 27B]

28 . Digests
28E . Journals
28J . Calendars

2A Legislative & executive documents, official documents
* Publications of the law-making institutions of the supranational jurisdiction. These are unlikely to follow the pattern found in national jurisdictions (legislature, executive, administration, judiciary) & adjustments may be necessary. For an example of what these institutions might be like, see European Union SG2 B.
* For the supranational body as a political organization (including official documents presenting its political & social policies & operation) see Class R Politics. This class takes only that literature which serves as primary material in studying the law of the jurisdiction.
* If in doubt, prefer Class S.
* For legislation, acts, etc., see 2L.
* Each institution or organ may be qualified as follows:
* Add to - (where the hyphen represents the classmark of the institution or its organ) as follows:
- 8E Journals
- 8J Calendars
- C General papers
- D Proceedings, debates
- G Bills
- H Working papers
- J Resolutions, opinions
  * If these have the status of secondary legislation, use 2NJ.
- M Committees
- S Official reports (general)
- U Other materials

2B . Legislature or quasi-legislature
2BY . Executive bodies
2C . . Governmental executive
* For example, Council of Ministers in EU.
2D . . Non-elected, administrative body
* For example, European Commission.
2EB . Other institutions general or near-general in scope
2EM . Special institutions
* Alternative (not recommended) to subordinating to special subject.

2F Treaties of formation
* Alternative (not recommended) is to locate these under the Constitution of the organization.
* Each treaty may be qualified as follows:

[Auxiliary Schedule S3]
[Treaties of formation 2F]

. * Add to - (where the hyphen represents the classmark of
. the treaty):
. - 5 Official texts
. - 6 Non-official texts, annotated, with commentary
. - G Related agreements, supplementary agreements
. - J (By country)
. * Add to J letters E/Z in Auxiliary Schedule
. 1.
. - L Drafts, advisory materials
. - N Other documents relating to the treaty
. - P By individual country (if applicable)
. - Q By other supranational jurisdictions (if applicable)

2G . Treaties (individual)
. . * By date.

2H Treaties of accession
. * By date, then country.

2I Other treaties (by date)

2JT International treaties
. * Alternative (not recommended) to locating in
. International law SD.

2JU . Multilateral treaties
. . * By date.

2JW . Unilateral treaties
. . * By date.

2K Conferences, meetings, etc.
. * By date.
. * With less legal force than treaties.

2L Legislation
. * Use this class when all or several types of legislation are
. included.

2M . Official acts & regulations
. . * Of general application, directly applicable to all member
. . states & binding on them.

2NB . Directives
. . * Addressed to (& binding on) one or more members &
. . requiring them to meet specified objectives & if necessary
. . amend their national legislation.

2ND . Decisions
. . * Addressed to corporate persons, etc. in member states &
. . binding on them.

2NH . Codes

2NJ . Secondary legislation, subordinate legislation
. . * May not be binding on members.

2NK . . Recommendations

2NM . . Opinions

2NP . . Declarations

2NR . Emergency legislation

2NX . National legislation applying the community law
. . * General works only; the preferred arrangement is to
. . locate the legislation of a particular member state under
. . that state.

[Auxiliary Schedule S3]
[Legislation 2L]
. [National legislation applying the community law 2NX]

2NY . . *By country*
. . . * Alternative (not recommended) to locating with the
. . . country for libraries wishing to keep this material here.
. . . If this option is taken, proceed as follows:
. . . * Add to 2NY letters E/Z in Auxiliary Schedule 1.

2P Court decisions, law reports, cases

2P9 . Individual cases
. . * General collections only, covering all courts.
. *By court*
. . * Each court may be qualified as instructed under 2PB in
. . Auxiliary Schedule S2 - e.g. Principal court - Special
. . tribunals within -2RN.
. . *By various characteristics*
. . . * Add to 2P letters D/W following S7 in S7D/S7W so
. . . far as applicable.

2R . . Principal court of the community or
. . organization

2S . . Other major court

2T . . Other courts
. . . * Arrange A/Z.

2U . . National courts' decisions
. . . * On matters of community or organization law.
. . . * The note at 2QX applies here also.
. . . * Add to 2V letters E/Z in Auxiliary Schedule 2.

2V . . Special subject courts'decisions
. . . * Alternative (not recommended) to locating under the
. . . subject - e.g. human rights courts. If this is taken:
. . . * Add to 2W letter A following S and letters B/W
. . . following S in SA and SBB/SBW.

2X Primary materials on specific subject areas
. * Alternative (not recommended) for libraries wishing to
. keep together all primary materials on subjects. If this
. option is taken:
. * Add to 2X numbers & letters 5/Y in Auxiliary Schedule
. S1; e.g. 2XN Economics & finance.

[Auxiliary Schedule S3]
. [Primary materials on specific subject areas 2X]

Auxiliary Schedule S4

. For an alternative arrangement of common
. law systems

. . * This is a guide for librarians wishing to adopt an
. . alternative arrangement (not recommended) for classes
. . SL/SQ. In this alternative, common law is treated as
. . one integral system, in which the individual national
. . jurisdictions (UK law, USA law, Australian law, etc.)
. . are treated as subclasses to be cited after the particular
. . branches of the common law.
. . * For example, all contract law based on common law
. . would be kept together, irrespective of the national
. . jurisdiction concerned. If it were thought necessary to
. . distinguish (say) an English treatment of the subject
. . from an American one, this would be effected by
. . qualifying the subject classmark by the country
. . classmark (introduced by 4). See SPE below for an
. . example.
. . * The alternative schedule is as follows:

SKY Common law systems
. * Completely general works only; for primary materials
. see SL/SO; for secondary materials, see SP.

. *Primary materials*
. . * Each jurisdiction is qualified as instructed in
. . Auxiliary Schedule S2.
SL . . English law, UK law
SMA . . Rest of British Isles
. . . * Add to SM letters A/M following SO in SOA/SOM;
. . . e.g. Eire SMF.

SMP . . Commonwealth, etc.
. . . * Add to SM letters P/T following SO in SOP/SOT.
SMV . . America,etc.
. . . * Add to SM letters V/X following SOO in SOV/SOX.
SN . . . USA
SO . . Caribbean
. . . * Add to SO letters B/U following SQ in SQB/SQU.

SP . *Secondary materials*
. . * Add to SP numbers & letters 3/9,A/W in Auxiliary
. . Schedule S1 - e.g.
SP4 E . . English law (general)
Y . . American (USA) law (general)
SP5 A . . Jurisprudence
SP6 . . Practice & procedure
SP6 4E . . . English procedural law (general)
4Y . . . American (USA) procedural law (general)
SP9 VB . . Substantive law
W . . . Private law
SPE . . . . Contract law
SPE 4E . . . . . English contract law

[Common law systems SKY]
[Secondary materials SP]
[Substantive law SP9VB]
[Private law SP9W]
. [Contract law SPE]
. . [English contract law SPE4E]

SPE 4Y . . USA contract law
SPW Criminal law
SPY Public law
SQ . Constitutional law
. . * Add to SQ number & letters 3/9,A/Y following
. . SC in SC3/SCY; e.g.
SQI . . Legislature
SQI 4E . . . British Parliament (general)
4Y . . . American (USA) Congress (general)

Making effective use of the A/Z Index

The context of law is implicit in all index entries; e.g. the entry for corporate financing means its law, not its economics.

Most terms in the index are elementary ones. No attempt has been made to index the huge number of compound classes which the schedules are capable of forming. For example, there is no entry for the compound class Criminal law procedure (SBW 6). Entries appear for both of the keywords present, but they are for the elementary classes whose combination produces the compound class:

Criminal law SBW
Procedural law S6

It is assumed that indexers know that the citation order in the law class cites the Subjects of law (substantive law) before the Processes of law (see Introduction, Section 7). So this compound will combine the elementary classes in the order Criminal law — Procedure, giving the classmark SBW 6.

Some class names cannot be expressed sensibly by a single word but need a phrase to express them — e.g. Mentally ill persons as offenders (SBW DM). In such cases a fundamental rule is observed: an entry term is never qualified by one of its own subclasses from the schedules. So entries appear for

Mentally ill persons as offenders SBW DM
Offenders SBW D

but not for:

Offenders, Mentally ill

The procedures observed above reflect the best-known and most effective method for economizing drastically on the number of index entries made whilst ensuring that all sought keywords still appear. This method is called chain indexing (see Sections 5.76 and 6.5 in the General Introduction to BC2).

It should be noted that in any given library most documents on law imply the law of the home country; so in an English library, a document on procedure in criminal law will usually be on English law (and go at SNW 6) and not the general class (SBW 6).

Never classify directly from the A/Z index. Always turn to the schedules, which show each term in its context; the context often affects the meaning. There may also be special instructions about building classmarks in the schedules; e.g. when normal synthesis is interrupted, as at SDD OPT Aliens (international law).

Index

E

H

K

L

N

Q

R

S

T

U

V

Printed and bound by CPI Group (UK) Ltd, Croydon, CR0 4YY
13/09/2026
14960860-0002